AGRICULTURE IN THE URUGUAY ROUND

Also by K. A. Ingersent

AGRICULTURE AND ECONOMIC DEVELOPMENT
(*with Subrata Ghatak*)
ECONOMIC ANALYSIS OF AGRICULTURE (*with B. E. Hill*)

Also by A. J. Rayner

CURRENT ISSUES IN AGRICULTURAL ECONOMICS
(*with David Colman*)
RESOURCE STRUCTURE OF AGRICULTURE
(*with K. Cowling and D. Metcalf*)

Also by R. C. Hine

GLOBAL PROTECTIONISM (*editor*)
THE POLITICAL ECONOMY OF EUROPEAN TRADE

Agriculture in the Uruguay Round

Edited by

K. A. Ingersent
Senior Research Fellow
Centre for Research in Economic Development
and International Trade
University of Nottingham

A. J. Rayner
Professor of Agricultural Economics
University of Nottingham

and

R. C. Hine
Senior Lecturer in Economics
University of Nottingham

St. Martin's Press

First published in Great Britain 1994 by
THE MACMILLAN PRESS LTD
Houndmills, Basingstoke, Hampshire RG21 2XS
and London
Companies and representatives
throughout the world

A catalogue record for this book is available
from the British Library.

ISBN 0–333–55340–3

Printed in Great Britain by
Antony Rowe Ltd
Chippenham, Wiltshire

First published in the United States of America 1994 by
Scholarly and Reference Division,
ST. MARTIN'S PRESS, INC.,
175 Fifth Avenue,
New York, N.Y. 10010

ISBN 0–312–10632–7

Library of Congress Cataloging-in-Publication Data
Agriculture in the Uruguay Round / edited by K. A. Ingersent, A. J.
Rayner, and R. C. Hine.
p.   cm.
Includes bibliographical references and index.
ISBN 0–312–10632–7
1. Tariff on farm produce.   2. Agriculture and state.   3. General
Agreement on Tariffs and Trade (Organization).   I. Rayner, A. J.
II. Hine, R. C.
HF2651.F27A233   1994
382'.41—dc20   93–29433
                                                CIP

Contents

List of Tables		vii
List of Figures		ix
Preface		x
Notes on the Contributors		xi
Abbreviations		xii

1. Introduction — 1
   K. A. Ingersent, A. J. Rayner and R. C. Hine

2. The Uruguay Round: Agenda, Expectations and Outcomes — 8
   David Greenaway

3. The US Perspective — 26
   Jimmye S. Hillman

4. The EC Perspective — 55
   K. A. Ingersent, A. J. Rayner and R. C. Hine

5. The Cairns Group Perspective — 88
   Rod Tyers

6. The Canadian Perspective — 110
   T. K. Warley

7. The Japanese Perspective — 140
   Kenzo Hemmi

8. The LDC Perspective — 157
   L. Alan Winters

9. The Food Industry Perspective — 182
   Simon Harris

Contents

10   Perspectives on EC Agricultural Policy Reform   203
     Secondo Tarditi

11   Agricultural Policy Reform after the Uruguay Round   223
     David Harvey

12   Agriculture in the Uruguay Round: an Assessment   260
     K. A. Ingersent, A. J. Rayner and R. C. Hine

Notes and References   291
Bibliography   302
Author Index   314
Subject Index   317

List of Tables

1.1	Net percentage PSEs, 1979–1986	2
1.2	Chronology of the Uruguay Round	4
2.1	The GATT negotiating rounds	10
2.2	Post Tokyo Round tariff reduction averages in principal industrialised countries (per cent)	12
2.3	Incidence of non-tariff measures in principal industrialised countries	13
2.4	Uruguay Round negotiating groups	16
2.5	Uruguay Round trade-offs	21
3.1	Total transfers associated with agricultural policies (in billion US dollars)	30
3.2	Summary of key elements of US agricultural proposal to the GATT, 15 October 1990	45
5.1	The Cairns Group, 1987–1989	91
5.2	The Cairns Group in world production and trade: a comparison with the 'Big Three'	92
5.3	The Cairns Group in world agricultural commodity exports	93
5.4	The Cairns Group as destination for 'Big Three' exports	94
5.5	Average food trade distortions in Cairns Group and other industrial countries	96
5.6	Effects of industrial country food trade distortions on Cairns Group food exports	97
5.7	Effects of industrial country food trade distortions on welfare in Cairns Group countries	98
5.8	Effects of EC unilateral reform, combined with EFTA membership, on international prices and on EC–EFTA production and net trade in 2000	104
5.9	Effects of EC–12 unilateral reform on production and net trade in 2000	105
5.10	The effects of unilateral EC Reform and EFTA membership on economic welfare in 2000	106
6.1	Canada's agrifood trade, 1989	114
6.2	Producer subsidy equivalents, Canada, 1979–1986 average, and 1987 to 1990, percentages	116

6.3	Aggregate measure of support, Canadian agriculture, 1987–1988, C$ millions	117
6.4	Aggregate net farm cash income, Canada, 1981–1992, $C million and percentages	119
7.1	Estimated farm size needed to reduce costs of production of rice	152
9.1	Aggregate levels of consumer subsidy equivalent by country (in % of consumer value)	188
9.2	Operation of EC export refund mechanism	197
10.1	Welfare effects of policy alternatives	220
11.1	Progress of MacSharry reform proposals, EC	230
11.2	Base data and primary illustrative calculations	240
11.3	Illustrative policy measures	241

List of Figures

6.1   A synoptic view of Canada's agricultural support
programmes and domestically-oriented negotiating
objectives   116

10.1   Economic development and agricultural employment
share in the EC   206

10.2   Farm assets and incomes per agricultural working unit
in the EC   206

10.3   Distribution of farms by family farm income per person   208

10.4   Relation between labour income and farm size   208

10.5   Structural impact of alternative prices   217

10.6   Welfare effects of alternative policy measures   219

10.7   Impact of non-tradable quotas at firm and industry
levels   221

11.1   Stylized representation of different support instruments
(EC, cereals)   239

11.2   Percentage adjustment of world commodity prices
towards free trade levels under PEGs at 100% and 80%
of 1986 quantities   252

Preface

The original inspiration for this book came from a one-day conference on 'Agriculture in the Uruguay Round' held in April 1990 at the University of Nottingham, under the auspices of the Centre for Research in Economic Development and International Trade (CREDIT). Three chapters of this book are based upon papers presented at that conference. A further six are by authors who were subsequently invited to make contributions. Publication has been held up longer than we would have wished due mainly to the unexpectedly protracted course of the Uruguay Round itself. It has been a pleasure working with our contributors and we are extremely grateful to all of them, not only for their hard work but also for their co-operation and patience with us in bringing this enterprise to a successful conclusion. We are also pleased to acknowledge our debt to Sharon Tipper who transformed a collection of heterogeneous manuscripts, produced in a variety of word-processing styles, into a harmonious whole fit to be sent to the publisher.

K. A.. Ingersent
A. J. Rayner
R. C. Hine

Notes on the Contributors

David Greenaway is Professor of Economics and Director of the Centre for Research in Economic Development and International Trade (CREDIT), University of Nottingham.

Simon Harris is Group Economist, British Sugar plc.

David Harvey is Professor of Agricultural Economics, University of Newcastle upon Tyne.

Kenzo Hemmi is Professor at Toyo Eiwa Women's University, Japan.

Jimmye S. Hillman is Emeritus Professor of Agricultural Economics, University of Arizona, USA.

R. C. Hine is Senior Lecturer in Economics and Research Fellow in CREDIT, University of Nottingham.

K. A. Ingersent is a Research Fellow in CREDIT, University of Nottingham.

A. J. Rayner is Professor of Agricultural Economics and Assistant Director of CREDIT, University of Nottingham.

Secondo Tarditi is Professor of Agricultural Economics and Policy, University of Siena, Italy.

Rod Tyers is Senior Lecturer in Economics, Australian National University, Canberra.

T. K. Warley is Professor of Agricultural Economics, University of Guelph, Ontario, Canada.

L. Alan Winters is Professor of Economics, University of Birmingham.

Abbreviations

AAA	Agricultural Adjustment Act
AD	Anti Dumping
AMS	Aggregate Measure of Support
BST	Bovine Somatatropin
CAP	Common Agricultural Policy
CDE	Consumption Distortion Equivalent
CG	Cairns Group
CGE	Computable General Equilibrium
CIS	Commonwealth of Independent States
COPA	Confederation of European Farmers' Unions
CUSTA	Canada–US Trade Agreement
CVDs	Countervailing Duties
EEP	Export Enhancement Programme
EFTA	European Free Trade Association
ERA	Effective Rate of Assistance
FAO	Food and Agriculture Organisation (of the United Nations)
FEOGA	European Agricultural Guidance and Guarantee Fund
FOGS	Functioning of the GATT System
GSP	Generalised System of Preferences
IBRD	International Bank for Reconstruction and Development
ICA	International Commodity Agreement
IMF	International Monetary Fund
ITO	International Trade Organization
LFAs	Less Favoured Areas
LUFPIG	Land Use and Food Policy Inter Group
MFA	Multi Fibre Agreement
MFN	Most Favoured Nation
MIPs	Minimum Import Prices
MPP	Market Promotion Program
MTN	Multilateral Trade Negotiations
NICs	Newly Industrialising Countries
NRP	Nominal Rate of Protection
NTB	Non-Tariff Barrier
NTMs	Non-Tariff Measures
PAG	Price Adjustment Gap
PDE	Price Distortion Equivalent

PEG	Producer's Entitlement Guarantee
PERTs	Political Economic Resource Transfers
PESTs	Political Economic Seeking Transfers
PSEs	Producer Subsidy Equivalents
QRs	Quantitative Restraints
SMUs	Support Measurement Units
SNOs	So-called Non-economic Objectives
TD	Trade Distortion
TDE	Trade Distortion Equivalent
TEs	Tariff Equivalents
TPRM	Trade Policy Review Mechanism
TRIMs	Trade Related Investment Measures
TRIPs	Trade Related Intellectual Property Rights
USDA	United States Department of Agriculture
VERs	Voluntary Export Restraints
VES	Variable Export Subsidy
VIL	Variable Import Levy
VRAs	Voluntary Restraint Agreements
WIPO	World Intellectual Property Organisation

1 Introduction

K. A. Ingersent, A. J. Rayner and R. C. Hine

The Uruguay Round launched at Punta del Este in 1986 was the eighth and most ambitious of the multilateral trade negotiations conducted under the auspices of the GATT (General Agreement on Tariffs and Trade). There were 105 contracting parties involved in 15 negotiating groups. As well as addressing traditional issues such as tariff liberalisation, the negotiators sought to extend GATT disciplines to the new areas of services, intellectual property and investment measures. In addition, a high priority was given to reforming trade in sectors such as textiles but especially agriculture, which had previously been subject to waivers from normal GATT rules and disciplines.

Previous rounds in the GATT had fostered a process of trade liberalisation in industrial products but had been unable to reduce agricultural trade barriers and distortions. The neglect of agriculture in the GATT stemmed from two main factors: first, the proliferation of market-distorting domestic farm programmes granting subsidies on domestic production, and second, exemption of agriculture from certain rules of the GATT prohibiting export subsidies and quantitative restrictions on imports.[1]

In the absence of effective international rules and disciplines, domestic pressures led to increased distortions in world agricultural trade in the period leading up to the launch of the Uruguay Round negotiations. This is substantiated by the monitoring activities of international agencies such as the FAO and the OECD, using the 'producer subsidy equivalent measure' or PSE (OECD, 1991). The percentage PSE, defined as a ratio of the total PSE to the gross value of production, is a convenient if imperfect measuring rod of support and protection. Table 1.1 shows PSEs in the principle OECD countries from 1979 to 1986 for the three broad aggregates of 'crops', 'livestock products' and 'all products'. There is a wide variation in results between countries, with support highest in Japan and the EC. However, the most notable feature is the upward trend in PSEs, reaching a peak in 1986, the year in which the Uruguay Round was launched. Even in major agricultural exporting countries like Australia, with a comparatively non-interventionist stance on agriculture,

1

Table 1.1   Net percentage PSEs, 1979–1986

	1979	1980	1981	1982	1983	1984	1985	1986
Australia								
Crops	3	5	8	15	8	9	13	19
L/S products	9	11	11	15	13	11	15	15
All products	7	9	10	15	11	10	14	16
Canada								
Crops	13	15	16	20	19	25	39	54
L/S products	36	34	36	36	37	40	39	45
All products	26	25	26	28	28	33	39	49
EC (10)								
Crops	45	25	30	42	26	24	44	66
L/S products	38	38	31	31	36	36	43	47
All products	40	35	31	34	33	33	43	52
Japan								
Crops	79	71	65	77	79	81	86	93
L/S products	52	49	51	46	50	48	47	53
All products	68	61	58	62	66	67	69	76
New Zealand								
Crops	2	4	10	13	8	9	10	15
L/S products	15	16	23	28	37	18	23	34
All products	15	16	23	27	36	18	23	33
United States								
Crops	8	9	12	14	34	21	26	45
L/S products	31	29	32	31	31	34	36	41
All products	21	20	23	23	33	28	32	43

Source: OECD, Up-Dating of PSE/CSE Analysis: Country Notes, Paris, 1989.

PSEs were again substantial by the mid-1980s. This reflects the defensive actions of governments in these countries, attempting to shield their farmers from the spillover effects of support policies in major nations or trading blocs, such as the EC and the US.

More generally, policy interdependence between countries linked by trade results in 'policy offsets'. Since protectionism by 'large' countries lowers international prices, a fraction of farm price support in one country is used to offset the impact of support in other countries. For example, the results of one empirical estimate suggest that in 1986/7 over 40 per cent of support to US farmers 'merely offset the losses created by policies of other industrialised countries' (Roningen and Dixit, 1989, p.27). Like the costs of open trade wars, the costs of agricultural policy offsets have been clearly wasteful on a grand scale, and attempting at least to reduce or even eliminate this waste was a major motive for placing agriculture at the centre of the Uruguay Round. But there were a number of additional reasons. First, the Round was initiated in response to concerns held by a number of countries that the general malaise in world trade in the early 1980s, combined with a rising tide of protectionism, might lead to a breakdown of the GATT system. In order to strengthen the multilateral trading system, it was thought necessary that unreformed sectors be included along with the extension of the GATT into new areas. Second, within a narrower agricultural perspective, the trade tensions created by the emergence of structural surpluses of major commodities by the mid 1980s and the budgetary and political costs of competitive subsidisation, brought agricultural protectionism to the forefront of the international economic policy agenda. Third, the domestic consumer and taxpayer burdens and the trade distortions stemming from domestic agricultural policies were made transparent by authoritative studies conducted both by respected individual analysts and institutions, such as the OECD, the World Bank and the USDA. Consequently, under internal and external pressures, agricultural policy makers were looking for ways to reform farm support policies and a 'window of opportunity' existed for nations to enter into negotiations to reduce agricultural subsidies and liberalise trade. As stated by Hathaway (1987) p. 3:

> At no time since World War II have so many countries been considering changes in their agricultural policies. It is in the interests of all countries that these changes take place with as little disruption as possible to their agricultural economies. Dislocations can be reduced if all major participants agree on directions and rules and the GATT is the only effective negotiating forum to include the various countries concerned.

The Uruguay Round was scheduled for completion in December 1990 at Brussels (see Table 1.2). A lengthy round was inevitable given that its scale and complexity would lead to protracted negotiations. However, the Brussels Ministerial Meeting ended in disarray because of wrangling over agricultural support. Deadlock over agriculture served to delay an agreement for another 2 years or more.

Table 1.2   Chronology of the Uruguay Round

Date	Event
November 1992	Washington Accord on agriculture between EC and US
September 1986	Launch at Punta del Este, Uruguay
December 1988	Mid-term Review, Montreal
April 1989	Geneva Accord
June 1990	Tabling of Aart de Zeeuw 'framework agreement'
December 1990	'Final' ministerial meeting, Brussels
February 1991	Formula agreed for resumption of negotiations
May 1991	US fast-track negotiating authority extended
June 1991	Negotiations resumed
December 1991	Tabling of Dunkel draft agreement on agriculture
May 1992	CAP reform adopted
November 1992	Washington Accord on agriculture between EC and US

There had been conflict in the agricultural negotiating group from the outset. The initial position of the major players – the US, the EC, the Cairns Group (CG)[2] and Japan – revealed deep divisions, particularly between the US and the EC, over the nature, extent and pace of reform. At the mid-term review (Montreal 1988) agriculture was identified as a major sticking point; the key issue being US insistence on a prior commitment to *eliminate* all forms of trade-distorting protection in the face of EC determination to preserve the mechanisms of the CAP (Common Agricultural Policy). In the Geneva Accord (April 1989), however, the US abandoned the 'zero' option whilst the EC also made certain concessions. The revised negotiating positions (post Geneva Accord) revealed some common ground between the US, supported by the CG, and the EC. Whilst all participants displayed a willingness to bring about substantive agricultural and trade policy reform, disagreements over the extent and speed of reduction in trade-distorting domestic and export subsidies and border protection led to the breakdown in Brussels. Subsequently, the negotiations were revived following an 'emergency' initiative by the GATT Secretary-General, Arthur Dunkel.

In February 1991 all contracting parties agreed to renew agricultural negotiations on the basis of reaching 'specific binding commitments to reduce farm supports in each of the three areas: internal assistance, border protection and export assistance'. This agreement on the objectives of the agricultural negotiations led to the resumption of negotiations in June 1991 in all 15 areas of the Uruguay Round. In addition, President Bush was able to persuade Congress in May 1991 to extend his 'fast track negotiating authority', effectively extending the US deadline for concluding the Uruguay Round until June 1993.

However, in 1991, as from the start of the Round, a resolution of the deadlock in the agricultural negotiations appeared to be linked to a reform of the CAP which moved away from providing trade distorting support. A paper on CAP reform – the MacSharry Plan – first tabled within the EC Commission in January 1991, and published in July 1991, proposed lowering support prices much closer to world market levels whilst supplementing farmers' incomes with direct income payments of two kinds. First, there would be payments to compensate for the support price reduction and, second, payments for compliance with arable land 'set aside' conditions.

Subsequently, the MacSharry Plan was revised and finally agreed in its revised form by the EC Council of Farm Ministers in May 1992. In the meantime, in December 1991, the GATT Secretariat put forward a draft agreement to hasten a conclusion to the Round. The so-called 'Final Act' highlighted four central issues in the agricultural negotiating group:

1 conversion of existing non-tariff measures to tariffs;
2 EC demands to be allowed to 'rebalance' lower protection of cereals against higher protection of cereal substitutes, particularly oilseeds;
3 US demands that the volume and cost of subsidised farm exports be limited;
4 EC demands that compensation payments to farmers under the MacSharry Plan be treated as 'decoupled' from production and not be counted as subsidies.

However, the Uruguay Round negotiations did not advance in the first nine months of 1992. The farm trade dispute between the US and the EC was at the heart of the impasse. Two issues were central. First, the EC regarded the MacSharry reform of the CAP, put into EC law in July 1992, as sacrosanct: any GATT agreement had to be compatible with the reform. Second, a technically separate dispute between the US and the EC on oilseeds, that had simmered for a number of years, threatened to erupt into a trade war. Since the beginning of the Round, US oilseed producers had been seeking action in the GATT in respect of what they claimed were the detrimental effects of EC oilseeds subsidies. In 1989, a GATT panel ruled that the EC subsidy impaired the benefits of duty-free access for oilseeds into the EC, to which the Community had agreed in the Dillon Round in 1960/61. In March 1992, the same panel ruled that a revision of the EC oilseeds subsidy scheme, linked to the MacSharry reform, did not eliminate the damage being done to US exporters. In September 1992, the US proposed binding arbitration on the amount of trade damage involved, put by the US at $1.5 billion and by the EC at no more than $400m. Subsequently, bilateral negotiations on the oilseeds dispute broke down, with the US seeking a GATT sanction for the unilateral imposition of retaliatory tariffs on EC farm and industrial exports to the US, these to be introduced in December 1992. The EC threatened in return to escalate the dispute into a 'tit-for-tat' trade war. Secretary-General Dunkel was called in to carry out a 'rescue mission' urging the two sides to settle the oilseeds dispute before the US deadline in December 1992 for the imposition of 'retaliatory tariffs'. He was also given a mandate to act as an intermediary between the US and the EC and other Uruguay Round participants, given the urgent need to restart negotiations. In the event, the threatened trade war was averted in the nick of time when, on 27 November, both the oilseeds dispute and the outstanding differences between the US and the EC on the Dunkel draft agreement on agriculture (on which the EC had reservations) were resolved simultaneously by a bi-lateral agreement, dubbed the Washington Accord . Apart from some EC disunity (led by France) concerning the compatibility of the Washington Accord with the recently agreed CAP reform, this shifted attention away from agriculture to the removal of remaining obstacles to reaching an overall Uruguay Agreement in other areas.

This book provides a perspective on the central role of the agricultural negotiations in the Uruguay Round. The core of the book concerns the stances adopted by five of the major players – the US, the EC, the Cairns Group, Canada and Japan – and how these shaped the course of the negotiations. The major chapters were written prior to the final stages of the Round and so do not allow for the benefit of hindsight. However, they do point up the differing objectives of the participants and the compromises made when faced with the reality of negotiating fundamental reforms in agricultural trade policy whilst attempting to retain national agricultural policy flexibility and autonomy.

Although the book is mainly concerned with efforts to reform the conduct of agricultural trade through the GATT, Chapter 2 (David

Greenaway) sets the scene by reviewing the origins of the Uruguay Round, the issues at stake and the prospects for success in a broader perspective, embracing all fifteen of the areas under which the negotiations were organised.

The next five chapters view the Uruguay Round agricultural negotiations from the national perspectives of the five major players. Chapter 3 deals with the US perspective (Jimmye Hillman); Chapter 4, the EC Perspective (the editors); Chapter 5, the Cairns Group Perspective (Rod Tyers); Chapter 6, the Canadian Perspective (T. K. Warley) and Chapter 7, the Japanese Perspective (Kenzo Hemmi).

A still broader view and analysis of the scope of the agricultural negotiations is given by four further chapters respectively dealing with the LDC Perspective (Alan Winters in Chapter 8); The Food Industry Perspective (Simon Harris in Chapter 9); Perspectives on EC Agricultural Policy Reform (S. Tarditi in Chapter 10) and Agricultural Policy Reform Options after the Uruguay Round (David Harvey in Chapter 11).

At the time of going to press (January 1993) the Uruguay Round had still not reached a final outcome. Thus conclusions about the likely outcome can only be tentative. Despite this proviso, in the final chapter the editors attempt to step back from the national perspectives covered by earlier chapters, in order to form a more detached view of Uruguay Round agriculture negotiations. That chapter, based in part upon a synthesis of the preceding national perspectives, includes an assessment of the achievements of the Round *vis-à-vis* agriculture, together with a review of the obstacles to faster progress with agricultural trade reform in multilateral negotiations, and lessons learned for any future GATT rounds.

Discerning readers will notice that different contributors to the book view its subject-matter from somewhat different standpoints in the spectrum ranging from purely normative to purely positive analysis of economic policy. Although we, the editors, chose to adopt a position towards the positive end of this spectrum, we think that it is inevitable that some of our contributors struck a more normative stance and we make no apology for this.

2 The Uruguay Round: Agenda, Expectations and Outcomes

David Greenaway

2.1 INTRODUCTION

The Uruguay Round is the eighth Round of multilateral trade negotiations (MTNs) convened under the GATT. It began in 1986 and was due to end in 1990. The Round may yet therefore yield a result, although at the time of writing that remains in doubt.

The Uruguay Round has been the most ambitious, and most complex of all the GATT Rounds thus far. As we shall see, it involved some 103 Contracting Parties (CPs) negotiating across 15 negotiating groups. Many of the topics addressed are new issues and some fairly complicated linkages between issues surfaced during the negotiations. The Round has come at a crucial time for the multilateral trading system, given growing pressures in the world economy towards regional trading blocs and the widespread erosion of respect for GATT rules and principles. Eventual success of the Round would serve to reaffirm the authority of the GATT and could pave the way for strengthened disciplines. By contrast, failure would be likely to accelerate further derogations from the GATT disciplines, encourage discriminatory trading arrangements and give a boost to bilateralism.

This chapter assesses the Uruguay Round. It begins with some brief background comments on the earlier GATT Rounds. Section 2.3 focuses on recent challenges to the GATT system. Section 2.4 then concentrates on the Uruguay Round itself, detailing the issues addressed and the problems which have surfaced. Section 2.5 assesses the prospects for agreement, evaluates the benefits of an agreement and the costs of failure.

2.2 THE GATT AND MULTILATERAL TRADE NEGOTIATIONS

The General Agreement on Tariffs and Trade has its origins in the Anglo-American grand design for post war reconstruction. The allies envisaged the creation of three key institutions – one to oversee commercial relations, one to provide an orderly framework for monetary relations and one to mobilise resources for reconstruction and development. The last two of these were dealt with at the Bretton Woods Conference which created the International Monetary Fund (IMF) and International Bank for Reconstruction and Development (IBRD – better known as the World Bank). The third institution was planned as the International Trade Organisation (ITO). Negotiations for the ITO culminated in the Havana Charter of 1948 (with 53 signatories). However, the Charter was never ratified by the US Congress and an enabling treaty which had been prepared to clear the way for the ITO became the set of rules for the governance of world trade. This was how the GATT came into being. It was initially signed in Geneva by 23 Contracting Parties (CPs) in 1947 and has since expanded to embrace 105 CPs.

The objective of the GATT is to provide a framework for the orderly conduct of trade, as well as a process within which trade liberalisation can take place. To this end, the key principles which underlie the Charter are non-discrimination, reciprocity and transparency. The first we have already mentioned. It is important because it discourages the swapping of favours between trading partners and thereby encourages CPs to the negotiating table – countries negotiate in the knowledge that the agreements reached apply to all parties. The principle of reciprocity is not actually in the GATT Charter as such but rather in the Preamble. This states that if one CP makes a trade concession to another (for example, by cutting a tariff), the party which benefits is obliged to reciprocate with an equivalent concession. As we know from basic trade theory, in the absence of distortions, reciprocity is not necessary for a country which is cutting tariffs to benefit. However, it is important to the trade liberalisation process. It encourages negotiators who are instinctively mercantilist to believe that 'fairness' is being achieved by both parties making concessions; it also encourages them to claim that there are double benefits from any agreement – lower prices of imports for consumers and better market access for exporters. Transparency dictates that when intervention is necessary it should be via visible instruments, rather than in opaque forms.

There are exceptions to both the non discrimination and reciprocity obligations. Under Article XXIV of the GATT Charter countries can engage in discriminatory trading arrangements if they form free trade areas or customs unions. A major exception to reciprocity is the waiver which developing countries enjoy. However, despite these, and other exceptions, non-discrimination and reciprocity have been central to the credibility of the GATT and the success of the pre-Uruguay Rounds of MTNs.

The mechanism instituted by GATT to promote trade liberalisation is the so-called 'Rounds' system. This process periodically brings CPs together to agree a package of trade measures. Table 2.1 lists the seven Rounds which preceded the Uruguay Round, the number of CPs involved in the negotiations, and the value of trade covered.

From 1947 to 1962 there were five Rounds concerned almost exclusively with tariff liberalisation. In the first two the tariff cutting was largely one way, with the United States offering concessions designed to assist Western European economies in their recovery from the Second World War. Later, reciprocity was required of the Europeans and tariff concessions were negotiated on a 'request–offer'/product by product basis. In other words, offers were made to cut tariffs on particular products and these were tied to specific requests for cuts on other products. Although these tariff cuts were geared towards the trade of industrialised countries and although certain sectors were completely excluded, most importantly agriculture which had effectively been given a waiver by provisions in Articles XI and XVI, these Rounds nevertheless achieved considerable trade liberalisation.

Table 2.1   The GATT negotiating rounds

Round	Dates	Number of countries	Value of trade covered
Geneva	1947	23	$10 billion
Annecy	1949	33	Unavailable
Geneva	1956	22	$2.5 billion
Dillon	1961–2	45	$4.9 billion
Kennedy	1964–7	48	$40 billion
Tokyo	1973–9	99	$155 billion

Source: Jackson (1990).

The Kennedy Round (1964–1967) was bigger in scale, in terms of the number of countries involved, the volume of trade it covered and the range of issues it tried to address. It was again largely concerned with tariff cutting. Since non tariff barriers were becoming more important (notably in textiles and clothing), there was some discussion about this and there was an intention to begin to think about liberalisation in agriculture. In the event the only real accomplishment was further tariff liberalisation, with average cuts on industrial products of around 35 per cent. Moreover the cuts were achieved through the application of a formula which applied to most products rather than on a request–offer basis. Although these were real accomplishments, there was some disappointment at the outcome on the part of developing countries which felt that their interests had not been fairly represented (see Whalley 1989).

The Tokyo Round (1973–1979) was yet more ambitious, with more than double the number of CPs involved and a much wider agenda. Tariff cuts on industrial products were once more an objective. In addition, the negotiators were concerned with agriculture, which still remained a sheltered sector, and a range of non tariff issues including subsidies, discriminatory government procurement and discriminatory use of import licences. These non tariff barriers assumed a major importance because the 1970s had seen a worrying growth in recourse to non tariff barriers. Moreover, much of that growth had occurred in so called 'grey area measures' over which the GATT has no direct jurisdiction – measures like voluntary export restraints. An aim of the negotiators was to discipline the use of such measures by making them subject to Article XIX, the safeguards clause. With so many items on the agenda, so many countries involved and bearing in mind that the Round occurred against the backcloth of the deepest post war recession to date, it is not surprising perhaps that the negotiations were protracted and complex. Agreement was reached in 1979. Again this involved major tariff cuts – on average around 38 per cent. Despite the fact that some product areas were excluded, this was an impressive cut. Moreover it was formula driven, the formula adopted achieving both liberalisation and harmonisation of nominal tariffs.[1] Nothing of any substance was agreed on agriculture. 'Codes' were introduced to deal with some non tariff barriers but it proved impossible to amend Article XIX in a suitable fashion to bring measures like VERs under GATT control.

As Winters (1990) points out, what one observes then is an evolution from a process which was initially solely directed at reducing tariffs to one which has become increasingly concerned with new issues raised by changing circumstances. Inevitably this has meant a growing preoccupation with constitutional matters.

2.3 CHALLENGES TO THE GATT SYSTEM

It is possible to identify real accomplishments of these first seven Rounds. The clearest symptom of achievement is the decline in average tariffs on industrial goods, in industrialised countries, from around 40 per cent in the late 1940s to around 5 per cent in the early 1980s (see Table 2.2). It is true that these are cuts in nominal rather than effective tariffs, that they exclude agricultural products and that average tariffs remain relatively high in many developing countries. Nonetheless, it would be churlish to underplay the extent to which tariffs have been reduced and, equally important, bound. Another obvious indicator of success has been the growing number of CPs involved in the process – a fourfold increase between the first Geneva Round and the Tokyo Round. Again there are obvious ways in which one might qualify this, for example the waiver given to developing countries has limited the concessions they have offered. Nevertheless, the fact remains that the doctrine of multilateralism has been progressively extended and new entrants presumably 'signed up' because they felt it in their interests to do so.

Against this, however, a number of stresses emerged in the 1970s which have developed into major cracks in the 1980s. These now constitute challenges to the GATT system and set the context against which the Uruguay Round was launched. Some of these actually have

Table 2.2   Post Tokyo Round tariff reduction averages in principal
industrialised countries (per cent)

	W	S
All Industrial Countries	4.9	6.5
United States	4.4	7.0
European Communities	4.8	5.6
Japan	2.6	6.0

W = weighted averages (weighted by MFN Imports)
S = simple average
Source: adapted from Greenaway (1983), Table 5.3.

their origins in the 1960s, although the historical context of the 1970s was important in bringing them to the surface. Specifically, the conjunction of the first major widespread recession of the post-war period, and the impact of shifting comparative advantage in a wide range of standardised manufactures towards the NICs and Japan, created a structural adjustment problem in the major industrialised economies.[2] This is not to argue that the rise in unemployment in industrialised countries was directly attributable to increased imports from the NICs and Japan. One can readily make a good case to the effect that this was *not* so. The point is that the conjunction of the two meant that inferences regarding causality that could be made *were* made, and fed the protectionist sentiments which invariably arise in times of growing unemployment and declining international competitiveness. Following that episode a number of challenges to the GATT system have surfaced and gained momentum.

First there has been the spread of grey area measures, that is, the proliferation of non-tariff measure (NTMs), sometimes referred to as 'the new protectionism' (see Table 2.3). The challenge here comes not from protectionist measures *per se* but rather from the form they have taken. Bhagwati (1990) has recently described this as the replacement

Table 2.3   Incidence of non-tariff measures in principal industrialised countries [1,2]

Importer	1981 Trade Coverage Developed	Developing	World	1986 Trade Coverage Developed	Developing	World
All Industrial	14.3	18.8	15.1	17.5	20.6	17.7
United States	9.7	15.5	11.4	16.6	19.1	17.3
European Communities	11.3	21.7	13.4	14.4	23.2	15.8
Japan	29.5	17.4	24.4	29.4	17.4	24.3

Notes:
1. Non tariff measures refers to: variable levies; product specific charges; quotas; prohibitions; non automatic licencing; VERs; MFA quotas. They do *not* include: health and sanitary regulations; packaging and labelling requirements; technical standards; minimum price regulations; tariff quotas.
2. Incidence is calculated as the share of total imports by value subject to non tariff measures.
Source: adapted from Laird and Yeats (1990).

of 'fix rule arrangements', with 'fix quantity arrangements'. Some of the derogations are legal (like the MFA), others are extra legal or illegal, like VERs. The sectors to which the measures are applicable have grown well beyond textiles and clothing to now embrace, *inter alia*, footwear, steel, automobiles and consumer electronics (for recent documentary evidence see Nogues, Olechowski and Winters, 1987). Although empirical evidence suggests that instruments like VERs are much more costly forms of protection than equivalent tariffs or subsidies (see, for instance, Pearson 1983, Greenaway 1986), their opacity makes them attractive to governments and producer lobbies alike. It is not hard to understand why they have spread therefore. But from the GATT's standpoint they constitute a danger because, in explicitly contravening the principle of non discrimination, they contribute towards an erosion of the system's foundations. This particular threat continues to grow: GATT (1990) identifies some 249 export restraint arrangements in existence.

A second challenge has come through a related route, namely the growing use of contingent measures like anti dumping and countervailing duty mechanisms as trade policy measures. Recent evidence suggests that dumping and export subsidies, in particular the former, are elastic terms and have become *de facto* instruments of trade policy (see Finger and Murray, 1990, on the US and Messerlin, 1990, on the EC). Indeed, as Hindley (1988) shows, it is comparatively easy to prove 'dumping' under EC rules. The same applies in the US, where Finger and Murray (1990) estimate the probability of an affirmative determination of dumping, once an action is initiated, at 0.9. This marginalises the GATT's role in the policing of alleged unfair trade practices. Insofar as the GATT mechanisms are less susceptible to capture than national provisions, this is unfortunate. Moreover, the evidence suggests that anti-dumping action generally leads to some kind of discriminatory price fixing arrangements. Thus, Messerlin (1989) reports that some 50 per cent of EC actions lead to a price-fixing agreement, whilst Finger and Murray (1990) report that almost half of all US countervailing duty actions in the 1980s resulted in VERs. Again, therefore, these are developments which contribute to the erosion of respect for basic GATT principles and rules.

A third source of pressure arises from the emergence of new issues. As tariffs have declined in importance in industrialised countries, attention has shifted away from a desire to negotiate tariff concessions on merchandise trade towards a desire to improve market access in services and investment, seek protection of intellectual property rights and so on. The GATT rules do not apply to these issues. Insofar as they are agenda items on the Uruguay Round, this may only be a temporary phenomenon. In the meantime, however, their profile has contributed to a growing preoccupation (especially in the US) with 'level playing fields'. The claim here is that a willingness to make concessions in one area (e.g. textiles and clothing) should be tied to progress in others (e.g. market access in tradeable services). In turn this has led to a gradual replacement of what Bhagwati (1991) calls 'first difference reciprocity', with a kind of intersectoral reciprocity. The challenge this poses to the GATT system is a serious one: negotiations which are driven by intersectoral reciprocity are likely to make bilateral negotiations more attractive than multilateral negotiations.[3]

These developments have at best led to an erosion of respect for the GATT principles; at worst a complete disregard for those principles. The sense that the GATT provisions are either outdated and/or ineffective has resulted in the principle of non-discrimination being honoured as much in the breach as in the observance, and there is now a real danger that multilateralism will be completely replaced by minilateralism based on the three big trading blocs, or greater bilateralism. With the 1988 Omnibus Trade Bill, and in particular Super 301 and Special 301 provisions, the US took a major step back from multilateralism in instituting a policy of 'aggressive unilateralism' (Bhagwati, 1990). The European Commission, in the context of post 1992 market access, has hinted at what might by analogy be called 'aggressive reciprocity', that is, mirror image reciprocity. It is against this backcloth that the Uruguay Round has been conducted.

2.4 THE URUGUAY ROUND AGENDA

We have already seen how the GATT Rounds have tended to become more ambitious through time, both in terms of country coverage and issues addressed. The Uruguay Round did not embrace significantly more CPs than Tokyo (103 compared to 99); however the range of issues covered was much more extensive. This was partly a consequence of there being a certain amount of unfinished business carried over from Tokyo, partly a consequence of certain constitutional issues being addressed for the reasons discussed in the previous section and partly a result of the fact that key parties would only give their assent to a Round being launched on condition that certain new issues were discussed. Table 2.4 sets out the full range of issues on the Uruguay

Table 2.4   Uruguay Round negotiating groups

Trade Barriers
  Tariffs
  Non-Tariff Measures

Sectors
  Natural Resource Based Products
  Tropical Products
  Textiles and Clothing
  Agriculture

GATT System
  Safeguards
  Subsidies and Countervailing Measures
  GATT Articles
  MTN Agreements and Arrangements
  Functioning of the GATT System
  Dispute Settlement

New Issues
  Trade-Related Intellectual Property Rights
  Trade-Related Investment Measures
  Services

Round agenda – fifteen negotiating groups in all, fourteen of which were concerned with various aspects of trade in goods, the other with services. As we shall see later, the fact that so many (old and new) issues were addressed has made the negotiations extremely complex and complicated. For the moment, however, let us briefly review the remit of each group.

Trade Barriers

Two separate negotiating groups were concerned with barriers to trade in goods, one on *tariffs* and the other on *non tariff barriers*. As we have already seen, the GATT MTNs have been remarkably successful in reducing tariffs. Nevertheless it was deemed appropriate to include tariffs as an agenda item. Not all products had been subject to liberalisation and tariff levels remained relatively high and unbound in developing countries (see Laird and Yeats, 1990). The objective of the negotiations has been to secure further trade liberalisation and, at least from the standpoint of some parties (e.g. the EC), to harmonise tariffs further. Thus, despite the fact that tariffs in industrialised countries were at historically low levels, this was seen as an area of potential gain. As well as liberalisation, negotiations have also addressed the issue of developing countries gaining credit for unilateral liberalisation undertaken in connection with World Bank conditionality.

Non-tariff barriers are essentially an item of unfinished business carried over from the Tokyo Round. As we have seen, growing reliance on NTBs in the 1970s has continued into the 1980s (see, for instance, Nogues, Olechowski and Winters, 1987). Although NTBs may be politically more convenient than tariffs, from an economic standpoint they are generally less efficient and contravene one of the key principles of the GATT, the most favoured nation provision. The group responsible for looking at NTBs was charged with establishing ways of constraining the use of NTBs and bringing them under the jurisdiction of the GATT. For example, one way of bringing a VER under the GATT is to calculate its 'tariff equivalent' and replace the VER with a tariff.[4] This tariff could then become the subject of the GATT negotiations in subsequent Rounds. From the standpoint of reaffirming the authority of the GATT, this is an important group.

Sectors

Four separate negotiating groups have focused on trade restrictions on a sector-specific basis, those concerned with *natural resource based products, tropical products, textiles and clothing* and *agriculture*. Natural resource based products and tropical products are relatively uncontroversial issues. Trade here is subject to fewer restrictions than agriculture, or textiles and clothing, and the potential gains from further liberalisation are relatively modest. The main issues have been tariff escalation in industrialised countries and the relative merits of GSP and MFN access. The same cannot be said of textiles and clothing. This is a sector of major significance to developing countries. For some thirty years, trade in textiles and clothing has been regulated by the so-called Multi Fibre Arrangements and their predecessors. The potential gains to developing countries of liberalisation are very considerable (Trela and Whalley, 1990), as are the potential gains to purchasers of clothing in the industrialised countries. The remit of the negotiating group is to provide a basis for eventual phase out of the MFA.

Trade in agricultural goods amounts to around 13 per cent of the total trade in goods. All of the major industrialised countries protect their agricultural sectors. There is now a substantial literature which attests to the costs of these policies (see Winters, 1987). Until now, agricultural trade has been completely immune from trade liberalisation. Pressure to have it included on the Uruguay Round came from those big producers which enjoy a comparative advantage in temperate zone agricultural goods – countries like Canada, Australia, Argentina and New Zealand and, most importantly, from the United States. Although the US supports its agricultural sector, it is not to the same extent as occurs in Japan or the EC. Negotiators here were, therefore, charged with the responsibility of taking action to improve market access and subjecting production subsidies to the GATT disciplines.[5]

The GATT System

Six of the fifteen negotiating groups addressed various features of the GATT system which the CPs felt were in need of review, namely *Safeguards, Subsidies and countervailing measures, GATT Articles, MTN agreements and arrangements, Functioning of the GATT system (FOGS)* and *Dispute settlement.* FOGS has delivered an important innovation, the so called trade policy review mechanism (TPRM). This is a process whereby the trade policies of CPs are monitored on a regular basis (every two to six years, depending upon the size of the country). It should therefore prove to be a valuable mechanism for highlighting changes in the trade policies of CPs. The group concerned with MTN Agreements and Arrangements has been reviewing the coverage and operation of the Codes introduced at Tokyo, as well as addressing the thorny issue of developing country participation in the GATT. The GATT Articles group is also addressing the latter through its review of developing country recourse to Article XVIII(b), which sanctions protection for balance of payments purposes. Other Articles are also under review, most notably XXIV (free trade areas and customs unions) and II(i) (tariff bindings).

Safeguards is another item of unfinished business carried over from the Tokyo Round. This refers to Article XIX of the GATT and the reluctance of CPs to use it. Article XIX sanctions temporary protection when a domestic industry suffers 'serious injury' from a sudden upsurge in imports. It is designed to provide governments with a safety valve against protectionist pressure. Instead of relying on Article XIX, many CPs have used grey area measures which are politically more attractive because they cannot be monitored by the GATT and can be used in a discriminatory manner (unlike Article XIX action). As in Tokyo, it is hoped that a suitable reformulation of Article XIX would not only encourage its use in the future but also allow pre-existing grey area measures to be made subject to the GATT disciplines. Articles VI and XVI of the GATT deal with anti dumping (AD), subsidies and countervailing duties (CVD). Countries have generally had recourse to national provisions rather than the GATT. Attention here has then focused on devising more effective criteria for discriminating between legal and illegal subsidies, as well as better procedures for policing their use. CPs do not always agree on what are legal/illegal measures. It is, therefore, necessary to have efficient dispute settlement mechanisms. There are actually two problems here. First, not all CPs are willing to have GATT adjudicate on disputes; second, *both* parties to a dispute have to agree to a Panel being set up and have to accept its findings for it to be followed up; it is easy to see then why the rulings of the GATT panels can be and have been ignored! As the jurisdiction of GATT widens to embrace new issues, the need for an efficient and effective dispute-settlement mechanism becomes increasingly important.

New Issues

Three issues are completely new to the GATT negotiations: *Trade related intellectual property rights (TRIPs), Trade related investment measures (TRIMs)* and *Trade in services*. As well as raising interesting analytical issues in their own right, all have proved to be contentious.

In industrialised countries, a number of institutional arrangements have been evolved to protect the creators of intellectual property – patents, copyrights and trademarks are good examples. Such property rights are not always enforceable outside the country of origin. In particular, most developing countries refuse to enforce intellectual property rights as copying is seen as a relatively cheap mechanism for technology transfer. Thus, in certain parts of the world, one can easily obtain cheap copies of Rolex watches, Gucci shoes, Lacoste T-shirts and so on. This lack of enforceability is a matter of great concern to the originators of these products, generally manufacturers in industrialised countries, as the transfers of income involved are reckoned to be substantial. Due largely to pressure from the United States, supported also by the EC, TRIPs were included on the Uruguay Round agenda. These countries hope that, by doing so, they can develop disciplines for bringing violators of intellectual property rights to book under the GATT.[6]

TRIMs refer to performance requirements imposed on multinational firms which engage in foreign direct investment. For example, the host government may only sanction the setting up of a subsidiary on condition that a certain proportion of required components are purchased locally – a local content requirement. Alternatively it may insist that a certain proportion of output is exported – a minimum export requirement. Investment measures such as these can have trade effects, they influence the amount of goods exported and imported. They are used largely, but not exclusively, by developing countries. Because they have trade effects, a negotiating group was charged with the responsibility of evaluating whether the existing GATT disciplines can be used to constrain their use and/or whether new disciplines need to be developed (see Greenaway, 1990).

Traded services include financial services like insurance and banking, transportation services, IT services and so on. The value of transactions in these activities is at least one fifth of the value of trade in goods. The GATT Articles only apply to trade in goods. Effectively then countries can intervene in international transactions in services with impunity. The US and EC see themselves as having a comparative advantage in services in general and financial services in particular. They argued strongly, therefore, that appropriate arrangements be developed for subjecting trade in services to multilateral disciplines. The argument is that there is no reason in principle why trade in services should be treated any differently to trade in goods and that further liberalisation of trade in goods, should have, as a *quid pro quo*, an agreement to deal with trade in services (see Balasubramanyam, 1991).

2.5 PROGRESS IN THE ROUND AND PROSPECTS FOR AGREEMENT

The schedule for the Uruguay Round envisaged a mid-term review in December 1988; the drafting of framework agreements (actually discussed at the Houston Summit in July 1990) followed by further negotiations on the final form of the agreement in autumn 1990. The formal signing of agreements would than take place in Brussels in early December 1990. As it happens, things have not worked out that way. The mid term review turned out to be a somewhat contentious affair with a number of CPs threatening to walk out of the negotiations; no draft agreements were in place for July 1990; and the Brussels meeting collapsed amidst recriminations about where responsibility for failure lay.

There are a number of factors which have contributed to the failure to reach agreement thus far and which could preclude eventual agreement. First the scale of the undertaking was quite enormous and, with hindsight, was bound to create difficulties. With 15 negotiating groups and 103 CPs, one had an agenda of truly gargantuan proportions. Second, and related to this, there are strong intersectoral linkages among many of the issues. When the Round was launched, it was believed that intersectoral linkages would in fact provide the key to a successful Round with deals being cut across groups. In the event it gave rise to what Mr Arthur Dunkel referred to as 'hide and seek' tactics. To illustrate this, consider Table 2.5, which identifies the main targets and concessions of the principal negotiating groups. For example, the United States was anxious to see progress

Table 2.5   Uruguay Round trade-offs

	'Targets'	'Concessions'
United States	Agriculture TRIPs Services TRIMs	Textiles & clothing Tariffs CVDs/AD NTBs
European Communities	TRIPs TRIMs Services Tariffs	Textiles & clothing Agriculture Safeguards CVDs/AD
Japan	NTBs TRIMs CVDs/AD Safeguards	Agriculture Services TRIPs
Developing Countries	Textiles & clothing NTBs Safeguards Agriculture Tropical products Natural resource based products	Services TRIPs TRIMs Tariffs

being made on agricultural liberalisation. A willingness to give way elsewhere, for example, on textiles and clothing, was contingent on a satisfactory outcome on agriculture. There are many examples of such linkages one could cite – the key point is that they complicated the negotiations. Offers of concessions in one area were held up by any lack of progress on other linked issues. This was particularly problematic in the case of agriculture. The United States took the view that agricultural liberalisation was central to any agreement. They wanted to see deep cuts in agricultural support measures in the EC, as well as dismantling of export subsidies. The European view was that changes of the sort proposed by the US would strike at the very heart of the Common Agricultural Policy and, as such, were wholly unacceptable. The gulf between the two sides ultimately proved unbridgeable. Whilst this dispute was festering, progress was arrested elsewhere. A third factor again tied in with the previous points was the difficulty of monitoring outcomes on some of the issues and measuring them against others. It is relatively easy to evaluate an offer to cut tariffs by x per cent; it is much more difficult to evaluate an offer to remove local content requirements. Moreover, there are problems of weighing one against the other.

Fourth, some of the new issues created unexpected difficulties, in part because they were new issues and there was no real track record of negotiating on them, in part because some of them raised constitutional problems. For example, developing countries argued that the GATT had no real jurisdiction in the matter of intellectual property rights and claimed this was the preserve of the World Intellectual Property Organisation (WIPO). Likewise they argued that since TRIMs were investment measures rather than border measures, they were instruments of national policy and not subject to the GATT jurisdiction. Services was another area where it was argued by some that national interest issues were at stake and the GATT had no real role to play.

A fifth factor which mitigated against an agreement was the intricacy of cross coalitional activity. Coalitions sometimes faced each other on a North–South basis (e.g. TRIMs, textiles and clothing); sometimes on a North–North basis (agriculture, tariffs), sometimes on both (agriculture). The point is that allies in one negotiating group may have been enemies in another (see Whalley, 1989). This made it more difficult to secure a winning coalition.

Sixth, the position of some of the key parties on some issues altered as the negotiations proceeded. US manoeuvring on services was particularly disruptive in this respect. The initial position was one which saw a framework agreement founded on MFN principles. Late in the negotiations, this position altered dramatically to one which not only proposed that MFN treatment be conditional but one which also identified sectors which should be excluded from any agreement. As soon as the US provided a list of excluded sectors, the EC responded with its own list.

Finally there were several important background developments which did not help. Thus, for example, a case can be made to the effect that the EC has been preoccupied to a greater extent with its single market programme than with the Uruguay Round. To a lesser extent the US has been preoccupied with negotiating free trade arrangements with Canada and Mexico. In addition, however, it has also introduced new trade measures founded on 'aggressive unilateralism' (Bhagwati, 1990). This sanctions (under US law) unilateral action designed to elicit changes in the trade policies of others. This action, which is based on discrimination and bilateralism, was unhelpful, to say the least.

For these reasons the Round collapsed in December 1990 – eighteen months later it has still not been completed. The Gatt Secretariat has attempted to force the pace of developments in various ways. For example, in the autumn of 1991, the number of negotiating groups was slimmed down to 8 'negotiating areas' in an attempt to bundle a larger number of issues together and expedite progress. When this failed to deliver an outcome, Mr Dunkel, the Director General, presented the CPs with the so-called 'Final Act', an agreement in draft, with appropriate 'square brackets' around controversial issues. The idea behind this was to concentrate attention on the key issues and thereby drive the negotiations forward again. Although most CPs saw the basis for an agreement in this text there were a number of key sticking points, most notably on agriculture. In particular the issues of whether compensation payments to European farmers were or were not decoupled from production was contentious.

Agriculture has continued to be at the heart of the failure to reach agreement. At the time of writing the US and EC are closer than they have ever been, following the apparent concessions made by the EC in the MacSharry Plan. This, together with impending US elections, could generate the momentum to complete the Round. Considerable uncertainty remains however, for several reasons. First, even when the US and EC reach agreement on agriculture, there remains unfinished business – Japan has not been an active participant in the agricultural negotiations and as yet has refused to budge on its controversial rice ban. Second, agriculture is not the only contentious area – services and intellectual property in particular also require work. Thus, it would be a mistake to assume that when agriculture is resolved, everything else falls into place. Finally, the time frame for agreement is now very tight having regard to the fact that US Presidential elections are upcoming in November 1992, and the US fast track negotiating authority expires the following Spring.

What would be the benefits of success, or costs of failure? This is a very difficult one to judge. A number of analysts have however attempted to estimate benefits using computable general equilibrium (CGE) modelling. For instance, Nguyen, Perroni and Wigle (1991) calibrate a multi-sector, multi-product, multi-country model to simulate the conclusion of a 'comprehensive' outcome and a 'face saving' outcome. The former comprises a 70 per cent cut in agricultural support, rapid phase out of the MFA, a 50 per cent cut in tariffs, a 20 per cent cut in protection of tradeable services and commitments to integrate TRIMs and TRIPs at some time in the future. The probability of this occurring is now zero. But for comparative purposes it is worth noting that the *net* welfare benefits of such an outcome are estimated at around $250 million, that is, around 8 per cent of the value of world trade.

The composition of the 'face saving' package is more modest: a 30 per cent cut in agricultural support, a commitment to phase out the MFA with the first steps being taken, a 50 per cent cut in tariffs and a longer term commitment to discipline TRIMs and TRIPs. This is actually not too far away from what a final agreement could look like. Nguyen *et al* estimate the net welfare benefits of this outcome at $100 billion – less than that of the comprehensive outcome, but still over 3 per cent of the value of world trade, and still worth taking rather than leaving.

Of course the benefits foregone of failure are not simply $250 or $100 billion (depending on the appropriate scenario). These should be regarded as *minimum* potential losses for the simple reason that there would be negative feedback associated with failure. We would not simply revert to where we were, or even stand still. The danger is that failure would result in further erosion of the GATT disciplines and credibility, and push the major trading nations/blocs to continue the drift towards regional, and away from multilateral, trading arrangements.

Although the effects of regional trade liberalisation on global economic welfare could, in principle, be second best only to those of multilateral liberalisation, it cannot be taken for granted that regional trading blocs will be liberal in their external trading relations. It is for this reason that the global welfare effects of the formation of regional trading blocs may actually be worse than maintaining the trading status quo.

3 The US Perspective

Jimmye S. Hillman[1]

'The only new thing in the world is the history we do not know.'
— Harry Truman

3.1 INTRODUCTION

Over the last two centuries the United States has suffered from isolationism, protectionism and lack of leadership in creating and maintaining consistent agricultural and trade policies. From the country's beginning an export market was taken for granted as the natural order of things and national trade policy consisted essentially of arguments over tariffs and customs duties. After more than a century of this, World War I should have awakened the United States to its potential for a new role in world affairs. Its answer was a rejection of the League of Nations in the early 1920s, followed by a reinforced protectionism throughout that decade, and by the disastrous Hawley–Smoot Tariff Act of 1929. Failed protectionist attempts to 'make the tariff effective for agriculture' centred on five McNary–Haugen Bills (1924–8) which included a two-price system. As an added negative effect on world trade, the United States for some years after WWI ignored its new role as the world's chief creditor.

In an attempt to reverse isolationism and failed trade policies the US Congress enacted the Reciprocal Trade Agreements Act (RTA) of June 1934 in which was incorporated the unique idea of Reciprocal Trade Agreements, an idea which has endured for more than 50 years of trade negotiations. The essence of that Act (initially enacted for a period of three years) empowered the President to order tariff cuts of up to 50 per cent on a bi-lateral, reciprocal basis, and that such cuts would be extended to third countries, on a most favoured nation (MFN) basis, provided that they were prepared to reciprocate by giving equally favourable treatment to imports from the United States. The fact that farmers, who had been particularly hurt by the shrinkage of their exports and the price slump accompanying it, needed large foreign markets to improve their situation was recognised in the reference in

26

the Act's introductory paragraph to trade expansion 'as a means of . . . establishing . . . a better relationship among various branches of American agriculture, industry, mining and commerce'.

The RTA was pushed through Congress, and the President was given this unprecedented authority, despite all the illiberal domestic policy (including farm programmes) which was being enacted at the same time. Die-hard protectionists in the farm sector who still favoured the high Hawley–Smoot tariffs and export dumping as principal agricultural policy tools lost the battle early with Henry A. Wallace, President Franklin Roosevelt's Secretary of Agriculture, who favoured the expansion of markets through tariff reduction.

Protectionists had not lost the war, however. Perhaps they considered the RTA an aberration which posed no real threat to their long term position. Also, RTA in one sense was a trade-off for the path-breaking elements of the Agricultural Adjustment Act (AAA) of 1933. Section 22, a part of the AAA, as amended in 1934 and the RTA were legislated more or less simultaneously, emphasising the political insight as well as the power of President Roosevelt. It was designed to protect the economic viability of domestic farm price supports.

The essence of Section 22 is that it legalised agricultural import quotas subject to certain constraints; that is, agricultural import quotas are legal provided a government support programme is in force covering the 'like domestic product'.[2] That is still the case. It authorises the President of the United States to restrict the importation of commodities by the imposition of fees or quotas if such importation would render ineffective, or materially interfere with, the policies of the Department of Agriculture in relation to agricultural commodities. The scope and permissible action of the original legislation was expanded by the Trade Agreements Extension Act of 1951, under which no trade agreement or other international agreement can be applied in a manner inconsistent with requirements found in Section 22. The Trade Expansion Act of 1962 also makes that exception. It will be shown later that the United States as part of its negotiating position in the Uruguay Round of multilateral trade negotiations expressed a willingness to negotiate the repeal of Section 22, but certain domestic farm interests continued vigorously to resist this change. If this piece of fundamental legislation were eliminated, and if no comparable substitute were put in place, the United States would, indeed, have taken a major step in removing the principal bulwark of its agricultural protection.

An additional disposition toward protection and trade distortion was contained in Section 32 of the 1933 AAA. Section 32 authorised the use of import duty revenues to subsidise the disposal of surpluses, domestically and abroad. Further, there was constant agitation in some agricultural quarters to legislate a marketing scheme with a discriminatory two-price system for farm products, domestic and foreign. Thus began a period of about 40 years (1933–73) of predominantly inward-looking, protectionistic agricultural policies, which became increasingly at odds with the United States position in the post-World-War II ambience and with its position in the post-war trade negotiations.

Rather than exercise a bold and liberal posture from its over-whelming economic status in the early 1950s, United States permitted the protectionistic views of farmers and farm organisations to prevail in the negotiation of waivers and exceptions to the GATT Article XI on the general elimination of quantitative restrictions. Adding to this and other protective devices was the Agricultural Trade Development and Assistance Act of 1954 (Public Law 480), the principal aspect of which was an expanded surplus disposal programme, some of it through export subsidies. Again a strong overall economic and political position of the United States was undermined and dissipated by rather narrow, vested interest groups.

Since World War II there have been eight GATT rounds of trade negotiations (Geneva 1947; Annecy 1949; Torquay 1951; Geneva 1956; Dillon 1960–1; Kennedy 1964–7; Tokyo 1974–9; Uruguay 1986–), most of which were devoted to reduction of tariffs on manufactured products. The Uruguay Round was the first to focus primarily on the agricultural sector and again the United States, which was the leader in insisting on that focus, found itself in the years immediately prior to 1986 in a position of qualified ambivalence with respect to its agricultural and trade policies. Even though the United States was, and still is, less culpable than its major trading partners, Japan and the European Community, it began the Uruguay Round with agricultural policies which resulted in total transfers to producers from taxpayers and consumers, less budget revenues (direct costs) of US$88 billion in 1986 and which total was still US$67 billion in 1989 (Table 3.1). The data in Table 3.1 demonstrate both the continuing enormity of the problems of agricultural policy distortion and the urgency of finding solutions for fundamental resource adjustment in the agricultural sectors of the world economy. This table emphasises that, amongst OECD countries, the lion's share of income transfers to farmers induced by agricultural policy are attributable to the European Community (12), the United States and Japan, in that order.

3.2 UNITED STATES URUGUAY ROUND OBJECTIVES

The Uruguay Round of the GATT negotiations, like most important historical events and phenomena, had factors underlying or leading up to it which are of vital importance for our understanding and objective analysis. As already suggested in the introduction to this chapter, the United States has had a long-standing, ambivalent position with respect to agricultural protection and international trade policy. The roots of conflict lie deep in the evolution of US economic development and occasionally manifest themselves negatively, as was the case with the 1947–8 negotiations over whether to include an International Trade Organisation (ITO) in the Havana Charter. United States interests and farm organisations led the opposition to the creation of an ITO.

Article XI, Section 1 of the GATT states:

No prohibitions or restrictions other than duties, taxes or other charges, whether made effective through quotas, import or export licenses or other measures, shall be instituted or maintained by any contracting party on the importation of any product of the territory of any other contracting party or on the exportation or sale for export of any product destined for the territory of any other contracting party.

But, due to the widespread incidence of agricultural protectionist sentiment around the world, including the United States, an exception to this general ban on the use of non-tariff barriers to trade was made in the case of agriculture. Thus, paragraph 2 was added to Article XI in order to make an *exception* in the case of agriculture to the otherwise general ban on the use of non-tariff barriers to trade. Sub-paragraph 2(c)(i) of Article XI effectively legalises an agricultural import quota, *provided* a supply control programme is in force restricting the production of the 'like domestic product'. However, the United States was not happy with sub-paragraph 2(c)(i) because the constraint it imposed on the use of an agricultural import quota was tighter than the constraint imposed by Section 22 of the 1934 amendment of the AAA.

Table 3.1 Total transfers associated with agricultural policies[1] (in billion US dollars)

Country	Transfers from taxpayers (1)				Transfers from consumers (2)				Budget revenues (3)				Total transfers (1) + (2) + (3)			
	1986	1987	1988	1989	1986	1987	1988	1989	1986	1987	1988	1989	1986	1987	1988	1989
Australia	0.4	0.3	0.2	0.3	0.5	0.4	0.4	0.4	0.0	0.0	0.0	0.0	0.9	0.7	0.6	0.6
Austria	0.4	0.5	0.6	1.1	2.2	3.0	2.7	2.2	0.0	0.0	0.0	0.0	2.6	3.5	3.2	3.3
Canada	4.4	5.7	5.1	4.2	3.6	3.6	3.1	3.1	0.1	0.1	0.1	0.1	7.9	9.2	8.6	7.2
EC-12	31.7	38.2	45.8	44.1	71.9	78.3	63.7	54.1	0.7	0.7	0.7	0.7	102.9	115.9	108.8	97.5
Finland	1.3	1.6	1.8	1.7	3.5	4.0	4.4	4.3	0.1	0.4	0.2	0.1	4.8	5.3	6.0	6.0
Japan	13.9	18.4	18.7	15.6	48.8	55.3	60.8	52.4	8.6	10.4	13.7	10.2	54.1	63.3	65.9	57.8
N. Zealand	0.9	0.1	0.1	0.0	0.1	0.1	0.1	0.1	0.0	0.0	0.0	0.0	0.9	0.1	0.2	0.1
Norway	1.5	1.8	1.8	1.8	1.4	1.8	1.8	1.6	0.2	0.2	0.3	0.2	2.7	3.3	3.4	3.3
Sweden	0.5	0.5	0.5	0.4	3.2	3.5	3.3	2.9	0.1	0.3	0.2	0.1	3.5	3.8	3.6	3.2
Switzerland	1.1	1.4	1.5	1.3	3.8	4.9	5.2	4.3	0.6	0.8	0.9	0.6	4.3	5.5	5.8	4.9
US	59.4	50.3	49.1	46.3	29.6	30.4	26.0	21.6	0.9	0.7	0.8	0.7	88.1	80.0	74.3	67.2
TOTAL	115.5	118.7	125.2	116.9	168.5	185.3	172.0	146.9	11.2	13.6	16.8	12.7	272.8	290.4	280.4	251.1

Source: OECD 'Agricultural Policies, Markets and Trade', Paris, 1990, p. 111, Secretariat Estimates.

Note to Table 3.1

1 Note that the total transfers shown in this table are broader than those covered by PSE and CSE calculations for two principal reasons. First, being confined to only twelve 'principal' agricultural commodity categories, PSEs and CSEs account for only part of the total value of agricultural production. Second, PSEs and CSEs exclude budget outlays on agricultural policy measures which do not benefit agricultural producers directly. Examples include subsidies specific to food processing and distribution, public expenditure on rural transport and other infrastructure, food consumer subsidies (such as food stamps in the US) and public stock holding expenditures. However, even these more comprehensive transfer estimates *exclude* the exchequer cost of administering agricultural policies. The difference between the total transfers associated with agricultural policies, as shown in this table, and the more frequently cited PSE and CSE transfers is not trivial. In recent years total transfers have been not much less than double the total of PSE and CSE transfers in most developed countries. For a fuller explanation of this point, see: OECD 'Agricultural Policies, Markets and Trade', Paris, 1991, p. 137.

Whereas Section 22 authorises the quantitative restriction of imports, subject only to a government support programme being in force for the 'like domestic commodity', Article XI.2(c)(i) of the GATT stipulates that the government programme must include *supply control*. Dissatisfaction with Article XI.2(c)(i) eventually led to the United States being granted a waiver to its commitments under those provisions. The celebrated Section 22 waiver was granted to the United States in 1955, as part of a wider revision of the General Agreement effected in that year. Although, in the strict letter of of the law, the 1955 waiver applied only to the United States, after it had been granted other GATT signatories understandably felt free to operate quantitative restrictions on imports of agricultural products *without* domestic supply control. By taking this action when it was at a comparative advantage and in a dominant position in world agriculture and trade, the United States sacrificed the high ground of international agricultural trade policy in round after round of the GATT trade negotiations for the next 30 years (Porter and Bowers, 1989).

These rounds of GATT negotiations since World War II resulted in significant reductions in industrial tariffs but not in agricultural protection. Instead, new methods of restricting agriculture arose, especially of the non-tariff type. The United States after a 40-year, inward-looking policy discovered it no longer dominated world agricultural commodity markets. After a respite of trade prosperity in the mid-1970s, increased market competition, lower farm prices and rural depression all succeeded in focusing American attention on foreign markets as a possible solution to farm distress. Unfortunately, a period of high exchange rates for the American dollar meant that its over-valuation would spell disaster for agricultural exports. In calendar year 1981 US agricultural exports had reached almost $44 billion, or 30 per cent of gross sales. From this peak exports dropped to $26 billion in 1986, or only 19 per cent of gross farm sales, and payments to US producers for farm price and income supports had skyrocketed to almost $30 billion. At least an equivalent amount in value was transferred from consumers as a result of agricultural policies then in existence. It was in this atmosphere that the United States led the way toward the Uruguay Round and in the process proposed a new departure in the negotiations: namely, the inclusion of domestic subsidies and import quota restrictions on the agenda, along with all other non-tariff agricultural trade barriers.

The United States, thus, had come a long way when it finally appeared willing in the mid-1980s to link, fundamentally, its agricultural policy with its international trade policy. A step had been taken in that direction in 1973 within the United States Department of Agriculture (USDA) when the domestic commodity programmes and international affairs were combined under a single Assistant Secretary for International Affairs. This did little to co-ordinate interdepartmental trade matters and concerns, however, and the ghost of agricultural protectionism quickly reappeared with the early 1980s downturn in exports.

The basic change, therefore, with which the United States appeared at Punta del Este, Uruguay in 1986 was the intent, not only to integrate its own agricultural and foreign policy objectives and to present a unified position, but also to insist that all the farm policies and related agricultural issues of each country or political bloc be put on the bargaining table. Robert Paarlberg in an excellent recent essay (Paarlberg, 1991) maintains that Reagan Administration officials, Clayton Yeutter, US Special Trade Representative, and Daniel Amstutz, Under-Secretary of Agriculture for International Affairs, after defeat on their free-market proposals in the 1985 Farm Bill, sensed an opportunity to pursue their domestic objective of reforming farm policy through an international negotiation abroad. No doubt both were deeply committed to basic restructuring of United States farm policy. In fact, seldom in the history of the GATT negotiations had the process and the potential outcome been so influenced by major US political personalities.

The United States had not had an abrupt conversion from protectionism and, in fact, there was much talk that its opening position in the Uruguay Round was a 'bluff'. Pressure groups campaigning for the retention of agricultural protectionism were still strongly entrenched in Washington DC. Nevertheless, there was a general recognition by the Congress and the Executive Branch of the high social costs of past mistakes in trade policies and the high price paid for uneconomic farm policies. But, in view of the strength of domestic opposition to major reform, the position on agriculture adopted by the US government in the Uruguay Round displayed considerable political courage.

The Tokyo Round, 1974–9, had been conducted during a period of unparalleled expansion of agricultural trade. Unfortunately, the Uruguay Round began at a time of declining agricultural trade and, for the United States, a declining relative share of that trade compared to a decade earlier. For example, the US share of world wheat exports varied between 40 per cent and 50 per cent for the decade 1974–83 but fell below 30 per cent in 1986–7 as the Uruguay Round started. The challenge to the US negotiators was to discover methods of negotiating farm programme changes throughout the world, including its own, which might rectify this situation.

A variety of proposals were tabled in late 1987 and early 1988 for the Uruguay Round of trade negotiations. The US proposal was for a sweeping elimination of *all* trade-distorting agricultural subsidies by the year 2000, or over a ten-year period (the so-called zero option). Was this position a bluff, or were the Americans naïve, or was this a bold politico–economic strategy? It seems unlikely that the US Administration really believed that the European Community and Japan would accept the zero option. If this interpretation is correct, the first negotiating proposal, tabled by the United States in Geneva in July 1987, was an ideological trial balloon launched by the Administration in the hope that political and economic winds would be favourable to achieving the desired result. As has already been stated, agricultural protectionism is deep-rooted; farm lobbies and their allies have always been the stumbling block to agricultural policy reform, both in America and other developed countries.

Paarlberg proffers the persuasive argument that, for their own ulterior motives, certain protectionism interests in the United States nevertheless supported the zero option in the secure knowledge that it would be rejected by other parties to the negotiations and that it might possibly torpedo the entire Round (Paarlberg, 1991, p.17). Though this strategy might appear a bit Machiavellian, one should never underestimate the latent physiocrats of rural America and the die-hard protectionist supporters of commodity programmes. There can be little doubt, however, that some elements in US agriculture, alarmed by adverse public sentiment and concern over the costs of current farm programmes, have for some time been in favour of substantial policy reforms.

The political opportunity arose in the Uruguay Round to attempt such reforms. Ambassador Yeutter, among others, was centre stage both in framing the proposals and in conducting the actual negotiations. Most knowledgeable policymakers agree on the disease; only the technical remedy was at issue. But few ever believed in the shock therapy of zero option. As with many of the ideological thrusts of the Reagan Administration, the vulnerability of the US position was overlooked, and the mechanics of executing the 'solution' was unsupported by the realpolitik of American farm programmes. To repeat, the political clout still wielded by agricultural protectionists, farm lobbies, farm fundamentalists and other opponents of freer agricultural trade was underestimated from the beginning of the Uruguay Round.

The US position has been for some time that it is impossible to free domestic agricultural markets while, at the same time, international markets continue to be distorted by the policy interventions of governments. Dale Hathaway, former Under-Secretary of Agriculture in the USDA, has observed that in the modern world domestic and international markets and policies are closely and inextricably interlinked (Hathaway, 1987). The United States with its opening salvo at Punta del Este appeared to be willing to forego its past 50-year reliance on regulating its internal markets for the greater goal of freer commodity and services trade on an international scale.

The theme of political expansion of markets was a recurring litany in testimony supporting the US position on the Uruguay Round. For example, Ambassador Hills, in a March 1991 testimony supporting fast-track extension, said: 'Agricultural reform of the kind the United States has proposed would allow world agricultural exports to expand by $100 billion, or by one-third' (Hearing: US House of Representatives Committee on Agriculture, 1991).

The ensuing process Paarlberg has skilfully described as an international negotiating venture at reforming US agricultural policy; as an attempt, conducted with like-minded officials abroad, both to weaken, then to finesse, the domestic farm lobby opponents of reform at home (Paarlberg, 1991, p.11). The problem with this plan to outmanoeuvre domestic opposition to reform was that it united the opposition. Thus, from the moment when the United States government chose to present agricultural reform as the central element in the overall Uruguay Round GATT negotiations, US domestic farm lobby groups, with some distinct advantages on their side, began their own strategy to protect themselves from this international effort to reduce farm subsidies.

Hence, initially the general objective of the United States in the Uruguay Round was to guide world agriculture and trade toward a market-oriented system which would be governed by stronger and more operationally effective GATT rules and disciplines, and ultimately fully to integrate agriculture into the GATT. Of major concern was long-range reforms in agricultural policies which would result in freer international markets for agricultural commodities. Ambassador Yeutter (later US Secretary of Agriculture), testifying before a key committee in the US House of Representatives on 25 September 1986 after the launching of the Uruguay Round, pointed out that the terms of the Punta del Este Declaration – following seven months of preparatory discussion in Geneva – had put all agricultural issues on the table in which 'at the top of our list is agricultural subsidies, which are hurting our efficient farmers and busting budgets around the world. We will also go after the full range of market access restrictions affecting agricultural trade, including those based on phoney health standards' (Yeutter, 1986).

Specifically, and in outline form, the US goals in the agricultural sector as of July 1987 might be summarised as follows:

1. To establish a discipline over the use of export subsidies. The United States sought to freeze existing subsidies with an agreed timetable for phasing them out over a period of years (the so-called 'standstill' and 'rollback' provisions).
2. To improve market access and to reduce trade barriers including quantitative restrictions. Non-tariff barriers, including animal health and plant inspection requirements, were singled out for special attention.
3. To strengthen the dispute settlement and enforcement processes including the development of improved arrangements for assuring compliance.

4. To phase out all trade-distorting domestic subsidies and import barriers over a 10-year period.

United States negotiators came away from the initial sessions of the Uruguay Round on an optimistic note, perhaps relieved that the 92 GATT member countries had at last launched a new round of multilateral negotiations. Ambassador Yeutter reported 'I am now pleased to report that we came away from the Punta del Este Ministerial meeting having achieved all of the objectives we identified. Multilateral negotiations will soon get underway on the full range of trade problems confronting us' (Yeutter, 1986).

Offsetting any undue optimism, however, was the memory of past negotiations and bargaining, particularly with the European negotiators, who are under constant pressure from hard-line farm organisations such as COPA and COGECA. The Uruguay Round negotiations were expected to be tough because there was much at stake and much work to be done. Producing a multilateral agreement on new trade rules and disciplines is always difficult. The United States, however, apparently deemed this latest effort necessary to open significant new opportunities for American agricultural exporters as well as to strengthen the global trading system so that all countries might compete on equal terms. In the background of the United States negotiating position lay its own farm policies, and there lurked US farm organisations and farm commodity groups which would be constantly on the alert to prevent an erosion of their interests during the coming years of negotiations. Many, including the author of this chapter, were not fully convinced that the US delegation would be permitted to 'go the distance' in substantially reducing its own farm support systems and the protection of commodity interests.

The original United States objectives and its bargaining position during the life of the Uruguay Round would be affected by two major forces: the reaction of other countries especially the European Community to its initial proposals; and the politics of agriculture in Washington. Whether by accident or design, for the first time in the history of the GATT a round of negotiations was scheduled to end simultaneously with the passage of a new Farm Bill in the fall of 1990.

During late 1987 and most of 1988 the US negotiation machinery was at work: (1) assessing the fallout from the initial proposals; (2) constructing proposals for future discussion and negotiations; and (3) undertaking economic analyses to document various scenarios for future bargaining.

3.3 PROCESS VERSUS SUBSTANCE

Often in international affairs the objectives sought by nations become so enmeshed and identified with the techniques for attaining those objectives that some unforeseen change in circumstances and events is needed to move things off dead centre and toward a conclusion. Such an anomaly, or cataclysmic occurrence, has never happened in the GATT negotiations. 'Rounds' have been opened, participants congregate at Geneva, negotiators jockey for position at a pre-agreed locale, and midway – or, usually, much later – through the Round some serious paper is surfaced by a country which ushers in a flurry of activities preparatory to the meeting of the deadline for concluding this particular Round. It has been no different with the Uruguay Round.

This is not to say that there has been no urgency in the current process, nor that the negotiating technique has been the same as in the Tokyo, the Kennedy and other Rounds. Indeed, the United States in particular, and the Cairns Group (Argentina, Australia, Brazil, Canada, Chile, Columbia, Fiji, Hungary, Indonesia, Malaysia, New Zealand, Philippines, Thailand, and Uruguay) alongside it, have utilised a variety of economic techniques and political tactics to move toward the accomplishment of objectives spelled out in the Ministerial Declaration at Punta del Este in 1986. From the beginning the United States said that agriculture was the top priority for the Uruguay Round. It also insisted that the scope of the negotiations be broader than in the past. That is, 'tariff reductions' was not the issue but, instead, 'substantial, progressive reductions in agricultural support and protection' must be achieved. This meant fundamental change in all agricultural and trade policies and programmes, domestic and international.

Implied in the United States position from the beginning was 'decoupling', or the separation of price or income payments to farmers based on production of farm commodities. The idea appears simple but is difficult of achievement and, contrary to implications in the current debate, it has been around at least 50 years. Academic economists in the United States were advocating decoupled payments as early as the 1950s, but Congress for the most part has always ignored proposals containing the concept (Reinsel, 1989).

The 1980s decoupling plan of Senator Rudy Boschwitz (Minnesota) – which did not include dairy and sugar – proposed to break the tie between production of agricultural commodities and income support by abolishing non-recourse loans, allowing prices to be determined in the market, paying farmers directly based on past production, and reducing payments annually to some lower level over time. However, farmers in the United States have always been quite sceptical of any concept that divorces their income from price, acreage and yield, and the equivalent phenomena on the animal side of production. As will be seen later in this chapter, on the other hand, the 1990s and the Uruguay Round were not 'normal' times, and the US policy makers were being forced into new avenues of thinking and action on farm issues and trade.

In November 1988 the United States submitted a Framework Proposal which was specifically designed to set the agenda for future negotiations and as a guide for the forthcoming Mid-Term Review of progress made during the first two years of the Uruguay Round negotiations and to outline a working plan for the final two years. A central element of the Framework Proposal was the 'tariffication' of all non-tariff barriers to agricultural trade, that is, that all NTBs should be converted to their tariff equivalents and bound. Combined with the tariffication proposal was its natural corollary that all tariff equivalents (TEs) be subject to a phased reduction leading to eventual abolition. Despite this attempt by the United States to advance the Uruguay Round by clarifying the agenda for the negotiations on agriculture, the contracting parties, meeting for the Mid-Term Review in Montreal in December 1988, could not agree upon objectives, let alone the procedures to be followed in achieving them. The United States, supported by the Cairns Group, wanted an agreement to achieve a market-oriented, barrier-free agricultural trading system. The US–CG proposal contrasted with that of the European Community which continued to refuse substantial alteration of its support policies and which, in line with European history, preferred market sharing arrangements. An impasse ensued, but not a complete breakdown in negotiations. A pause was convenient in any case, to permit the 'digestion' of the US election results (including the election of a new President) in November 1988.

3.4   YEUTTER AND THE US COMPREHENSIVE PROPOSAL

At one critical point prior to the ill-fated Montreal Conference Ambassador Yeutter, still as Special Trade Representative (STR), signalled a willingness to move away from the zero option and, with the Cairns Group, compromise towards a more realistic position of a short-term roll-back of agricultural supports, export subsidies and trade barriers. United States farm groups led by sugar and dairy protectionists lobbied successfully to have Yeutter persist with the zero option. Specifically, the chief economist of the National Milk Producers Federation expressed concern that a short-term reduction in support barriers and price supports of 10 per cent for two years could cost the US dairy industry $2 billion. He added: '. . . why should US agriculture not be alarmed at the administration's talk of possibly embracing something less than its long-term objective? Why should we think something different is going to happen, given that this administration has been more critical of basic agricultural programs than previous administrations? Why should we not be concerned this time around?' (Vitaliano, 1988).

Early in 1989 the appointment by the incoming Bush Administration of Dr. Clayton Yeutter as Secretary of Agriculture, moving him from the post of Special Trade Representative under the Reagan Administration, appeared to reinforce the resolve of the United States toward hard bargaining to lower agricultural supports and to foster liberal agricultural trade policies. Yeutter's unique background *vis-à-vis* European farm groups, his excellent knowledge of US agribusiness and trade, his well-known ability at achieving political compromise, all coupled with his toughness at insisting on movement toward fundamental change when the economic facts warrant such change, placed him in a strong auxiliary position in the new US Administration. Yeutter's new appointment was a signal of the strength of the US commitment to agricultural policy reform, as well as testing how acceptable a reduced level of protection might be to agricultural interests in the United States. If political support for his position became uncertain, which it ultimately did, the US commitment would inevitably soften.

The new Special Trade Representative, Ms Carla Hills, along with Yeutter, could and would continue to urge negotiators in the Uruguay Round to reduce substantially agriculture supports, and to ensure more liberal agricultural and trade policies for the future. Over the next two years one could accurately predict inexorable pressure both at home and abroad by the United States to adopt the appropriate political techniques in order to attain its basic objectives. As was soon evident, some modifications in those objectives themselves would be tabled in order to keep the negotiations moving.

The delayed Mid-Term Agreement of April, 1989 in Geneva salvaged the negotiations from complete break-down. In order to preserve the basic objectives agreed to in the Punta del Este Declaration, particularly that of establishing 'a fair and market-oriented trading system', the United States accepted what was characterised as a language change from 'elimination of *all* trade distortions' to 'substantial, progressive reductions in agriculture support and protection sustained over an agreed period of time'. Actually, this form of words was a cover for a basic shift in the US position. The new President, George Bush, had fudged away from the zero option in agriculture in order to buy time on other aspects of the Uruguay Round negotiations, but a tough stance on agriculture persisted.

The Mid-Term Agreement at US insistence also called for strengthened GATT rules pertaining to agricultural trade and it established a work plan for the rest of 1989. In addition to the fundamental issue of market access and subsidies, participants were to advance proposals on a variety of topics, including food security concerns, special and differential treatment for developing countries, and ways to counter the possible negative effects of the reform process on net food importing countries (Deaton *et al.*, 1990). The agreement also stated that by the end of 1990 participants would agree to a long-term reform programme and the period for its implementation. In keeping with the programme established in the Mid-Term Agreement the United States submitted a paper in July, 1980 which outlined a procedure to convert all non-tariff barriers to tariffs with the understanding that tariffs would be substantially and progressively reduced. The rationale for this approach was that tariffs have been, historically, the preferred means of protection under the GATT (Deaton *et al.*, 1990, p. 5).

Also, in accordance with the terms of the Mid-Term Agreement, the United States tabled at Geneva on 25 October 1989 its Comprehensive Agricultural Proposal, the first nation to do so, preparatory to the final 14 months of negotiations. This latest proposal outlined in considerable detail policies to be included in the phase-out of agricultural protection over a ten-year period. The US zero option remained intact in the Comprehensive Agriculture Proposal. Ideological positions, once taken by great powers, die reluctantly. But many observers, including the author, had little doubt that the United States would ultimately retreat from the hard-line zero option. This Comprehensive Proposal in the words of Secretary Yeutter 'is designed to level the playing field for farmers, so they compete fairly against one another instead of against governmental treasuries, in order to feed this growing population with a rational set of international trade rules' (Yeutter, 1989).

The US Comprehensive Proposal was tabled after one of the most intensive periods of agricultural and trade policy analysis in the history of the GATT. The Economic Research Service, USDA, alone lists 228 studies done by that agency as of September (Nabbs-Zeno and Swann, 1991). Many other major and minor analyses were done by public and private, domestic and international agencies. The salient feature of most of these studies was a general support of the United States position: that agriculture is, indeed, the most protected and distorted sector in the global economy; that governments spend billions of dollars, each year, to fund policies which are detrimental to the welfare of farmers, consumers and taxpayers; and that the entire world would benefit by agricultural trade liberalisation, though some farmers and consumers (e.g., in LDCs) would lose.

Despite all of the 'proof' by research studies of resource misallocation, of the protection of vested interests and of the enormous costs of farm programmes, lobbyists and politicians select only those that support their own positions. Hence, US opponents of agricultural trade liberalisation continued their efforts at demonstrating the ill effects of a rapid dismantling[3] of government farm programmes. Results of two studies were selected for particular prominence by farm groups. By one estimate (Roningen and Dixit, 1989), even in a world of multilateral liberalisation, the elimination of farm subsidies would still cost US farm producers $17 billion; and by another study (Drabenstott *et al.*, 1989) more than $5 billion. These types of data were gleaned from the numerous models and research by academic, government and private economists and were fodder for the anti-liberalisation lobbyists. Added to these, special interest group commissions formed their own studies. Unfortunately, in such periods, objective analysis gives way to convenient fact-finding and often the data needed to support objectivity is difficult to find.

An entire chapter could be devoted alone to an analysis of the US Comprehensive Proposal of October 1989 (US GATT Delegation, 1989). Suffice to say the document repeated the US commitment to a more market-oriented trading environment in which all countries would be able to compete on relatively equal terms, according to their comparative advantage, and not by government support. It reaffirmed the belief of the US Government that trade liberalisation would increase the volume of agricultural trade and eliminate artificially low prices which are the result of subsidised overproduction.

The Proposal was presented in a 21-page, single-spaced document. Four main sections comprised an integrated package and were designed to prevent reforms in one area from being offset by programmes in another. A special section on differential treatment for developing countries was designed for those countries which can demonstrate a special need. Three annexes outline product coverage, types of subsidies to be prohibited, and a classification of internal policies.

Its Comprehensive Proposal formed the political and economic basis for the United States argument during the last scheduled year of the negotiations. Particularly important, the United States continued to press its tariffication proposal during this period. In the meantime, United States farm politicians spent a good part of that year in Washington drafting the 1990 Farm Bill. Even though US GATT negotiators had let it be known, 'We are not writing the 1990 Farm Bill in Geneva', the simultaneous processes and the interlocking considerations could not be ignored. The United States, as if to strengthen its position in Geneva, in late October 1990 passed a farm bill which drove home two relevant points for European observers. First, there were large spending cuts – an estimated $40 billion over 5 years – through a variety of changes in programme operation. In this the United States was 'leading by example', although at least part of the spending cuts were forced by the over-riding necessity of reducing the federal budget deficit. Second, there was continued authorisation of export subsidies through a re-authorisation of the Export Enhancement Programme (EEP) and a Market Promotion Programme (MPP). All this was buttressed, of course, with a continuation of Section 22 which the United States had as 'decision bait' in its Comprehensive Proposal. These aspects of the Farm Bill might be viewed as counter-attacking foreign agricultural export subsidies, and might be interpreted as, 'If we can't negotiate the elimination of export subsidies and similar supports, then we shall match your spending!'.

3.5 PRESSURE FOR NEGOTIATING MAINTAINED

As time fast slipped away, specificity in the negotiations was urgently needed. Again the United States, after temporary delays caused mainly by domestic budgetary problems, led the way by tabling, on 15 October 1990, its 'final' proposal to reduce trade-distorting domestic agricultural subsidies by 75 per cent over a 10-year period. An integral part of this proposal was the call for a 90 per cent reduction in export subsidies over two years. Thus the proposal assumed a more urgent nature with respect to export subsidies, a position in stark contrast with that of the

European Community which argued that export subsidies should be reduced only in terms of overall levels of support.

Another specific part of the US proposal was the renewed emphasis on the tariffication of market access barriers. All non-tariff barriers would be converted to tariffs expressed in *ad valorem* percentages, and would be 'bound' along with other existing tariffs. The major innovation was that whereas until then the United States had pressed for the *elimination* of import barriers within 10 years, the goal was now reduced to a 75 per cent cut over the same period (one facet of abandoning the zero option) with a final ceiling rate of not more than 50 per cent *ad valorem* by the year 2000. Tariff quotas would be used as a transitional mechanism for products currently subject to non-tariff barriers, or subject to an import tax in particular cases such as rice to Japan. In such cases a minimum access level of 3 per cent (of total domestic consumption) would be established and subsequently expanded by 75 per cent over ten years. The proposal allowed for a tariff 'snapback' to prevent market disruption if imports of a particular commodity exceeded 120 per cent of the imports of that commodity during the previous year.

Although this US proposal was less aggressive than earlier positions taken, and even though the United States continually falls short of living up to its own stated farm policy objectives, the proposal fitted the overall strategy of removing government from the market by decoupling income support from the production of agricultural commodities. As stated earlier in this chapter, the original strategy of the Reagan Administration was to use the Uruguay Round as a negotiating forum to pursue the objective of domestic agricultural policy reform. Decoupling was a part of that strategy. Decoupling as offered by the US Office of the Special Trade Representative in the negotiations, however, took on yet another different meaning: for negotiating purposes trade distorting programmes must be removed, but direct payments to farmers could still be made if they were not tied to production and did not distort trade. It is important to reiterate that the concept of decoupling is complex and carries with it a variety of meanings and potential ramifications.

Negotiations on subsidies proceeded on the basis of the negotiating framework reached at the mid-point of the Uruguay Round, that is, whether to categorise subsidies as prohibited (red light category); permissible but actionable or countervailable (yellow light category); or permissible and nonactionable (green light category). The United States focused most of its attention on the red light and so-called dark amber categories (a variation on yellow which would make remedial action more automatic when certain kinds or levels of subsidisation are present). In contrast, others focussed on the rule for developing and expanding the green light category.

As the Uruguay Round progressed, US farmers and farms groups obviously visualised successful negotiations as pre-empting their birthright, or price–income franchise, and as inimical to their long term welfare. The vital difference between current attempts (including Uruguay Round negotiations) and former proposals to decouple payments to farmers from production is that never before have direct payments based on production been so large, the linkages among domestic and world markets so complete, and the concentration of payments so focused on large and seemingly financially successful producers. It might be added, also, that never before in the United States have farm programmes and their costs been under greater scrutiny by the media and by the general public. The basic question still remains: how do we permit the market to set prices and to signal the need for changes in resource use, while offering some assistance to farmers to deal with vagaries of weather and problems caused by structural excess capacity and other issues? (Reinsel, 1989).

A summary of the basic elements of the US proposal as of 15 October 1990 is shown in Table 3.2. In addition to the decoupling idea there was the milder provision of low-level protection through the transparent means of tariffs, and equal treatment of agricultural commodities under the GATT with other traded goods. Consistent with its overall approach, in this proposal, the United States advocated the eventual removal of the exceptional treatment of agriculture under the GATT, including Article XI.2(c)(i) which allows countries to impose quantitative import restrictions as part of supply-management systems. The United States reiterated a willingness to part with its beloved Section 22 (not a specific part of its latest proposal) in order to obtain its general strategic goals of the Uruguay Round, which was to phase out all import barriers, provided trading partners reciprocate.

Yet, substance was once again giving way to process in the GATT. As pressure from the United States increased on the European Community to table a meaningful proposal to reduce agricultural support, farmers, farmers' organisations and farm supporters in many European countries mounted demonstrations against change. In France, Italy and even England during late October, 1990 the object of such demonstrations appeared to be to block concessions to the

Table 3.2　Summary of key elements of US agricultural proposal to GATT, 15th October, 1990

Export subsidies
- reduce export subsidies on primary agricultural products by 90 per cent over 10 years, relative to 1986–8 and starting in 1991–2.
- export subsidies on processed products to be phased-out in 6 years.
- negotiate specific commitments on quantities exported and budget outlays regarding such subsidies.

Market Access starting in 1991–2.
- abolish Article XI.2(c), convert all non-tariff barriers to bound tariffs, and bind all tariffs
- reduce all tariffs, including newly converted ones, on average by 75 per cent over 10 years, relative to 1986–88 and starting in 1991–2
- the final tariff ceiling would not exceed 50 per cent.
- for products now subject to non-tariff barriers establish minimum access commitments of 3 per cent of domestic consumption and expand access by 75 per cent over 10 years using a tariff rate quota,
- eliminate tariff quotas after 10 years.
- allow tariff snapback provision using a price or a quantity trigger, as a safeguard for the transition period.
- allow developing countries that are net importers of a commodity, depending on their per capita GNP, up to 15 years to implement the commitments.

Internal support
- support policies directly linked to the production or price of a specific commodity would be reduced by 75 per cent over 10 years, relative to 1986–88 and starting in 1991–2.
- other trade-distorting measures to be reduced by 30 per cent in developed countries and according to agreed criteria for developing countries
- reduction commitments to be commodity specific and implemented using an AMS.

Sanitary and phytosanitary measures
- develop new rules to settle trade disputes,
- use the Chairman's legal text for these commitments.

Source:　Summarised by W. M. Miner in 'The GATT Negotiations and Canadian Agriculture', Discussion Paper, Centre for Trade Policy and Law, Carleton University, Ottawa, Canada, 22 November, 1990.

American proposal. Despite all this, United States negotiators and their Cairns Group allies maintained the pressure for reform.

At the same time, one could sense that the United States was positioning itself for some type of compromise. An important question arises as to why the United States waited so long to back away from the zero option. There is no single answer. It will be remembered that Ambassador Yeutter and the US negotiators entered the Uruguay Round with great determination to use the international bargaining forum to restructure US farm policy, along with a liberalising of world agricultural commodity markets. A strong opening position was taken to that effect. Yeutter continued to argue forcibly for that position at Montreal in December, 1988; he also gave it his 'best shot' at Geneva in the spring of 1989. Later, when he indicated a willingness to compromise, certain US farm lobbies got busy and he was advised to stick to the zero option. Thus, one answer to the above question is that apparently Yeutter and the United States team miscalculated on the Europeans, underestimating their strength and tenacity. On the American side, he was betrayed by the unwillingness of some US agricultural interests to compromise. There was no political intrigue to undermine the US position in the GATT. There is no great 'mystery' as to this outcome, unless there be mystery in the political activities of a democratically elected government.

3.6 THREATS, CRISES AND DELAYS

By 1 November 1990, negotiations had deteriorated into a war of nerves after the European Community had failed to produce a trade liberalising offer, which had been due by 15 October in Geneva. The United States threatened trade war in an attempt to force the European Community to table its proposals. Secretary of Agriculture Yeutter threatened that US farmers would keep their taxpayer support to ensure access to international markets in the face of subsidised EC competition. 'The probability is we're going to have a war of subsidies. That is almost inevitable' (Knight and Dow Jones, 1990).

Supporting Yeutter's thesis were data released from the General Accounting Office (GAO) which pointed out that the United States had spent $US32 billion on farm supports of all kinds in 1989, compared to the EC's $US53 billion and Japan's $US33 billion. But, with the passing of the US 1990 Farm Bill the GAO pointed out that the US farmers *could* get up to $US40.8 billion per year (Knight and Dow Jones, 1990).

Thus, at the 'countdown' of the Uruguay Round the United States had a strong agricultural position on the table that would represent a major advance by gradually removing most policies that disrupt trade and which would treat agriculture equally with industrial goods under GATT rules. An apparent softening of the United States position on export subsidies, however, worried some countries in the Cairns Group. There was concern in some quarters that in order to negotiate a deal with Europe the United States would have to make even further compromises and to retreat substantially from its proposal of 15 October. Certain elements in United States agriculture, moreover, were not eager for any agreement that would eliminate the protection which had been part of their expectations and planning processes for many decades.

Countdown became 'breakdown' at the December, 1990 meeting of the GATT in Brussels which had originally been intended to conclude the Uruguay Round. The flurry of events that occurred and followed the breakdown are indicative of the agricultural trade reforms that might ultimately occur from the Uruguay Round of negotiations. The United States sent several of its top trade officials to that meeting and, even though fruitful discussions were held outside of agriculture, a deadlock in that area provoked a suspension of the talks. Deadlock centred around the so-called Hellstrom proposal which, essentially, proposed 30 per cent reductions on internal support, border protection and export subsidies over five years (Hellstrom, 1990).

Even though this proposal fell short of United States objectives in a number of areas, including the level of reduction commitments, the United States joined other countries in expressing willingness to negotiate on the basis of the Hellstrom text. That might lead to serious talks, it was thought. The European Community was unwilling to accept this as the basis for negotiations on agriculture and at that stage the Cairns Groups and some LDCs walked out of the meeting.

In sum, as to process, or tactics, it can be said quite confidently that, up to and including the December 1990 meeting of Ministers in Brussels to negotiate final results, the United States had been more comprehensive and more methodical in the Uruguay Round with respect to the economics and politics of agricultural trade than at any time in the history of trade negotiations. The United States entered the final phase of bargaining in a very strong position to press for long-term agricultural reform and for more liberal agricultural trade policies. Nevertheless, the Americans, as well as the Cairns Group, probably underestimated European intransigence toward change in agriculture, embodied in the Common Agricultural Policy. This issue is debatable. The writer's position is that they should have been prepared for all contingencies in light of past GATT rounds and in view of the history of high agricultural protection in much of Europe (Tracy, 1982), fortified in many regions by physiocratic philosophy and reinforced recently by the prominence given to issues such as self-sufficiency, food safety and 'green' or environmental arguments – all demanding a *status quo* on the farm and in rural areas.

3.7   TRADE POLITICS AND THE NEW FAST TRACK

At the beginning of 1991 the attention of the United States and the world was temporarily diverted to the Gulf War and away from the GATT Uruguay Round and other matters. But not for long. It would be inappropriate in an account such as this chapter to attempt to analyse or to describe all the issues bearing on the United States agricultural position as the year began, and as the parties attempted to re-establish a negotiating dialogue after the breakdown. Several events, however, are worthy of brief treatment and this final section will centre on them. These will be designated as the Dunkel Shuttle, the MacSharry Plan, the Yeutter Resignation, the new Fast Track and the implication of a GATT agreement for United States agriculture.

Most agricultural interests in the United States, whether or not in support of the Administration's position in the Uruguay Round, nevertheless expected some movement toward the reduction of protectionism through the negotiations. The same could be said of European agricultural interests, though their bargaining position had not been so well defined. At this time, the United States had the advantage of having just enacted the 1990 Farm Bill which further reduced domestic assistance to the agricultural sector and called for a billion dollar increase in export subsidies if the GATT were to fail.

In this atmosphere the GATT Director General, Arthur Dunkel, began a series of discussions aimed at the resumption of the Uruguay Round talks. His shuttling between negotiation groups and other officials, and his effective diplomacy, helped promote technical discussions in Geneva which were necessary prior to the resumption of political talks. Such technical discussion, had they been held prior to the ill-fated Brussels meeting in December, 1990, might have clarified the meaning of just what the negotiating parties had put on the table. Dunkel on one occasion in early 1991 stated bluntly, 'Agriculture: the situation cannot continue . . . the reform of agricultural trade has become a central point not only in the Uruguay Round agenda, but also in the internal debates on economic and social policies practically everywhere' (Dunkel, 1991). On another occasion, his patience wearing thin, he expressed exasperation at United States and European Community attempts to place blame on the other for lack of progress on agricultural talks (Dunkel, 1991a).

Simultaneously with the Dunkel Shuttle, Mr Ray MacSharry, EC Farm Commissioner, was busy prescribing his proposals for reform of the Community's Common Agricultural Policy. The 'reflections' paper entitled 'Communication of the Commission to the Council: the Development and Future of the CAP' raised all the old questions of assistance to agriculture in Europe and its costs (European Commission, 1991). Meanwhile, in the United States the politics of the GATT were centring on the position of Secretary of Agriculture and Congressional debate about extension of Fast-track legislation.

The translation of United States Secretary of Agriculture Yeutter to Chairman of the Republican Party on 1 March 1991 sent mixed signals on the state of the GATT negotiations. Was this a signal of retreat or of slow down by the Americans? His knowledge of the agricultural issues, his position relative to trade policy and his long-time association with the European 'mind' on agriculture had made him a formidable factor to be dealt with by all parties in the Uruguay Round. His departure no doubt pleased many European farm groups as well as those commodity groups in United States agriculture who had basically opposed the Yeutter position on farm policy for many years and who favour high levels of assistance and protection.

Secretary Yeutter's move to a new position must be interpreted as inspired by the stage reached in the Uruguay Round. He had directly and indirectly been involved with the negotiations and the agricultural agenda since 1 July 1985, first as STR and from January 1989 to March 1991 as Secretary of Agriculture. He had led the fight to reform fundamentally US farm policy, first on a domestic level, then through the GATT negotiation. On occasion he appeared willing to compromise the Untied States' hard line position in Geneva but that seemed politically inexpedient or unacceptable. There appeared to be no mystery about his departure other than a question whether President Bush and Mr Yeutter's successor, Mr Edward Madigan, would pursue agricultural policy reform and trade liberalisation with the same zeal and vigour.

No doubt, Mr Madigan, who became US Secretary of Agriculture on 12 March, 1991, could speak with more political authority about farm issues, having been elected from a farm district in Illinois for eighteen years. For sixteen of those years, he was on the Agriculture Committee, eight as the ranking Republican. His standing with farmers was high at the time of appointment, which was reinforced by the fact that he occupied an elected office, a matter with which Dr. Yeutter, who had not, sometimes had to deal. Madigan was faced immediately with a major problem in the dairy industry and had to argue against quick fixes in US dairy policy (Madigan, 1991). The dairy lobby took advantage of this short-term crisis to restate their opposition to the liberalising provisions of the US Uruguay Round proposal (Vitaliano, 1991).

Other farm lobbyists and farm groups hostile to the Administration in the GATT had won a victory of sorts and would inevitably expect a softening of the hard line. The zero option was history. As domestic and foreign policy issues came and went in 1991, the Uruguay Round was no longer the priority issue of the Bush Administration and Mr Madigan's profile on trade issues would be kept low. At the Washington agricultural establishment, emphasis was on prevention of further damage to the US negotiating position from within. The bureaucracy was quiet.

Thus, the question can be raised again as it has been at other places in this chapter: for all the talk about freer international trade, the lowering of government assistance, and the restructuring of agriculture policies, just how committed were United States negotiators? How far was the United States willing to go in order to attain their objectives? To be sure, the United States farm bills of 1985 and 1990 moved unilaterally in the direction of freeing up markets and toward reducing the cost of farm programmes. In the 1990 bill, yields continued to be 'frozen' on base acreage, but with the yield base updated, thus partially supporting the decoupling of income from farm production. The US Congress had agreed to reduce farm support by $13.5 billion over the next five years. At the same time, however, the Export Enhancement Program (EEP) had an open faucet, and Section 22 as well as Section 301[4] were fully operative.

At the same time the Fast-track[5] debate revealed much of the protectionist sentiment that has existed for a long time in rural America. Fast-track authority for an additional two years, until June 1993, was given by the Congress to the President in late May 1991. So another major hurdle was overcome toward keeping the Uruguay Round negotiations on course. From a United States perspective, attention could now be turned to the negotiations and, more seriously, to the implications for the United States agricultural sector of an agreement at Geneva. What that agreement would be, of course, would have to be negotiated before its impact could be assessed. In the meantime, the domestic farm lobby was taking advantage of the stalled negotiations and the two-year US Fast-track extension by pursuing subsidy guarantees for various farm groups (Paarlberg, 1991).

Academics, government economists, farm organisations and commodity groups in the United States in the spring and summer of 1991 continued their politico–economic analyses of the Uruguay Round: the potential fallout; the possible gains and losses from various scenarios. A study undertaken principally to clarify the last US proposal in the Uruguay Round (that of 15 October, 1990), and to present an analysis of its economic implications for US agriculture, is particularly relevant to this chapter (USDA, 1991).[6]

Specifically, the United States was not proposing that support to producers be eliminated. As has already been pointed out, in the Uruguay Round GATT negotiations the United States never proposed the elimination of all producer support, only that which is tied to output-increasing incentives (in the GATT parlance, 'green' policy instruments do not present a problem).

Another vital implication of the US proposal is that a reduction in farm subsidies does not necessarily imply commensurate reductions in producer prices – because market prices are expected to rise. This aspect of the proposal is so important that the section of the USDA report explaining it is reproduced verbatim as Appendix 3.A1. This is a key element of the United States position in the ongoing attempt at policy reform, which has been emphasised both for the domestic agenda of US farm groups as well as for other GATT negotiation participants, particularly in Europe.

This report, which obviously had been written to assuage the anxieties of the US farm community, goes into further analytical detail as to how US agriculture will benefit significantly from a Uruguay Round agreement along the lines of the US proposal. The principal clarifying features are:

1. Even though support levels might remain higher elsewhere, United States producers would gain from subsidy reductions;
2. United States competitiveness would be enhanced;
3. A GATT agreement would not expose United States producers to large market shocks;
4. An agreement would not change United States food safety regulations;

5. The agreement would give credit to the United States for actions taken in the 1985 and 1990 farm bills to reduce subsidies.;
6. Authority over United States agricultural policy decisions would remain in Washington.

The study makes a 5-year projection of the US proposal of October 1990 from 1986–8 base period levels of support, but with implementation deferred until 1992–6. Moreover, the study results indicate projected budget savings over 5 years in excess of the losses suffered by adversely affected producer groups like sugar and dairy, that is, a net welfare gain would remain even after the gainers had compensated the losers. Finally, the aggregate effects of a GATT agreement along the lines of the US proposal would permit an increase in US farm income because prices and production would be generally higher. By 1996, cash farm income for United States agriculture would be at least $1–2 billion higher than under baseline assumptions. United States farm product exports would be $6–8 billion higher (USDA, 1991, pp. 31–2).

3.8 CONCLUSION

The United States, despite a checkered and dubious record on agricultural protection dating back to the 1920s, nevertheless, came into the Uruguay Round of the GATT in 1986 apparently determined to change things. It was determined to change not only its own but also the world's propensity toward subsidies, supports and all types of assistance which had seen the average level of protection in agriculture rise substantially since World War II. The United States was apparently willing to place everything, including Section 22, on the bargaining table in order to effect domestic agricultural policy reform; that is, to reduce public commitment for costly farm price and income support policies of the past. The United States Administration, with backing from Congress, passed Fast-track legislation; and its negotiators, along with the Cairns Group, pressured the European Community to move its agricultural sector forward toward a freer trade era for agricultural commodities.

Only with the departure of Secretary of Agriculture Clayton Yeutter did the United States seem to falter in its determination to move into a new era in its combined agricultural and trade policies. Many of the old questions about the power of the United States farm lobbies began to resurface. How could it be that agricultural subsidies continue to be large even with the decline in farm numbers and with the reduced agricultural vote? Some would find it strange that the political power of agriculture seems to increase with the diminution in its relative size. Traditional economic science seems unable to explain this phenomenon.[7] Would the outcome of Geneva be worth the effort of the past five years?

The last half of 1991 was highly important for the Uruguay Round of GATT as well as for the future of United States agriculture. Considerable understanding had been generated about the problems and issues, and some progress was made on resolving differences, but these would be swept aside unless there were an agreement. The daily ebb and flow of the GATT developments as this is being written (November 1991) provides little information to an outsider as to what is going on in Geneva. One good sign for the Americans, however, is that there appear to be strong differences developing between the European parties.

What if there is a less than successful outcome in the Uruguay Round? The United States can point to the large adjustments in internal farm subsidies made since 1986–8 as a result of the 1985 and 1990 farm and budget legislation. Moreover, it can contend that US agricultural tariffs and import protection for most products are low. And, on the important subject of farm export subsidies, United States agriculture, while substantially dependent on foreign markets, especially in cereals, can survive in a continuing struggle with its chief competitors.

APPENDIX 3.A1

Subsidy Reductions do not Mean large Cuts in Support Prices*

First, internal subsidies subject to reduction include market price support, direct payments tied to production and input subsides. For market price support and direct payments, the level of support to be reduced is the product of the price gap (between the support price and a fixed reference price) and the quantity that receives support. Thus, this form of support could be reduced by cutting the support price or the quantity receiving support. Alternatively, other subsidies could be reduced. Therefore, a reduction in internal subsidies does not mean that support prices such as target prices and loan rates would necessarily be cut.

Second, even if the cut were made only in the support price, the percentage reduction would be applied to the price gap, not the support price. For example, if the support price were $100/ton and the reference price $60/ton, the price gap would be $40/ton. A 75 per cent reduction in the the price gap would result in a support price of $70/ton [$60/ton + (.25 × $40/ton)]. Therefore, a 30 per cent reduction in the support price would achieve a 75 per cent reduction in the price gap.

For United States producers of wheat, feed grains, rice and cotton, the quantity of production receiving support declines as market prices rise and programme participation falls. To the extent that a GATT agreement raises market prices and programme participation falls, computed support automatically declines. For voluntary programmes, this tends to lessen or eliminate the need to reduce the price gap or reduce production eligible for support by other means to meet GATT commitments.

Source: Office of Economics, USDA, 'Economics Implications of the Uruguay Round for US Agriculture', Washington DC, May 1991, p. 7.

4 The EC Perspective

K. A. Ingersent, A. J. Rayner and R. C. Hine

The opening section of this chapter provides a historical background to the Uruguay Round dealing with the involvement of the EC in recent changes in the structure of world agricultural trade and earlier rounds of GATT negotiations. This is followed by a short section on the Punta del Este Declaration which launched the UR in 1986. There next follows a longer section dealing with the evolution of the EC stance on agricultural policy and trade reform during the negotiations. A fourth section discusses the convergence of negotiating positions, particularly between the EC and the US, as well as the late drive for CAP reform, ostensibly for purely domestic reasons. A fifth section outlines the Dunkel draft agreement on agriculture and discusses the obstacles to its acceptance by the EC. In the concluding section we attempt to compare what the EC hoped to achieve from the Uruguay Round agricultural negotiations with the actual outcome.

4.1 BACKGROUND

As the world's largest single importer, and the second largest single exporter of agricultural products, the EC could not avoid playing a key role in the Uruguay Round agricultural negotiations.[1] In terms of world market *import* shares, the EC's major imports (excluding intra-EC trade) have, in recent years, been soybeans (nearly 50 per cent), butter (nearly 20 per cent), cheese (over 20 per cent), sheepmeat (nearly 50 per cent), and beef and veal (nearly 15 per cent).[2] The largest EC world *export* market shares (excluding intra-EC trade *except* for sugar) have been sugar (nearly 20 per cent), wheat (about 16 per cent), dried skim milk (nearly 30 per cent), butter (nearly 50 per cent), cheese (about 45 per cent), beef and veal (about 25 per cent) and pork (about 20 per cent).[3] A notable feature of EC agricultural trade is that certain commodities, like butter, cheese, beef and veal, appear as both major exports and major imports, reflecting factors such as the butter and cheese import quotas accorded by the EC to New Zealand, as part of the British Accession Treaty, and qualitative differences between imports and exports of commodities like meat.

Overall, the EC moved from being an *importer* of most agricultural products after the EC(6) expanded to EC(9) in the early 1970s, to being a net *exporter* of most in the mid-1980s. This transition, due to the combined effects of the CAP and rising productivity rather than Community expansion as such, had critical implications for the EC budget. This was due to the adverse effect of declining import levy revenues combined with the rising costs of export refunds needed to dispose of surplus production on world markets. Thus, at the outset of the Uruguay Round in 1986, the EC was under pressure to reform its agricultural policy from two directions. First, there was pressure from agricultural trading partners who wanted improved access to the EC market for their exports, as well as an end to subsidised competition in third country markets. Second, there was internal pressure for reform for mainly budgetary reasons.

The EC's position in the Uruguay Round needs to be viewed against the background of three earlier GATT rounds, namely the Dillon Round (1960–1), the Kennedy Round (1964–7) and the Tokyo Round (1973–9). Because, under Article XXIV:6, the GATT is required to examine the impact of any customs union or free trade area on third countries, the impetus for the Dillon Round came partly from the formation of the EC(6) in 1957. As far as agriculture was concerned, the crux of the Dillon Round was that the EC intended to switch protective instruments from specific national bound rates of import duty to variable import levies. This change was expected to reduce access to the EC market for third country exporters, such as the US. The US tried but failed to gain guaranteed access to the EC market for its existing level of agricultural exports. However, very significantly in view of later developments, the EC did agree to bind rates of duty on oilseeds, oilseed products (such as oil and meal) and cereal substitutes (such as manioc and corn gluten feed) at very low or even zero levels. Moreover, the common external tariff on sheepmeat (for which no Community Regulation existed at the time) was bound at 20 per cent. Later, as the EC approached self sufficiency in the commodities concerned, these concessions re-emerged as a serious constraint on the EC's ability to modify the CAP in response to budgetary and political pressures.

During the Kennedy Round (1964–7) more emphasis was given to the liberalisation of agricultural trade than in earlier rounds of MTNs. The EC's negotiating position on agriculture had two main planks. First, a proposal that all agricultural support measures be reduced to a common denominator prior to *binding* the margin of support, termed the '*montant de soutien*'.[4] Second, concerted market organisation and market sharing amongst major agricultural exporters, including a 'World Commodity Agreement', covering cereals, beef and veal, some dairy products and sugar, to stabilise prices at fair and remunerative levels and control product surpluses (Tracy, 1982, p. 376). These EC proposals were rejected by the US and other exporters of temperate agricultural products, ostensibly on the grounds that they failed to offer any *reduction* of existing levels of agricultural protection. However, it has also been suggested that a more fundamental reason for the rejection was that some of the EC's agricultural trade competitors were unwilling to accept external constraints on their domestic agricultural policies (Tracy, 1982, p. 277, quoting Warley, 1976, p. 385). Also, the EC's desire for extending the adoption of ICAs had little international appeal in the early 1960s. The main upshot of the Kennedy Round was that the EC could claim that it had succeeded in defending the CAP against attempts by the US and other countries to see its major instruments, such as the variable import levy, outlawed under the GATT. But, for its part, the US could claim to have avoided 'legitimising the CAP' (Harris *et al.*, 1983, p. 277).

As far as agricultural trade was concerned, the agenda for the Tokyo Round (1973–9) was little changed from the preceding Kennedy Round. Whereas the US and other agricultural exporting countries still sought to improve their access to the EC market, the EC continued to defend using the CAP to protect farmers from the pressures of external competition. The EC's negotiating mandate was now quite explicit in insisting that the CAP's principles and mechanisms could not be the subject of international negotiations. With the CAP now firmly established, the EC was no longer willing to consider quantifying and binding levels of agricultural protection along the lines of its own *montant de soutien* proposal during the Kennedy Round. Rather, it revived its ideas for stabilising commodity prices and expanding agricultural trade through international agreements to manage markets, whilst leaving domestic agricultural policies intact. In the event, virtually no progress was made during the Tokyo Round to resolve the basic disagreements between the EC and its agricultural trade competitors led by the US concerning the objectives of agricultural MTNs under the GATT. On international market management, limited 'arrangements' for dairy products and beef were concluded, but a major attempt at an international grains agreement ended in failure.

Another product of the Tokyo Round was agreement on a Subsidies Code committing governments to ensuring that their subsidies do not harm the trading interests of other countries. As far as agriculture was concerned it was hoped that the Subsidies Code would strengthen the application of Article XVI in disciplining the use of export subsidies. Article XVI:3 of the General Agreement specifies that no contracting party may apply a primary product export subsidy so as to capture more than an equitable share of world export trade in the product concerned, *judged by historic shares during a previous representative period.* Article 10:2(c) of the 1969 Subsidies Code specified that a 'previous representative period' should normally be the *three most recent calendar years in which normal market conditions existed* [authors' italics]. However, due to its lack of legal precision, the application of this criterion did little to improve the resolution of agricultural trade disputes concerning the use of export subsidies (Warley, 1988). The Tokyo Round ended in 1979 with no major advances made either in the liberalisation of trade or agreement upon bringing trade-distorting domestic production subsidies under international discipline. No progress had been made in defining the status within the GATT of newer trade policy instruments such as variable import levies, and older instruments such as import quotas, and variable export subsidies still lacked effective international control, despite the existence of articles covering their use.

During the period immediately preceding the inauguration of the Uruguay Round in 1986 the European Community's attitude to agricultural trade reform was ambivalent. Budgetary pressures for the reform of the CAP were intense, as evidenced by the introduction of milk quotas in 1984. In 1985, a green paper was published by the Commission under the title 'Perspectives for the Common Agricultural Policy'. This document emphasised that Article 39 of the Treaty of Rome remained fully valid: no revision or re-interpretation of the objectives stated there was required. But, at the same time, the CAP could not remain insulated from the influence of world markets where competition formed the framework within which European agriculture had to operate. Thus a more market-oriented approach to pricing and other aspects of the CAP was essential to keep agricultural expenditure within the prescribed financial guidelines (as determined by the Dublin Summit in December 1984). The objective of aligning Community support price levels with those of competing exporters was recommended as being consistent with this approach, but only in the long-term with appropriate complementary measures to safeguard producer incomes. In referring to the alignment of price support levels, the Commission appeared to be thinking of market management by international agreement rather than actual price reductions. Thus it expressed the hope of convincing trading partners of the need for better organisation of world markets to the general benefit of all countries, including LDCs, and to avoid the 'unjustified costs of cut-throat competition'. The green paper also reiterated the Community's long-standing objective of achieving more 'balanced' levels of protection amongst different commodities, specifically relative to cereals and livestock (highly protected) and oilseeds and cereal substitutes (very low or zero protection).

The 1985 green paper was, of course, no more than a statement of the *Commission's* thinking on the direction of needed adjustments to the CAP, including agricultural trade policy: conservative as it might look to exponents of market liberalisation, its tone was in fact quite liberal compared with any reforms upon which the Council of Ministers was then likely to agree. Unlike the Commission, the Council is a decision making body within which no agreement can be reached without reconciling the conflicting interests of the Community's member states.

4.2 THE INITIATION OF THE URUGUAY ROUND AND THE ROLE OF THE EC

The principal instigator of the Uruguay Round was the US. For this reason its agenda reflected largely American priorities, including the liberalisation of trade in services and high technology goods, the protection of intellectual property rights and the reduction of trade privileges accorded to Newly Industrialising Countries (NICs), committing them to liberalising their imports. On agriculture the top US priority was to regain its market share of world trade in cereals and other agricultural products, which had declined during the early 1980s, by negotiating through the GATT to abolish all forms of agricultural support and protection. The US was strongly supported in this aim by other major exporters of temperate agricultural products, such as Australia, New Zealand, Canada and Argentina. But some other GATT contracting parties, including the EC, had major misgivings about the focus on agricultural trade issues. Within the EC it was suspected that an unstated aim of the US was to destroy the CAP. But, if the EC refused to negotiate on agriculture its wider trading interests could be severely damaged by the raising of protectionist barriers to EC exports, particularly in the US. In the run-up to the Uruguay Round the EC therefore attempted to limit the scope of the negotiations to the modification of existing agricultural policies rather than radical reform. This strategy was successful to the extent that the Punta del Este Declaration which launched the Uruguay Round made no specific reference to ending agricultural export subsidies. Had it done so the EC would have been implicitly committed to dismantling the CAP system of support.

The Punta del Este Declaration, which launched the Uruguay Round in July 1986, stated that the central objective for reforming the conduct of agricultural trade was to 'bring *all* measures affecting import access and export competition under strengthened and more operationally effective GATT rules and disciplines' [authors' emphasis]. This clearly committed all the GATT signatory countries, including EC member states, to allowing their domestic agricultural policies to be the subject of international negotiation, as well as trade policies aimed directly at restricting imports and expanding exports at the expense of foreign competitors. Thus, the EC could no longer withold import levies and export refunds, the basic instruments of the CAP, from GATT negotiations. Moreover, this initial statement of the Uruguay Round's agricultural objectives specified both the subjection of agricultural policies to the GATT rules and disciplines and the reduction of agricultural protection. Thus the Declaration referred to 'improving the competitive environment by increasing discipline on the use of all direct and indirect subsidies and other measures affecting directly or indirectly agricultural trade, including the phased reduction of their negative effects and dealing with their causes'. However, countries were clearly divided on how far and how fast they were prepared to go in reducing the support of domestic agriculture. Although all governments were committed to making some reduction in the level of agricultural support, the Punta del Este Declaration did not commit any country to the phased *abolition* of support. The subsequent tabling in Geneva of 'position papers' on agriculture, would reveal how far apart the main participants in the Uruguay Round negotiations were on this issue.

4.3 EVOLUTION OF THE EUROPEAN COMMUNITY'S STANCE ON AGRICULTURAL POLICY AND TRADE REFORM DURING THE NEGOTIATIONS

For the most part, the EC's stance on agriculture during the Uruguay Round was reactive rather than innovative. Rather than coming forward with its own proposals for reform, the Community chose to react to proposals for reform tabled by others, most notably the United States and the Cairns Group of agricultural exporting countries. This stance may be explained by the Community's determination to protect the CAP, as far as possible, from *external* reform pressures. However, towards the end of the negotiations, the EC stance became more flexible in certain respects, largely as a result of rising *internal* pressures for fundamental reform of the CAP. But, even then, the Community spokesmen were unwilling to admit that proposals for reforming the CAP were being influenced by external pressures generated by the Uruguay Round negotiations.

4.3.1 Initial position, 1987–1988

The EC's initial position papers, in 1987–8, were largely in reaction to the opening gambit of the US calling for the *abolition* of all trade distorting agricultural support and protection within 10 years – the so-called 'zero option' (see Chapter 3 for a detailed explanation of the US position). Unsurprisingly, the EC took the view that the US proposal was too extreme to be taken seriously. The EC's own position at this early stage of the negotiations emphasised the difference between short-term and long-term policy reform priorities. For the *short-term*, two types of reform were proposed: first, action to reduce instability in particular commodity markets and, second, action to reduce excess supplies overhanging international markets. The policy instruments proposed by the EC for achieving these goals were, first, a GATT agreement on international market management affecting cereals (and cereal substitutes), sugar and dairy products, in order to achieve improved market stability. Second, in order to achieve the goal of reducing excess supplies, the EC wanted some negotiated reductions in levels of support affecting the 'most problematic commodities', namely, the three in the managed market group, plus rice, oilseeds and beef. Under the heading of *longer-term* reforms, the EC floated the idea of a concerted move towards the reduction of domestic support over a wider range of commodities, allied with a reduction of external protection. Also, with knowledge of a later development – the major CAP reform promoted by Agriculture Commissioner MacSharry and adopted by the Council in 1992 – it is pertinent to note that as early as 1987 the EC's position paper referred to the possibility of compensating producers for reduced price support with 'decoupled payments', by resorting to 'direct methods of supporting farmers' incomes which are not linked to output'.

The EC was also willing to consider the possibility of reduced levels of protection being *bound* in the GATT subject to two provisos. First, the aggregate measure of support (AMS) employed to measure protection must be such as to give explicit credit for domestic supply constraints imposed by the government and to allow for the effects of world price and exchange rate fluctuations. The economic rationale of this proviso was that trade competitors benefit from domestic supply control and that support measurement needs to be insulated from the effects of short term price and exchange rate instability to facilitate monitoring of longer-term reduction commitments. Second, any agreement on binding levels of protection must be flexible enough to permit the protection of some individual commodities to be *increased*. The intention of this so-called 're-balancing' provision of the EC's negotiating position on agriculture was clearly designed as an escape route from the low or zero level tariff bindings on oilseeds and cereal substitutes to which the EC had committed itself in the Dillon Round. The high priority given to finding such an escape route may be attributed to the rapidly rising budgetary costs of the EC cereals and oilseeds support regimes. Other things being equal, the budgetary costs of cereals support (the combined costs of intervention and export refunds) rise directly with the size of the cereals surplus. The size of the surplus is, in turn directly correlated with the volume of imports of cheap cereal substitutes, like citrus pulp and maize gluten. The EC oilseeds support regime is a deficiency payment scheme, with the producer price set well above the price of imports. Thus, assuming a flat rate unit subsidy (or deficiency payment), the budgetary costs of support rise directly with the volume of EC production, which has steadily increased under the support regime.

It was also clear that, despite having signed the Punta del Este Declaration, the EC was still not prepared to yield, at this stage, on the fundamental principles of the CAP. In particular, it was resolved to continue using the instruments of the variable import levy and the variable export subsidy in order to maintain internal price stability at a high level, including Community Preference giving domestic production a permanent price advantage over comparable imports. Thus, despite some signs of greater readiness to consider concerted and reciprocal reductions in agricultural support levels, the EC's negotiating position on agriculture at the beginning of the Uruguay Round was little changed from the position taken up and defended in the Tokyo

Round, that is, that radical changes in the CAP pricing system, which both insulates and protects EC producers from world prices, cannot be conceded in the GATT negotiations.

In a later suggestion, tabled in Geneva in October 1988, the EC wanted the GATT signatories to agree to progressive reductions in domestic agricultural support over five years from a 1984 baseline (the year in which EC milk production quotas first took effect). Note that this unquantified 'offer' related only to domestic support and not to border protection. This suggestion also included details of the measurement device which the EC wanted to use both for monitoring progress in the reduction of agricultural support and for binding support levels in any new GATT arrangement. The EC's 'support measurement unit' (SMU) was much more restricted in conception than the PSE (see OECD, 1987).

The SMU excludes direct payments for supply control (such as set-aside payments) and allows credit for the effects of quotas and similar restrictions on production. Moreover, the SMU would be based not on the difference between domestic and current world prices, but the difference between the domestic price and a *fixed* external reference price at a constant exchange rate (EC Commission, 1988). Where a quota is in force, the *unit* SMU is defined, *not* as the difference between the support price, P_s, and the external reference price, P_r, but as the difference between the *shadow* price, P_u, due to the quota, and P_r. Moreover, the *aggregate* SMU is defined, not as the unit SMU times actual production, but as the unit SMU times the *quota*, i.e. aggregate SMU $= (P_u - P_r)Q$, where Q is the quota quantity. By comparison, aggregate PSE $= (P_s - P_w)Q_s$, where P_s = support price, P_w = world price in foreign currency, and Q_s = actual quantity supplied. Note that since milk production quotas were introduced in the EC actual production has consistently exceeded the quota.[5]

4.3.2 Mid-Term Review and Geneva Accord

By the end of 1987, when six countries or groups of countries had tabled their initial negotiating positions on agriculture in the Uruguay Round, it was clear that the outcome would largely depend upon whether the strongly opposed positions of the EC and the US could be reconciled. The position of the Cairns Group of agricultural exporting countries was too close too that of the US, though less extreme, for the CG to play a mediating role. The position of Japan, another major player, was too close to that of the EC, particularly with respect to border protection. Thus, due to the lack of common ground between the major contestants, serious negotiations in the Agricultural Negotiating Group (NG5) had not commenced by the time of the Mid-Term Review of the Uruguay Round, held in Montreal in December, 1988.

It may have been hoped that the trade ministers attending the Mid-Term Review would give political impetus to the agricultural negotiations. But that hope failed to materialise. The chairman of NG5 made a valiant effort to break the stalemate by preparing a statement of major issues for decision. Ministers were invited to decide whether the ultimate goal should be the *elimination* of trade-distorting agricultural support and protection, or only its substantial *reduction*. But the polar positions taken by the EC and the US on this issue resulted in deadlock at Montreal. Whereas the US demanded a prior commitment by all parties to the eventual elimination of support, before negotiations could begin on merely reducing it in the short-term, the EC remained implacably opposed to the zero option on any time-scale. Although the EC was prepared to contemplate modifying the CAP, it would not consider phasing it out. The Cairns Group attempted to mediate between the US and the EC by urging the US to drop its insistence on the zero option. But this attempt failed and ministers were unable to find any compromise between the US and EC positions upon which they and other GATT participants would agree. So, in Montreal, the agricultural negotiations reached an impasse which threatened the continuation of the Uruguay Round as a whole. However, since tentative agreements had been reached in 11 of the remaining 14 negotiating areas, it was decided to adjourn for three months to give the GATT Secretary-General time to explore whether the disagreements in each of the four problem areas, including agriculture, could be resolved sufficiently to enable the Uruguay Round itself to continue. The remaining three problem areas were intellectual property rights (TRIPS), textiles trade and safeguards.

The threat of imminent collapse produced by the Montreal debacle was sufficient to produce a compromise which broke the deadlock on agriculture. When the negotiators reconvened in Geneva at the beginning of April 1989, the GATT Secretary-General was able to produce the text of an acceptable draft agreement on agriculture based upon the statement of issues for decision presented by the Chairman of NG5 in Montreal. However, the text of the 'Geneva Accord' contained no reference to the *elimination* of trade-distorting support and protection, but only to its progressive *reduction*, with credit being allowed for measures already taken since 1986 (the year of the Punta del Este Declaration). The Geneva Accord represented concessions both by the US in implicitly abandoning the zero option, and by the EC in accepting that credit would allowed for actions taken to reduce support only since 1986, instead of from 1984 as previously claimed. The Geneva Accord also declared that, henceforth, *all* internal policy measures which affect trade should be subject to the GATT disciplines. Thus, very significantly for the EC, it was agreed that measures such as variable import levies (VILs) and voluntary export constraints (VERs), not previously covered by the GATT articles,were now firmly on the negotiating table.

4.3.3 Revised position post the Geneva Accord, 1989

Under the terms of the Geneva Accord negotiating parties were required to submit their proposals for achieving the agreed objectives of long-term reform by December 1989. This obligation gave rise to the tabling in Geneva of a fresh batch of position papers. The US was the first in the field (October, 1989) with a revised position asking for separate and specific commitments to be made to reducing support in each of the three inter-related areas of internal support, import access and export subsidies. On *internal support* the US proposed a 3-tiered approach to greater discipline based upon degrees of trade distortion. On the top tier were the *most trade distorting* or 'red' policies, identified as providing support linked directly with production, such as administered commodity prices and deficiency payments. On the bottom tier were the *least trade distorting* or 'green' policies, identified as those giving rise to agricultural budget expenditures *not* linked with production, such as research and extension, environmental protection and conservation, and bona fide food aid. Intermediate between these extremes were middle tier or 'amber' policies, defined by the US as including generally available producer input and investment subsidies. The US pressed for top tier policies to be phased out completely over ten years. Bottom tier policies could be permitted to continue without discipline. Middle tier policies would be subject to monitored reduction and the GATT discipline. It is significant that, despite having signed the Geneva Accord earlier in the year, the US continued, at this stage, to press for the zero option *vis-à-vis* the most trade-distorting policies.

On *import access*, the US proposed that all import barriers not explicitly covered by the GATT, such as VILs, VERs and minimum import prices (MIPs) be prohibited. But 'permitted' NTBs (that is, import quotas authorised by Article XI of the General Agreement) might be allowed to continue subject to their conversion to tariff quotas in the short run and simple tariffs in the long-term. The tariff quotas would be phased out over ten years after which a bound tariff (at a relatively low rate) would be the only form of protection. On *export subsidies*, the US proposed that, apart from bona fide food aid, these should be phased out completely over five years.

The EC's revised position paper in the aftermath of the Geneva Accord was delayed until the dying days of 1989. This conceded that current agricultural support levels were 'too high' and offered their gradual and balanced reduction over five years in the first instance. But the EC still held back from actually *quantifying* the cuts in support and protection it was prepared to contemplate. Moreover, it declined to accomodate the US position by making separate and specific commitments to cut support in the three areas of internal support, import access and export subsidies. The EC was prepared only to commit itself to a reduction of internal support, which it claimed implied parallel support reductions in the remaining two areas. Thus, it is only for analytical convenience that we here summarise the EC's December 1989 position paper under these headings. On *internal support*, the EC wanted a gradual reduction, measured in terms of its own AMS, the support measurement unit (SMU), relative to 1986 as the base period. However, this 'offer' was qualified by a reiteration of the EC's long-standing demand for the 'rebalancing' of *higher* protection of oilseeds and cereal substitutes against lower protection of other commodities. On *import access*, the EC responded to the US tariffication proposal with a *partial* tariffication proposal of its own. The basis of this proposal was that border protection should consist of two elements, a fixed tariff calculated relative to an external reference price (effectively the world price expressed in domestic currency at a fixed exchange rate) and a 'corrective factor' to offset world price and exchange rate fluctuations beyond certain limits. Also, unlike the US and the CG countries, the EC favoured the retention of a reformulated Article XI in the General Agreement to permit the use of agricultural import quotas in exceptional circumstances, but only in conjunction with domestic supply control programmes. On *export subsidies*, the EC would not make any specific reduction commitment or countenance phasing them out. But it argued that they would be *reduced* as internal prices and the fixed tariff came down with the negotiated reduction in the SMU.

In sum, revisions of negotiating positions following the Geneva Accord revealed some common ground between the EC and the US, particularly on the issue of replacing all other barriers to agricultural trade with tariffs. But the EC's partial tariffication proposal was much more cautious than the US proposal that, apart from a low bound tariff, border protection be phased out completely within ten years. Moreover, whereas the US was pressing for separate and specific commitments to the reduction of internal support, border protection and export subsidisation, the EC was unwilling to be committed to this approach but only to a 'formula approach' to reduced support and protection based upon the SMU.

4.3.4 'Final' position, 1990

The Uruguay Round participants had agreed that all 15 negotiating groups, including the negotiating group on agriculture (NG5) would produce 'framework agreements' by mid-1990. Approximately six months would then remain for the negotiators to settle the fine details of agreement in each area in preparation for the conclusion of the Uruguay Round at a ministerial meeting scheduled to be held in Brussels early in December. In pursuit of this plan, on 27 June 1990, Mr Aart de Zeeuw, Chairman of NG5, delivered a draft Framework Agreement on Agriculture to the negotiators in Geneva. This document identified internal support, border protection (including tariffication) and export competition as the major issues upon which decisions were still needed. But unlike the Chairman's report going into the Mid-Term Review, which emphasised issues rather than decisions, the Framework Agreement did propose solutions to which the NG5 negotiators were invited to agree.

On the issue of trade distorting *internal support*, the Framework Agreement invited a commitment to substantial and progressive reductions of support on a commodity-by-commodity basis and expressed in terms of a total AMS, using 1988 as the base year. But it was suggested that policies of decoupled support, such as research and environmental conservation, be excluded from this commitment. On *border protection*, a commitment to the application of the principle of tariffication to all protective measures was invited. All tariffs would be substantially and progessively reduced and tariff quotas expanded over a period of years from 1991–2, in line with internal support reductions measured in terms of an AMS. On *export competition* the Framework Agreement invited a commitment to running down export assistance faster than other forms of support and protection, though with provision for the survival of some residual level of export assistance governed by strengthened and more operationally effective GATT rules and disciplines.

By endorsing the formula approach to implementing and measuring the reduction of *internal support*, the Framework Agreement steered closer to the EC than to the US on that issue. But no concession was made to the EC demand that an AMS 'credit' be allowed for domestic supply control other than opting for a *total* AMS, rather than a unit AMS not reflecting the volume of production. On the issue of *border protection* the framework document's endorsement of tariffication was nearer to the US position, with few qualifications to meet EC concerns about world price and exchange rate fluctuations. No reference was made to the possibility of 'rebalancing' levels of protection, consistently a key element of the EC negotiating position. On the issue of *export competition*, the Framework Agreement also steered rather closer to the US than to the EC position by calling for export assistance to be reduced more rapidly than other protection.

Despite the best endeavours of its author, Aart de Zeeuw, the draft Framework Agreement on Agriculture failed to advance the pace of actual negotiations in its immediate aftermath. Rather its principal impact was to underline the continuing deep divisions within NG5, particularly between the EC and the US. The impasse on agriculture in the Uruguay Round found its way on to the agenda of the G7 Economic Summit held in Houston, Texas, in early July 1990. The Summit's final communiqué endorsed the call for substantial and progressive reductions in farm support and protection, referring specifically to the three areas of internal support, market access and export subsidies, and commended the draft Framework Agreement to the negotiators as a suitable basis for successful negotiations. But, despite this high-level political intervention, no success was achieved in reducing the wide gaps between the positions of the EC and the US, with Japan and the CG playing somewhat subsidiary roles. However, the negotiators did agree to adhere to a procedural timetable set by the GATT Secretary-General for continuing the agricultural negotiations after the summer. Specifically it was agreed, first, that by 1 October, all contracting parties would submit to the GATT Secretariat 'country lists' detailing their current levels of agricultural support, on a commodity-by-commodity basis, expressed in terms of PSEs: second, that by 15 October, all parties would table papers giving details of the reductions in support and protection they were prepared to offer and the period over which they were ready to make them.

US position

As in earlier stages of the negotiations, the US was first in the field with a revised position paper on agriculture, this time in response to the Secretary-General's request to all contracting parties for quantitative details of the amounts by which they were prepared to reduce support and protection and over what period. The US proposal of 15 October 1990 was based upon the NG5 Chairman's draft Framework Agreement but with quite numerous deletions and amendments. As expected, the offers tabled by the US were ordered under the headings of internal support, border protection and export competition.

Internal support

Four major proposals were made under this heading, as follows:

1. The most trade-distorting domestic support measures, such as market price supports, deficiency payments and production-linked input subsidies, to be cut by 75 per cent from 1986–8 average levels over 10 years, starting in 1991–2.
2. Less trade-distorting domestic support, such as credit subsidies and non-commodity-specific input or investment subsidies, to be reduced from the same base year and over the same period, but only by 30 per cent.
3. All support reduction commitments to be commodity-specific, expressed in terms of an AMS denominated in national currency and based on the gap between the current support price and a fixed external reference price derived from 1986–8 base period data.
4. Non-trade-distorting agricultural programmes, such as environmental protection, resource retirement and diversion, income safety-net programmes and bona fide food aid, to be exempt from any reduction commitment.

In advancing this set of proposals for reducing internal support of agriculture, the US made two very significant concessions to the EC position. First, the zero option of *eliminating* trade-distorting support over 10 years was at last abandoned in favour of a 75 per cent reduction over the same period. Second, the principle of using an AMS to express and monitor commodity-specific cuts in support and protection was conceded. Moreover, in agreeing that the AMS could be based upon the difference between the current support price and a *fixed* external reference price, the US moved towards endorsing the

SMU as being the appropriate AMS, but without allowing full credit for supply control.

Border protection

Five major proposals were made by the US under this heading, as follows:

1. All NTBs to be converted into tariff equivalents (TEs) derived from the average gap between external and internal prices during the base period 1986–8.
2. All tariffs and TEs to be bound and then reduced by 75 per cent over ten years from 1991–92: no tariff to exceed 50 per cent *ad valorem* after ten years.
3. Base period import access opportunities to be guaranteed with tariff quotas, to be expanded by 75 per cent over ten years and removed completely thereafter.
4. An initial minimum access level equivalent to 3 per cent of domestic consumption to be guaranteed, to be expanded to 5 per cent over ten years with unrestricted access (other than tariff protection) thereafter.
5. Importing countries to be permitted to resort, under specified conditions, to a tariff snap-back mechanism to provide emergency relief against market disruption caused by sudden import surges or exceptional price movements, but only during a ten-year transition period. The snap-back could be invoked by either a *price* or a *quantity* trigger.

This proposal on the reduction of border protection was slightly less radical than the previous US position which had called for the *elimination* of tariffs and tariff quotas within ten years. But the requirement that quota restrictions be eliminated *after* ten years remained. The addition of the price-trigger tariff snap-back provision appeared to be a concession to the EC demand for a 'corrective factor' to shield producers in importing countries from the full impact of major reductions in world prices.

Export competition

The most important US proposal under this heading concerned subsidised exports of *primary* agricultural products. It was proposed that, relative to the base period 1986–8, aggregate budgetary outlays on export assistance and the total quantity of exports assisted should *both* be reduced by 90 per cent over ten years from 1991–2.

On subsidies applied to exports of *processed* agricultural products, the US wanted these to be eliminated over 5 years from 1991–2.

Producer-financed export subsidies would be exempted from the more general provisions only under tightly defined conditions.

The only major exception to the virtual phasing out of subsidised agricultural exports which the US was prepared to accept was the provision of bona fide *food aid* to LDCs.

The final US position on export competition differed from the previous one in abandoning the objective of eliminating export subsidies in favour of a 90 per cent reduction (except for processed products) and by extending the implementation period for primary agricultural product exports from five to ten years.

EC position

The EC responded to the final US position on agriculture by offering to reduce internal price support of main products by 30 per cent over 10 years, from a 1986 base and expressed in terms of an AMS wherever practicable. On border protection, the EC reiterated its partial tariffication offer, subject to rebalancing. On the reduction of export assistance the EC responded by offering 'a concomitant adjustment of export restitutions'. Each of the three main elements of the EC's final offer requires some more detailed explanation.

Internal support

The EC proposed to neutralise the effects of world price movements on levels of support by calculating the AMS relative to *fixed* reference prices based on average 1986–8 data. Moreover, the Community would claim credit for reductions of internal support already undertaken and implemented between 1986 and 1990. Thus its commitment to reducing internal support during the five years from 1991 to 1995 was confined to implementing the 'residual' reductions needed to honour the commitment to a 30 per cent cut over ten years from 1986. For most commodities this residual cut in support would be considerably less than 30 per cent, compared with the 75 per cent cut over 10 years from 1991–2 sought by the US. Thus major discrepancies remained between the EC and US positions on reducing internal support. First, although both offers nominally covered a 10-year period, the lack of agreement on dates meant that the common ground between them was confined to the five year period from 1991 to 1995. Second, the depth of the cut in support which the EC was prepared to contemplate making over this shorter period was, for most commodities, much less than half the 7.5 per cent per annum which the US was seeking.

Border protection

The EC clarified with additional details its earlier offer to transform NTBs, such as variable levies, into 'partial tariffs' consisting of a 'fixed component' and a 'corrective factor'. The *fixed component* was defined as the difference between the internal support price (usually the intervention price) and a fixed external reference price (as used in calculating the AMS) *increased by 10 per cent* [authors' italics], supposedly to reflect Community preference. No specific reduction in the fixed component was offered beyond stating that the 30 per cent reduction in the AMS 'will provide a reduction of border protection'. The *corrective factor* was described as being designed to offset all exchange rate movements (relative to a fixed base level) plus a proportion of world price fluctuations (denominated in national currency) depending on their extent. The Community also insisted that its tariffication offer was contingent upon the acceptance of its demand for 'rebalancing'. Specifically it proposed to replace the duty-free or near duty-free admission of oilseeds, oilseed products and cereal substitutes with tariff quotas based upon existing import levels. Tariff quota imports would be subject to low rates of import duty (6 per cent for oilseeds and protein crops and 12 per cent for cereal substitutes). Thus some similarities existed between the EC's partial tariffication offer and the US scheme for converting all NTBs into their tariff equivalents (TEs), with provision for resort to a tariff snap-back mechanism to give emergency relief against market disruption caused by sudden import surges and exceptional price movements. But large gaps remained between them on issues such as the rate at which tariffs would be brought down (with the EC unwilling to be committed in advance to any specfic reduction of the fixed element of its tariff) and continued EC insistence on the rebalancing of border protection to restrict imports of oilseeds and cereal substitutes.

Export competition

The EC did not offer any specific reduction in agricultural export assistance in terms of either budgetary expenditure on export subsidies or the quantities subsidised. Rather it limited itself to making the general statement that 'the proposed reduction of support and protection will lead to a considerable reduction of export subsidies in (terms of) global expenditure, as well as in unit terms, on the assumption that world prices remain stable'. It also stated 'the Community is ready to quantify the results flowing from the reduction in internal support, the limiting of subsidies to the level of the import charge and the effective implementation of the principle of equitable market shares'. The last-mentioned point reiterated the Community's commitment to revising Article XVI of the General Agreement in order to make its equitable market shares provision more effective. Thus the Community's final offer on the lowering of barriers to export competition fell a long way short of the US demand that exports of primary agricultural products be reduced by 90 per cent over 10 years in terms of both budgetary expenditure on export assistance and the volume of exports subsidised.

The main difference between the Community's final position paper on agriculture and its predecessors was that it offered a quantitative reduction in internal support, expressed in terms of an AMS over a specific time period. However, although it did not oppose the principle of also reducing border protection and export assistance, it was not prepared to offer any quantitative reduction in either of these areas over any specific time period. Thus with the US pressing hard for major quantitative commitments to reduce support in all three areas, the two major protagonists in the Uruguay Round agricultural negotiations remained far apart after 'final' position papers had been tabled in Geneva with only a few weeks to go before Ministers were due to meet in Brussels in order to conclude the Round as a whole.

4.4 THE CONVERGENCE OF THE GATT NEGOTIATIONS AND THE DRIVE TOWARDS CAP REFORM TO REALISE DOMESTIC POLICY OBJECTIVES

What was intended to be the final meeting of the Uruguay Round, duly held in Brussels early in December 1990, ended in fiasco. No agreement could be reached on agriculture and failure there brought the entire Round to an abrupt halt. The crux of the lack of agreement on agriculture was that the US and CG were unable to accept the EC's refusal to offer specific quantitative commitments to lowering border protection and reducing export assistance. Although those opposed to the EC's position were apparently prepared to negotiate on the depth of reductions in support and protection and the associated time-scale, they were not prepared to compromise on the issue of making specific commitments in each of the three main areas of contention. The Community's agricultural trade competitors were not prepared to accept the argument that in view of how the CAP works, a specific commitment to reducing internal support, expressed in AMS terms, is a sufficient assurance that border protection and export assistance will be cut commensurately. They suspected that, one way or another, the EC would manipulate its AMS calculations in such a way as to avoid making matching reductions in these two areas, whenever this suited EC interests. The US and the CG also wanted cuts in export assistance to be deeper, and at a faster rate, than in the remaining two areas. Another deep-seated disagreement was that the US and the CG would not accept the EC's insistence that its quantitative offer to lower internal support, expressed in AMS terms, was contingent upon getting approval for rebalancing increased protection of oilseeds and cereal substitutes against lowered protection of other commodities.

Yet, despite the fundamental disagreements on agriculture between the EC and the US, which were largely responsible for the debacle in Brussels, in December 1990, significant pressures existed on both sides to resolve the agricultural problem. In addition to the benefits of reaching an overall GATT agreement also involving the remaining 14 areas, the major incentive for the EC to seek agreement on agriculture was to reduce budgetary pressure. Despite the adoption of 'stabilisers' early in 1988, by the end of 1990 rising budgetary costs of the CAP were again causing serious concern in the Community. Whereas a successful outcome to the Uruguay Round might help considerably in containing the agricultural budget, particularly in the longer-term if world prices rose, failure could easily result in unmanageable budgetary pressures, especially if this resulted in an agricultural export subsidy war. But the EC Commission took the view that, regardless of the final outcome of the Uruguay Round, further measures of CAP reform were urgently needed for reasons of purely domestic concern.

Shortly after the collapse of the Uruguay Round negotiations in Brussels, the EC Agricultural Commissioner, Ray MacSharry, presented to the Commission a green paper on CAP reform under the title 'Development and the Future of the CAP: Reflections Paper of the Commission'. This document reiterated the fundamental imbalance inherent in the CAP system of income support, as well as its inequity. It argued that these flaws derived from guaranteeing product prices rather than incomes per se, and maintaining support prices above market clearing levels, with the result that agricultural output had grown at a rate 'increasingly beyond the market's absorption capacity'. The growing costs of holding rising stocks and subsidising a growing volume of exports had both borne heavily on the budget. The stabiliser measures, which the European Council decided to enforce in February 1988, may have had some temporary success in holding back the rising tide of agricultural expenditures, but were no more than a palliative since they involved no fundamental reform of the CAP. The green paper argued that the only way to remove the incentive to ever higher production inherent in the present system of support was to lower market prices. But this was not politically viable unless accompanied by direct income aids. Another constraint upon CAP reform was that 'sufficient numbers of farmers must be kept on the land'. But support needed to be tilted in favour of those in greatest need, in order to achieve 'real financial solidarity' (a basic principle of the CAP). For this reason the green paper suggested the 'modulation' of direct income aids, according to farm size, income, regional situation or other relevant factors.

The crux of the 'MacSharry Plan', to give the Commission green paper its popular title, was headed 'Guidelines for the Future'. This contained the details of suggested support price reductions, together with proposals for modulated direct income compensation, on a sector by sector basis. So, for example, in cereals production growers not classed as 'small producers' would qualify for direct income payment support *only* on condition that they set aside a designated proportion of their arable land. Land which was set aside could only be fallowed or used to grow biomass crops. Thus, for set aside participants, the scheme would effectively dilute the degree of income support they received as compensation relative to their *total* crop acreage. Similar proposals were made having the effect of making major cuts in support prices matched by full compensation for small producers and partial compensation for larger ones, for oilseeds, protein crops, milk (allied to quota restrictions), beef and sheepmeat. The plan stressed that livestock producers should benefit considerably from the reduction in the price of cereals used in feed.

The MacSharry Plan was sufficiently controversial, even within the Commission, for it to remain unpublished for several months. According to reports leaked to the press, some commissioners thought that the suggested reductions in support prices were too drastic, and the bias in the distribution of compensation payments towards small producers 'unfair' to larger producers as well as penalising efficiency (Green Europe, February 1991, p.15). However, although in the version finally released for publication and communicated to the Council in February 1991 [COM(91)100 final] no actual quantities were included in the section headed 'Guidelines for the Future', the essential spirit of the document remained unchanged. Several months then followed in which member states of the Community and numerous interested organisations communicated their views to the Commission. This process culminated with the publication of a revised version of the MacSharry Plan in July 1991 [COM(91)258 final].

The revised document proposed cutting the Community's administered market price of *cereals* by some 35 per cent, phased over the 3-year period, 1994–6. Similar arrangements would apply to oilseeds and protein crops. Compensation for the reduction of price support would take the form of a fixed acreage payment based on the'gap' between the old and new support prices and the regional average yield. But, except for 'small producers', eligibility to receive compensation would be conditional upon participation in 'voluntary' set-aside, initially set at 15 per cent of the total farm acreage of cereals, oilseeds and protein crops. 'Small producers' were defined as those with an annual production of not more than 92 tonnes of cereals (or approximately 20 ha. at the Community average cereal yield). The document was ambiguous concerning whether otherwise eligible producers must actually plant the whole, or even a minimum proportion of their permitted acreage in order to qualify for full compensation.

In addition to qualifying for direct income payments on their permitted cereals acreage, set-aside participants would also qualify for additional compensation in the form of a set-aside acreage payment. But this would be limited to 7.5 ha. of set-aside land per farm. Above this maximum set-aside would be uncompensated.

As well as advancing plans for reforming CAP crop regimes, the revised MacSharry Plan also made proposals for dealing with milk, beef and sheepmeat. The milk proposal amounted to no more than a small reduction in the Community-wide quota leaving some scope for redistribution to priority classes of producer within member states. The quota reduction was to be combined with a small (10 per cent) reduction in dairy product support prices (to reflect the effect of lower cereals prices on the cost of feedingstuffs). But smaller-scale producers would be eligible to receive an annual cow headage payment in compensation for the price cut. Larger-scale producers would also be eligible to receive the headage payment up to a maximum of 40 cows, provided they complied with maximum stocking rate conditions.

The proposal for beef involved a reduction in the intervention price to reflect the lower price of cereals. But producers complying with maximum stocking rate conditions (less stringent in less favoured areas [LFAs]) would qualify for headage payments on steer cattle and suckler cows up to a maximum herd size limit. The proposal for sheepmeat was similar, except that in this case there would be no support other than ewe headage payments, subject to a maximum flock size limit modulated in favour of flock owners in LFAs.

The revised plan also discussed budgetary implications. The Commission estimated that, despite the high budget costs of compensating farmers for the reduction of *consumer* financed price support in the short-term, when the new arrangements came fully into force in 1997 annual FEOGA guarantee expenditure would be some 1000million ECU *less* than the agricultural guideline based on existing rules. The Commission proposed a one-off increase of 1500 million ECU in the base of the agricultural guideline to cover additional short-term expenditure, including the costs of German unification as well as MacSharry.

Thus, from an EC perspective, by the middle of 1991 the ultimate fate of the Uruguay Round agricultural negotiations appeared to be tied up with the fate of the MacSharry Plan, since both were ultimately concerned with reducing the incidence and costs of agricultural support, especially trade-distorting support. However, any connection between MacSharry and the Uruguay Round was officially denied by Community spokesmen: the MacSharry Plan was concerned only with reforming the CAP to realise purely domestic objectives. However, most independent observers saw a very real connection. Although the prospects for reforming the CAP along the lines of the MacSharry Plan appeared quite good, mainly for long-term budgetary reasons, the big unanswered question was whether internal Community agreement on the details of the reform could be reached in time to save the Uruguay Round.

Breaking the historical sequence of events followed in this chapter so far, it is germane to observe at this stage that the legal text of a somewhat modified version of the MacSharry Plan was finally adopted by the Council of Agriculture Ministers on 30 June 1992. There were two main changes from the revised draft version of the plan. First, the cereal support price reduction (over 3 years) was cut fom 35 per cent to only 29 per cent. Second, the proposed modulation of compensation for set aside was abandoned: *all* producers, regardless of scale of production, would qualify for compensation, subject only to their agreement to set aside the designated proportion of their arable land. Some further discussion of the final version of the MacSharry Plan, and its implications for the GATT negotiations, appears in Chapter 12.

4.5 DUNKEL DRAFT AGREEMENT ON AGRICULTURE: OBSTACLES TO ACCEPTANCE BY THE EC

The Uruguay Round agricultural negotiations were revived in February 1991 when, at an emergency meeting in Geneva called by the GATT Secretary-General, all the contracting parties agreed to the resumption of negotiations on the basis of reaching 'specific binding commitments to reduce farm supports in each of the three areas: internal assistance, border protection and export assistance'. By not objecting to this form of words, the EC softened its previous hardline refusal even to consider the possibility of acceding to the US demand for specific support reduction commitments in all three areas. However, despite this initiative, the agricultural negotiations made little further progress in 1991, even with some apparent further relaxation of US demands for subsidy (internal and export) and border protection reductions at a US–EC summit on 9 November 1991. But, on 20 December 1991, GATT Secretary-General Dunkel attempted to force the Uruguay Round to a successful conclusion by presenting the negotiators with a comprehensive draft agreement including all areas of the negotiations, including agriculture (GATT, 1991).

In areas other than agriculture, the provisions of Dunkel's 'Final Act' were based upon provisional agreements already reached in the relevant negotiating groups. But in agriculture, where no consensus view had emerged on the critical issue of 'numbers', that is, the *amounts and time-scale* of cuts in government support and protection, Dunkel had to devise his own draft agreement for consideration by the negotiators.

The main body of the Dunkel text on agriculture dealt specifically with improving market access, reducing domestic support and improving export competition. In addition, criteria were specified for use in identifying 'green' domestic support policies permitted to be exempted from support reduction commitments, including decoupled income payments. A common *implementation period* of 1993–9 applying to all cuts in support and protection was proposed. But two different *base periods* of 1986–8 and 1986–90 were proposed, respectively applying to (i) domestic support reduction and improved market access, and (ii) export subsidy reduction. In the three main areas of contention the key provisions were:

1. Improved market access: an average reduction of 36 per cent in customs duties, including those resulting from the tariffication of NTBs, such as import quotas and variable levies, subject to a minimum reduction of 15 per cent in every tariff line. Customs duty reductions to be supplemented by *minimum access opportunities*, set at 3 per cent of the importer's base period consumption in the first year of implementation and rising to 5 per cent in the final year. *Special safeguard provisions* were also included to cushion the effects of unusually large import surges or reductions in import prices.

2. Domestic support reduction: a uniform cut of 20 per cent, expressed in terms of an AMS and applying individually to all supported commodities, with credit allowed for actions already taken since 1986. But in defining the AMS simply as the difference between the internal price and the external reference price (expressed in domestic currency) times the quantity supported, that is, $(P_s - P_r)Q_s$, Dunkel did *not* allow as much credit for supply control as envisaged by the EC's SMU proposal. Exempt 'green box' policies were defined as those 'having no, or at most minimal, trade distortion effects', including publicly financed R & D, early retirement schemes for farmers and land retirement (subject to a minimum retirement period of three years). Dunkel also prescribed a set of criteria for use in determining whether particular schemes of direct payments to farmers qualified as *decoupled payments* eligible for green box treatment. A common feature of these criteria was that where direct income payments related to prices, production volumes or the employment of factors of production, only fixed *base period* values could be used. In addition, eligibility to receive payments could *not* be made conditional upon the continuation of production after the base period.

3. Export competition improvement: twin requirements that *budgetary outlays* on export subsidies be cut by 36 per cent and the *volume* of subsidised exports by 24 per cent. Dunkel also categorised six different forms of export subsidy to be subject to reduction commitments.

Dunkel's 'Final Act' also included a timetable for the successful conclusion of the Uruguay Round. This set 1 January 1993 as the target date for the implementation of a Uruguay Round Agreement. To allow the minimum time needed for ratification and implementation by national governments, a deadline of 15 April 1992 was set for concluding negotiations. But the timetable for *agriculture* required all participants to submit product-specific lists of their base-period positions and support reduction commitments, drawn up in terms of the parameters of Dunkel's draft agreement in each of the three critical areas of market access, domestic support and export competition. These lists were to be tabled in Geneva by not later than 1 March 1992.

Being ready to accept the Dunkel draft agreement on agriculture as the basis for a successful conclusion of the Uruguay Round agricultural negotiations, the US and most of the CG countries (but not Canada) were prepared to adhere to this timetable. But the EC held back for a number of reasons. First, on improved import access, Dunkel made no concession towards permitting the Community to include the rebalancing of oilseed and cereal substitute protection in its overall commitment to reduced protection. Moreover, the formula proposed by Dunkel for converting NTBs into tariff equivalents made no provision for maintaining a margin of Community Preference (long regarded as a fundamental principle of the CAP). Second, on domestic support reduction, Dunkel's definition of AMS to be used to measure reduction commitments failed to recognise the EC's desire to have full credit given for supply control. Third, and perhaps most importantly, the EC was extremely reluctant to be committed to any restriction on the *volume* of subsidised exports. It is easier to control the size of the CAP budget (of which export restitution payments form a part) than the volume of production. Because of these difficulties, in responding to Dunkel's 1 March deadline the EC confined itself to submitting lists showing its commodity-specific base period positions in each of the three critical areas, but without making any new support reduction commitments, either on the terms of the draft agreement or otherwise.

Due to the failure of the EC and a number of other countries including Canada and Japan to adhere fully to the conditions he had laid down for moving swiftly to an agreement on agriculture, Secretary-General Dunkel was compelled to abandon the timetable set by the Final Act for the conclusion of the Uruguay Round negotiations by 15 April 1992. No new target date was set to replace it.

Apart from the 24 per cent cut in the volume of subsidised exports, the quantitative reductions in support and protection proposed by

Dunkel, in each of the three areas, did not appear to be a major problem for the EC, with two provisos. First, it appeared unlikely that the proposed 'compensatory payments' at the centre of the MacSharry Plan would meet the criteria laid down by Dunkel for direct income support to be classed as 'decoupled' and therefore exempt from reduction. Second, even if MacSharry's *proposed* compensatory payments did qualify for 'green box' treatment by the GATT, the awkward problem remained that the MacSharry Plan itself was still only a blueprint which still had to be agreed and adopted by the Council of Ministers. Domestic opposition to MacSharry's proposals for CAP reform was still very active, particularly from farm organisations throughout the Community which continued to campaign for tighter supply control as an alternative to lower market prices with compensatory payments. Farmers continued to be highly distrustful of direct income support as well as resenting having to depend on 'charity'. A further obstacle to Council acceptance of the MacSharry Plan was that some member states were opposed to the proposed modulation of compensation in favour of small producers on the ground that this discriminated against 'efficiency' and international competitiveness. It was also argued by some that the final decision on the MacSharry Plan could not be taken in advance of the final outcome of the Uruguay Round negotiations, though this was clearly inconsistent with the EC's official stance that CAP reform was being actuated only by domestic considerations.

The EC shared with the US the problem of trying to find a way round Dunkel's strict criteria for according 'green box' treatment to their preferred scheme of direct payments. Whereas the US claimed that its existing deficiency payment scheme for cereals and certain other crops bore many of the hallmarks of 'decoupled payments', the EC claimed that, despite being linked to set aside, US deficiency payments were an implicit export subsidy. For its part, the US was unlikely to agree to the EC's proposed compensatory payments under the MacSharry Plan being accorded green box treatment. In April 1992 unofficial sources were suggesting that a so-called 'blue box' compromise might be reached whereby the EC and the US were both permitted to continue non-decoupled deficiency payments at their base period level for a limited period. After the expiry of the grace period, the payments would either have to be modified to accord with the Dunkel decoupled payment criteria, or be placed in the 'amber box' for phased reduction. Although delaying the attainment of the policy objective of breaking the link between farm income support and production and trade, such a compromise might have the advantage of buying more time in which to assess the *political* feasibility of truly decoupled farm income payments. In particular, it remains to be demonstrated that taxpayers are prepared to subsidise people who were farmers in the past but have no current obligation to produce for the market.

Differing national positions within the EC greatly complicate the Community's stance in the Uruguay Round agricultural negotiations, as well as in trying to find internal consensus on the MacSharry proposals. But, since the internal debates preceding key Council decisions on both issues have taken place behind closed doors, little information about this exists in the public domain. However, it is generally considered that France, as a major cereals exporter, is particularly opposed to tight limits on export subsidies, as well as to the erosion of Community Preference. For a mixture of political and historical reasons, Germany is very strongly committed to the defence of German farmers' incomes. The farm vote remains a particularly powerful force there. With its relatively liberal agricultural trading traditions before entering the Community, the UK has supported the EC's highly protectionist stance on agriculture in the Uruguay Round with considerable misgiving. On the MacSharry Plan, the UK and the Netherlands, with their relatively favourable farm structures, have argued most strongly against discriminating against larger-scale producers in the provision of compensation for the reduction of price support and participation in set aside.

Despite their traditional opposition to 'renationalising the CAP', were it not for the GATT, the Community's agriculture ministers might now be tempted to ease their budget problem by transferring part of the cost of compensating farmers for the reduction of price support back to *national* governments and budgets. However, this is scarcely feasible since, for the purpose of honouring support reduction commitments, no distinction between national and Community support measures in the same category would be accepted by the GATT.

4.6 CONCLUSION: WHAT DID THE EC EXPECT FROM THE URUGUAY ROUND AGRICULTURAL NEGOTIATIONS? WHAT DID IT ACHIEVE?

The EC originally regarded the Uruguay Round agricultural negotiations as a damage limitation exercise. As in previous GATT rounds, it aimed to defend the CAP and minimise the effects of external pressures to change its character. But from the beginning of the Uruguay Round in 1986, and even from some years before that, it was widely accepted within the EC that change was needed to bring the agricultural budget under more effective control. From the beginning of the latest round of GATT negotiations the EC's preferred option for agriculture was some kind of market sharing agreement amongst the world's largest producers and exporters of temperate agricultural products. That way, product price support could remain as the principal basis of farm income support, albeit at the cost of more stringent production constraints. But the EC's main adversaries in the negotiations were not at all amenable to this strategy. The US took up the extreme position of the 'zero option' calling for the complete abolition of all trade-distorting support and protection within ten years. The Cairns Group of agricultural exporting countries took up a less extreme position, but one which was much nearer to that of the US than the EC.

During the course of the negotiations the US proposed the gradual liberalisation of agricultural markets through the tariffication of all NTBs. This proposal was clearly aimed at getting rid of, inter alia, the variable import levy. Despite the VIL being a central instrument of the CAP, the EC chose to respond with a partial tariffication proposal of its own. However, the EC continued to emphasise throughout the negotiations that any offer it made to ease the entry of agricultural imports would be subject to rebalancing *increased* protection of oilseeds and cereal substitutes against lower protection of other products. Although the reason for this strategy was primarily historical – the EC had agreed to accord duty-free or near duty-free status to these products in an earlier GATT round – it was also actuated by the objective of stimulating domestic EC demand for home-produced cereals for use as livestock feed.

The EC eventually succeeded in forcing the US to abandon the unrealistic zero option, but this alone was insufficient to unblock the way to a Uruguay Round agreement on agriculture. A necessary though not sufficient condition of attaining this objective was a fundamental reform of the CAP. Unless and until this was achieved the EC could not depart from its inflexible rearguard stance in response to US and CG initiatives. The break came in December 1990 when the EC Agriculture Commissioner unveiled a plan of fundamental CAP reform. The principal feature of the Commissioner's proposals was the replacement of farm product price support with direct income support to a substantial degree.[6] Although EC officials maintained that the reasons for embarking on this course were purely domestic, particularly the necessity of improving control of the agricultural budget, it so happened that the MacSharry proposals appeared to fit in quite well with CAP reforms of a type which might be acceptable to the Community's agricultural trade competitors, especially the US and the CG. From their point of view the most decisive feature of the MacSharry Plan was the proposed switch from price support to direct income support at least partially divorced from production and trade.

The EC reaction to the draft agreement on agriculture, tabled by the GATT Secretary-General at the end of 1991 in an attempt to force a conclusion to the Uruguay Round negotiations, was rather overshadowed by the unfinished internal debate on the MacSharry Plan. Whilst the EC did object to some aspects of the Dunkel agreement, particularly the proposal to force down the *volume* of subsidised exports at a predetermined rate, as well as budgetary expenditure on export assistance, the Community's main object appeared to be to play for extra time both to reach internal agreement on the details of the MacSharry Plan and to clarify the compatibility of some of its features with Dunkel's proposals. In particular, it was important for the EC to know whether if it accepted Dunkel's proposed 20 per cent reduction in domestic support, MacSharry's 'compensatory payments' would count as 'amber' or 'green'. Obviously, if they were permitted to be counted as green, or possibly 'blue' as an interim measure, this would greatly ease the task of reconciling MacSharry with Dunkel.

Early in 1992 unofficial press reports suggested that the EC was willing to water down its rebalancing demand as a negotiating counter. This would involve abandoning the objective of imposing a tariff on imports of oilseeds and oilseed products. But imports of cereal substitutes would be subject to regulation by quota. With this exception, the EC does not appear to have fought very hard for the retention of import quotas, as currently permitted by Article XI.2(c) of the GATT under specific conditions. In view of the Community's earlier attempt to obtain full credit for domestic supply control, and the possibility of using this to 'justify' the use of import quotas (as strongly argued by Canada), this seemed slightly surprising. However, the import quota question may have been overshadowed by a common desire on the part of the EC and the US to ensure that *production* quotas receive green box treatment in AMS measurement, particularly in the specific case of land diversion, that is, set aside.[7] This may also explain why, towards the end of the negotiations, the EC appeared to be no longer pressing for more AMS credit to be given for supply control.

In April 1992 agreement on agriculture between the EC and the US appeared to be quite near. But the actual clinching of an agreement appeared to hinge upon three key issues:

1. Internal EC agreement on the MacSharry Plan, with possible modification of detail, but without changing its major thrust.
2. Resolution of the issue of the GATT classification of direct income payments to farmers both in the EC and the US, with agreement on the creation of a 'blue box' possibly clinching the issue.
3. Compromises on the two linked issues of (i) quantitative reductions of subsidised exports, and (ii) the restriction of EC imports of cereal substitutes by quota.

The primary obstacles to the striking of compromises to resolve these issues were obviously *political*. But with powerful sectional interests on both sides of the Atlantic still opposed to the lowering of agricultural trade barriers, and important elections pending, it was by no means certain that a final agreement on agriculture could be struck before Dunkel's 'Final Act' began to unravel.

4.7 POSTSCRIPT

The EC and the US resolved their Uruguay Round differences on agriculture by striking a bilateral agreement on 20 November 1992. Readers are referred to the end of Chapter 12 for an outline of the main provisions of the 'Washington Accord'. However, although this development appeared to remove a major obstacle to the conclusion of an overall Uruguay Round agreement, the EC position on agriculture remained ambiguous due to the dissent of France, which claimed that commitments under the Washington Accord were inconsistent with the MacSharry CAP reform, particularly with respect to quantitative limits to subsidised exports. However, the EC Council decided not to risk isolating France by taking a vote on this issue alone, but rather to defer voting until a decision was needed upon whether to accept a complete Uruguay Round Agreement in which the trade-offs were clearer between concessions given on agriculture and gains made in other areas of the negotiations.

Summary of EC concessions on agriculture during the Uruguay Round

The concessions made by the EC during the course of the agricultural negotiations up to the Spring of 1992 can be summarised briefly. It could be held that by signing the Punta del Este Declaration, which stated that the central objective of agricultural policy reform was to 'bring all measures affecting import access and export competition under strengthened and more operationally effective GATT rules and disciplines' the Community finally gave up insisting that the CAP could not be the subject of international negotiations. However, this concession appeared to be beyond dispute when, in April 1989, the EC subscribed to the Geneva Accord declaring that *all* internal policy measures which affect trade should be subject to GATT disciplines. A second concession under the Geneva Accord was that the EC agreed to shift the baseline for any agreed cuts in internal support from 1984 to 1986.

In its first position paper tabled in the aftermath of the GA (in December 1989), the EC yielded some ground on border protection by putting forward its partial tariffication proposal. In response to a US proposal for converting all NTBs to simple tariffs (or tariff quotas) prior to reduction and eventual elimination, the EC suggested a two-part scheme of border protection consisting of a fixed tariff, subject to negotiated reduction, and a 'corrective factor' to cushion the impact on domestic market prices of major fluctuations in external prices (measured in domestic currency).

The 'final' EC concession on agriculture before the major break-down of negotiations in Brussels, in December 1990, was the offer to reduce internal support by 30 per cent over 10 years from a 1986 base. The EC's refusal to go beyond this concession to make parallel commitments on the reduction of border protection and export assistance was the major reason for the Brussels breakdown.

In the aftermath of the Brussels stalemate, at an emergency meeting held in Geneva in February 1991, the EC softened its previous hardline refusal even to consider making specific commitments to the reduction of border protection and export assistance by not objecting to a form of words proposed by the GATT Secretary-General for restarting the agricultural negotiations. This form of words committed all the contracting parties, including the EC, to the resumption of negotiations with a view to reaching 'specific binding commitments to reduce farm supports in each of the three areas: internal assistance, border protection and export assistance'.

Under a bilateral agreement struck between the US and the EC in November 1992 (the Washington Accord) the EC effectively abandoned 'rebalancing'. It was agreed that EC imports of oilseeds and oilseed products would not be subject to a tariff, as the EC had earlier demanded. Further, it was agreed that EC imports of cereal substitutes would remain unrestricted, subject only to bilateral consultations taking place should such imports rise in the future to a level 'inconsistent with the implementation of CAP reform'.

5 The Cairns Group Perspective

Rod Tyers[1]

Although there are few countries which leave incentives in their farm sectors undistorted, there are many in which the economy-wide pattern of protection does not favour agriculture as a whole. Convention in the theory of trade protection (Anderson and Hayami, 1986; Vousden, 1990) would lead us to expect that most agricultural exporting countries would be members of this latter group. The principal modern exceptions, of course, are the EC and the United States, both of which now protect exporting agricultural sectors. These exceptions aside, the predominant agricultural exporting countries are indeed among those whose patterns of protection do not assist agriculture.

Since the origin of the GATT, it is this group of countries which have watched powerlessly as exceptions to the GATT principles have accumulated, sanctioning increasing distortions against their exports. The collapse of international food prices in the 1980s and the ensuing trade war between the EC and the United States provided the stimuli which brought many of them together, overcoming the developing country solidarity barrier for the first time, to form the Cairns Group of comparatively efficient agricultural exporting countries.

This chapter addresses the interest of this group of countries in the Uruguay Round, their influence over it and the potential gains to them which might stem from it. The section to follow briefly summarises the origins of the group and its composition. Section 5.2 offers a quantitative assessment of the impacts on the group of food trade distortions in other industrial countries. Section 5.3 then reviews the role of the group in the Uruguay Round to date. Section 5.4 examines the potential gains from likely trade reforms in Western Europe; in particular those which would stem from the EC's unilateral agricultural reforms and which are implicit in the anticipated expansion of the EC to include the five continental members of the European Free Trade Association (EFTA). Finally, Section 5.5 offers brief conclusions.

5.1 ORIGINS

From its inception, the GATT has been weak in disciplining agricultural protection. Exceptions began with the over-riding of the general prohibition of quotas where these were associated with programmes ostensibly restraining domestic agricultural production. Then, in 1955, the United States obtained the 'Section 22' waiver of the GATT rules applying to parts of its agricultural sector. Switzerland's entry into the GATT in 1966 came at the price of exemptions for its agricultural sector. Finally, although export subsidisation is banned by the GATT, the 1960s also saw exceptions to this general rule applying to agriculture. The latter exceptions might have seemed innocuous enough at the time, but they became particularly important in the 1970s as the EC was transformed by the CAP from a net agricultural importer to net exporter.

When, following the 1985 Food Security Act, the United States ceased holding stocks to support cereal prices and established its Export Enhancement Program, to try to win back some markets lost to the EC, average real food export prices fell to levels unprecedented this century.[2] Since both the EC and the United States had persisted in either blocking or ignoring the GATT dispute settlement on agricultural issues, other agricultural exporting countries faced substantial and continuing deterioration in their terms of trade with no effective opportunity for redress.

In 1985, as a new round of trade negotiations loomed, the Australian Minister for Trade, John Dawkins, sought to gather a group of the trade ministers from thus disadvantaged agricultural exporting countries. Collaboration was canvassed in Geneva and, early in 1986, the Uruguayan government hosted a meeting of officials from Argentina, Australia, Brazil and New Zealand in Montevideo. Separate discussions between the governments of Australia and Thailand led to a follow-up meeting of a wider group in Bangkok later that year. This was preliminary to a full gathering of trade ministers in Cairns, a small resort town in Northern Australia, just prior to the establishment of the new Round in Punta del Este. The group of countries represented at that meeting have since been known as the Cairns Group.[3]

The initial concern of the group was to keep agriculture on the agenda for the Round. For the first time in the modern history of the GATT a group comprising industrial, developing and centrally-planned economies worked together to advance a common aim. And it succeeded, overcoming opposition from within the EC and ensuring that agriculture would receive unprecedented attention during the remainder of the Round. It did so because of the solidarity of the group on that issue. The recent decline in agricultural export earnings was a political priority in all Cairns Group countries. Through the Group and the Round, their governments could be seen to be taking action, where previously their small country status had rendered them impotent in the face of the EC–United States conflict.

The Cairns Group's solidarity on the agricultural trade issue in those early years contrasted with its heterogeneity in other respects and hence with the contradictory positions its members might be expected to take on other areas in the Round. Some of this heterogeneity is clear from Table 5.1, which lists the member countries along with indices of their economic size, level of development and of the importance of agriculture in their exports. The Group comprises two very large developing countries, Brazil and Indonesia, a number of smaller developing and industrial countries, one Eastern European centrally-planned country and Australia and Canada, the latter pair being described by Higgott and Cooper (1990) as 'middle powers'.

All members have shares of agriculture in exports which are substantially higher than the world average, four with the majority of their exports coming from that sector. Although the member with the greatest economic clout is Canada, it has the least dependence on agriculture for its export earnings. This, combined with high rates of protection of its dairy and livestock sectors, has caused some ambiguity in Canada's position on agricultural trade reform, a point discussed in some detail by T. K. Warley in Chapter 6. Although Canada put the point of view of the Cairns Group countries at the 1987 Venice summit of the 'big seven' economic powers, the leadership of the Cairns Group has fallen predominantly to Australia.

Despite the predominance of developing countries in the Group, a source of its influence is its economic size compared with the EC(12), Japan and the United States (the 'big three'). This is quantified in Table 5.2. Its population is almost as large as theirs combined. It has a tenth of global GDP and this share is expanding with rapid growth in several of its member developing countries. While it has a tenth of global manufacturing output, compared with the quarter produced in each of the big three, its share of global agricultural value added is larger than that of any big three member.

In international trade, the Cairns Group has about the same value of merchandise exports as Japan. Although it is a comparatively small exporter of manufactures, it is responsible for about a quarter of global

Table 5.1 The Cairns Group, 1987–1989[a]

	Population (millions)	GDP Total (1987 US$bn.)	GDP Share of agriculture (%)	Exports[b] Total (1987 US$bn.)	Exports[b] Share of agriculture (%)
Argentina	32	78	13	8	62
Australia	17	192	4	28	37
Brazil	144	307	8	29	35
Canada	26	433	4	102	20
Chile	13	22	8	6	35
Colombia	32	38	18	5	45
Fiji	.72	1.3	23	.24	82
Hungary	11	26	16	9	23
Indonesia	175	81	23	19	22
Malaysia	17	32	20	21	36
New Zealand	3	16	10	8	69
Philippines	60	37	24	7	29
Thailand	54	55	15	14	41
Uruguay	3	8	10	1	55
TOTAL	586	1324	9	257	30
Global averages			5		13

a Annual averages for the interval 1987-89.
b Merchandise only.
Sources: Population, GDP and value added are from World Bank *World Tables*, various issues, except for Fiji, where these data are from East West Centre (1986) and Asian Development Bank (1991). All trade data are from the United Nations International Trade Statistics, as provided in computerised form via the ANU International Economic Databank.

agricultural exports, about the same share as the big three combined. This pattern is disaggregated in Table 5.3 which shows that the prominence of the Cairns Group extends over all agricultural commodity groups. Its dominance is nevertheless outweighed in important product groups: by the United States in cereals and oilseeds and by the EC in dairy products.

On the import side, Table 5.2 indicates that the Cairns Group has about a tenth of world manufacturing imports. This is roughly the

Table 5.2 The Cairns Group in world production and trade: a comparison with the 'big three'[a]

	Cairns Group		World shares (per cent) due to EC-12		Japan		USA	
	1980–2	1987–9	1980–2	1987–9	1980–2	1987–9	1980–2	1987–9
Population	12	13	8	7	2	3	6	5
Production[b] GDP	8	9	30	29	15	17	30	31
Agriculture	16	17	16	16	10	9	13	13
Manufacturing	10	10	31	26	21	24	28	30
Merchandise exports,[c] total	10	10	16	16	7	10	12	12
Agriculture	24	23	11	11	1	1	14	12
Manufacturing	6	7	22	19	13	13	18	14
Merchandise imports[c] total	10	9	19	17	7	7	13	17
Agriculture	6	6	13	15	9	12	9	10
Manufacturing	11	10	21	19	3	4	13	18

a The 'big three' are the EC, the United States and Japan.
b Agriculture and manufacturing value added.
c EC trade excludes reported intra-EC trade.

Sources: The population, GDP and value added shares are based on World Bank: *World Tables*, various issues. The trade data are from the United Nations International Trade Statistics. Data were provided via the ANU International Economic Databank.

Table 5.3   The Cairns Group in world agricultural commodity exports

	Cairns Group		World shares (per cent) due to EC-12		Japan		USA	
	1980–2	1987–9	1980–2	1987–9	1980–2	1987–9	1980–2	1987–9
Meats (SITC 01)	30	24	10	11	–	–	7	9
Sugar (SITC 06)	29	20	19	19	.2	.4	3	3
Oilseeds and nuts (SITC 22)	17	21	.3	.6	–	–	67	47
Dairy Products (SITC 02-025)	12	10	31	21	4	3	2	2
Textile Fibres (SITC 26)	22	28	7	8	.3	.2	20	13
Vegetable oils (SITC 42)	46	41	12	14	4	5	13	9
Rubber (SITC 23)	43	44	7	9	4	.5	8	9
Beverages (SITC11)	7	5	42[a]	39[a]	1	1	2	3
Other agriculture	23	24	8	7	1	1	13	13

a   Presumably large because it included processed imports
Source: United Nations International Trade Statistics, as provided via the ANU International Economic Databank.

same as Japan's share of world manufacturing exports. Indeed, although there has never been any suggestion that the Group exploit punitive power on the import side to achieve its negotiating aims, it is interesting to observe that the potential exists for the exercise of such power.

A closer look at this potential requires an examination of the pattern of bi-lateral trade between the big three and the Cairns Group. This is summarised in Table 5.4. Although the United States sends about a third of its exports to Cairns Group countries, the corresponding fraction is only about a tenth for the EC and Japan. Given that agricultural protection in the latter pair is more damaging to Cairns Group exports than that in the United States, rather more leverage than this would likely be needed for retaliatory import restrictions to influence successfully their trade policies. In any case, as Higgott and Cooper (1990) point out, the Cairns Group has taken the view that the principal source of the agricultural trade problem is disputation between the EC and the United States and that its role is to facilitate resolution.[4]

5.2   THE EFFECTS OF INDUSTRIAL COUNTRY DISTORTIONS

To estimate the effects of industrial country distortions on agricultural exports from Cairns Group countries it is simplest to use an established global trade model. In this case the model of Tyers and Anderson (1992) is used. It is a dynamic simulation model of the global markets

Table 5.4   The Cairns Group as destination for 'big three' exports

Share (%) of exports of	EC-12[a]	USA	Japan
All merchandise			
1980–2	9	25	15
1987–9	9	30	12
Manufactures			
1980–2	10	30	15
1987–9	8	34	11

a   Share of EC-12 exports *not* directed to other EC countries.
Source: United Nations International Trade Statistics as provided by the ANU International Economic Databank.

for seven food commodities (wheat, coarse grain, rice, sugar, dairy products, ruminant meats and non-ruminant meats) which identifies 30 countries and country groups. In a newly updated and expanded version (Tyers 1992a, Appendix 1), its base period is 1990 and simulations extend through the year 2010.[5]

There is also a static equilibrium version which is used in combination with the full dynamic model to analyse the effects of existing distortions. This works in the following way. First, a full dynamic simulation is made through, say, 2000 on the assumption that broad policy *regimes* will remain unchanged. Then, for particular years, solutions are made of the static equilibrium version in which all parameters are set to medium-run adjustment levels and underlying exogenous shifters, such as population levels, GNP and technology, are advanced accordingly. Explicit in the latter simulations is the absence of the distortions subject to analysis. The path mapped by the static solutions is that which would be followed without those distortions once all transitional dynamics had settled down. The effects of the distortions are then simply measured by comparing the prices and quantities produced, traded and consumed in the reference dynamic simulation with the corresponding values in the static equilibrium solutions.

The policies of Cairns Group countries tend either to offer comparatively little support to their agricultures, or, through the protection of other tradeable goods sectors and the overvaluation of exchange rates, to be biased against them. The only important exception to this generalisation is Canada, which offers high rates of assistance to its dairy and livestock sectors. By contrast, industrial countries generally distort their economies in ways which offer substantial net assistance to agriculture.

In the Tyers–Anderson model the level of protection observed in any year is endogenous.[6] The most accurate historical indication of this pattern of distortions is available through 1990 from the OECD (1992, and supplements) for industrial countries and Webb et al. (1990) for others. It is also useful to illustrate the pattern using simulated distortions for 2000, assuming no changes of policy regime, since it is in this period that reforms will be effective.[7] The resulting distortions, expressed as average nominal protection coefficients, are listed in Table 5.5. With the single exception of Canada, the measured levels of protection in the Cairns Group countries are very much less than those in the industrial countries as a group. The pattern of distortions would therefore be expected to retard the growth of agriculture in Cairns Group countries while accelerating it in other industrial countries.

Table 5.5   Average food trade distortions in Cairns Group and other
            industrial countries

	Simulated nominal protection coefficients[a]		
	1990	1995	2000
Selected Cairns Group countries			
Argentina	0.74	0.74	0.75
Australia	1.04	1.07	1.06
Brazil	0.91	0.94	0.94
Canada	1.28	1.35	1.38
New Zealand	1.07	1.10	1.10
Thailand	1.04	1.08	1.08
EC	2.05	2.24	2.21
Average for all industrial market economies[b]	1.80	1.89	1.83

a   These are simulated coefficients (ratios of producer to border prices
    adjusted for marketing margins). Averages are for wheat, coarse grain,
    rice, sugar, dairy products, ruminant meats and non-ruminant meats,
    calculated as the value of output at domestic prices divided by the
    corresponding value at home currency border prices. Figures in parenth-
    eses measure protection in terms of *consumer* price distortions.
b   In addition to Australia, New Zealand and Canada, these include the
    United States, the EFTA (5) countries and Japan.
Source: Simulations using the Tyers-Anderson food trade model.

The simulated effects on Cairns Group exports are listed in Table
5.6. They are large overall, with the net value of food export earnings in
the Cairns Group being reduced by about three quarters. The volume
of dairy product exports is reduced by more than 100 per cent in several
Cairns Group countries since distortions abroad shift their terms of
trade so that they become net importers of dairy products. The effect
on the Group's net cereal exports is small, however, because the
protection in other industrial countries is highest in their livestock
sectors and this enhances the consumption of cereals as feed. Reform in
those countries would therefore raise direct cereal consumption but
lower indirect consumption.

The corresponding welfare effects on Cairns Group economies are
summarised in Table 5.7. Farmers are generally worse off by amounts
averaging about a quarter of the gross value of staple food production.
The largest proportional effects are in New Zealand, where the loss to

Table 5.6 Effects of industrial country food trade distortions on Cairns Group food exports

	Change in exports volume, %				Change in net food export value %
	Cereals	Meats	Dairy products	Sugar	
Argentina	−23	−50	−74	−	−60
Australia	−8	−35	−82	−5	−40
Brazil	−51	−57	−162[a]	−72	−88
Canada	−10	−	−	−	−3
Other Cairns Group	−25	−44	−95	−45	−66
Total, Cairns Group	−16	−44	−115[b]	−38	−55

a   Net foreign exchange earnings from trade in the food groups listed.
b   Reductions larger than 100 per cent indicate that net exporters without industrial country distortions become net importers in the presence of those distortions.
Source: A comparison of simulations of the Tyers–Anderson model, with and without industrial country food trade distortions, in 1990.

farmers is at least as large as the 1990 value of food production there, and in Australia where it is about a third. It is also high in Canada, but Canadian farmers are more highly protected than those elsewhere in the Group. Indeed, the net effect of foreign agricultural protection on the one hand and offsetting home protection (not reformed in the experiment under discussion) on the other is just favourable to Canadian farmers (Tyers 1992b, Table 5.7).

In all cases, the net effect of foreign agricultural protection on overall economic welfare is smaller to the extent that home consumers gain from the lower prices which result. Again the case of Canada is extraordinary. The net welfare effect of a change in a country's terms of trade depends on its pattern of comparative advantage and not on its pattern of trade under the influence of distortions (Tyers and Falvey, 1989). In the absence of its own protection, Canada would be a substantial net importer of all livestock products, so much so that its food agriculture would be a net consumer of foreign exchange, rather than a net provider of it. Since foreign protection reduces the international prices of livestock products by proportionally more than it does those of cereals, industrial country protection is actually

Table 5.7 Effects of industrial country food trade distortions on welfare in Cairns Group countries[a]

| | *Average annual income-equivalents[b] of changes due to industrial country policies (1985 US$ billion)* | |
	Farmers	*Net economic welfare*
Argentina	−2.4	−3.5
Australia	−3.3	−1.8
Brazil	−4.8	−1.8
Canada	.8	−1.1
Other Cairns Group[c]	−7.4	−2.8
Total Cairns Group	−18.7	−11.0

a   This analysis covers the cereals, meat, dairy and sugar sectors only.
b   The sum of the changes in the equivalent variations in income. The net effects incorporate changes in equivalent variations in farmer and consumer income, changes in stock profits and net government revenue from food policies. See Tyers and Anderson (1992) Appendix I. The results presented here ignore indirect distortions due to exchange controls and protection in other sectors. The effects of these are examined in Tyers and Anderson, Chapter 6.
c   This includes Indonesia, Malaysia, New Zealand, the Philippines and Thailand, as well as Chile, Colombia, Fiji, Hungary and Uruguay. Since the latter five are not represented individually in the model, the impacts on these countries are approximated by apportioning within country aggregates using GDP shares.
Source: A comparison of simulations of the Tyers–Anderson model with and without industrial country food trade distortions in 1990.

favourable to Canada in net economic welfare terms. As its own protection reveals, however, farm interests have a larger than proportional influence over Canadian economic policy. For this reason, provided it is able to retain a good part of its own farm protection, Canada can be expected to support the rest of the Cairns Group in pressing for reform elsewhere.

Nevertheless, for the Cairns Group as a whole, net economic welfare is impaired by agricultural protection elsewhere. This impairment is greatest in Argentina, Australia, Brazil and New Zealand, where it exceeds a tenth of the gross value of their food production. Thus, the contractionary effect of foreign agricultural protection on Cairns Group agriculture, and on the Group's overall economies, is indeed substantial. Their collective interest in less distorted agricultural trade is clear.

5.3 THE ROLE OF THE GROUP IN THE NEGOTIATIONS

In its original declaration, adopted in Cairns in 1986, the Group committed itself to working collectively to ensure the inclusion of agriculture in the Round, called for standstill and rollback provisions in agriculture and ensured that the Group would liaise with other affected developing country groups and interests.[8] Their first detailed proposal was presented to the Negotiating Group on Agriculture in October 1987. While that proposal supported the complete removal of distortionary policies, as had that of the United States, it also sought early relief (in the form of a freeze on market access restrictions) for exporters hurt by the policies to be disciplined. It also allowed for a protracted phasing out of distortionary policies while attaching priority to export subsidies and quantitative import barriers.

This proposal contrasted with the US 'zero option' proposal, which advocated the complete removal of distortionary policies over a short phase-out period. Reliance by the Cairns Group proposal on aggregate measures of support, such as producer and consumer subsidy equivalents (Hertel, 1989), and a longer phase-out period left their proposal less dogmatic about the mix of policy instruments. Where the United States proposal was radical, that of the EC represented the opposite extreme. It emphasised stabilisation of prices and its commitments to reform were limited to budget ceilings on CAP programmes. Its effects would not have enhanced the role of market forces in the EC agricultural sector.

Despite the elements of compromise in the Cairns Group proposal, and the adoption of most of its provisions as the basis for discussions at the Montreal mid-term review in December 1988, the positions of the United States and the EC were too far apart for agreement and any early harvest. It was not until April 1989 in Geneva that movement appeared in the positions of the EC and the United States and a new round of proposals was sought.[9]

The new United States position retained the short phase-out period for export subsidies and taxes but it now emphasised the conversion of import restrictions to bound tariffs and their phasing out over ten years. Measures of support were to be classified as 'red', 'amber' or 'green' depending on their potential for distorting international trade.

Again the EC was far more modest, claiming that stable domestic markets would be threatened by 'tariffication', and offering reductions in its own 'support measurement unit' over an initial three years, from levels achieved in 1986.[10] Some limited tariffication was accepted in principle in the hope of winning agreement from the United States for 'rebalancing' (the unbinding of the low tariffs on some products, such as the cereal feed substitutes cassava and corn gluten).

Again a conciliatory approach was sought by the Cairns Group. Despite their collective power in many agricultural markets they recognised that their interest lay in a more complete subjection of agricultural trade to the GATT disciplines, which could only come from commitment by the United States and the EC to the outcomes of a successful Round. While maintaining the objective of complete reform and adopting the conversion of import restrictions to tariffs in the meantime, it offered a long phase-out period for existing export subsidies and accepted a case for some modest support of farmers in poorer countries.

The gulf between this and the current EC proposal remained substantial, however, prompting frustrated criticism of the EC by representatives of the Group during meetings in 1990. But the United States also came under fire from the Group for its 1990 Farm Bill, which cemented some farm support programmes in ways apparently inconsistent with its GATT proposal. Furthermore, the increased budget for the United States Export Enhancement Program, ostensibly to 'win back' markets from the EC, was particularly unpalatable to the Group.

The Round was now drawing toward its planned conclusion, in Brussels in December 1990. Accumulating frustration over the continuing trade war and the apparent intransigence of the EC had led the position of the Cairns Group away from the middle ground and toward that of the United States. An important internal division began to develop. Canada's desire to retain the protection of its dairy and poultry sectors, preferably through non-tariff barriers currently permitted under Article XI for agricultural products, led it to offer a separate proposal to the final meeting.[11] This did not lessen the influence of the Cairns Group over the Round, however, since it was they who blocked its completion in Brussels.

The final proposals of the United States and the Cairns Group sought extensive tariffication and 75 per cent reductions in support rates, to a maximum *ad valorem* tariff of 50 per cent. Both proposals persisted with separate consideration of export subsidies and guaranteed access limits for exporters in markets such as that of the EC. Again, the EC offered a comparatively modest commitment to reduced support, without specifying the ultimate rate to be achieved. Critically, it rejected explicit agreements on export subsidies. A compromise offered at the meeting was rejected by the EC, whereupon the Cairns Group withdrew from negotiations in all areas. Given the importance of the developing countries in the Cairns Group to the negotiations on services trade and intellectual property rights protection, this effectively prevented the conclusion of the entire Round.

The Round was restarted in February 1991 and, in May, the United States Congress extended its 'Fast-track' negotiating authority by up to two years. Meanwhile, the United States and the EC continued bilateral negotiations in search of a settlement on agriculture. In early 1992 the EC adopted a set of unilateral reforms (often titled the MacSharry reforms, after the then EC Commissioner for Agriculture) which, although they were driven substantially by internal budgetary pressure and the search for new sources of overall economic growth in Europe, went some way toward consistency with the Dunkel proposal (EC Commission, 1991). Indeed, in the 1990s the unilateral grain market reforms offer more substantial cuts in domestic production than would have been necessary under the Dunkel proposal and hence reduced trade distortions (Josling and Tangermann, 1992; Helmar *et al.*, 1992). Significantly, though, like the corresponding EC proposal to the GATT, it ignores access by exporting countries outside the EC and any separate discipline over export subsidies.

In subsequent bilateral negotiations with the United States, the more conservative EC countries were not prepared to go beyond these unilateral reforms in any commitment to the GATT. These private negotiations were further impeded by the refusal of the EC to honour a separate ruling under the old GATT code against its barriers to oilseed product imports. Nevertheless, a bilateral agreement was eventually achieved in November 1992. The 'Washington Compromise' reached is unlikely to be palatable to the Cairns Group. It goes little further in the EC than the already committed unilateral reforms and in the United States much of the trade effect of its protection had been offset in any case by quantity controls (Guyomard *et al.*, 1992). Nevertheless, the Group is likely to see further obstruction of the Round as undesirable given the presence on the table of measurable concessions, not to mention the value to it of the associated agreements on trade in manufactures and services.

5.4   THE CAIRNS GROUP INTEREST IN LIKELY REFORMS IN WESTERN EUROPE

Central to any collective reform of distortions affecting world food trade will be reform of the CAP. This is because the sheer size of the EC's agricultural economy, combined with its high levels of protection, render it the most substantial single contributor in distorting the international terms of food trade (Tyers and Anderson, 1992, Table 6.2). The recent Washington Compromise took the form of revised rules of conduct with which the EC's already-agreed unilateral reforms are largely compatible (Josling and Tangermann, 1992; Guyomard et al., 1992). The specific effects on agricultural trade policy in the United States are limited to reductions in the Export Enhancement Program (EEP), which primarily affects trade in wheat and the average international effects of which to date have been small (Roberts et al., 1989 p. 87). For this reason, the analysis to follow emphasises the unilateral EC reforms. Moreover, it includes the other significant development in economic policy which is likely to affect Western Europe in the 1990s: the enlargement of the EC to include the continental EFTA countries (CEPR, 1992). This will enhance the liberalising effect of CAP reforms, since protection of food production in the comparatively wealthy EFTA countries has been considerably higher than in the EC. Indeed, the average EFTA equivalent nominal protection coefficient for food agriculture in 1990 was twice that in the EC (Table 5.5).

The key components of the EC's unilateral reforms are substantial reductions in the internal prices of agricultural products (which are to be offset by deficiency payments to producers), combined with a tightening of supply control mechanisms such as global quotas and land set-asides. Specifically, support prices would fall by 35 per cent for cereals and 15 per cent for beef and 4 per cent for butter. Although more substantial cuts in dairy product prices were included in the original MacSharry proposal, at the time of writing these are not yet agreed to by the member states. The corresponding deficiency payments to producers would be proportional to areas planted and the sizes of animal herds. Except on very small farms, land set-asides would be enlarged to 15 per cent of the area planted to cereals and oilseeds and the global milk production quota would be reduced by 4 per cent. These reforms will be phased in quickly: the complete reforms should be in effect by 1997.[12]

To estimate the welfare effects of these reforms, combined with the concordance of the EFTA countries' agricultural policies with that of the EC, a further simulation is made using the trade model introduced above in Section 5.2. In this simulation the main elements of the EC reform proposal are represented and the reformed CAP is introduced in the EFTA countries over the interval 1993–6.[13] The effects of these changes on EC and EFTA food production, exports and international prices by the year 2000 are summarised in Table 5.8.

Food production in the expanded EC would continue to grow through the decade, but more slowly than in the reference scenario. Lower cereal prices cause increased consumption, especially in the only partially reformed livestock sector. The net result is lower EC net exports (or higher net imports) and hence higher international prices. The only exception to this rule is the non-ruminant meat sector. Since the reforms thus far agreed affect that sector least, resources tend to migrate to it from the now less protected ruminant meat sector. And on the demand side, the relative price of beef falls, reducing non-ruminant meat consumption. A similar change occurs in the dairy sector of the EC-12, production incentives in which are impaired only slightly by the reforms. But this is offset by reduced production in the EFTA countries.

The parallel effects of CAP reform on food production and net exports from the EC 12 alone, without EFTA countries, are summarised in Table 5.9. As expected, the results of excluding the EFTA countries are quite small. For most products, reductions in production and exports attributable to CAP reform are slightly smaller for the EC 12 than for the larger EC–EFTA grouping. But dairy products and non-ruminant meat are a little different in that *positive* rates of growth in production and exports are accentuated. The effect of these small differences in production and exports between the EC-12 and EC–EFTA on *world prices* (not shown in Table 5.9) can only be correspondingly small.

The corresponding economic benefits to Cairns Group countries from the EC reforms are modest but significant.[14] Table 5.10 lists estimates of the changes in annual net food export earnings and economic surplus which would stem from the EC's unilateral reforms and its incorporation of the EFTA countries. For the Cairns Group as a whole, net food export earnings would be larger following the reforms by 33 per cent, the main gains coming in net cereal exports, which increase by almost 60 per cent, and beef exports, which increase

Table 5.8 Effects of EC unilateral reform, combined with EFTA membership, on international prices and on EC–EFTA production and net trade in 2000 (per cent changes, unless otherwise specified)

	Rice	Wheat	Coarse Grain	Sugar	Dairy Products	Ruminant Meat	Non-ruminant Meat
Change in World Price: 2000: reform over reference	5	10	7	2	1	7	–1
Production Growth: 2000 over 1990							
Reference	16	29	19	24	20	20	29
Reform	5	11	8	23	21	5	41
Change in Production: 2000: reform over reference	–10	–13	–10	–1	0	–13	9
Change in net exports:[a] 2000 reform over reference, million metric tons	–4	–22.9	–10.3	–.3	–.3	–2.5	2.9

a In 2000 the EC (extended to include the EFTA-5) is actually projected to be a net importer of rice and coarse grain. Where positive a change in 'net exports' indicates increased exports or a reduction in net imports, depending on which prevailed in the reference simulation.

Source: A comparison of two simulations through 2000, using the Tyers–Anderson world food trade model. Again the reference assumes no change of policy regime. The other incorporates unilateral reforms in the EC along with the concordance of EFTA-5 agricultural policies with the reformed CAP.

Table 5.9   Effects of EC–12 unilateral reform on production and net trade in 2000 (per cent changes, unless otherwise specified)

	Rice	Wheat	Coarse Grain	Sugar	Dairy Products	Ruminant Meat	Non-ruminant Meat
Production Growth: 2000 over 1990, %							
Reference	16	30	19	23	19	20	30
Reform	5	16	10	22	21	5	44
Change in production: 2000: reform over reference, %	−9	−11	−8	−.4	2	−12	11
Change in net exports:[a] Reference over reform, Million metric tons	−.5	−18.2	−9.7	−0.	3.0	−2.2	3.6

a   In 2000 the EC is actually projected to be a net importer of rice and coarse grain. Where positive, a change in 'net exports' indicates increased exports or a reduction in net imports, depending on which prevailed in the reference case.

Source: Results from the analysis discussed in the text.

Table 5.10 The effects of unilateral EC reform and EFTA membership on economic welfare in 2000[a] (1990 US$ billion)

	Change in net food export earnings	Approximate annual welfare gains[b]	
		Farmers	Net
Argentina	.8	.4	.4
Australia	.9	.9	.4
Brazil	.5	1.7	−.5
Canada	.8	1.7	.2
Other Cairns Group[c]	.8	1.6	−.2
Total Cairns Group	**3.8**	**6.3**	**.4**
EC–12	−5.2	d	2.5
EFTA–5	−4.6	d	10.7
USA	2.8	2.3	1.8

a This analysis omits unilateral EC reforms to the oilseed sector, but all other elements of the proposal are represented approximately. See EC Commission (1991), Josling and Tangermann (1992) and Helmar *et al.* (1992).
b The sum of changes in equivalent variations in income of consumers and farmers with changes in stock profits and net government revenue from food policies. See Tyers and Anderson (1992) Appendix 1.
c This includes Indonesia, Malaysia, New Zealand, the Philippines and Thailand, as well as Chile, Colombia, Fiji, Hungary and Uruguay. Since the latter five are not represented individually in the model, the impacts on these countries are approximated by apportioning impacts within country aggregates using GDP shares.
d The proposal offers substantial compensation to farmers for reduced support prices, land set-asides and reduced livestock herds. this compensation is too complex to represent accurately here. Suffice it to say that the net losses to farmers would be small by comparison to the net overall gains within and outside the EC.
Source: Comparison of simulations using the Tyers–Anderson world food trade model, as for Table 5.8.

by 40 per cent. The gain in cereal exports is large compared with the degree to which Cairns Group cereal exports have been restrained by all other industrial country policies (Table 5.6) because the reforms only marginally reduce EC protection to the livestock sector, while they make cereals considerably cheaper in the domestic market.[15] This change redresses about half of the adverse impact of all industrial country distortions on the net food export earnings of the Cairns Group (Table 5.6).

The corresponding gains in producers' surplus which accrue to Cairns Group farmers sum to about US$ 6 billion per year, redressing about a fifth of the annual loss due to industrial country distortions.[16] Canadian farmers are clear and substantial gainers and these gains outweigh consumer losses from higher food prices, confirming the wisdom of their stance with the Cairns Group in favour of CAP reform (absenting, of course, reciprocal reforms in Canada). Brazilian farmers also gain but the net change in aggregate welfare is unfavourable. Higher food prices cause consumer losses which are slightly larger than the producer gains. Indeed, the membership of the Cairns Group includes other large developing countries which are net importers of the cereals most affected by unilateral EC reform even though they are net exporters of agricultural products. Indonesia and Malaysia, for example, are also net losers from unilateral EC reform. For the Cairns Group as a whole, then, the gains to farmers from higher international food prices are mostly offset by corresponding losses to consumers.

Of course, had the analysis included the market for oilseeds and oilseed products, the estimated net gain to Brazil would almost certainly have been positive and those to other Latin American food exporters larger. Moreover, since no substantial reforms of the EC dairy and sugar sectors were agreed to in 1992, Cairns Group members are denied the additional stimulus to their exports which would flow from such reform (Table 5.6). But such further reform (or, at least, increased quantity control) is likely, considering that productivity in the livestock sector in general has been increasing in most countries and that closer links between the EC and the Czech Republic, Hungary and Poland could yield substantial increases in Western European livestock output.

Against these omissions which could be favourable to the Cairns Group, however, must be set the effects of unilateral reforms in many developing countries which have hitherto discriminated against their agricultural sectors (Valdes, 1992). Food production could rise in these countries, offsetting the upward pressure on prices due to the industrial country reforms. Of more significance still are the even more dramatic reforms taking place in Eastern and Central Europe and the former USSR. The potential for increased food productivity in that region is very great indeed (Tyers, 1992a). If only a part of that potential is realised in the next decade, it will be sufficient to more than reverse any upward pressure on international food prices due to Uruguay Round reforms.

5.5   CONCLUSION

The Cairns Group was formed out of frustration among comparatively efficient agricultural exporting countries over a series of changes in the conduct of world agricultural trade over which they, as individual countries, could have no influence. They are a diverse group of countries; some are industrialised, some are developing; some are large and others small; one is East European and formerly centrally planned. But they are collectively significant as producers of agricultural products, with more value added in agriculture than either the EC or the United States, and as agricultural exporters, with more such exports than the EC and the United States combined. They are also responsible for a tenth of the world's imports of manufactures, though this does little to enhance their punitive power in world trade since these imports tend not to come from the EC or Japan, the Group's principal adversaries in the Round.

There is no doubting that the Cairns Group has a legitimate grievance against countries with high agricultural protection. The net value of their agricultural exports is reduced by more than half as a consequence of agricultural protection in industrial countries alone. The net cost of this protection to their farmers is about US$ 26 billion per year, or about a fifth of all current value added in Cairns Group agriculture.

The strength of this common interest has been sustained during the Round by the continuing trade war between the EC and the United States which has further impaired their terms of trade. Thus cohesive, the Group has had a profound influence on the conduct of the Round, denying the EC and the United States the opportunity to come to terms bilaterally in a way which could harm the interests of other exporters. They have been aided in this by the new importance of developing countries in other aspects of the Round: in the negotiations on services trade and on intellectual property rights. The developing countries in the Cairns Group have been able to make progress in these areas conditional on progress on agriculture.

In the final stages of the Round, however, agreement on agriculture has depended on success in bi-lateral negotiations between the United States and the EC. Those negotiations concluded in November 1992 with an agreement which falls far short of the Cairns Group proposals during the Round. Its effects on trade in food products will be dominated by the unilateral reforms of the CAP, agreed upon early in 1992. Nevertheless, considering that the bilateral agreement offers the potential for measurable reductions in EC net food exports, and that EC distortions have been dominant in affecting their terms of trade adversely, it is unlikely that the Cairns Group will further delay the conclusion of the Round.

6   The Canadian Perspective

T. K. Warley

Canada is an example of a medium-sized economic power whose comparative advantage in agriculture has long been frustrated by the subsidy and protection policies of other nations. More recently, Canada's economy and taxpayers and the crops sector of its agriculture have been the victims of the competitive subsidization of grain and oilseed exports by the agricultural super-powers, the United States (US) and the European Community (EC). Canada therefore has an immense stake in the attempt being made in the Uruguay Round (UR) to bring about substantial and progressive reduction in agricultural support and protection on a global basis and to subject trade in farm and food products to strengthened and more effectively applied GATT rules and disciplines.

On the other hand, parts of the Canadian agrifood complex are domestically-oriented and heavily protected, and the ability to continue support and protection for the dairy and poultry sectors has a bearing on national political unity and the survival of the nation.

The dichotomy between the attempt to foster the interests of its export sectors – mainly grains, oilseeds and red meats – while preserving protection for less competitive sectors is the central challenge facing Canada's agricultural negotiators. It has shaped Canada's proposals in the GATT on agricultural and trade policy reform, and determined Canada's position and influence in the Cairns Group.

Canada's agricultural trade policy is part of the country's overall trade policy and its broader international economic relations. These are dominated by Canada's economic relations with the United States. Because Canada's regional and multilateral trade policies are intertwined, there is a relationship between Canada's proposals on agriculture in the GATT and the agricultural provisions of the Canada–US Trade Agreement (CUSTA).[1]

The agricultural negotiations in the Uruguay Round are designed to reshape national agricultural policies in ways that recouple domestic and international prices, reduce support for high-cost production, decouple support for farmers' incomes from their production decisions, and change the trade arrangements and practices that accompany

110

national farm policies and programs. The re-focusing of agricultural policy objectives and re-instrumentation of farm programmes that might be internationally mandated as a result of a UR agreement will interact with changes in agricultural policy that are being undertaken in Canada primarily for domestic reasons. While national reforms are not GATT-driven, they are intended to be compatible with the agreement on agricultural policy and trade reforms being sought in the UR. By the same token, their completion will facilitate national accommodation to an international accord.

These themes are developed in the pages that follow. The chapter is organized in six parts. Section 1 sketches Canada's trade and agricultural policies and relates these and the agricultural content of the CUSTA to Canada's approach to the agricultural negotiations in the GATT. This serves as a backdrop for Section 2 in which Canada's broad negotiating objectives for agriculture in the UR are spelled out. Canada's negotiating tactics are examined in Section 3. Consultative arrangements for seeking the views and support of national constituencies are briefly described, but the major subject of this section is Canada's position in the Cairns Group of Fair Traders in Agriculture. Canada's agricultural offer of 15 October 1990 is described in Section 4. The content of the offer is related to the nation's agricultural policies and interests and to proposals made earlier in 1990 on the strengthening and clarification of Article XI of the General Agreement and on improvements in the code on subsidies and countervail duties. The implications of a UR accord for Canada's agricultural trade, for economic conditions in the farming component of the agrifood industry, and for the future development of agricultural policies and programmes are sketched in Section 5. In the absence of an agreement at the time of this writing, this section is necessarily tentative. Section 6 concludes the chapter by offering a judgement on Canada's negotiating position on agriculture in the Uruguay Round.

6.1 THE SETTING

Broad trade policy

'Canada is a relatively small, trade-dependent nation, with its exports heavily concentrated in a narrow range of products exported to one big market' (Hart, 1989, p. 110). This sentence aptly describes the Canadian economic condition and explains the fundamental thrusts of Canada's commercial diplomacy. With 30 per cent of national income derived from trade, Canada's present and future prosperity is inextricably linked to open and secure access to world markets. As a small country without the power of retaliation, Canada must rely on a rules-oriented international trading system to protect and advance its interests. On both grounds, Canada practises active multilateralism in the GATT. However, with 70 per cent of its exports going to the United States, Canada must always focus also on the bilateral trade relationship. Thus Canada follows a two-track trade policy – multilateralism in the GATT and bi-lateralism with the United States. The two tracks are inter-connected for, historically, because of the disparity in the size and power of the two neighbours, Canada has sought to secure and improve its access to the US market and manage bi-lateral trade frictions through the trade liberalizing initiatives taken in successive GATT Rounds and by appealing to the universal rules and dispute settlement mechanisms of the General Agreement. Another consequence of the orientation of Canada's trade towards the US is that, because of the most favoured nation principle and the mercantilist bargaining that occurs in GATT Rounds, Canada has been able to benefit from the concessions exchanged between 'the big three' – the US, Europe and Japan – while directing most of its own access concessions to the US.

The decision by Canada to enter into a comprehensive bi-lateral trade agreement with the US was therefore an important discontinuity in national trade policy. It acknowledged that the GATT is no longer adequate to provide the assured and improved access to the US market that is so vital to Canadians' prosperity, or to handle the frictions that inevitably attend such a huge and complex bi-lateral trade flow.[2] It also marked the acceptance by Canada that it must prepare for global competition by learning to compete successfully in a continental free trade area. Hence, for Canada the CUSTA is both a bulwark against resurgent US protectionism and a catalyst for the adjustments needed to make Canada competitive in the global economy.[3]

The significance of these features of Canada's overall trade policy for Canada's position on agriculture in the UR is as follows.

First, a successful outcome of the multilateral trade negotiations (MTNs) is important to Canada in its own right for it would reaffirm multilateral liberalism, strengthen the GATT as an institution (particularly in dispute settlement), permit expansion of Canada's exports and diversification of its markets, and extend trade liberalization to agriculture and resources – two hitherto neglected areas that are still very important in the national economy.

Secondly, from a Canadian perspective the MTNs are also critical to the bi-lateral relationship with the US, in that they can provide solutions to two systemic problems that could not be resolved in the limited context of the CUSTA. The first of these is the strengthening of international disciplines on the use of subsidies and the response of governments to them through the countervail provisions of national trade remedy laws. This is crucial since the aggressive use of trade remedies seems to be the weapon of choice for a Congress bent on reasserting its authority over US trade policy and indulging its protectionist proclivities. It has particular agricultural relevance since Canadian agrifood exports to the US have been materially and increasingly hampered by US countervail actions against farm products. The second area that could not be addressed in the CUSTA is the global problem of trade distortion in agriculture, and, more particularly, the distortions that exist in production and trade in commodities in which both countries have a comparative advantage, notably grains and oilseeds.

A third aspect of Canada's overall trade position and strategy in the MTNs flows the other way, from the CUSTA to the UR. Three agricultural matters should be noted. Firstly, the future prospects and present reality of freer continental trade in a range of farm and food products have already catalyzed a review of Canada's agricultural policies and programmes. The adaptations that have been made or are being contemplated to fit the sector for continental free trade are in line with those which would be required by a global agreement on agricultural policy and trade. Secondly, in giving the US improved access to the Canadian market for products for which the US is the major supplier, Canada has already expended part of the negotiating coinage it might have used in the MTNs. The most important examples are the phased elimination of tariffs on fruits and vegetables and processed foods and the ending of grain import licensing by the Canadian Wheat Board (CWB). Finally, the CUSTA has provided innovations in dispute settlement mechanisms and the harmonization of technical standards that could be precedent-setting models for a global agricultural agreement.[4]

Agricultural trade policies

Overall, and by international standards, Canada has a highly productive and competitive agrifood industry which assures afford-able abundance to food consumers, provides good incomes to its participants, and makes a falling but still significant contribution to the nation's trade and national income. The value and composition of Canada's agricultural trade are summarized in Table 6.1. Canada has a merchandise trade surplus in agriculture and is a net exporter of many temperate zone agricultural products. Grains, oilseeds and red meats are the big ticket items, and some 75, 60, 40 and 25 per cent of the output of wheat, barley, canola (rapeseed) and hogs, respectively, are exported. However, Canada also exports a wide variety of other products ranging from root vegetables to flowers. Farm product exports are numerically equal to around 50 per cent of farm cash receipts nationally, and this high level of export dependence is destined to grow in the future as domestic population plateaus and per capita consumption is satiated, and as productivity and resource fixity continue to expand supplies. The Prairie provinces – which contain the majority of Canada's farm land and half its farmers – are especially

Table 6.1   Canada's agrifood trade, 1989

	Exports	Imports	Balance of Trade
		(C$ Millions)	
All goods	134 511	134 903	−392
Agricultural and food products	8 834	7 113	1 721
Grains, grain products and animal feeds (except oilseeds)	4 005	672	3 333
Oilseeds and oilseed products	1 162	456	706
Live animals	532	95	437
Red meats	949	588	361
Other animal products	506	310	196
Dairy products	176	150	26
Poultry and eggs	68	174	−106
Fruits and nuts	103	1 693	−1 590
Vegetables (except potatoes)	279	899	−620
Potatoes and products	186	105	81
Seeds for sowing	96	80	16
Sugar and maple products	143	301	−158
Tobacco, raw	58	5	53
Vegetable fibres	–	97	−97
Plantation crops	–	707	−707
Other	571	781	−210

Source: *Food Market Commentary*, 12, 3 January 1991, Table 2, Ottawa, Agriculture Canada.

dependent on access to foreign markets. This high level of trade dependence means that Canadian agriculture as a whole (and more particularly its producers of export-oriented commodities) is extremely vulnerable to other countries' subsidy and trade practices. Accordingly, Canada's commercial diplomacy in agriculture is concerned to lower the market access barriers and the import-displacing domestic subsidies of importing countries and to reduce the production and export subsidies of competitors that displace Canada's exports in third markets.

Under normal conditions, the major exported products (which account for around 60 per cent of the gross value of farm output) are not heavily subsidized, though they do benefit from the availability of economic safety nets provided by various stabilization programmes[5] and, in the case of grains and oilseeds, from significant transportation subsidies[6].

By contrast, products which are oriented to the domestic market receive substantial and continuous support and protection. The extreme cases are milk, poultry meats and eggs, which constitute some 25 per cent of output. Canada has chosen not to compete with foreign suppliers in the production of these products. Prices are set according to full costs of production (including a return to farmer-provided resources but excluding a return to the investment in quotas), and the administered prices are implemented through domestic supply controls and insulated from much lower external prices by import quotas. The CUSTA provided for the continuation of Canada's Article XI import quotas on supply managed products. The production and processing of many fruits and vegetables are protected by tariffs, and the grape and wine industry by the practices of provincial liquor monopolies. However, under the CUSTA, these measures are being phased out, and by 1998 there will be continental free trade in fresh and processed horticultural products and wine. Continental trade in processed foods will also be tariff-free by 1 January 1998.

The basic instrumentation of Canada's agricultural price and income support and stabilization programmes is shown in Figure 6.1. The recent level of support and protection as measured by the OECD in 'producer subsidy equivalents' (PSEs) and by Canadian authorities as an 'aggregate measure of support' (AMS) are shown in Tables 6.2 and 6.3 respectively.

The data on support levels for the grains and oilseeds sector in the latter half of the 1980s are clearly at odds with the above assertion that 'the major exported products ... are not heavily subsidized'. A combination of three developments — market imbalances, the lowering

Figure 6.1   A synoptic view of Canada's agricultural support programmes and domestically-oriented negotiating objectives

Commodity Group	Dairy	Poultry	Horticulture	Grains and Oilseeds	Red Meats
Degree of regulation and support	Most		- -		Least
Major support instruments	Supply management and import quotas			Tariffs	Safety nets
					Transport subsidies
Major domestically-oriented negotiating objectives	Retain administered pricing and QRs, and clarify Article XI		Exemptions for key products	'Green' status for income stabilisation programmes WGTA treated as domestic subsidy Discipline others' trade remedies	

Table 6.2   Producer subsidy equivalents, Canada, 1979–86 average, and 1987 to 1990, percentages[1]

	1979–86 av.	*1987*	*1988*	*1989(e)*	*1990(p)*
Crops	26	48	31	24	35
Wheat	26	54	39	26	43
Coarse grains	27	49	25	23	26
Oilseeds	20	30	20	23	21
Livestock products	38	50	50	45	45
Milk	66	81	72	73	79
Beef and Veal[2]	32	49	51	35	36
Pork	12	11	18	24	16
Eggs	25	23	37	27	20
All products	32	49	42	37	41

1   The percentage PSEs are gross for crops and net for livestock products.
2   The high figures result from comparing Canadian fresh beef prices with international prices for lower quality grades.
(e)   Estimate
(p)   Provisional
Source: Organisation for Economic Co-operation and Development, 1991, Agricultural Policies, Markets and Trade: Monitoring and Outlook, 1991, Annex Table 111.6, Paris.

Table 6.3 Aggregate measure of support, Canadian agriculture, 1987–1988[1], C$ million

Commodity	Market Price Supports[2] Amber	Direct Payments Amber[3]	Direct Payments Green[3]	Reduction of Input Costs + General Services Amber	Reduction of Input Costs + General Services Green	Total Amber	Total Green	Total Amber + Green
Wheat	270	1121	71	585	307	1976	378	2354
Barley	30	388	16	117	65	534	82	616
Corn	14	154	2	2	55	170	57	227
Canola	0	246	18	79	102	325	120	445
Soybeans	0	2	0	1	32	2	32	34
Sugarbeets	3	2	0	0	5	6	5	10
Dairy	1869	99	12	5	451	1973	463	2436
Beef	48	163	67	2	528	213	595	807
Pork	0	207	2	8	234	215	236	451
Poultry	336	5	1	1	127	342	128	470
Eggs	166	−8	0	2	56	161	56	217
Sub-total	2736	2379	191	800	1961	5915	2152	8067
Apples	0	18	6	1	20	18	26	44
Potatoes	0	0	5	2	52	2	56	58
Other Crops	0	173	44	99	290	272	333	605
Sheepmeat	1	4	0	0	6	4	6	10
Other l'stock	nc	2	2	0	41	2	43	45
Sub-total	1	196	56	101	408	298	464	762
All Commodities	2737	2575	247	901	2369	6213	2616	8829

Notes to Table 6.3

1 The data generally apply to the 1987/8 crop year for arable crops and to the 1988 calendar year for livestock

2 Market price supports are calculated using a 1986–88 average reference price

3 The categorisation or programmes as amber or green follows paragraph 8 of MTN.GNG/NG5/W/170. No 'credits' are given for supply controls. The 'AMS' is therefore not a 'trade distortion equivalent'.

nc Not calculated

Source: External Affairs and International Trade Canada.

---

of US grain loan rates and the enactment of the Export Enhancement Program (EEP) under the 1985 Food Security Act (and the US–EC subsidy war' that ensued thereafter) – resulted in the collapse of export prices and a precipitous decline in market receipts to Canadian grain and oilseed producers. With market returns barely sufficient to cover the variable costs of production, Canada's federal and provincial governments were compelled – despite large budget deficits – to provide massive assistance to the grains and oilseeds sector under existing safety net programmes and to introduce new ad hoc schemes (notably the 1986 Special Canadian Grains Program and its successors) in order to prevent an economic holocaust amongst grain farmers and the collapse of the agricultural economies of the Prairie provinces. The extent of this assistance – in terms of soaring direct payments to agriculture, and the high proportion of aggregate net farm cash income that these payments constituted – is shown in Table 6.4.

6.2 AGRICULTURAL NEGOTIATING OBJECTIVES

Canada's objectives for agricultural policy and trade reform in the UR are determined both by its position as a net exporter of farm and food products and by the differential interests of its export and domestically oriented commodity sub-sectors and the different domestic programmes that support these.

- As a net agricultural exporter, Canada needs a reduction of support and protection in other countries so as to achieve a number of goals. These include the strategic objectives of:
- ensuring that future growth in world food consumption is met from low-cost sources;

Table 6.4 Aggregate net farm cash income, Canada, 1981–92, $C million and percentages

	1981	1982	1983	1984	1985	1986	1987	1988	1989	1990	1991	1992f*
Grains and Oilseeds												
Market Receipts	6650	6521	6,909	6,942	5034	5212	4682	5409	5603	5585	5254	4332
Cash Expenses	3754	3934	4156	4589	4657	4195	4108	4426	4636	4700	4659	4973
Market Income	2800	2587	2753	2353	1377	1016	554	984	967	885	595	−641
Direct Programme Payments	280	242	361	730	1145	1655	2593	2190	1793	994	1358	2718
Net Cash Income	3176	2829	3115	3082	2522	2671	3147	3180	2760	1879	1953	2077
Payments as % of Net Cash Income	9	9	12	24	45	57	82	69	65	53	70	131
Other Commodities												
Market Receipts	10983	11430	10999	11935	11760	12748	13052	13247	13866	14071	13727	13681
Cash expenses	9341	9787	9647	9995	10188	10548	10633	10933	11819	11584	11317	11330
Market Income	1642	1843	1351	1986	1579	2202	2429	2314	1847	2487	2410	2351
Direct Programme Payments	839	951	837	1060	1108	1317	1261	1597	1974	1331	1384	2040
Net Cash Income	2481	2604	2188	3048	2651	3519	3689	3911	3821	3818	3794	4391
Payments as % of Net Cash Income	34	37	38	35	41	27	34	41	52	35	36	46
All Products												
Market Receipts	17633	17951	17908	18895	17800	17960	17904	18656	19269	19656	18981	18013
Cash Expenses	13095	13721	13803	14474	14845	14743	14741	15359	16455	16284	15976	16303
Market Income	4538	4430	4104	4321	2956	3218	2983	3298	2814	3372	3005	1710
Direct Programme Payments	1118	1193	1198	1790	2253	2972	3854	3793	3767	2325	2742	4758
Net Cash Income	5657	5433	5303	6130	5209	6190	6836	7091	6581	5697	5747	5468
Payments as % of Net Cash Income	20	22	23	29	43	48	56	53	57	41	48	74

f Forecast 23 December 1991.

* Includes payments under GRIP, NISA and Farm Support and Adjustment Measures I and II, but not payments to cover deficits in the Canadian Wheat Board's pool accounts for the 1991/2 crop, which will approach $750 million.

Source: Agriculture Canada.

- re-shaping Europe's common agricultural policy (CAP) in advance of the creation of a Pan-European entity;
- preventing the emergence of a second wave of agricultural protectionism amongst the newly industrialized countries;
- reinforcing the political democratization and economic liberalization of the former communist countries by incorporating them into a market-driven international economic order;
- strengthening the integrity of the multilateral trading system by bringing agriculture into the GATT.

These are in addition to the more immediate objectives of:

- realizing the economic benefits of Canada's comparative advantage in agriculture by reducing the level of support and protection in other countries;
- permitting the sector to flourish without the need for the present high level of support, which is unsustainable and unjustifiable in the longer term.

Canada's instrumental agricultural negotiating objectives for achieving these ultimate ends are (Gifford, 1989):

- a substantial reduction of tariff and non-tariff import barriers;
- a substantial reduction of trade distorting subsidies, including the elimination of export subsidies;
- the articulation of strengthened and more effectively applied GATT rules, equally applicable to all countries;
- a system to ensure that health and sanitary measures are not used to inhibit trade.

These objectives are couched in terms of Canada's agricultural export interests. Securing them would provide improved and more assured access to other countries' markets, greater opportunities for adding value to raw farm products, higher and more stable prices, and lower support costs.

With respect to products which are oriented to the domestic market, Canada's negotiating objectives are essentially defensive. There is no disposition to extend to other countries the improved market access granted to the US under the CUSTA for horticultural products, processed foods and wines. More importantly, Canadian authorities seek to retain the quantitative import restrictions that underpin the market price supports provided to the dairy and poultry industries.

6.3 CONDUCTING THE NEGOTIATIONS

Governments that embark on international negotiations negotiate on at least three fronts. Abroad they engage other countries with whom concessions will be exchanged. Secondly, they seek to coordinate their positions with those of other like-minded countries, and where possible develop common strategies and proposals. Thirdly, they must negotiate at home with affected constituencies and among governmental agencies and departments – some of which regard private sector groups as clients. Canada's experience in negotiating on agriculture in the Uruguay Round has been that the descending order of difficulty among these three has been obtaining a domestic consensus, conducting alliance politics and negotiating with economic adversaries.

Domestic mechanisms and policy adaptations

The institutional structure created to handle Canada's participation in the Uruguay Round (and the negotiation of the CUSTA) has been described by Skogstad (1990). Sufficient to note here that the federal government has sought the policy advice and consent of the provinces through a Federal–Provincial MTN Committee and provided information on agriculture to the provinces through a Federal–Provincial Agriculture Trade Policy Committee. The advice and support of private agrifood sector groups is provided through a Sectoral Advisory Group on International Trade (SAGIT) for agriculture, food and beverages. Major general farm organizations and commodity groups are represented on the agrifood SAGIT and are well placed to influence Canada's negotiating position.

At the same time as Canada's international agricultural trade policy objectives and tactics were being established, the federal government initiated a comprehensive review of 'domestic' agricultural policies and programmes. These, of course, have international dimensions through their effects on production and consumption (and therefore on net import requirements and net export availabilities), and because in Canada, as elsewhere, trade arrangements for farm and food products are the external instruments of domestically-oriented policies. An agricultural policy review was conducted by the newly elected

Progressive Conservative government in 1984 and radical reforms were proposed (Ministerial Task Force, 1985). But their implementation was put aside as the government was forced to cope with the deepening financial crisis in agriculture and the deterioration in agricultural trade conditions in the 1980s. By 1989, however, a combination of continuing disenchantment with domestic policies and the need to adapt them to the agricultural provisions of the CUSTA, together with the prospect of multilateral agricultural policy and trade reforms in the GATT, required that the agricultural policy review process be restarted. A base paper (Agriculture Canada, 1989) and a national conference held in December 1989 signalled that the government required the agrifood sector to become more market-oriented and self-reliant, and a set of task forces met through 1990 to develop proposals for achieving that end.[7] While it was repeatedly stated that the policy review was not 'GATT-driven', it was obvious that policy changes must be 'GATT-friendly' in that national policy and programme changes must be supportive of the multilateral agricultural trade reform initiative, result in the use of policy instruments which were internationally acceptable, and prepare farmers and agribusinesses to compete successfully in an environment of reduced support and protection.

The domestic consultations on the UR agricultural trade negotiations and the national policy review were of course intertwined in that they addressed a common set of pivotally important programmes and issues, involved many of the same people, and because the recommendations of the various task forces took account of Canada's UR negotiating position on agriculture. In particular:

- new farm income safety net programmes were introduced in 1991 that were intended to be both more effective domestically, more likely to be accepted in the GATT as being production and trade neutral, and, potentially, less likely to attract US countervail duties;
- a commitment was made to retain supply management and quantitative import controls as the primary mechanisms for supporting the Canadian dairy and poultry industries (though measures were proposed for creating a 'second generation' of supply management systems with fewer negative impacts *on Canadians*);
- decisions on the subsidies paid on the costs of transporting western grains and oilseeds to export positions were postponed, partly because of the political sensitivity of the issue and partly to await the treatment of transportation subsidies in the UR;

• recommendations were made that are aimed at improving farmers' management skills, farm finance and the competitiveness of the food processing industry: these are designed to prepare the agrifood sector to survive increased competition in the domestic market and to gain market share abroad.

The commitment to continue supply management systems for the dairy and poultry industries – which emerged from the SAGIT and the domestic policy review, and which has been repeatedly reaffirmed by Ministers – is particularly important since it shapes Canada's negotiating position in the UR on market access and domestic subsidies. The reasons for this stance have less to do with the formidable lobbying skills of dairy and poultry producers, or with an admiration of formula pricing, supply controls and quantitative restrictions (QRs) on imports as policy instruments, than with the political imperatives that flow from the agricultural and political geography of the country. In brief, milk and poultry products are produced primarily in Central Canada and, more especially, they account for about 45 per cent of gross farm income in Quebec. Federal and provincial politicians of all parties who antagonize farmers in Quebec's 50 rural seats court electoral disaster. More importantly, at a time when the separatist movement in Quebec is strong, and is supported by the Union des Producteurs Agricoles (UPA),[8] Canada's negotiating position on Article XI is driven in large measure by the imperative of preserving national political unity and ensuring the very survival of the country.

Canada and the Cairns Group[9]

The story of the role of the Cairns Group (CG) of Fair Traders in Agriculture in the UR is told elsewhere in this volume. The limited task undertaken here is to explain the often-ambiguous and increasingly uncomfortable position of Canada in the Group.

The characteristics Canada shares with other members of the Cairns Group are that it is a medium-sized agricultural exporter,[10] is dependent on trade for the prosperity of its agrifood sector, and is being victimized by the subsidy policies and trade practices of the superpower triad, particularly the EC.

Lacking individual retaliatory power, the CG partners hoped that a coalition of aggrieved and like-minded countries could ensure that agricultural trade would be made the centrepiece of the MTNs and not be left aside – after a preliminary skirmish between 'the big three' – as occurred in previous Rounds.

The collective influence of the CG flows from four factors. As exporters of 25 and 10 per cent of world shipments of temperate zone agricultural products and manufactures respectively, the Cairns countries together have some weight in world trade. Secondly, their political influence derives in part from the fact that membership is drawn from 'the four quadrants of the globe'. Thirdly, the CG has consciously sought to define a middle ground of constructive content and good process that, on the one hand, would persuade the EC and Japan to commit to agricultural reform and, on the other, would provide the US with a fall-back position as it inevitably retreated from its non-negotiable initial 'double zero' proposal. Finally, as was demonstrated at the 1988 Montreal Midterm Review and the 1990 Brussels Ministerial Meeting, the CG has the power to block completion of the Round if the member countries' trade policy priorities are not addressed in a meaningful way.

On agricultural trade reform Canada shares the view of the Group as a whole that the key to the negotiations is to secure change in the agricultural and trade policies of Europe and Japan, if the US Congress is to go along with reform of the trade distorting policies of the United States. Furthermore, Canada also takes the view that the route to lasting reform lies in a combination of strengthened GATT rules and explicit commitments on staged reforms, with the latter being expressed in country- and commodity-specific commitments on domestic subsidies, market access and export competition.

However, from the beginning there were differences between Canada and the other members in their commitment to the Group, on the objectives of agricultural policy and trade reform, and on the means by which these might best be attained.

Canada differs from the other CG countries in the larger size of its economy, in the greater compositional diversity and geographic concentration of its exports, and in its ability to pursue its international economic policy objectives through the G7 economic summits, the Quadrilateral Group of Trade Ministers and the CUSTA. Canada is also the only CG member which is a significant importer of farm products. Furthermore, since agricultural exports account for only 7 per cent of Canada's total exports – a much smaller share than the other members of the Group – Canada's interest in successful outcomes in other areas of the MTNs dilutes its interest in the single issue of agricultural trade and makes it more reluctant than other CG countries to hold the whole negotiations hostage to progress in this one area.

More particularly to our purposes here, on one key matter Canada's views on agricultural trade reform differ from those of other members of the Group, and especially those of Australia. Whereas the other CG countries want rapid progress towards a world in which there would be only 'green' service programmes and decoupled income supports in national agricultural policies, and no exceptional treatment for trade in agricultural products under the General Agreement, Canada's immediate political imperative, and perhaps the ultimate vision of its authorities, requires the retention of market price supports for milk and poultry products. This leads Canada's negotiators to argue that import quotas should continue to be legal under the GATT if used in support of national supply management programmes.

The difference over whether Article XI's QRs for agriculture should be phased out or be retained, clarified and strengthened has been evident throughout the history of the CG. The rift was one of the reasons that Canada made a separate initial proposal in 1987 on how agriculture should be negotiated. It was at the centre of early debates on the nature of an AMS and Canada's advocacy of the use of a 'trade distortion equivalent' (McClatchy, 1988). And the difference became increasingly evident as the negotiating process moved from general proposals to specific offers, as attention swung from subsidies to market access, and as the CG moved progressively from the middle ground towards the position of the Group's natural ally, the United States.

Canada's negotiators were successful in avoiding the CG coming out with an outright condemnation of Article XI:2(c)(i) and the QRs it permits, though they could not persuade the alliance to endorse Canada's position. Successive formal CG proposals and ministerial communiqués after CG meetings used language which called only for the elimination or reduction in market access barriers 'not explicitly provided for in the GATT', and as late as November 1989 the Group went no further than indicating that it 'favoured' the tariffication of non-tariff market access barriers (Cairns Group, 1989). In July 1988 Canada endorsed the Group's proposal that there be an immediate freeze in support and a 10 percent reduction in its total value in 1989 and 1990 as stepping stones to a final agreement (Cairns Group, 1988). Canada insisted, however, that this not be expressed in commodity-specific terms lest it be prevented from making formula-based price increases for milk producers and be required to concede that market price supports achieved through supply controls were candidates for reduction. The task of setting milk prices was also shifted from the federal cabinet to the Canadian Dairy Commission so as to circumvent the CG proposal that governments should refrain from increasing support prices for farm products where they had administrative responsibility. The texts prepared by the Chairman of the Negotiating Group on Agriculture in December 1988 for the Mid-term Review and in June 1990 for what were expected to be the final phases of the negotiations left the matter of Article XI unresolved.

The rift in the alliance was publicly acknowledged in the clarification exercise conducted in early 1990 on the country proposals submitted in November 1989 (GATT 1990), and with the tabling by Canada in March 1990 of a proposal for the clarification of Article XI (Government of Canada, 1990a). But separation did not occur until October 1990 when the CG submitted an offer (which Canada did not initial) requiring the elimination of Article XI (Cairns Group, 1990). Canada's own offer called for the retention of Article XI and the tariffication of only those QRs that were not consistent with revised GATT rules. Canada also rejected the use of an AMS that used differences between national and international prices as a basis for reducing the level of domestic subsidization provided by market price supports and import barriers.

There can be little doubt that Canada's influence on the MTNs via the Cairns Group has been compromised by its preoccupation with maintaining protection for its import-competing interests. But, history may record that this was of little consequence in that Canada's ambiguous position did not get in the way of the Group making its major contributions to the Uruguay Round process. These were to give agricultural trade due prominence in the run-up to the launch of the MTNs at Punta del Este, to chart an early course in agriculture on which the Community could set sail, and to insist to the end that the voyage to a trading system for the 21st century could not be completed unless agricultural trade was included in the 15-ship armada that reached safe harbour. The fact that Canada lagged behind in a group led by Australia and the Latin American members is regrettable, but fortunately was not decisive.

6.4 CANADA'S OFFER[11]

Canada's formal offer on agricultural policy and trade reform followed the framework laid down in the draft of an agricultural agreement prepared by the Chairman of the Negotiating Group on Agriculture in June 1990 in that its proposals covered internal support, market access and export competition.[12] It proposed that an agricultural accord consist of specific agreements enshrined in a set of stronger GATT rules and disciplines (Government of Canada, 1990b).

Export competition

Canada's most important single agricultural negotiating objective is to bring an end to the use of the export subsidies that take markets away from efficient suppliers. Accordingly, the proposal on export subsidies is the most ambitious and unqualified. It calls for a ban on new export subsidies, the phasing out of existing government-funded export subsidies over 10 years, and additional disciplines in the transition period to ensure that countries do not increase their market shares over those held in 1986–8. To close the potential loop-hole provided by food aid, it is proposed that the FAO's 'usual market requirements' be observed and that only grant aid be permitted.

Canada does not make much use of direct, publicly-funded, export subsidies, so this proposal was easily made. The freight subsidies paid under the Western Grains Transportation Act (WGTA) act as export subsidies. However, transport subsidies were not counted as export aids in the AMS data submitted by Canada on 1 October 1990, and it appears that Canada seeks to have 'the Crow Benefit' treated as a domestic subsidy and therefore subject to a 50 per cent reduction rather than elimination. The singling out of government-financed export subsidies for abolition is designed to allow the producer-financed export schemes operated by some marketing boards to continue.

The position taken by Canada on export subsidies in the group negotiating a new subsidies code is consistent with the agricultural proposal: government-funded export schemes would be identified in a definite list, removed from the exemption for agriculture in Article XVI and banned or, if used, subject to countervail duties (CVDs) without proof of injury (Minister of International Trade, 1989).

If its proposals on export competition were accepted, Canada would be relieved of the burdens placed on its grains and oilseeds sectors in third markets by the EC's export restitutions and by the Export Enhancement Program and other aids to exports operated by the US, would face fewer pressures from subsidized exports in the Canadian market (for instance, of beef, canned ham and dairy products), but would be free to continue the WGTA, price pooling by the Canadian

Wheat Board, and some small but useful Canadian producer-financed export schemes operated by various marketing boards.

Internal support

On domestic subsidies Canada proposes that programmes be categorized according to the degree of trade distortion that they cause. 'Green' programmes would not be subject to either reduction commitments or countervail duties. They would include all the usual 'generally available' programmes – collective services, environment and resource conserving measures, adjustment assistance, regional development aids and, most importantly, crop insurance, disaster relief and other farm income safety net schemes that meet criteria to be agreed. It is proposed that *government expenditures* on trade distorting 'amber' measures be reduced by 50 per cent over 10 years according to country and commodity-specific schedules to be negotiated. The AMS is not seen as a suitable mechanism on which to base commitments to reduce domestic subsidies. The official reason is that differences between national support and international transaction prices have only a tenuous relationship with production and trade effects. More important is the fact that use of an AMS would require changes to be made in the market price supports provided to the supply managed products. However, where an AMS is used as a measure of the equivalence of commitments, Canada proposes that credits be given for effective supply control programmes.

Though some adaptations of farm income safety net programmes might have to be made to conform with 'green' criteria, and import access commitments would influence the amount of milk and 'feathered product' output that received support, acceptance by other countries of Canada's offer on internal support would leave two of its major domestic support programmes – safety nets for export products and market price supports for the dairy and poultry sectors – essentially intact. The direct subsidy paid on industrial milk ($6.03 per hectolitre and some C$ 280 million total) would have to be halved, but it has long been a target for elimination by governments bent on reducing expenditures.[13] The subsidy of C$ 720 million paid annually under the WGTA that covers some 70 per cent of the cost of transporting Prairie-grown grains, oilseeds and special crops to export positions would also be halved. But this too is a programme which the federal and some provincial governments, agribusiness and many farm groups wish to change because of its adverse effects on farm resource use and value-adding processing.[14] The expenditure cut required by Canada's GATT offer could well trigger economically desirable but politically sensitive changes in the WGTA, such as the payment of lump-sum compensation to present beneficiaries, or the conversion of the programme into a scheme to improve the overall transportation infrastructure of the Prairie region.

There is an important link between Canada's proposals on domestic subsidies made in the groups negotiating on agriculture and on subsidy-countervail issues. It is proposed that a definitive list of carefully circumscribed 'green' programmes be not only absolved from support reduction commitments but also be classified as non-actionable under the countervail provisions of national trade remedy laws. It is hoped that Canada's farm income safety net programmes would qualify on both counts, thereby permitting the continued provision of 'stop-loss' assistance to farmers in periods of extreme market stress and ending the threat of countervail duties being imposed by the US on exported Canadian farm products that have benefited from stabilization schemes. If Canada's farm income safety nets do not meet agreed criteria for production and trade neutrality, or if there is no coincidence between 'green-ness' for reduction commitments and 'actionability' under trade remedies, then there is an even greater need for clearer rules and better procedures that will discipline national countervail duty actions. To this end Canada has proposed strengthening international disciplines on such matters as the standing of complainants, sterner tests of causation and injury, higher *de minimis* levels, limiting countervail duties to subsidy differentials, and improved dispute settlement mechanisms (Meilke and van Duren 1990). The clarification of the status of farm income safety nets is necessary both to guide the future development of Canada's farm programmes and to resolve an issue that could not be settled under the CUSTA and which is impeding the development of Canada's trade with the US.

Border protection

Canada's offer on market access is dominated by its desire to have other countries provide improved and more assured access for its exports whilst itself retaining and making more predictable the quantitative import controls that underpin Canada's supply control programmes. There is also a reluctance to add further to the adjustment pressures faced by Canadian growers and processors of products who already face increasing competition from US imports under the terms of the CUSTA.

The proposal calls for: all terms of access to be bound; all existing tariffs to be reduced by about one-third over 10 years or to a bound ceiling rate of 20 per cent by applying a harmonizing formula;[15] all non-tariff measures other than the QRs authorized by revised GATT rules (particularly Article XI) to be converted to equivalent tariffs and reduced by formula by 50 per cent or to a ceiling binding of 20 per cent; and minimum access commitments to be implemented through rising tariff rate quotas. It is also proposed that countries with meat import controls eliminate them and rely instead on the normal safeguards against legal but disruptive imports provided by the GATT's Article XIX. The Canadian offer says nothing about new safeguard measures to accompany tariffication, but the Cairns Group's proposal that temporary and limited tariff increases be permitted in response to import surges and large world price movements would probably be supported by Canadian authorities. (The CUSTA provides for a tariff 'snap-back' for horticultural products.)

Canada proposes that QRs on imports continue to be permitted under Article XI:2(c)(i). However, because of the uncertainties created by the 1989 GATT panel ruling against Canada's placing quantitative restrictions on imports of ice-cream and yogurt (GATT, 1989) and the earlier ruling against Japan's quantitative import controls on 12 food and agricultural products (GATT, 1987), there is a clear need to change the substance and the language of the Article so as to clarify which products may be subject to import controls in support of supply management systems. Canada's supply management schemes are in danger of being undermined by rising imports of processed food products bearing reduced (under GATT) or zero (under CUSTA) tariffs. The Canadian government's GATT proposal for amending Article XI follows closely the changes demanded by organized milk producers (Dairy Farmers of Canada, 1989). The proposal is that the product coverage of Article XI:2(c)(i) be spelled out in an agreed list or by defining 'like product' 'in any form' as those in which there is not less than 50 per cent by weight of the fresh product produced under supply controls. At the same time as it seeks to confirm the legality and strengthen the efficacy its own use of QRs, Canada wants to guard against the promiscuous invocation of Article XI and the proliferation of GATT-legal import quotas by other countries that claim to be placing production under control. Accordingly, Canada's proposal also seeks to tighten the conditions that must be met for supplies to be deemed to be 'restricted' and would confine the right to use the Article to net importers.

Having closed the gaps in Article XI:2(c)(i), and reduced its use by others, Canada acknowledges that it too must provide some measure of improved and assured access to its market to foreign suppliers of products under import controls. It therefore offers a minimum access for imports equal to 5 per cent of production for a commodity sector (e.g., milk) and 1 per cent for specific products (e.g., butter).

Acceptance by others of Canada's offer on border protection would result in an end to all country-specific exceptions (including the US waiver) and the tariffication of the EC's variable import levies, the US' Section 22 quotas and many of Japan's agricultural import controls. Canada, however, would be authorized to continue to use a GATT-aberrant instrument – the import quota – and be able to continue fully to insulate its administered producer prices for milk, poultry meats and eggs from international market conditions.

The concessions Canada offers on import access are awkward but not onerous.

The minimum access commitments of 5 and 1 per cent, and the ending of import embargoes on dairy product substitutes,[16] would entail contraction of the Canadian dairy, turkey and egg industries by 2 or 3 per cent but have little effect on chicken producers. Confining the use of Article XI's QRs to net importers, if importer status is measured in value terms, might require curtailment of Canada's practice of dumping skim milk powder and evaporated milk abroad. Structural surpluses of these products would have to be diverted to secondary national uses or given to poor countries as food aid.

The effect of Canada's tariff offer on the horticultural and food processing industries – which get most of their protection from tariffs – is tempered by the modesty of the proposal that tariffs be cut by only a third over a 10-year period, and by the expectation (though it is not in the initial offer tabled in Geneva) that Canada will seek exemptions from its tariff offer for such import-sensitive products as fresh fruits and vegetables, cut flowers, and canned tomato paste, mushrooms and apple juice. Producers will still have to compete with US suppliers in a tariff-free continental market under the CUSTA (and later with Mexico under a North American Free Trade Area), but they would be spared intensified competition from off-shore suppliers of these products.

The Canadian proposal that countries which limit meat imports under national legislation rely henceforth on the safeguard provisions of Article XIX of the General Agreement would result in the elimination of the US Meat Import Law and the voluntary export restraints that are the *de facto* controls on beef imports into the United States. As long as unrestricted access to the US market was assured and other countries provided minimum access commitments, Canada's own Meat Import Act could be readily sacrificed since permitted beef imports under the formula in the law (or under the minimum import access granted in the Tokyo Round) are regularly greater than actual imports. The law has been triggered only once.

Other matters

Though they are not part of Canada's October 1990 offer, Canada has tentative positions on other matters that permeate the negotiations on agriculture. For instance, its interest in the European market for oilseeds and their products makes it oppose the Community's wish to rebalance protection. While Canada acknowledges the legitimacy of such 'non-trade concerns' as food security, food safety, environmental protection, rural viability and the like, it is resolved that, to the maximum degree possible, these matters should not be addressed by policy instruments that cause trade distortions. On 'special and differential' (S&D) treatment for the less-developed countries (LDCs), Canada shares the view of other developed countries that the LDCs should not emerge from the UR with the same 'free ride' in agricultural trade as they have had hitherto in trade in manufactures.[17] Accordingly, it prefers that S&D take the form of longer periods to accede to common reduction commitments and universal rules and that the extensions be related to individual LDC's degree of development.

There is an agricultural component to other areas of the MTNs, and Canada has made proposals in other negotiating groups that complement its formal agricultural offer. The relevance of its proposals to the group negotiating a new subsidies code to Canada's position on the retention of its farm income safety nets and its wish to see other countries' export subsidies outlawed has been noted above. On access to supplies, Canada would likely support the phasing out of the right to use export restrictions under Article XI:2(a) in return for improvements in import access, and the export restriction provision in Article XX(j) might be qualified (as in the CUSTA) to give importers access to the same proportion of supplies when export restraints are in effect. If Article XIX is to substitute for meat import laws – and eventually for the special safeguards that may accompany tariffication during a transition period – then Canada would like to see improvements in the Article's provisions with respect to non-discrimination and digressivity. One expects also that the discussions in the Negotiating Group on GATT Articles are being watched carefully since new requirements regarding the 'transparency' of the activities of state trading entities could influence the operations of the Canadian Wheat Board and other national marketing agencies.

6.5 IMPLICATIONS

Due to the impasse in Brussels in December 1990 and the uncertainties about when substantive negotiations might be resumed and the nature and 'reach' of a final accord, it is difficult even to speculate on the effects on the Canadian agrifood sector of a UR agreement on agricultural policy and trade reform.

Early empirical modelling reported by the OECD (1987), Tyers and Anderson (1988), Roningen and Dixit (1989), and others, and summarized by Meilke and Larue (1989) and Blandford (1990), all agree that under complete agricultural de-subsidization and trade liberalization Canadian taxpayers and consumers would experience lower expenditures, while Canada's farmers would suffer a loss in producer surplus since increases in market prices would be insufficient to offset reduction in the income transferred by existing policies. Overall there would be a significant net gain in national economic welfare, even if farmers were fully compensated for their income losses. The adjustment costs to Canadian producers would be considerably lower under multilateral liberalization than under unilateral reform. A more recent study confirms these broad conclusions (CARD, 1991). These results are similar to those forecast for other developed countries, and the absolute magnitudes of the various economic changes are only of national interest.

None of these studies tell the full story of the adjustments that free trade in agriculture might entail. Compensation payments might not be made and, even if they were, decoupled payments for income losses would not prevent a massive reduction in the capital value of farm assets.

Most of the analytical work that has been done by Canadian government analysts has not been published. One study that was released modelled the effects of national policy and international price changes on representative farms, and showed that if reform was comprehensive, adjustments would be most severe for farms producing supply managed products (see, for example, Narayanan *et al.*, 1989). However, other studies (for example, Graham *et al.*, 1990) have suggested that – free of supply controls and other constraints which increase industry cost structures – the Canadian dairy and poultry industries could become exporters at competitive prices of some products, at least to northern US states.

Most of the empirical analyses of the economic effects of agricultural trade and policy reform have assumed complete liberalization. This will clearly not result from the current MTNs. Due to the 'linearity' of most models, the estimated economic effects of some lesser level of cut in subsidies and access barriers would be proportionately lower. But this is not realistic either, for the policy changes countries will be willing to make will be a non-linear function of the degree of reform agreed. For instance, Canada might be willing to retreat from its stance on the Article XI QRs that protect its market price supports for supply managed products if a 'big' GATT result in agriculture was on the cards, but it is likely to stick closely to the offer described in Part IV if all that the triad and CG countries can agree to is an accord that is somewhat better than that rejected by the US and the CG in Brussels in December 1990 but still well short of complete reform.

A second study released by Agriculture Canada (Cahill, 1991) estimated the effects on Canadian agriculture of a more limited agreement. It was assumed that a UR accord would involve halving export subsidies, reducing internal 'amber' support by one-third, and cutting by one-third existing tariffs and the tariff equivalents of non-tariff measures not approved by the GATT. However, though it was assumed that (subject to 'credits' for supply controls) market price supports for supply-managed products would have to be reduced, it was also assumed that import quotas for milk products, poultry meats and eggs would remain in place though with a 3 per cent minimum access commitment. Under this scenario, Canada's grains, oilseeds and milk producers would suffer a net loss in income compared with a 1986–8 base period situation, whilst cattle, hog and poultry producers would have experienced net income gains. Government expenditure reductions would have been 20 per cent larger than the sum required fully to compensate the losers for their income losses.

Estimates of income changes under partial liberalization relative to 1986–8 levels of assistance are of interest but are not definitive, for it is unlikely that Canadian governments will be able to sustain direct payments to farmers at the levels reached in the period since 1986. In this sense, even a limited agricultural agreement would be beneficial to Canada's export interests in that it would begin a GATT-bound process of opening markets, restraining subsidized competition and, perhaps, placing improved multilateral disciplines on US countervail practices. The endogenous budgetary and other forces that are causing the European Community and the United States to undertake unilateral reform of their agricultural policies would continue to work internally and be locked in and reinforced by the international agreement. The combination of multilateral commitments and internal reform pressures would reduce the risk of competitive subsidy wars breaking out again.

The major obligations placed on Canada to reduce support for its export commodities would be to cut expenditures on transport subsidies under the WGTA and perhaps to make changes in its farm income safety net programmes. The first has been discussed earlier. On safety nets, recent developments have been supportive of the GATT-process in that an attempt is being made to replace industry-wide, commodity-specific, price or margin-oriented stabilization pro-grammes with schemes that stabilize the gross and net incomes of individual farmers. One of these – Net Income Stabilization Accounts (NISA) – may well be 'GATT-able' in its present form:[19] indeed it may be a model that other countries would want to emulate. The initial version of the other program – the Gross Revenue Insurance Plan (GRIP)[20] – is too 'rich' and too much linked to individual commodities to be ruled production- and trade-neutral. However, reductions in the level at which average gross revenue per acre is supported, and stabilization of the revenue earned from a 'basket' of products rather than from individual crops, are changes that will likely be made in the future for domestic reasons. They would almost certainly be required by an international agreement on domestic subsidies.

Changes are also afoot in policies that affect Canada's ability to accept international obligations on the border measures that protect some of its import-competing products. Full application of the CUSTA and the eventual implementation of a GATT panel ruling on the treatment of imported wines will mean that during the 1990s Canada's horticultural, grape and wine and food processing industries will become more competitive. There will then be less internal pressure to seek exemptions from tariff reductions for some of the sensitive products of these industries.

Canada's position on Article XI is more complicated. A huge federal budget deficit makes a switch from market price supports to direct payments to milk and poultry producers unattractive. Two industry advisory groups that were charged with the task of determining how a 'second generation' of supply management schemes might be created acknowledged the need to reduce the costs of producing milk and poultry products so as to lower the difference between national and international prices, but they took as given that supply controls and quantitative import restrictions would continue into the future. And the prospect of a vote on separation being taken in Quebec not later than October 1992 virtually compels the federal government to be unyielding in Geneva on Article XI at the present time. One can speculate that under a 'big' agreement on agriculture in the MTNs Canada would likely have sought a continuation of Article XI's QRs when used to support effective supply controls by net importers, but finally acceded to this being granted only as a special and time-limited exception. With only a limited agricultural agreement in prospect, Canada can be expected to adhere to its position on Article XI and seek the support of the EC, Japan, Switzerland and others for the retention of this particular agricultural exception.

6.6 CONCLUSIONS

Despite the immense stakes of Canada and its agrifood sector in fundamental and far- reaching multilateral agricultural and trade policy reform, it is apparent that, to this point (mid-1991), Canada has offered few contributions to the attainment of that end.

To advance the interests of its agricultural export groups, Canada has ambitious objectives – for others. These include the proposals that other countries tariffy, bind and reduce their import barriers, halve their internal support expenditures, abandon their use of export subsidies, and accept stronger disciplines on the trade remedies they apply to counter Canada's own farm 'assistance' programmes. Canada's only significant concession that affects its agricultural exports is to offer to halve the transport subsidies paid under the Western Grains Transportation Act – which most Canadians believe should be changed or abandoned anyway.

On behalf of its dairy and poultry import-competing sectors, Canada refuses to use an AMS, declines to reduce its administered prices, rejects tariffication of the QRs that underpin its market price supports, and proposes that it be allowed to apply Article XI:2(c)(i) QRs to a wider range of products. For major import-competing farm products that are not under supply management, Canada will probably seek exemptions even from the modest tariff reduction it has proposed.

A sympathetic view of this seemingly-hypocritical negotiating position would list at least the following four factors. First, because Canada's policies do not cause the problems in world product and factor markets Canada has little to contribute to their solution. Since, under normal circumstances, Canada is not a big subsidizer in agriculture, the demands made on other countries for policy changes will necessarily be larger. And once others cease distorting world grains and oilseeds markets Canada will no longer need to pay the off-setting subsidies that allow its own producers to survive. Second, the low-slung, market-responsive farm income safety nets that socialize a part of normal production and market risks – which would then remain as the principal direct assistance provided to agriculture – should be internationally acceptable because they are production and trade-neutral, particularly in the improved versions being developed. Thirdly, some Canadian interest groups and public authorities genuinely believe that high market price supports are trade neutral if backed up by effective supply controls and appropriate minimum access arrangements for imports. (Defenders of this position are untroubled by the fact that it was never intended that Article XI should provide permanent protection; that there is a demand-side distortion; that consumption is met from high cost domestic sources while efficient suppliers are denied remunerative market opportunities; and that Canada dumps abroad its structural surpluses of supply managed products while protesting its right to restrict their importation). Finally, defenders of Canada's position on agriculture in the Uruguay Round claim – with some justification – that in no other country is national political unity and survival so directly affected by the timing and content of its offer on agriculture.

A less charitable judgement on Canada's stance would acknowledge that – like other countries – Canada is only interested in pursuing its national interests in an international setting as those interests are perceived by national political leaders. A starting point of this realpolitik is that the scope of the UR agreement on agriculture will be determined by a bargain between the United States and the European Community and be little affected by a 'small' offer from Canada, either in its own right or by its weakening the influence of the Cairns Group. Furthermore, a limited UR agreement would provide significant benefits for Canada's farm exports while relieving the pressure to make major changes in its import arrangements. Thirdly, insofar as national trade policy has two elements, foreign trade policy (which is focused on getting other countries to make changes that will improve your welfare) and domestic trade policy (which is designed to make your own economy more competitive by forcing it to adjust to international competition) (Hart, 1990, p.6), Canada's leaders seem to have concluded that the agrifood sector is already being required to make all the adjustments it can tolerate under the national policy review and the CUSTA. On this view, Canada might be ready to accept stronger obligations in the second half of the decade when the constitutional crisis is resolved, when the CUSTA has stimulated productivity, and when the national agricultural policy reform agenda is well advanced – but not yet.

It is possible, of course, that Canadian authorities are playing a waiting game, and anticipating that they can delay until the final hours of the negotiations acceptance of those international obligations that will force the changes in unloved national farm programmes that they are politically unable to initiate themselves. However, such subtlety in manoeuvre will not be evident until the negotiations are completed.

An alternative view would be that Canada is 'a nation of artful chiselers', 'one of the more adept exploiters of multilateral mercantilist bargaining' and 'the quintessential free rider, whether by accident or design' (Hart, 1990, p. 22).[21] To this point, this judgement could not be rejected on the basis of Canada's offer, the statements of its Ministers, and the positions they have required the country's negotiators to take.

The problem with such unprincipled behaviour is that national trade policy should have a third objective – system building. Smaller countries like Canada, individually and collectively, have a particular responsibility for the creation and strengthening of a rules-based multilateral trading system. Big countries can look after their own economic interests by the exercise of power: smaller countries must seek protection in their ability to appeal to a set of clear trade rules that are universally applied. The fundamental criticism to be made of Canada's negotiating stance on agriculture is that the country is not offering a contribution to global agricultural reform commensurate with its stake, and that, by seeking exemptions for its aberrant behaviour, it is weakening the effort being made to create the rules appropriate to a more open world agricultural economy. And to the extent that the attempt at agricultural trade reform comes up short, then so too will be the accomplishments of the Uruguay Round as a whole. Yet no country has a greater stake than Canada in the success of this unparalleled opportunity to create a more open, lawful and predictable multilateral trading system which can deliver prosperity, equity and harmony in the remainder of this millennium and beyond. That the short-run economic interests of 50 000 dairy and poultry producers could be permitted to jeopardize this over-arching national purpose is a measure of how low the conduct of national affairs in Canada has fallen.

7 The Japanese Perspective

Kenzo Hemmi[1]

7.1 JAPANESE ATTITUDE TO THE URUGUAY ROUND NEGOTIATIONS

Due to the rising tide of protectionism in the industrial world, especially in the US, which threatened Japanese exports in particular, Japan generally welcomed the initiation of the Uruguay Round of multilateral trade negotiations in September 1986. Even the Japanese farm lobby, under strong bi-lateral pressure from the US to open the Japanese rice market to external competition, sought to use the Round as a shelter from this pressure. It was hoped that because of Japan's huge export surplus with the U.S., the protection of Japanese agriculture might emerge more favourably from multilateral than from bi-lateral negotiations, due to the support of other major food importers, such as the European Community. This explains why, in April 1986, the Japanese government stated that it was not prepared to deal with the rice issue bi-laterally, but only through the Uruguay Round of multilateral trade negotiations.

Japanese farm interests have been extremely reluctant to countenance any further liberalisation of access to their domestic market, asserting that with Japan being the world's largest importer of agricultural goods the huge export surplus is the result not of insufficient agricultural imports but of unnecessarily large exports of manufactured goods. They see Japanese farmers as being victims of the greed of compatriot manufacturers and traders.

The farm lobby's opposition to the relaxation of agricultural protection is, with some exceptions, supported by non-farm opinion, particularly that of Japanese housewives. Because of their rapidly increasing disposable real incomes, housewives have been increasingly tolerant of high food prices. It is a widely held view that excessive dependence on imported food supplies is unduly risky, as international food markets have been unstable and some imported foods might be contaminated with dangerous chemicals. The results of public opinion polls have suggested that the Japanese public favours maintaining a fairly high ratio of food self-sufficiency.

But, despite the internal opposition to reduced agricultural protection, the Japanese government, since the Uruguay Round negotiations started in September 1986, has taken some steps to relax barriers to agricultural imports. Thus, in February 1988, Japan agreed to the removal of quantitative restrictions on 8 out of a total of 22 agricultural and marine products to which such restrictions then applied. Shortly afterwards, in June 1988, it was decided that, as from April 1991, quota restrictions on beef and fresh oranges would be abandoned. These steps were taken partially in response to continued bi-lateral pressure from the US. But, in the opinion of the Japanese government, there is no room at present for the further liberalisation of border measures affecting agricultural trade. In taking this position the Japanese government has been influenced by the knowledge that farmers in the EC and the US also enjoy substantial government support and protection, and that the international prices of a number of agricultural commodities are depressed by their subsidised exports.

The following extract from a publication by the Ministry of Foreign Affairs summarises the Japanese stance in the Uruguay Round very well.

Japan's motivation for participating in the Round is, briefly, to slow down the rising tide of protectionism, and, in turn, to restructure the world trading system as the basis of peace and prosperity in the world in approaching the 21st century.

We recognise the Uruguay Round as being the cornerstone of the movement towards reduced protection.

Launching the Round helps not only to save the GATT system from weakening but also the world trading system from being increasingly dominated by protectionism and shrinkage.

We recognise that Japan plays an important role in the Uruguay Round negotiations and that the free trading system of the world has in the past formed the basis of the prosperity of the Japanese economy, and will continue to do so in the future. The success of the Round is of vital interest to Japan despite the existence of difficult issues like agriculture. It is necessary for Japan to negotiate positively on these difficult issues and to do our best in making difficult adjustments in the domestic economy affecting both the government and non-government sectors. (Ministry of Foreign Affairs, 1988, pp. 15–16)

Three further points should be added. First, the author believes that the government is prepared to make such necessary but minimum concessions on agriculture in the negotiations as are needed to ensure the success of the Round as a whole. This strategy is reflected by Japan's passive approach to the agricultural negotiations, contrasting with the much more active role played in other fields such as trade in services and safeguarding intellectual property rights. Second, the belief is widely held in Japan that in the past the primary aim of the GATT negotiations on agriculture was to benefit exporters at the expense of importers. But, as the world's largest importer of agricultural products, it is Japan's duty on this occasion to defend the interests of food importers. Third, a single commodity, rice, dominates domestic discussion of the GATT agricultural negotiations. By comparison, issues such as the harmonisation of sanitary and phytosanitary regulations, or even the relaxation of border measures affecting dairy products, scarcely attract public attention.

7.2   PROGRESS MADE BY THE END OF JUNE 1991

In the opinion of the author the Uruguay Round has made a significant impact upon Japanese agricultural policy. But Japan's stance in the agricultural negotiations has been influenced by a number of background issues and developments. Three of the most decisive issues, as discussed in this section, are: the timing and length of the Round in relation to changes in domestic agricultural policy; limited public awareness in Japan of the issues at stake in the agricultural negotiations; and the rationale of the Japanese government's minimalist strategy for negotiating the lowering of agricultural protection.

7.2.1   Timing and length of the Round in relation to changes in domestic agricultural policy

At the end of WW2 Japan experienced a severe food shortage but succeeded in recovering food supply stability within the remarkably short period of ten years. The focus of Japanese agricultural policy then gradually shifted from increasing food production to developing a more efficient agricultural sector. After several years of deliberation, the Basic Agricultural Law of 1961 was enacted. This law laid down that the two basic objectives of agricultural policy should be to increase agricultural productivity and to maintain farm income at a level comparable to non-agricultural sector income. But, by launching the Doubling National Income Plan simultaneously with the enactment of the Basic Agricultural Law, the government effectively decreed that these policy objectives for agriculture must be attained within the context of a rapidly growing economy. Agricultural development programmes under the Basic Agricultural Law became disrupted by a spurt of economic growth, and agricultural support programmes played a much larger role than originally anticipated or intended. Although the government pursued an ambitious plan for the liberalisation of agricultural imports, by 1970 the Japanese level of government support for agriculture had risen considerably higher than the support levels of major European countries.[2] The world grain supply shortfall of 1972–3, combined with the embargo on soybean exports by the US at the same time, and the establishment of 200-mile fishing limits by many countries, reminded the Japanese of their severe food shortage after WW2. Resolutions calling for an increase in domestic food supply capacity were unanimously adopted in both Houses of the Diet in April 1980. Since then the food security issue has become a primary objective of Japanese agricultural policy. But at the same time the emphasis of government agricultural programmes has shifted quietly away from increasing production to enhancing productivity. The increasing abundance of food supplies on world markets has also been recognised. The Third Report on the Administrative Reform (July1982) recommended a reduction in the support price of rice. Moreover, in a report on food security published in June 1985, the Keidanren (Japanese Federation of Economic Organisations) expressed the view that programmes of increasing domestic food supply capacity were unrealistic. As Japan's trade surplus continued to increase after 1984, the prime minister appointed a Committee on Measures for the Promotion of Economic Restructuring for the Improvement of External Economic Relations (the so-called Maekawa Commission). The Commission's report, published in April 1986, recommended that, except for a few key products, the gap between domestic and international market prices should be narrowed through permitting a steady increase in imports. Further, that in preparation for the coming round of the GATT negotiations, access to the market for products subject to quantitative import restrictions should be improved. In the light of these recommendations the actual launching of the Uruguay Round negotiations in September 1986 was timely for Japan. In May 1986 the Japanese government undertook to carry out the Commission's recommendations in a declaration entitled 'The Guideline for Promoting Economic Restructuring'.

The support price of rice was frozen after 1984 and was in fact reduced in 1987, for the first time since 1957. The nominal value of agricultural product imports increased from US$16.8 billion in 1985 to US$29.7 in 1989. Japanese farmers were, of course, very unhappy with these policy changes, as revealed by the results of the Upper House election in July 1989, when the ruling Liberal Democratic Party lost 23 out of 26 single member districts, most of which are in farming areas. This election result at least temporarily reduced the government's enthusiasm for the further liberalisation of agricultural imports and continued lowering of the rice support price. For this reason the (unexpected) extension of the Uruguay Round negotiations after December 1990 may be viewed as being beneficial to those Japanese who are genuinely in favour of a final agreement which includes the further liberalisation of agriculture.

7.2.2 Limited public awareness in Japan of the issues at stake in the agricultural negotiations

Mainly because of the language barrier, discussions of the GATT agricultural negotiations in Japan have been isolated from those going on in the outside world. Even research personnel obtain information mainly from domestic sources, such as the Japanese mass media, or farm lobby spokesmen, but especially from the government through the Ministry of Agriculture, Forestry and Fisheries. Foreign information sources, either printed or broadcast, are rarely used. The main source of information used by the Japanese mass media on the progress of the Uruguay Round has been the Japanese government. Although all high level GATT meetings have been attended by journalists representing the Japanese mass media, these representatives have relied for information mainly upon press conferences held by Japanese delegates. Foreign delegates and foreign journalists have rarely been approached.[3] Since Japanese journalists rely almost exclusively on Japanese sources for information, and because the press briefings given by Japanese delegates tend to be biased in favour of Japanese agricultural interests, the journalists inevitably get a myopic view of the issues involved in the negotiations. Broad issues, which are of interest to all countries involved in the negotiations, easily get confused with proposals advanced by the US government.

Similarly, discussions of Cairns Group proposals are easily neglected, as also are discussions of proposals advanced by other major food importing countries. The Japanese press appears to be barely aware of the potential benefits of reaching a balanced overall agreement in the Uruguay Round negotiations in which, for example, concessions might be made affecting agriculture in exchange for the potential gains from agreeing to bring trade in services within the ambit of the GATT.

Both agricultural research personnel and agricultural journalists in Japan tend to interpret all discussion of the issues at stake in the agricultural negotiations as implicit criticism of Japanese agricultural policy. Although a few voices have criticised the Japanese government for its passivity in the agricultural negotiations, the majority of commentators have supported the attitude of the Japanese government and the Japanese farm lobby. A final point is that most Japanese farmers subscribe to two newspapers which have published many articles criticising all proposals that agricultural protection be reduced. These newspapers, both published by agricultural producer organisations – the National Federation of Agricultural Co-operatives and the National Chamber of Agriculture – have also often published articles on farmers' organisations in other countries campaigning against the reduction of agricultural support and protection.

7.2.3 Rationale of the Japanese government's minimalist strategy for negotiating the reduction of agricultural protection

The Japanese government is anxious to avoid the stigma of being blamed for sabotaging the entire Uruguay Round of multilateral negotiations through an unwillingness to be sufficiently flexible on lowering agricultural protection. But, at the same time, the government is extremely sceptical whether, quite apart from its own negotiating stance, the Round will in fact result in any very significant reduction of agricultural protection world-wide. It therefore wants to avoid making any greater concession on agriculture than the minimum necessary to ensure the success of the Round as a whole.

There are a number of reasons for the Japanese government's scepticism regarding the ability of the Uruguay Round participants to deliver a significant reduction of agricultural protection. First, there is the failure to make significant progress with liberalising agricultural trade in past GATT rounds. Second, there is the observation that the European Community's efforts to reform the CAP have been making only very slow progress. Agricultural protectionism in France, Germany and Italy in particular is thought to remain sufficiently strong to block more rapid progress for at least a few more years. Third, the Japanese government observes that, even in the US, there is strong political resistance by producers to the reduction of agricultural export subsidies as well as to liberalizing imports of such products as peanuts.

7.3 AGRICULTURAL PROTECTION AND PRODUCTIVITY IN JAPAN

Japanese agricultural policy is based upon the premise that the government's ability to reduce agricultural protection depends upon the rate of improvement in agricultural productivity. It is for this reason that, since the early 1980s, the emphasis of government policy has shifted away from increasing production to increasing productivity. The core of the economic analysis upon which the government's productivity enhancing programmes are based is as follows (Hemmi, 1987, pp. 33–7). The farm population is ageing and growing numbers of farmers are retiring without successors. Others have to reduce the sizes of their farms. In order to realise the government's productivity enhancing objectives it would be necessary to transfer 0.7 million hectares of agricultural land between 1980 and 1990 from retiring farmers, and those wishing to reduce their farm size, to those wanting to expand their operations. Another 1.1 million hectares would need to be transferred on a similar basis between the years 1990 and 2000. It was also projected that, resulting from these transfers, by the year 2000 there would be substantially increased numbers of 'large' 10–15 hectare rice farms and 'large' 20–35 hectare dairy farms. On this basis it was projected that over the 20-year period from 1980 to 2000 it might be feasible to lower the level of agricultural protection in Japan to the EC level. But such a modest target might fail to satisfy the demands of the US or the CG. Between 1986 and 1991 the support price of rice was in fact reduced by about 12 per cent in nominal yen. The government has tried to accelerate the rate of price reduction by revising the price support formula, but without success.[4] It seems that the feasible rate of price reduction depends almost entirely upon the rate of structural improvement.

7.4 JAPANESE PERSPECTIVE ON THE PROGRESS OF THE AGRICULTURAL NEGOTIATIONS UP TO MID-1991.

Three comments are apposite pertaining to the Mid-Term Review Agreement (Geneva Accord); Japan's offer of September 1990; and more recent developments.

7.4.1 Mid-Term Review

On the Mid-Term Review Agreement, the Japanese government was pleased that other participating governments agreed to recognise 'food security' as a possible objective of national agricultural policy. This appeared to acknowledge the legitimacy of the Japanese request for giving basic food commodities special treatment, even though approval of Japan attempting to maintain self-sufficiency in rice was likely to be withheld. Under the Mid-Term Review Agreement Japan was committed to undertaking substantial and progressive reductions in trade-distorting farm support. This helped considerably in activating discussions on the Uruguay Round in Japan.

7.4.2 Japan's agricultural offer of September 1990

The Japanese government formulated and presented its 'final' offer on agriculture within a few weeks following the Trade Negotiation Committee meeting of the GATT in Geneva and the parallel G7 Summit Meeting in Houston, Texas, during July 1990. The offer reflected Japan's basic position on food security, that is, the need to agree special border protection adjustment rules for basic food commodities (such as rice in Japan) and to review and clarify GATT Article XI: 2(c)(i) relating to agricultural import quotas. The offer also stated that 'it is a prerequisite of Japan's offer that all participants make equitable commitments on a reciprocal basis'.[5] On commitments based on AMS reduction, the Japanese offer stipulated that proportionate increases in the AMS should be permitted 'in order to compensate for the effects of such exogenous factors as inflation': also that 'the base year for the reduction of support should be 1986'. Subject to these provisos, the specific Japanese commitment to the reduction of internal support, using the AMS, was that 'rates of reduction should be calculated based on the target (basic) reduction rate of 30 per cent for the period 1986 to 1996, taking into account import ratios of the products and the production restriction ratio of the basic food commodities (rice)'. Soybeans, beef, pork, poultry and eggs were not included amongst the products subject to AMS reduction since, in the case of soybeans, the ratio of imports to domestic production has been very high and the effect of domestic production on trade is therefore thought to be negligible. In the cases of beef, pork, poultry and eggs, AMS reduction is considered irrelevant since, for these products, Japan's protective measures are all border measures. The following specific AMS reduction offers were made relating to two groups of commodities: 1. For wheat, barley and rice combined as a cereal sector the target total AMS reduction value will be from 3197.2 billion yen in 1986 to 2347.5 billion yen in 1995 (26.6 per cent reduction). 2. For sugar and milk/dairy products unit AMS reduction targets will apply. For milk/dairy products the target reduction is from 39.8 yen/kg in 1986 to 29.2 yen/kg in 1996 (26.7 per cent reduction). For sugar no specific offer was made at the time but promised later.

On the reduction of border protection, Japan offered commitments of two types: elimination of import quotas; and reduction of tariff rates. On the first of these two counts, Japan claimed credit for action already taken to eliminate import quotas since September 1986 relating to processed cheese, ice cream and some other dairy products, some beans, tomato juice and other tomato products, fruit juice and some other fruit products: also the decision taken in June 1988 to eliminate import quota restrictions on beef and fresh oranges by April 1991. No additional offers to eliminate import quotas were made. On tariff rate reduction the offer stated that 'Japan is prepared to consider reduction of tariff rates for those commodities for which commitments using the AMS are not offered and for which quota restriction on imports is not imposed. The target rate of tariff reduction will be equivalent to the average rate of tariff reduction for all agricultural products implemented by Japan in the Tokyo Round'. On the reduction of tariff rates on tropical products, Japan offered to consider proposals on a request/offer basis.

Although Japan's September 1990 proposal contained almost no specific mention of rice, it is clear that the AMS reduction offer concerning cereals definitely includes rice. This can be interpreted as signifying that the Japanese government is prepared to relax present import restrictions on rice, even though there has been no official statement to that effect. This judgment is made despite the fact that as recently as 1988 the Diet passed a resolution confirming self-sufficiency in rice as a policy objective, and that during the 1989 Upper House election campaign some LDP candidates asserted that not a single grain of rice would be imported. The government has not concealed the fact that in recent years Japan has been importing some 50 000 tonnes of rice annually (admittedly only a very small fraction of total consumption). Moreover, several leaders of the LDP, including a former prime minister, have hinted that Japan might agree to import a quantity of rice equivalent to some fraction of domestic consumption. But the government has repeatedly rejected the tariffication of the internal rice support price. The Japanese government argued that if it were to accept the US proposal of converting all internal support measures into their tariff equivalents, then to be eliminated in 10 years, there would be almost no support thereafter. The government maintained that to the Japanese public such a radical change of policy appears highly dangerous due to the vulnerability of the Japanese rice market to climatic changes and other factors liable to cause wide fluctuations in supplies and prices on the world market. The weakness of the government's case on this issue is that the rates at which tariff equivalents are reduced is negotiable, that there is room to institute a safety mechanism, and that a palpable advantage of tariffication is that all government support measures are made transparent.

Based upon this summary of the agricultural policy and trade reforms the government offered in September 1990, it may be concluded that Japan has been a rather passive participant in the negotiations. But, broadly speaking, Japan is prepared to make concessions equivalent to those conceded by the EC. However, Japan is trying to maintain residual agricultural import restrictions at about their present level.

7.4.3 More recent developments

Although the official Japanese position on agriculture has not changed since September 1990, members of the ruling party were present at the abortive 'final' meeting of the Uruguay Round held in Brussels early in December. The author interpets the presence of Japanese politicians in Brussels at that time as indicating that they expected the EC to make some further concessions on agriculture in exchange for gains made in other areas of the negotiations and to ensure the success of the Round as a whole. They needed to be 'on the spot' in case Japan needed to consider making last minute adjustments to her own position in response to moves by the EC. In the event, the Japanese delegates may have been reassured by the EC Agricultural Commissioner's statement in Brussels that other participants in the negotiations failed to grasp the magnitude of the sacrifice which the EC's offer to cut domestic agricultural support by 30 per cent implied for Community farmers and, further, that 'unless and until they reduce their expectations there will not be progress on agriculture'.

The granting by the US Congress of the President's application to have his 'fast-track' authority for dealing with trade legislation extended by two years until mid-1993 was reported in Japanese newspapers. But this has not yet prompted any shift in the official Japanese position either. It is reported that the US government is still asking the Japanese government to accept the tariffication of all measures of protecting and supporting domestic rice production. The acceptance by Japan of this proposal still appears unlikely. It appears equally unlikely that the US would be satisfied by any possible offer by Japan to admit imports of rice by quota equivalent to some small fraction of domestic consumption.

7.5 THE POSSIBLE EFFECTS OF GLOBAL AGRICULTURAL POLICY AND TRADE REFORM ON JAPANESE AGRICULTURE AND FOOD SUPPLY

Speculation about the possible effects of an eventual 'positive' outcome to the Uruguay Round negotiations must be based upon certain assumptions. First, it is assumed that the EC will finally go no further than extending its original offer of a 30 per cent cut in domestic farm support to one of about 40 per cent. Second, it is assumed that the base year for agricultural support or AMS reduction will be 1986 and not 1990 as proposed by the Hellstrom compromise paper circulated at the Brussels meeting in December 1990. In view of the AMS reductions already implemented by Japan between 1986 and 1990, as detailed earlier in this chapter, the combined effect of these twin assumptions is that the additional AMS reductions needed to meet the Hellstrom target of an overall reduction of 30 per cent between 1990 and 1995 would only be quite small. Official Japanese estimates of the relevant figures are 5.4 per cent for cereals and 8.6 per cent for milk/dairy products (MAFF, 1990, p.13). Third, it is assumed that the issue of the tariffication of border measures will be crucial for Japan. Although the EC has partially accepted the principle of tariffication, with significant reservations, Japan has repeatedly rejected the tariffication of domestic rice support measures, for the reasons already explained. For this reason, the author proposes to examine separately the effects of a GATT agreement on Japanese agriculture both with and without the tariffication of rice support measures. Fourth, it is assumed that, during the next few years, both Japan and the rest of the world will escape the effects of either a severe economic depression or a pronounced boom.[6] Projections by the FAO and others signify that by the year 2000 the production of cereals will significantly exceed consumption in the developed world, whereas in developing countries the reverse situation will prevail. It is assumed that, due to a shortage of foreign exchange in LDCs, developed country exporters of cereals will be unable to dispose of their export surpluses in LDC markets.

For the purpose of this exercise, no assumption is made concerning the extent of any possible reduction of agricultural export subsidies. Japan does not subsidise her own exports and favours their elimination elsewhere. It must be recognised, of course, that the abolition of export subsidies could affect Japanese agriculture by raising the world market prices of heavily subsidised products like wheat and dairy products. But the author chooses to avoid addressing this question here.

Most Japanese agricultural economists are of the opinion that Japanese agriculture would be adversely affected by the liberalisation of agricultural imports, that is, as a result of liberalisation there would be irreversible declines both in the number of farmers and the area of land in crops.[7] But differences of opinion do exist on this issue and a minority of Japanese economists believe that Japanese agriculture could cope with import liberalisation without irreversible adverse consequences (e.g. Kano, 1987).

A recent study entitled 'Costs of Production of Rice in 2000 and 2010' is enlightening on the issue of the potential ability of Japanese agriculture to reduce costs of production (Chino, 1991). This study includes an estimate of the decrease in the costs of rice production which might be caused by the combined effects of technical progress and an increased scale of operation. The effects of technical progress are estimated relative to large rice farms of 3 hectares (compared with an average size of only 0.882 ha.). It is estimated that on such farms production costs will decline by 6.6 per cent between 1988 and 2000 due to technical progress, and by a further 4.2 per cent between 2000 and 2010. These figures are not impressive and appear to cast serious doubt upon the ability of Japanese rice producers to withstand rapid reduction of government support and protection from the current level. However, if account is also taken of the estimated effect of increasing the average scale of operation on rice farms a different picture emerges. In 1988, the average cost of producing rice on the average sized rice farm of 0.882 ha. was 20 367 yen/60 kg. Starting from this baseline, and taking account of both technical progress and increasing scale of operation, the various 'target' average farm sizes at different dates needed to match various hypothetical rates of reducing average costs may be estimated. In Table 7.1 are shown the hypothetical average farm sizes corresponding with rates of cost reduction ranging from 10 per cent to 40 per cent at two target dates, the years 2000 and 2010. The figures in the table indicate that if the policy objective was to reduce the average costs of rice production by 30 per cent by the year 2000 this might be achieved through successful measures to raise the average size of farm to 5.28 ha. This does not look like an impossible task. But the more ambitious task of reducing costs by 40 per cent or more, by the same date, would entail a radical programme of structural reform and be difficult to achieve.[8]

Japanese agriculture is by no means confined to the production of rice. Whereas rice is of major importance to part-time farmers, who depend mainly upon non-farm economic activities, full-time farmers depend more for their income upon other lines of production, such as livestock and horticulture. Moreover, whereas producers of rice and other energy food crops are very dependent upon government support to maintain their farm income, due to stagnant demand for these products, producers of other kinds of agricultural and horticultural products are much less reliant on government intervention. Crops other than energy food crops, including flowers and other ornamental plants, are produced mainly by progressive full-time farmers. The demand for such crops is increasing. During a period of 22 years ending in 1987 the consumption of flowers and other ornamental

Table 7.1 Estimated farm size needed to reduce costs of production of rice

Rate of reduction (%)	Average costs (Y per 60 kilos)	Needed farm size (ha.)	
		2000	2010
10	18 330	1.29	1.03
20	16 294	2.35	1.83
30	14 257	5.28	3.92
40	12 220	19.31	12.50

Source: J. Chino, 1991, p. 142.

plants increased by as much as 637 per cent. More and more farmers, especially full-time operators, are moving away from growing government-controlled products to the production of uncontrolled ones. Even among rice growers there has been a shift in emphasis away from the production of directly controlled standard rice to indirectly controlled quality rice.[9] It is apparent that, in general, Japanese farmers are gradually becoming less reliant on government support programmes (Hemmi, 1990). In the author's opinion the reduction of government support and protection would encourage the acceleration of these socially beneficial shifts in the pattern of agricultural production in Japan which have already started.

On the basis of the recent developments and changes in the pattern of Japanese agriculture which have just been described and analysed, it is judged by the author that the 30 per cent reduction of domestic support and protection over 10 years, based upon 1986, as contained in Japan's offer of September 1990, could be absorbed without serious difficulty. But if a higher cut of as much as 40 per cent had to be conceded in the GATT negotiations, an ambitious programme of structural improvement would probably be entailed. The possibility of at least partially compensating farmers for the reduction of price support with direct income payments, preferably decoupled from current production, could also be considered.[10]

On the question of border protection, the Japanese government appears to be prepared to permit some rice imports, possibly amounting to between 300 000 and 500 000 tonnes per annum. According to a recent Japanese government projection, the total demand for rice is likely to decline from 10.65 million tonnes in 1987 to only 10.10 million tonnes in the year 2000 (Study Group on Japanese Agriculture in the 21st Century, 1990, p. 102). However, despite the projected decline in total demand there is thought to be room for an additional 300 000 tonnes of lower-priced rice for processing, and domestically produced rice displaced by the possible rice imports might fill this niche. But of course, rice imports would aggravate the problems of the Staple Food Control System.[11] If Japanese rice imports reached 1 million tonnes drastic reform of this system would be needed.

The above speculation concerning Japan's ability to absorb imported rice is based on the assumption that imports will be sold on the domestic market at the government-supported price. Any difference between the price of imported rice and the domestic selling price will be siphoned off by the government and be used in helping to finance the deficit on the Staple Food Control Account. However, if the difference between the domestic support price and the landed price of rice imports was to be tariffied, the present Staple Food Control System, which is designed to stabilise the internal price both for producers and consumers, would be unworkable. If the Japanese government wished to continue to insulate the domestic price of rice from external price movements a system of variable import levies and export subsidies similar to the present CAP system would need to be introduced.

The abandonment of quantitative import restrictions in favour of tariff protection could also have serious effects upon local agricultural economies. For example, the liberalisation of starch imports would adversely affect local agriculture in Southern Kyushu, as well as in some parts of Hokkaido. However, except for the case of wheat, the budget costs of compensating producers for their likely income losses might be acceptable. But the compensation of wheat producers would be much more difficult for reasons similar to those already discussed relating to rice.

Finally, there is the issue of food security. It is possible that Japan's attempt to have food security treated as a 'special case' in order to retain protection from food imports will be rejected by the remaining parties to the GATT negotiations. In that case there is no doubt that the immediate effect of any sudden cut in the domestic producer price of rice would be a quite significant reduction in the area under rice, with the supply shortfall being met by imports. However, it is also likely that, after a transitional period, the idled rice fields would be absorbed by more efficient and much enlarged rice farms with the ability to survive at the lower price. Rice fields are too wet to produce non-rice crops economically. Thus, it may reasonably be hypothesised that, in the long run, the volume of rice production in Japan will remain at approximately its present level. But that volume will be produced by a much smaller number of more efficient producers. This hypothesis is supported by the results of a recent statistical study of internationl trade in grains (Fujita, 1991), which assumes that international patterns of production and trade in grain are primarily determined by resource endowments and income levels, and that deviations from the 'normal' pattern of trade reflect government policy distortions . Compared with the average grain trade patterns of 20 developed countries and a total of 41 countries in the world, Japan deviates slightly from the average in the direction of 'excess' grain imports. This implies that Japan's present ratio of self-sufficiency in grain is primarily due not to government policy but to resource endowments.[12]

Agriculture is one sector of a very dynamic Japanese economy and is well able to adjust its structure to changing economic conditions. A government projection indicates a decline in the number of farmers and other farmworkers aged 60 or less, and working more than 150 days per year, from 2.06 million in 1988 to 1.05 million in the year 2000. It is inferred from this decline in the size of the full-time agricultural labour force that the minimum size of efficient rice farms will increase from 3 ha. (6.3 ha. in Hokkaido) in 1987 to 8 ha. (11 ha. in Hokkaido) in 2000 (Study Group on Japanese Agriculture in the 21st Century, 1990, pp. 115–6). The structure of Japanese agriculture is changing and will continue to change quite rapidly up to the end of the present century and beyond, whatever the outcome of the Uruguay Round.

7.6 POSTSCRIPT: NOTE ON DEVELOPMENTS FOLLOWING THE RELEASE OF THE DUNKEL TEXT ON AGRICULTURE[13]

The Draft Final Act was reported by various Japanese mass media immediately after its release in December 1992. Among various parts of the Draft the agricultural part attracted Japanese mass media most. There were 4 kinds of immediate Japanese reactions. First, agricultural people voiced their opinion strongly against the Text, and expressed their deep disappointment with proposed conversion of all non-tariff import barriers to bound tariffs (tariffication), especially with inclusion of the measures permitted under Article XI:2(c) into tariffication. Second, non-agricultural people, generally speaking, expressed a view favourable to the Text, and urged the government to accept the Draft Final Act. Their observation was that the Draft not only reflected a good compromise among various conflicting positions in the negotiating group, but also provided the last chance for success with the Round. Third, the government made its stance clear that the government could not accept the Text, and would continue attempting to persuade other governments, including the US government, to understand the Japanese position. The government also tried to calm down the Japanese fear of being isolated by making it clear that Canada, Israel, South Korea, Mexico and Switzerland too were rejecting tariffication. Fourth, Professor Yujiro Hayami and others drew attention to the proposed minimum rate of reduction of tariffs resulting from tariffication. The Text proposed that tariffs resulting from tariffication should be reduced at a minimum by 15 per cent in 6 years from 1993 to 1999, that is, 2.5 per cent a year. Hayami claims that Japanese rice could survive a tariff reduction of this magnitude since government support of the price of rice has been reduced by 2.5 per cent a year during the past 5 years (Policy Reform Forum, January 1992).

The last observation initiated a series of heated discussions on the effect of the tariffication, as specified in the Text, on Japanese rice production. For example, Professor Masaru Morishima and others published an article on 'The Effects of Rice Tariffication'. They argued that if all non-tariff rice protection measures were converted into tariffs the price would fall by as much as 51 per cent due to the abolition of rice production controls. Japanese imports of rice would be 3 070 000 tons in 1999. This represents 29 per cent of the rice consumed in the country (Rice Policy Study Group, February 1992, pp. 2–3). The discussion also considered the questions of whether tariffication and the reduction of tariffs as specified in the Text would necessitate abolition of the Food Control System.[14]

Leading cabinet ministers including Michio Watanabe, Vice Premier and Minister for Foreign Affairs, openly expressed the view that the government should work hard on adjusting Japan's stance to the new situation. Also that given a current tariff on rice of 600 per cent and the proposed rate of reduction of 15 per cent over 7 years, the resulting impact on the Japanese rice market would not be serious (*Asahi Shimbun*, 14 and 21 January 1992). Of course, officials of the Ministry of Agriculture, Forestry and Fisheries rejected this view immediately by claiming that such a high rate of tariff reduction on rice could not be permitted, and that under the present Food Control System the liberalisation of rice imports would result in a large increase in stock held by the System (*Asahi Shimbun*, 21 January 1992). These discussions continued until 13 April 1992, when the most recent meeting of the Trade Negotiations Committee of the GATT came to an end.

Another recent development is worthy of note. In June, 1992 the Japanese Ministry of Agriculture, Forestry and Fisheries published its New Food, Agriculture and Rural Programme (*Atarashii Shokuryo, Nogyo to Noson Seisaku Tenkai no Kihonteki Shiten to Hoko*). The programme aims to develop 10–20 ha. rice farms by 2000. It seems that the Ministry has decided to accelerate the process of increasing farm size.

8 The LDC Perspective

L. Alan Winters[1]

8.1 INTRODUCTION

This paper concerns the developing countries' interests in the liberalisation of world agricultural trade. The industrial countries' current
batteries of protectionism have a number of obvious consequences for
world agricultural markets, and thus for developing countries. It is
hoped that the Uruguay Round will reverse the tide of protectionism,
and so alleviate some of the harm done, but as I shall argue below not
every ostensibly successful conclusion to the Round will be beneficial in
these respects. Thus it is important for the developing countries how
the industrial countries address their own problems, and the prime
purpose of this paper is to identify ways in which developing countries
might influence the outcome of the GATT trade talks in agriculture in
the direction of mutual advantage.

8.2 INDUSTRIAL COUNTRY OBJECTIVES

Industrial countries claim a wide range of objectives for their
agricultural policies. The principal one, *de facto* if not *de jure*, is
simply to raise incomes in the farm sector, but this is buttressed by a
whole series of what I have termed SNOs – So-called Non-economic
Objectives – Winters (1990).[2] These include shifting the distribution of
income towards farmers, preserving the environment, maintaining
viable and vital rural communities, and guaranteeing secure and
stable food supplies.

These are legitimate objectives for governments, and indeed also
figure prominently in the developing countries' aims, but they are
neither non-economic nor greatly enhanced by current agricultural
policy. They are important, however, for two reasons; first, they
describe, at least to some extent, the genuine aspirations of, and
constraints on, industrial country negotiators – that is, they define part
of the pay-off matrix in the negotiating game. Second, they are
selectively appealed to by negotiators as *ad hoc* objections to various

reform proposals, and thus define issues to which developing country negotiators should have answers.[3]

In considering industrial countries' policies a genuine constraint must be added to the list of SNOs: the public budget. Budgetary pressure is the most obvious and, to date, most potent source of pressure for agricultural reform. Farm policy nearly bankrupted the European Community in the mid-1980s, but as soon as the pressure was relieved in 1988/9 by a mixture of small reductions in support and significant increases in world prices, Commissioner for Agriculture MacSharry started talking about increased farm aid. Similar pressures have been felt in Japan – for example, over the rice programme in the 1970s – and in the USA and EFTA countries. The budget is among the most transparent, and hence controversial, aspects of farm support, and for politicians and bureaucrats the trade-off between budgetary savings and economic efficiency is almost always settled in favour of the former.

Although they have eased recently, budgetary pressures are still likely to play an important role in the completion of the Uruguay Round talks. For example, the EC's Common Agricultural Policy has got a very bad press because of its voracious appetite for public money. It not only requires significant taxation to maintain, but, because the EC authorities are tightly constrained in the total resources that member-states make available to them, it effectively blocks EC initiatives in other dimensions. Thus nearly every Community policy statement promises/demands that agriculture's share of expenditure be scaled down in favour of the regional and structural funds – that is, general industrial subsidies. As the process of completing the internal market approaches its climax other claims on EC funds will become stronger – for example, for R & D, training, infra-structure, and so on – and a number of political compromises requiring public subvention will probably be necessary. Taming the agricultural monster will not only win friends directly, but will also allow the Commission more latitude elsewhere.

The budgetary dimension has also been important in the USA and will become increasingly so. The budget deficit is the largest single malaise in the US (and world?) macro-economic position, and yet the Administration has promised no new taxes and along with Congress regularly finds new and deserving causes for expenditure. As the need for macro-economic action increases, so will the political pressure to shuffle more of the costs of farm support on to consumers both at home and abroad.[4] The full liberalisation of agricultural trade is not a feasible outcome of the Round; budgetary considerations will make it more difficult to ensure that those farm policies which remain are economically efficient (that is, second-best). An additional tactical objective in industrial countries is the need to make agricultural support politically acceptable. High implicit taxes on consumers are only occasionally politically embarrassing, but stories of fraud, rotting stock-piles and huge payments to rich farmers appear to worry the politicians much more. The propensity of the Common Agricultural Policy to generate surpluses is thus an important issue bureaucratically; it figures strongly in the minds of EC negotiators, and pushes them further toward solutions based on managed supply.

8.3 DEVELOPING COUNTRY INTERESTS

The principal effect of industrial country protectionism is to reduce the world prices of most agricultural commodities. Precise figures are impossible to calculate, and the range of estimates is very large. At one extreme Tyers and Anderson (1988) suggest that OECD liberalisation would raise wheat prices by about 25 per cent, beef by 50 per cent and dairy by 100 per cent in 1995, while at the other extreme other commentators argue that liberalisation could even lower some world prices. The most likely outcome is that liberalisation will induce mild price increases. This would clearly have economic implications for developing countries, although not all in the same direction. Exporters of the temperate products whose prices are most affected by industrial liberalisation – for example, Argentina and Thailand – have strong and direct interests in the dismantling of protection; their revenues and income would increase significantly. On the other hand chronic food importers – for example, Bangladesh – would undoubtedly suffer. A third group of developing countries, however, falls into an intermediate category: at the current low prices for temperate goods they are net importers but would be self-sufficient or net exporters at free trade prices.[5]

Some commentators argue that developing countries as a group would gain from OECD liberalisation – eg. Loo and Tower (1988) – while others – e.g. Matthews (1985), Parikh *et al.* (1987) and Tyers and Anderson (1988) – are more pessimistic. At the most extreme, allowing time for liberalisation to occur, and extrapolating current trends until then, Tyers and Anderson estimate that the effect on developing countries as a whole of the liberalisation of temperate crops would be a net loss of welfare of $14 billion at 1995 quantities and prices. This is among the most pessimistic estimates, but in fact there are several reasons for questioning it now, and even more for questioning its relevance to the 1990s and 2000s.

First, the result is based on historical responses to changes in prices, estimated on data from an era when industrial country policy was increasingly interventionist and when developing country governments penalised and discouraged agriculture. If industrial country liberalisation were genuine, and bound under the GATT, developing country production responses could be stronger than past evidence suggests. For example, Maddala (1990) has shown that supply elasticities estimated without taking into consideration the disequilibrium effects of price supports and/or buffer stocks can be seriously biased downward. Moreover, if in addition, developing countries liberalised their own agricultural regimes, many of which entail taxing farmers, supply responses would be further enhanced. For several reasons, however, it would be possible to exaggerate the direct supply response of developing country farmers to liberalisation-induced price rises: for example, in the past developing countries have not generally allowed their agricultural policies to be strongly influenced by external factors, the price changes deriving from liberalisation are expected to be smaller than the secular declines over the 1980s; and a number of developing country import competing sectors are protected rather than taxed (Krueger, Schiff and Valdes, 1988). Thus, while increased developing country supply may be anticipated, it is less through the direct channels of price responses than through the indirect channels to which I now turn.

The second reason for expecting stronger liberalisation effects on output than Tyers and Anderson allow is that greater price stability and/or higher price levels plus a more secure atmosphere and policy environment for developing country agriculture would encourage infra-structural investment and research and development, none of which figure in existing models' supply functions. Third, Tyers and Anderson deal only with seven temperate product groups. Price rises in these would, at least to some extent, spill over into tropical product markets in which developing countries are already net exporters. Moreover, if agricultural liberalisation also included tropical products directly, its effects on developing country export earnings and income would be redoubled, as Valdes and Zeitz (1980) showed.

A fourth, and critical dimension, of the analysis concerns stability. Most industrial country policies are designed to insulate domestic consumers and producers from changes in world prices. The effect is to increase world price instability, because fewer countries adjust their supply and demand to any particular quantity shock, the effects of the shock on world prices is increased. It is common ground among commentators that industrial country liberalisation will reduce world price instability, and Tyers and Anderson suggest it might do so by factors of two for wheat and dairy and four for beef. Model-builders do not, however, allow instability to feed back into production decisions. In part this is justifiable, for farmers in both the developed and developing world are insulated from most instability. But insulation shifts the burden of risk on to the government and in developing countries such burdens are large relative to overall public sector resources.

For the governments of actual and potential agricultural exporters the assumption of increased risk means (a) that long-term insulation is much less feasible in developing than in industrial countries; (b) that agricultural shocks tend to destroy macro-economic equilibria when insulation breaks down and thus are shifted on to other sectors (especially their capital transactions), and (c) that, fearing such shocks, developing country governments tend to under-value agriculture. The last point represents perhaps the most pernicious effect of industrial country policies on developing countries. Industrial country interventions distort world markets and encourage (in their own eyes, oblige) developing country governments to intervene in their economies beyond desirable levels and far beyond their ability to do so effectively. The result is the promotion of industry above agriculture, the consequent distortion of normal patterns of savings, investment and development, and the extension of bureaucracy, inefficiency and, frequently, corruption. If only industrial countries would stabilise world markets by trading openly, developing countries would have much less to fear in liberalising their own agricultural sectors. This, in turn, would curtail the pressures to promote industry artificially and may, as a result, reduce some of the competitive pressure on industrial countries' manufacturers.

The effect of world price instability on food importers is more complex than that on exporters. It may well result in a higher degree of self-sufficiency for the sake of insulation. If this is achieved by subsidising agriculture or by taxing it less than other sectors, and if the subsidy–tax rate is maintained in the face of world liberalisation, locally produced quantities may increase with industrial country liberalisation, but this may not be welfare enhancing. If, on the other hand, importing governments respond to the improved world price stability by reducing their net support for agriculture, then local output may fall, but welfare is likely to increase. Krueger, Schiff and Valdes (1988) found a surprising amount of support for import competing agriculture in developing countries and so developing country liberalisation may tend to off-set some of the output-enhancing effects of industrial country liberalisation. This may – but need not – increase developing countries' overall import dependence.

A fifth problem for developing countries arising from industrial country intervention is that it replaces risk by uncertainty. Agricultural supply and demand are inherently variable, and while free world trade cushions and spreads the risks, the latter are, nonetheless, still there. However, they are risks in Knight's sense; they are amenable to probabilistic quantification and are thus at least partly addressable by contingent decision-making and at least partly ameliorated through the law of large numbers. Current intervention, on the other hand, gives rise essentially to Knightian uncertainty. It is just not predictable what trade policies Congress or a budget-stressed Administration will dream up, nor when; moreover, policy decisions tend to be long-lived rather than serially uncorrelated like weather shocks. Thus having politics rather than commerce in the driving seat changes the nature of the environment, making it much more dangerous for developing countries to rely on exports of agricultural products.

The previous paragraph suggested that developing countries are generally unable to influence the critical political decisions affecting their trade. This is more so in agriculture than in manufacturing, for the former has always lain farther beyond the grasp of the GATT and is cursed with remarkably powerful domestic lobbies in the industrial countries. Thus for so long as intervention is the rule, developing country producers can expect to do badly from it. The evolution of US sugar quotas or the existence of VRAs on EC imports of feed-grain substitutes are sufficient to prove the point.

The conclusion of this analysis is that developing countries have differing interests in the reform of industrial countries' agricultural policies. While some would suffer from a terms of trade deterioration, others would benefit from a movement towards free trade and the imposition of commercial discipline in the making of agricultural policy. For some, liberalisation will improve their food trade balance and for others worsen it, but there is no simple link between the quantities of trade and economic welfare: much depends on how those changes in quantities are brought about. I shall argue below that focusing on the amount and direction of trade as criteria of success – as negotiators are prone to do – would be most misleading for the longer run. The true requirement is for genuine liberalisation defined as the reduction of distortions, not market discipline defined by increases or reductions in trade. Indeed, I shall argue that, despite their possibly differing interests in liberalisation, developing countries should nearly all be able to agree to resist a 'quantity-based solution' to the agricultural trade problem.

8.4 THE BACKGROUND TO THE GENEVA ACCORD

As preparations were made for the Uruguay Round, agriculture figured low on the agenda of the EC, EFTA and Japan. Although the EC had some minor objectives in the agricultural talks it would probably have been happy to have seen the sector ignored altogether, and, when that proved impossible, sought to scale down expectations about what could be achieved. Thus the EC maintained – and ostensibly still maintains – that the basic structure of the Common Agricultural Policy is non-negotiable. The pressure to include meaningful talks on agriculture was of two sorts. The budgetary strain and popular derision of the CAP forced the EC's hand internally, while, rather less importantly, the USA and the Cairns Group exerted effective external pressure.

The creation of the Cairns Group of non-subsidising exporters has been one of the most interesting and innovative features of the Uruguay Round of negotiation relative to previous ones. It has pursued a single issue – agricultural reform – in a clear but politically realistic fashion: by building bridges between the two protagonists it has first kept the issue alive and second, at least to some extent, kept the broader economic issues – that is, liberalisation rather than market-sharing – on the table. Although it is widely recognised that any settlement in agriculture must meet the requirements of the EC and the USA, one still reads of there being three significant parties to the negotiations. The emergence of the Swiss formula in the Tokyo Round shows the possible role of an intermediary, and it is not difficult to envisage some advantage accruing to that party. While the presence of Canada and Australia increases the Cairns Group's political power, the Group's mere existence provides a useful reminder that, in major set-piece negotiations, developing countries are not altogether impotent. That said, however, developing countries and the Cairns Group are going to have to make concessions if they are to cash in their influence in any concrete way, and they are going to have to maintain a fairly unified stance.

The Punta del Esta Declaration of July 1986 dealt with agriculture very fulsomely. It talked of 'correcting and preventing distortions', 'greater liberalisation . . . of import access and export competition' and 'strengthened GATT rules and disciplines'; a far greater degree of commitment than any previous Round had made. On the other hand, the Declaration was sufficiently imprecise to permit widely varying interpretations of what its signatories were committed to and what means of solution were to be considered.

Much of 1987 and 1988 was taken up by the preparation of basic positions and the analysis of technical issues. Of the latter perhaps the most important was the advocacy of Producer Subsidy Equivalents (PSEs) as a measure or even as a target for the degree of protection. PSEs attempt to calculate the extent to which the full range of protective policies increase producers' incomes. They were originated by Josling (1973), have been calculated by OECD (OECD, 1987) and other official bodies, and championed as a negotiating tool by Tangermann, Josling and Pearson (1987).

Tangermann, Josling and Pearson suggest that PSEs could be both negotiated and bound. Bound PSEs, they say, would form a basis for an orderly reduction of protection which could not be undermined by the introduction of new policies, and which did not have to make explicit trade-offs between the very disparate forms of intervention used by different countries. Negotiations are not yet at the stage of quantitative offers and requests, but it looks increasingly unlikely that PSEs will be anything more than an information measure, if that. Their inability to separate the extent of trade distortion from the degree of income support, and their inevitable fluctuation when fixed internal prices are compared with variable world prices have been the principal stumbling blocks. On the former, the EC has been particularly anxious to obtain 'credit' for its recent quantity controls which, while boosting farm incomes, are claimed to reduce the disruption of world markets.[6] For this reason the EC invented its own measure – the support measurement unit (SMU) – which, among other things, allows credit for quantity controls. At the risk of caricature one could summarise the three major parties' basic objectives in their initial statements as follows:

EC: a completely regulated system of agricultural trade,
US: the complete abolition of import restrictions and subsidies affecting trade (the 'zero' option);
Cairns Group: the reduction of supports affecting trade, but with remaining discretion over (some) domestic policies.[7]

The Japanese and smaller European countries were also reluctant to liberalise – ostensibly because of their SNOs – and certain developing countries (including some Cairns Group members) also put forward positions of varying liberality.

During 1988 the US and the EC showed little sign of compromise and took part in an acrimonious debate terming each others' proposals as 'disappointing' and 'unrealistic'. Fundamentally the question was about whether the basic structure of the CAP was negotiable. The EC had maintained ever since the Kennedy Round that it was not, while the US insisted that it should be and began to argue that without genuine agricultural reform (at that time defined as the USA's 'zero' option) the whole Round would fail.

With such gaps to span, it is hardly surprising that the Montreal mid-term talks of December 1988 foundered over agriculture. However, within days of the break-down, signs of a possible conciliation were evident. The break-down was presented as a means of increasing the time for consultations, contingent progress in other areas was recognised as such, and bilateral US–EC meetings occurred once the two administrations had changed. At a more fundamental level, it became clear that Congress was not wholly behind the US 'zero' option. This eased the passage of negotiation towards the Geneva Accord, although in the long run the active interest of Congress in negotiations is hardly a recipe for agricultural liberalisation. By March 1989 the US had moderated its position a little – talking of 'ratcheting down' farm policy rather than abolition – but the EC was still inflexible. Indeed the EC argued that far from further reform of the CAP, the modifications made since 1984 should attract credit in the negotiations – that is, be reciprocated by other parties over and above concessions made to win any further EC reforms. The Cairns Group, however, threatened that they would abandon the Round if the US and EC could not reach agreement over a text on agriculture. This was a more realistic threat than the earlier US insistence that the zero option was the *sine qua non* of the Round, quite simply because agriculture figures more prominently in the Cairn's Group's objective function than the USA's. Thus it probably helped to create an atmosphere in which settlement was possible. This again illustrates the role that can be played by an intermediary committed to obtaining a solution.

With this background, the Secretary General of the GATT, Arthur Dunkel, presented his first compromise document. This was not acceptable itself but provided a focus for negotiations. The latter mostly had the effect of weakening the document's reform content by such means as introducing a studious imprecision about base-years from which to measure reforms.

The final agreement emerged a week later with the following *long term* principal conditions:

1. 'progressive substantial reductions' in agricultural support, defined to be all measures bearing directly and indirectly on import access and export competitiveness, and expressly including QRs, tariffs, internal and export subsidies, and export restrictions;
2. special treatment for developing countries, including 'taking into account'. any negative effects of reform on food importers;
3. taking account of non-trade objectives (basically SNOs);
4. a timetable in which reform plans were to be presented by the end of 1989 and the first step of reform executed in 1991. The plans were to cover *inter alia* the application of aggregate measures of support, the application of GATT rules, tariffication and decoupling; and
5. the reform programme to be subject to multilateral surveillance.

The *short-term* dimensions were said at the time to have been the more contentious to negotiate, but having once been agreed they have largely dropped from sight. They included:

6. a freeze on price support levels and import restrictions, but not on those changes already negotiated; price support levels were to be defined in national currency (ECU in the EC) with a 1989 base, while access was to be assessed on the average of 1987 and 1988, with reductions defined either commodity-by-commodity or on an AMS (aggregate measure of support);
7. plans for reductions in support aid and improvements in access to be presented to the Agriculture Negotiating Group by October 1989, with six monthly reports on progress starting in December 1989;

8. exemption for developing countries; and
9. a waiver from the provisions under 'exceptional circumstances'.

The short-term requirements did not require much adjustment of the major parties. Using the current year as the base from which to measure support 'validates' the US's recent relaxation of set-aside and allows her to claim credit for a future tightening of limits to their former levels; export subsidies figure in the text of the accord but no mechanism for measuring or freezing them is recorded; there are no targets for short-term de-escalation, so that existing EC plans to reduce cereals excess production through the stabiliser will receive negotiating credit; and the calculation of support prices in ECU will disguise the protection inherent in the EC's green money system.[8] The Cairns Group claimed that the short-term agreement represented a down payment on liberalisation. In truth, however, it was not much more than a means of keeping agricultural bush-fires under control while the rest of the Round proceeded, as the lack of action since March 1989 has confirmed.

The long-term agreements also fall short of the aspirations voiced at the beginning of the Round. For example, some of the countries of EFTA publicly registered their misgivings about the accord. The significance of this is not yet clear, but given that EFTA's support might be important for US or EC objectives over other elements of the Uruguay Round, and particularly given the current explorations of further EC and EFTA integration in the context of 1992 and Common European Economic Space, EFTA objections on agriculture might turn out to be quite important.

Prima facie the outcome of the interim talks appeared very close to the EC's original objectives. The basic mechanisms of the CAP were unchallenged, the EC had to make few short-term concessions beyond the reductions in support mandated by its own budgetary situation, and there was an implicit acceptance that supply management is acceptable (that is, that it earns credit). The US effectively surrendered its zero option − encouraged by Congress and the farm lobby − and little remained of the Cairns Group proposals for de-escalation. Nevertheless, there were a few grains of comfort, and the challenge now is to bolster the US and Cairns Group positions sufficiently to allow them to impose some rationality on the Europeans (EC and EFTA) and the Japanese. It will require considerable political skill and compromise by the developing countries to cement the liberal coalition, not only against international market managers but also against the US farm lobby.

8.5   AFTER GENEVA

The Geneva Accord hardly represents a pinnacle of liberal trading nor even of short-term agricultural de-escalation. It did, however, contain a few grains of hope, such as a commitment to progressive substantial reductions in the internal support and protection of agriculture, and a commitment to the surveillance of agricultural policy under the GATT. Moreover, by allowing a further nine months for the preparation of final positions it permitted further debate both within and between contracting parties.

It is not yet clear how much progress has been made towards a final agreement. As Tangermann (1990) has noted, in some respects the final position papers presented late in 1989 retreated from the Geneva Accord, rather than extended it. In other respects, however, they were sufficiently vague and confusing to allow more optimistic commentators, such as Tangermann himself, at least to hope for a satisfactory outcome. Zero options can no longer be seriously contemplated, but Tangermann argues that the EC position – the key one – leaves scope for significant liberalisation in the areas of market access, export subsidies and domestic support. He bases his hope on the studied imprecision of the EC text, which while hawkish in tone leaves some doors ajar. I take a slightly less bullish view of the text, but it is clear that the EC Commission, and still more the Council of Ministers, is divided on the stance to take. Such division makes the final outcome impossible to predict – it could, for instance, easily depend on the compromises struck over non-GATT issues such as the treatment of Eastern European agricultural sales – but the uncertainty also allows outside parties a degree of influence. The remainder of this chapter discusses how developing countries might seek to influence the US–EC–Cairns negotiations in their favour or at least away from their detriment. The US proposals are not of unalloyed benefit to the developing world, but in their present form they are a substantial step in the right direction. Developing country negotiators then will generally need to find ways of supporting the US and Cairns Group positions against the pressures from the European (EC and EFTA), the Japanese and the (heavily lobbied) US Congress. This section considers some of the issues arising from the final position papers, although it does not go through them and their reception blow-by-blow; the next section notes some potential pitfalls in the negotiations.

One of the most promising routes to trade liberalisation in agriculture is so-called tariffication followed by negotiated tariff reductions. Tariffication has been suggested by several commentators in the past – for example, Zeitz and Valdes (1988) and the Dutch Minister of Agriculture (see *Agra Europe*, 18/11/88) – but was not seriously considered in the negotiations prior to Geneva. It gets only a subsidiary mention in the Accord and at that stage was thought by many commentators to be dead. In mid-July, however, the USA revived the issue as a practical approach to the relaxation of import–access restrictions. The US proposed (a) that a base level of imports should be subject only to bound tariffs, (b) that imports above the base level should be subject to additional extraordinary tariffs, and (c) that over the course of ten years the base level of imports should expand and the extraordinary tariff fall until all trade faced only the bound tariff. The US suggested that actual 1990 imports and nominal protection co-efficients would provide suitable definitions of base imports and the extraordinary tariff respectively, but these aspects remained negotiable.

The tariffication of barriers to agricultural imports would have several advantages: transparency (domestic and international), restored sensitivity of domestic supply and demand to market signals, and simplicity of administration. The first two of these advantages cause difficulties for the EC given its explicit and implicit objectives, but, significantly, the EC has not entirely ruled out tariffication. The EC's final position paper suggested that border protection might comprise both a fixed component (a tariff) and a variable component adjusted to allow for exchange rate changes and developments in world prices. If the variable component precisely off-sets external shocks, we are effectively back with variable levies and tariffication is dead, but to the extent that the off-set is incomplete, the world market will influence internal agricultural conditions. Tangermann (1990) notes that the EC document does not explicitly specify complete offset and argues that if the other negotiating parties exploit that fact, the EC may make concessions, at least so far as the transmission of world prices is concerned. Other commentators, on the other hand, feel that completeness was implicit (for example, *Agra Europe*, 2/2/90) although of course that may change with pressures.

The simplicity of administration will also make obstacles for reform. All industrial countries have large agricultural bureaucracies to administer the present detailed market regulations. Tariffication would threaten some bureaucratic jobs directly and would serve warning on others, because it will be more difficult to defend detailed internal regulation in the face of a market-driven international trade sector. Moreover, not only will the bureaucracies themselves mistrust tariffication, but so too will farm groups, whose lobbying power is at least partly related to the size and power of their related bureaucracies. Thus if tariffication is to succeed it must be pursued at the political level, or at least at the level of 'general' ministries such as the Ministries of Finance and Foreign Affairs. This, in turn, suggests that tariffication will be most likely to be taken seriously during the later stages of the negotiations, when cross-sectoral deals are being struck and governments are assessing their attitudes to the Round as a whole.

A fourth advantage frequently claimed for tariffication is that precedents and well-tried procedures exist for the subsequent negotiation of tariffs. This is true, but it is not guaranteed that the trick which unlocked industrial tariffs in the 1950s and 1960s will work on effectively for agriculture in the 1990s. The key to the GATT's early success was its members' political acceptance of the need for liberalisation coupled with the use of reciprocity to hitch the mercantilist tractor to the free-traders' wagon. The driving force of real-world trade policy is almost invariably mercantilist – the desire to increase sales.[9] By providing a means whereby exporters' aspirations could match or overcome import-competing sectors' apprehensions, the GATT allowed governments to put together sufficient coalitions for liberalisation. Agriculture is potentially more difficult than this. First, the desire for liberalisation is not entirely certain and, second, the scope for reciprocity within agriculture is severely limited. Other than the diffuse general-equilibrium effects, known to economists but apparently to no-one else, there are virtually no producer groups in Japan or Europe who would gain from agricultural liberalisation. Thus there is no well-focused opposition to the farm-lobby's resistance to change. Such opposition will emerge only if agriculture is linked to other issues which, while possible, is not generally seen as part of tariffication.

Even if tariffication does not lead to an immediate reduction in protection, however, it would still be desirable in stabilising world markets by allowing market signals to permeate domestic agricultural decision-making. It would be even more desirable if it were coupled with a ban on export subsidies, as Zeitz and Valdes (1988) suggest, for trade reversal due to policy intervention would then be virtually impossible.[10]

This analysis has several implications for the way in which developing countries should approach tariffication. First, since it is so clearly in their interests – especially with respect to stabilising world markets – they should promote it, and be willing to undertake tariffication themselves. Second, the principle is more important than the numbers involved. It would be unwise to allow negotiations to become stuck on precise numbers before the principle is agreed. Third, given that tariffication is on the agenda, work should start on calculating suitable levels for base imports and extraordinary tariff rates and for the rate of relaxation, in order that the proposal is not stymied by the apparent practical difficulties of implementation.[11] Finally, developing countries must explore linkages between tariffication and non-agricultural issues in order to be able to take advantage of late-stage cross-issue negotiation at senior ministerial levels.

The US position paper also made outline proposals for liberalising other elements of agricultural policy. It proposed a complete ban on export subsidies and export restrictions and a three-fold classification of internal measures. The first group of measures comprises production and price-based policies (including some marketing policies) which should be phased out over ten years. The second group comprises 'permitted' policies which include, *inter alia*, *bona fide* food aid, income support and environmental policies. The third, intermediate, group of policies would be defined as a residual and would include policies such as certain uniform input subsidies which have some, but not direct or strong, impacts on international trade. The US proposes that these be subject to 'discipline' through the binding and negotiated reduction of an aggregate measure of support. Given that the 'discipline' group excludes the measures that cause the most difficulty in defining an AMS, for example, quotas, set-asides and environmental programmes, settling an appropriate measure for this limited purpose should not be too difficult.

It is interesting that in one respect the US proposal for this intermediate category of measures follows traditional GATT practice. Having defined the sets of measures which are either definitely legal or definitely illegal, the proposal requires that remaining policies should be subject to discipline 'to prevent their use in ways that would nullify or impair concessions'. This is the wording of the existing Article XXIII of the GATT. In the absence of a satisfactory list of transgressions, the GATT is enforced by (a) the explicit recognition of each contracting party's right to the benefits stemming from the implementation of the GATT by other contracting parties; and by (b) the rights of any party to complain against any act or situation which interferes with the delivery of those benefits regardless of whether that act or situation figures at all in GATT regulations. Thus it is the effects of the GATT, not the procedures of trade policy, that are protected. This formula postpones the full elaboration of GATT responsibilities until concrete cases arise, and in so doing helps the process of negotiation and initial implementation. It probably offers the best hope of alleviating the suspicions surrounding and ambiguities inherent in industrial countries' agricultural policy sufficiently to allow an agreement to be struck. Moreover, providing that not too many policies fall into the intermediate category, and that negotiations on GATT disciplines (in the FOGS Group) allow confidence in future rulings, the use of this traditional approach may well represent a major step towards liberalisation.

The US proposal was acceptable to the EC but it may turn out to contain enough scope to allow negotiation. Tangermann (1990) again sees a ray of compromise in the EC paper in this direction, but it is buried very deep. If the EC does not reject the suggestions out of hand, and thus risk the opprobium of sabotaging the Round, it may seek to shift policies from the 'phasing-out' to the 'discipline' group and from there to the 'legitimate' group. Such a procedure has clear political attractions – the US 'wills' the procedural points but concedes enough 'substantive' ones to the EC to allow the latter to maintain its own 'honour'. If the process gets out of hand, however, it also has the potential to legitimise much agricultural protection for the next several decades. Thus developing countries should seek to ensure that not too much redefinition of policies occurs, and in particular that a market-based, as opposed to a quantity-based, outcome is achieved.

Although it concedes the need for some measure-specific bindings, the EC paper foresees a more prominent role for aggregate measures of support than does the US, proposing that they be used to provide a central means of disciplining agricultural policy. Through its support measurement unit (SMU) the EC seeks to define the AMS in a fashion that (arguably) more closely reflects policies' impacts on the world market (the discipline motive) and is more amenable to direct policy control (the management of markets objective). The EC's SMU differs from the PSE in making allowance for quantity-reducing measures such as quotas, and also for fluctuations in exchange rates and world prices. The EC also proposed that changes in AMSs be measured from a 1986 base, which would grant it credit for its more recent reductions in support. Finally, the EC suggested, in a tortuous piece of prose, that the price from which SMUs were measured might be adjusted periodically, and that the degree of reduction in support might depend on world price developments, that is, the same world price changes might be (partially) transmitted to the domestic economy. However, the political nature of the EC's periodic readjustments of its own green currency rates (which are somewhat similar in concept to the SMU references prices) hardly bodes well for future SMU adjustments. Moreover, while the transmission of world agricultural forces appears acceptable to the EC, that of exchange rate changes seems quite unacceptable.

If AMSs are to be an important part of the final outcome, as opposed to a measure of residual policy effects as in the US proposal, it is highly desirable that PSEs are favoured over SMUs. If the EC is allowed to apply SMUs it will receive credit for existing and future quantity-controls, which can only encourage the sort of implicitly market-sharing arrangements that the Community so earnestly desires. Such market-sharing will almost inevitably operate in favour of the major parties. It will prevent developing countries from expanding their market shares of industrial country markets, for as they come forward to do so individually they will be picked off one by one, while on the other hand, individual quotas may well still be subject to unilateral or bilateral (US/EC) adjustment, just as the sugar or butter restrictions are dealt with, at present.

Even, putting their political weakness aside, developing countries would suffer from a regime of quantitative restrictions because it would almost inevitably worsen market instability. Coupled with market-sharing would be fixed internal prices in the industrial world, rigid patterns of production, and, most probably, rigidities in world trade patterns. These would concentrate the effects of natural supply shocks on to residual world markets on which developing countries will find themselves dependent for their marginal trade. Finally, quantitative constraints are designed to raise prices, without allowing the quantities supplied to follow suit. If ever developing country net exporters became part of a 'market stabilisation' scheme they would find themselves prevented from increasing their sales while net importers would still face higher prices than presently. Thus developing countries should all be able to agree to resist quantitative market-sharing arrangements.

Certain developing countries have expressed reservations about the PSE measure, fearing both its complexity and its inability to take account of their SNOs [Runge and Stanton, 1988). Such objections apply to any mechanical aggregate measure, and so as a matter of tactics if not of principle, developing countries should throw their weight behind PSEs in any negotiation of AMSs. If the GATT surveillance of agriculture is to achieve anything it must have clear summaries of the degree of protection with which both to confront the negotiating parties and to alert public and political opinion to the continuing distortions of trade. Although the calculation of PSEs is complex (even contentious), their message is clear: should we be boosting farmers' incomes by x per cent? The importance of these points is illustrated by the EC's cereals policy during the eighties. While the EC was pursuing a 'prudent' price policy (since 1981) and a reform package (1985–6), the PSE on wheat doubled from 28 per cent to 58 per cent. If countries can negotiate using no more than their own rhetoric, international surveillance will be a sham.

An attractive goal of the Round would have been to bring agriculture back into the (strengthened) GATT by making it subject to clauses XI and XVI banning quantitative import restrictions and export subsidies. For so long as agriculture remains special it will be difficult to liberalise. For this reason it is important that negotiations ultimately deal directly with policy instruments rather than just with PSEs or other aggregate measures. Thus while AMS may be used to monitor progress and possibly to measure degrees of reciprocity, in the end commitments will have to be written on specific policies. Moreover, while formulae may be used to define the skeleton of a solution, the final package will require considerable amounts of commodity-specific negotiation. It is important for developing countries, therefore, to consider the scope they have for easing the process of measure-specific negotiations.

In Winters (1987a) I argued that developing countries may have more influence in bi-lateral negotiations than they realise, for they maintain negotiable QRs on a large number of items for which the main industrial countries were principal suppliers. Indeed I identified significant scope for industrial-developing country negotiations over QRs on a principal–supplier basis. Returning to that exercise, it is plain that a fair number of the developing country QRs are in the agriculture and food sectors, which suggests that even within the Agriculture Negotiating Group developing countries have something to offer.[12] Moreover, Finger's (1979) analysis suggests that countries offering reciprocal concessions are in a far stronger position to influence the outcome of negotiations than are those which just sit by and complain.

8.6 PITFALLS IN NEGOTIATIONS

The Uruguay Round is an immensely complex set of negotiations. At the same time as grand concepts such as general liberalisation, tariffication and aggregate measures of support are being discussed work proceeds on detailed matters such as the precise specification of particular policy instruments and the definition of certain classes of goods. At an intermediate level lie a series of technical economic issues which, while not part of the concept of liberalisation, are part of its implementation, and which, if they are not appropriately handled, have the power to subvert and undermine the process of agricultural de-escalation. This section briefly discusses four such issues and suggests how they may be circumvented. It observes the old maxim that 'forewarned is forearmed' and attempts to alert economists on developing countries' negotiating teams to the dangers that may await them during negotiations.

Exchange rate variability poses problems for negotiators in defining the level of support for an agricultural product if a fixed internal price is compared with a variable world price. This difficulty led the EC to propose that, for the purposes of calculating support measures, reference prices should be fixed in terms of local currencies; that is, for each producer country, protection should be measured relative to the domestic-currency equivalent of internationally agreed prices with the conversion from the latter to the former made at a single historical exchange rate rather than at the current market rate. Thus 'reference prices' will not reflect subsequent changes in exchange rates, so that as, say, the ECU appreciated, the EC's internal ECU price of imported agricultural goods would remain fixed while the prices of other EC tradeable goods fell. The resulting distortions between each country's internal prices for agricultural and other tradeable goods are obvious and unavoidable, and the scope for political chicanery in the periodic re-negotiations to reset reference prices or reference exchange rates is evident. The parallels with the EC's complex green-currency system are close, and just as that system is manipulated for protective purposes, so too could be the proposed international system. Moreover, fixing local currency prices, as the EC proposal implies, would perpetuate current insulation policies and the world price instability they engender. As was noted above, there are signs of EC movement over fixing the world price components of the reference price (that is, world price changes may percolate through to the domestic economy), but no such concession appears likely on exchange rates.

A different response to exchange-rate fluctuations has been the argument that, since exchange rate movements can swamp all but the largest sector-specific interventions, it is more important to get the world monetary system right than to worry about trade policy. A similar impression might be gained from a superficial reading of some of Schuh's writing (that is, 1988) on the macro economic influences on farming; viz, until we have macroeconomic stability, farm policy is of second-order importance.[13] These arguments are both misleading and distracting. Trade policy affects the relationships between different tradeable goods, and artificial wedges between marginal rates of transformation between different tradeables are almost always harmful. The exchange rate and macroeconomic variables, on the other hand, affect trade-offs between tradeable and non-tradeable goods or between goods and money, and while distortions in these links may be harmful they are largely independent of the trade policy issue. Moreover, macroeconomic conditions change rapidly, so that a trade distortion designed (or permitted) as an off-set to a macroeconomic problem in one year would very probably be inappropriate to macro conditions a few years later. Thus the reduction or removal of distortionary trade policy will be beneficial in the long run almost regardless of what happens macroeconomically, and any claim to the contrary is probably best seen as obstructionism.

A second potential stumbling block is *preferential trading arrangements*. An apparent concession by the US and EC would be to allow the Cairns Group and other developing countries a greater share of their markets while maintaining their basic protective structures in place. Such an offer might seem attractive to the parties concerned, but it would not generate the market shares available under liberal trade and would, anyway, set an extremely dangerous precedent for future trading relations. First, it would further enforce the mercantilist notion of trading efficiency and even if the initial allocations were welfare-improving in increasing the relative shares of efficient producers, the rigidities so introduced would almost guarantee that distortions increased in later years. Second, because only existing producers would be considered in the negotiations, the outcome would inevitably favour them (including those in the US and EC) over those who are merely potentially efficient. Third, the rent transferred to developing countries by such a means would be limited. Fourth, increased rents would accumulate to existing producers in the developing countries, or would entail increased government intervention if they were to be distributed in some other way; rents generated in such a fashion would have quite different development implications from those associated with increased export earnings deriving from increased supply at world prices. Fifth, preferential access for certain producers at given prices has insulation effects and thus increases price variability in the unrestricted residual world market; moreover, unless in return for increased market access the US and EC reduced their output, the residual world price would inevitably be reduced by such a scheme. Finally, the quotas agreed in 1990 could not be guaranteed for future years.

The disadvantages of such preference schemes are manifest first in the General System of Preferences (see, for example, Langhammer and Sapir, 1988) and second in the history of world sugar trade. Both the US and the EC grant preferential market access to certain developing sugar producers. The US has reduced its quotas steadily since the mid-1970s; and, although the EC has maintained its quotas, they are very unevenly distributed and at least to some extend accrue to countries which have no natural advantages in sugar production. Much of the revenue-enhancing effect of preferential quotas, even for the few lucky countries holding significant quotas, is undermined by the reductions in the residual world price that the quotas induce by increasing world supply and by the variability in world prices that market rigidities entail.

None of the documents pertaining to the Uruguay Round suggests that preferential arrangements are being considered, but that does not mean that they will not figure at a later stage. Preferential market access can be more attractive than free trade to the favoured producers, and such schemes have the negotiating advantage of internalising nearly all the gain. That is, all the 'cost' to the EC or US of increasing imports through a preferential quota can be presented as a benefit (increased exports) to particular and identifiable negotiating partners. These partners can then be expected to offer concessions in return – in this case, to back the final mercantilist market-sharing package. This is in direct contrast to genuine market liberalisation in which, although it is plain that efficient suppliers as a whole can gain, it is not clear *ex ante* which among them will. Thus it is much more difficult to extract reciprocal concessions and build coalitions for genuine liberalisation than for market-sharing arrangements. Put crudely, the negotiators from the major markets can bribe certain producers to connive with them by offering fat pickings from their consumers' pockets. In the face of deadlock, and particularly if the rest of the Round comes to depend on agriculture, the political attractions of preferential access schemes may become very strong.

Ultimately very few if any developing countries would gain from preferential trading, but avoiding it will require a high degree of co-ordination and co-operation. In this regard, groups such as the Cairns

Group and the Group of 77 may be important, as will the GATT
Secretariat, who should make it clear that preferential access agreements will not be acceptable solutions to the issue.

A third distraction is *special and differential treatment*. This has
become something of an icon for developing country negotiators, but it
serves their interests very poorly. Not only is their own protection
almost always economically harmful, but insisting on maintaining it
amounts to non-reciprocity and so emasculates developing countries in
negotiation: because they are offering so little, they are offered so little.
Finger (1979) shows the advantages accruing to developing countries of
full participation in the Kennedy Round, and Winters (1987a) shows
that developing countries have 'concessions' to offer, even in bi-lateral
principal–supplier negotiations and even in agriculture. If developing
countries wish to break down the restrictions of US, Japanese and
European agricultural policies they have to be prepared to make
concessions in their own policies. Otherwise reluctant liberalisers,
especially within the EC, will be able to shelter behind the excuse of
reciprocity.

A more serious issue which may yet serve to subvert the process of
negotiating agricultural reform is the position of the major *developing
country importers of food*. According to most analyses OECD
countries' farm policies have lowered the world prices of temperate
products, and through their substitution effects, also those of tropical
products; these reductions are clearly beneficial to net importers. I have
argued above that these benefits can easily be exaggerated, especially in
the medium to long run, but that some of the world's poorest countries
are vulnerable is undeniable. So far as this chapter is concerned,
however, the issue is less whether any countries will actually suffer,
than how to prevent the fear that they may from being used as an
excuse for no action.

First, the overall size of the problem must be put in perspective. The
OECD model (OECD, 1989) suggests that liberalisation would reduce
grain prices, and Loo and Tower (1988) find developing countries
gaining from industrial country liberalisation. Even Tyers and Anderson (1988), who overstate the problem, find net benefits from OECD
liberalisation of $20 billion for industrial countries offset by net costs of
only $2 billion for developing countries at 1980–2 prices and quantities,
and figures of $51 billion and $14 billion respectively at projected 1995
values. Thus there is plenty of net benefit to go round. This observation
amounts to saying that current agricultural policies are an appallingly
inefficient way of supporting developing country food imports.

The obvious way of addressing the distributional consequences of agricultural reform is through increased aid flows. These should come from the beneficiaries of any reform – consumers in the OECD countries and producers in the potential exporting countries like the Cairns Group. A useful way of easing the path of the negotiations would be for the latter group of countries to pledge, say 5 per cent, of their export earnings to aid very poor food importers.[14] For the OECD countries the politics are more complex, for, especially among agricultural negotiators, they perceive themselves as already making major sacrifices by contemplating reform: thus the attractions of making additional fiscal transfers are not overwhelming. First, this is a matter of presentation – the huge potential consumer benefits must be publicised. Second, during the transitional period of any reform, OECD countries are still going to be taxing consumers quite heavily. A commitment to funnelling, say, 2 per cent, of this implicit or explicit tax to food importers would be feasible.[15] As reform proceeded the amount of transfer would decline; this would be attractive politically and would marginally aid the process of reform. It would also perhaps focus attention in recipient countries on the need to address long-term food requirements independently of aid, and, to the extent that aid is needed for longer periods, the proposal above would at least allow time for its gradual introduction into the general tax base.

Two further elements would ease the apparent burden of increased aid to OECD countries. First, the increases in world food prices would increase the incentives for research and development applicable to production outside the protected OECD markets. Much of this is conducted inside OECD, so a modest increase in support for it would be a (politically acceptable) internal transfer rather than an external one. Second, food and other aid flows are currently distributed in a perverse and inefficient fashion. Large amounts of aid go to relatively well-off middle-income countries (for example, Egypt) while the very poor receive little. Rationalisation of these flows would further reduce the burden of any increment required as the result of agricultural reform.

A major problem of bi-lateral aid flows is their use for political rather than economic purposes. This is reflected both in their direction (see the comments above) and, frequently, their nature. For example, food aid flows owe more to donors' needs to find outlets for surpluses than to recipients' needs. For this reason, the problems faced by the very poor food importers should be addressed on a multi-lateral basis with revenue commitments made to an aid institution and disbursement made quite independently of political objectives. While the process of establishing such an institution would be a GATT one (in collaboration with development organisations such as UNCTAD and the World Bank), the natural location for it would probably be UNCTAD. Moreover, it is important to note that it would be a temporary body established as part of the transitional arrangements of the Uruguay Round, and would cease to exist when those arrangements were complete.

To be effective the transitional aid would need to be directed carefully within recipient countries. Cheap food benefits the urban poor at the expense of the rural poor and it would be necessary to ensure that any reverses were off-set in the right quarter. This difficulty does not appear to be insurmountable, however, for the urban sections of society are frequently more articulate and more easily reached than are rural communities. The problem will be to prevent aid from being captured by the middle-classes. As with so much that has gone before in this chapter, however, the urban poor are not a reason for preventing liberalisation: any claim to the contrary should be met by the demonstration that they may be protected while still leaving positive benefits for other sections of society.

8.7 CONCLUSIONS

The developing countries are not major players in the Uruguay Round agriculture negotiations. They are nonetheless seriously affected by the talks' outcome and hence have an interest in exerting as much constructive influence as possible. This paper highlights a number of issues which developing country negotiators should consider in formulating their position over the critical period of the next year.

- Developing countries will reap few benefits from a 'quantitative solution' to world agricultural problems. Quantity controls would raise prices, offer little scope for increased exports and exacerbate market instability.
- Tariffication will address developing countries' interests in stabilising world prices.
- Aggregate measures of support will not define liberalisation but may help to measure it; the PSEs is preferable to the SMU.
- Developing countries should negotiate fully on agriculture as on other issues. Special and differential treatment promises very few

direct economic benefits and amounts to little more than non-participation in negotiation.

- World food prices may rise slightly with liberalisation – it is difficult to tell by how much – but the correct response to any resulting hardship is aid and adjustment, not blocking liberalisation.

9 The Food Industry Perspective

Simon Harris[1]

Since the publication of the draft 'Final Act' of the Uruguay Round of the GATT negotiations in December 1991 (GATT, 1991), the Round's likely final shape has been clear, on the basis that agreement is ultimately reached. As a consequence, it has been possible to start drawing up a provisional assessment of how far the food industry's aims have been met in the Round. The assessment had to remain provisional as the text of the agricultural part of the Final Act had not been finalised at the time of writing (November 1992): important participants, including the European Community (the EC) and Japan had not accepted it in full.

Again the detailed negotiations on the participants' Commitment Schedules had yet to occur. As the old saying has it: 'The Devil lies in the Detail'. Only when the details have finally been established will a full assessment be possible.

9.1 THE SIGNIFICANCE OF THE FOOD INDUSTRY

While a principal focus of attention in the Uruguay Round was agriculture, it should be recognised that the vast majority of agricultural production in the developed world has to be processed by food manufacturers before it can be sold to the final consumer. For example, it has been estimated (Slater, 1988) that in the UK 'nearly 80 per cent of farm (food) output is processed by domestic food manufacturers'. This means that the linkages between agriculture and food manufacturing are extremely close, with food manufacturers being heavily dependent on agricultural producers for their principal raw materials. Agricultural producers are equally dependant on food manufacturers, however, to transform their production into forms desired by the final consumer.

Yet – and this will be a recurring theme of this chapter – attention in the GATT negotiations has reflected the biases in domestic policy and government institutions (Harris, 1989) with attention focused on agriculture and not the food industry, without whom agricultural production would be unusable by modern consumers.

Although this focus reflects traditional preoccupations, it ignores the increasing significance of food manufacturing. Estimates prepared for the EC food and drink industry representative organisation in Brussels – the Confederation des Industries Agro-Alimentaires de la CEE (CIAA) – and cited in a submission to the Community's GATT negotiators (CIAA, 1988) suggest that food and drink manufacturing in the European Community directly employs some 2.6 million people and that some ten million people are dependant, directly or indirectly, on the industry. In terms of gross output, food and drink manufacturing is the EC's largest industry, accounting for 15 per cent of total industrial value added (Eurostat, 1992). Estimates prepared for the European Parliament (cited by Marsh, 1991) suggest that the food sector 'accounts for some 10 per cent of its GDP and for 20 per cent of its work force'.

It is important to note also that over time, as agriculture declines in significance in terms of both employment and as a share of GDP, food and drink manufacture rises in importance as consumers demand a higher processing element in their food to match modern life styles. Thus Slater (1988) has estimated that in 1985 agriculture's contribution to British GDP at 1.8 per cent was less than a third of the total of agriculture and food taken together, at 9.1 per cent. This is at the opposite end of the spectrum to a country like Greece where, in 1979, agriculture accounted for four fifths of the total value added of agriculture and food taken together (Harris, 1989).

Again, in terms of its significance in international trade, the food and drink industry is the EC's fifth largest exporter. It consistently runs a surplus on its trade with the rest of the world. International trade is of major significance to the EC food industry, with third country exports accounting for 6 per cent of turnover, equivalent to the industry's net profit margin.

A major contrast with agriculture lies in the nature of the products exported. Agricultural exports tend to be of bulk commodities, which can only be sold on over-supplied world markets with large export subsidies – in GATT parlance. (In Community parlance these are referred to as export restitutions or refunds.) In contrast, food industry exports are of high value added products, often branded, which are marketed. Thus, manufacturers may take years creating markets for their products. This contrasts with the opportunistic nature of agricultural sales on world markets which may be characterised as surplus disposal. The Community's dumping of its agricultural surpluses on world markets was responsible for many of the trade tensions in the first half of the 1980s. These, in turn, were a primary factor in the decision to embark on the Uruguay round of GATT trade negotiations in 1986.

The contrast with the Community's manufactured food exports could not be more marked, with Community food and drink manufacturers being among the most competitive in the world. Apart from the food industry's political significance as a major employer, it should be recognised that increased economic wealth is generated by exporting value-added processed products rather than bulk agricultural commodities. For example, the USDA has estimated (Schluter and Edmondson, 1989) that one million dollars' worth of maize exports, as such, generates 75 jobs in the US economy. Exported as processed poultry, however, the same amount of maize generates 658 jobs.

9.2 THE FOOD INDUSTRY'S AIMS IN THE URUGUAY ROUND

In the initial phases of the Uruguay Round, the European (CIAA, 1988) and British (FDF, 1988) food industries issued statements expressing their support for the aims of the negotiations and setting out what they hoped would be achieved. These objectives may be broadly summarised as:

- the consideration of the food industry's interests as a whole, rather than particular aspects impinging on food industry competitivity being considered in separate negotiating groups;
- the adoption of agricultural support systems which would lead to cheaper domestic raw material prices and improved access to imported raw materials;
- improved access to Third Country markets for EC exporters;
- the avoidance of production quotas domestically and market sharing arrangements internationally as market distorting mechanisms;
- the elimination of existing non-tariff barriers to trade and the prevention of the emergence of new barriers;
- a successful outcome to the negotiations as a means of avoiding international trade disputes, where retaliation principally falls on processed food products;

- 'special and differential' treatment for developing countries to be confined to the least developed and access to raw materials produced in developing countries not to be denied to developed country food manufacturers;
- for so long as EC agricultural raw material prices are above world levels, the maintenance of a system of compensation for EC exporters of processed products;
- improvement in the protection available for investment in Third Countries and for intellectual property such as trade marks and patents;
- an adequate transition period for changes agreed in the Uruguay Round to give food manufacturers (and agricultural producers) adequate time to adjust.

9.3 THE INCLUSION OF AGRICULTURE IN THE URUGUAY ROUND

Although comments in the following sections may appear rather qualified, it should be recognised that it was a major achievement for the health of the global economy, as a whole, to have widened the scope of the GATT to include areas long excluded – in particular agriculture and textiles – as well as the completely new area of services. In the area of agriculture undoubtedly more could have been achieved, but to suggest therefore that the outcome was a disappointment is to underrate the size of the achievement in having brought agriculture within the scope of the normal GATT disciplines.

That it should have been widely suggested in the USA that the outcome in the agricultural area was not good enough to ensure an easy passage through Congress was, it may be suggested, rather a reflection on the unrealistic negotiating objectives set by the US government. It was never realistic to pretend, as the US Administration did, that it would have been feasible to eliminate all agricultural support in ten years (the so-called 'double zero' option) which was the initial US negotiating stance (GATT, 1989).

There are several reasons for this judgement. First, if after forty years of GATT negotiations stretching over seven rounds prior to the Uruguay Round, there were (and still are) significant levels of industrial protection left – particularly so in 'sensitive' sectors – then why should it have ever been considered possible to eliminate all agricultural protection in a single round? Indeed, in the area of industrial protection, it should be noted that while there have been major successes in eliminating quantitative restrictions on imports and lowering levels of import tariffs, there has been a spread of less formal trade restricting instruments, such as Voluntary Export Restraints (Blackhurst, 1977) to achieve support by other, non-tariff mechanisms.

Two further reasons for believing it would have been unrealistic to eliminate all agricultural protection in a single round lie in the sensitivity of governments to adequate levels of food supply as a continuing prime objective for their people, and the fact that most agricultural protection arises from domestic support policies.

The importance of food security as a prime objective can most easily be illustrated by reference to the EC's common agricultural policy (the CAP), whose origins lie in the starvation widespread in Europe after the Second World War. Again, the concerns of the net food importing developing countries in the Uruguay Round are a current reflection of the over-riding priority of food security for governments, including their demand for increased food aid to offset the expected impact of trade liberalisation in raising world commodity prices (Group W/74, 1989).

The sensitivity of negotiating on agriculture protection has always been aggravated for governments by the erosion of sovereignty embodied in the fact that domestic support policies have to be put on the international negotiating table. In the past, this was always regarded as a major stumbling block to reducing levels of agricultural protection.

Finally, it should be recognised that the limited degree of agricultural trade disarmament arising from the Uruguay Round is only the start of what is meant to be a continuing process. In the draft 'Final Act', further agricultural negotiations are specifically provided for towards the end of the six year implementation period for the Uruguay Round outcome. The last Article of the 'Final Act' is explicitly entitled 'Continuation of the Reform Process'.

9.4 THE FOOD INDUSTRY VIEWED AS A WHOLE

The structure of the Uruguay Round negotiations reflected the traditional structure of government departments, with their emphasis on agriculture and the complete absence of the food industry's interests as being of any significance. Thus, in the Uruguay Round the food industry's interests were covered in several GATT negotiating committees dealing with agriculture (of course), but also those dealing with tropical products, tariffs, non-tariff barriers, trade-related investment measures (TRIMs) and trade-related intellectual property rights (TRIPs).

Yet the food industry had been most concerned to avoid this outcome. It had lobbied for the negotiations to consider its interests as a whole, saying that only if this were done would it be possible to consider its effects for food industry competitivity. The underlying concern was that the competitiveness of the food and drink industry should not be jeopardised by decisions taken in relation to purely agricultural considerations.

The British food industry (FDF, 1988) said that 'the interests of the food and drink industry [should be] considered in a properly co-ordinated manner in the current round of negotiations and that it [should] not [be] treated just as an adjunct of agriculture. The food and drink industry is a separate industry in its own right which should be regarded as such'.

It is a salutary reminder of the agro-centricity of most politicians that the Uruguay Round negotiations were held on traditional lines with all the emphasis placed on agriculture.

9.5 CHEAPER DOMESTIC RAW MATERIALS

A major consideration in the food industry's support for a successful Uruguay Round negotiation was the cheaper domestic raw material prices it would bring and, it was hoped, the improved access to imported raw materials from Third Countries. In the EC, as in many other developed countries, government support for its domestic agriculture has resulted in the prices paid for domestically produced agricultural raw materials being higher than they otherwise would be. In effect, the EC runs a 'two price' system with its food manufacturers paying one price for raw materials used in processed foodstuffs consumed domestically, and another lower price (in net terms) where products are to be exported to world markets.

Without venturing into the argument as to what world prices would be for agricultural raw materials under 'free' trade scenarios, it is clear that the Community's food industry is substantially penalised in terms of the cost of the higher raw material prices it has to pay, where its output is going for domestic consumption. Thus the sort of estimates produced for consumer costs (OECD, 1992) suggest that EC consumers paid an extra 29.94 billion ecu, on average over the period

1979–86, as a result of the CAP. This was equivalent to approximately 30 per cent of the consumer value of the commodities covered (wheat, coarse grains, rice, oilseeds, sugar, milk, beef, pigmeat, poultrymeat, sheepmeat, wool and eggs). The levels of consumer subsidy equivalents by country vary widely, however, as shown by Table 9.1.

The concern about the price of raw materials applies not so much at the aggregate level, because there the demand for food as a whole is price inelastic. But at the level of individual products – such as a chocolate bar – demand is highly price elastic. Here the cost of raw materials can be extremely significant accounting, in some products, for over half total costs.

Against this background, the Uruguay Round will have delivered a useful cut in raw material costs. Quite clearly, however, in the interests of getting an agreement it was felt better to go for a relatively small level of cut which would be accepted, rather than a larger level of cut which risked there being no agreement at all.

In economic terms the effective level of cut depends on what is the key parameter determining market prices in an individual country, whether it is internal support or levels of import protection and/or ability to export surpluses. In nominal terms, however, the 'Final Act' provides for the following cuts, in percentage declines, over the six year implementation period:

Table 9.1 Aggregate levels of consumer subsidy equivalent by country (in % of consumer value)

	1979–86 average	*1991*
Australia	−7	−8
Austria	−28	−50
Canada	−22	−31
EC	−30	−42
Finland	−55	−72
Japan	−39	−46
New Zealand	−10	−3
Norway	−40	−63
Sweden	−37	−60
Switzerland	−46	−55
USA	−18	−19
Total OECD	−28	−37

Source: OECD, 1992.

GATT Agriculture Cuts

Internal Support

- Reference period: 1986–8;
- To be measured using the Aggregate Measurement of Support (AMS);
- Reference level AMS to be cut 20 per cent.

Export Competition

- Reference period: 1986–90;
- Subsidised export volumes to be cut by 24 per cent (this was revised down to 21 per cent by the US/EC deal at the end of November 1992);
- Budget spending on export subsidies to be cut 36 per cent.

Import Access

- Reference period: 1986–8;
- Frontier measures affecting import levels to be converted to tariffs ('tariffication');
- Tariffs, on average, to be cut by 36 per cent, with a minimum 15 per cent cut;
- Minimum import access to be set at 3 per cent of consumption: to rise to 5 per cent over the period.

A major issue arising from the 'Final Act' is the lack of coherence between the proposed differing levels of cut. Thus, a 20 per cent cut in the level of AMS for a particular commodity is likely, in practice, to translate to a cut of around half that level in internal institutional support prices. If, as has been suggested, the AMS cut for cereals means a cut of 10 per cent to 12 per cent in EC intervention prices, then this could, in turn, be undermined by the size of the cut in the levels of external protection and/or the need to cut subsidised export volumes.

The concern from the food industry's point of view is that while spending on export refunds for processed products has to be cut by 36 per cent, the prices for the domestic raw materials used in the manufacturing process might only fall by, say, one third of this level with obvious implications for EC food manufacturers exporting to Third Countries. The differing structures of countries' varying agricultural and food situations mean that differing levels of cut, in terms of the various parameters addressed, would be necessary to ensure greater consistency. It is likely, however, that the final proposal at the December 1990 GATT meeting in Brussels would have given a more satisfying outcome (Helstrom, 1990). Here it was suggested that there should be a flat rate cut of 30 per cent in all the elements being negotiated – internal support, export competition and import access.

9.6 IMPROVED ACCESS FOR THIRD COUNTRY IMPORTS

The most significant development here is the change of principle embodied in a switch from the EC's minimum import prices (Threshold Prices), enforced by variable import levies, to import tariffs as applied for all other products entering international trade. No matter that initial levels of import tariffs will be extremely high and that, on average, they will be cut by only 36 per cent during the Uruguay Round implementation period. It is the change of principle which is important as a precedent for future GATT rounds.

Whether the changes will have any significant impact for particular products in the Uruguay Round implementation period will depend essentially on how close EC domestic market prices were to Threshold Prices before tariffication occurred. In cases where there was a large gap (that is, there was a lot of 'water' in the tariff) the impact of the change will be small. In cases where the gap was smaller, potentially duty-paid import prices could impact on domestic EC market prices. Whether this would be allowed to happen would also depend, however, on which products the EC chose to cut its import tariffs by the minimum permitted amount of 15 per cent, rather than the required average of 36 per cent.

The opening-up of markets, in volume terms, seems unlikely to have much effect for the EC. The minimum access requirements provided for in the Uruguay Round are relatively minor: 3 per cent, rising to 5 per cent over the period. For most mainstream agricultural commodities the EC already imports at, or above, these minimum levels as a result of earlier rounds of GATT negotiations and/or separate negotiations arising from the accession of new countries to the EC. For example, the EC import arrangements for ACP sugar and New Zealand lamb and butter are the direct results of UK accession to the EC in 1973. Again, the import quotas for 'Hilton' beef are a result of the Tokyo Round of GATT negotiations.

The food industry's generalised wish to have access to cheaper Third Country imports has not been addressed as such in the negotiations, as this is bound-up in the mainstream agricultural negotiations. The food industry has lobbied specifically, however, on improving import access for more minor products which are either not produced in the EC at all or where the required qualities are not produced. Items included in these categories cover tropical beverages, some nuts, herbs and spices, dried fruit (on this, see Harris and Swinbank, 1991), true long grain rice and manufacturing quality beef. It has long been recognised that the EC's maintenance of import tariffs for tropical products (such as beverages and spices) is not because of any domestic production, but because of the need to maintain a margin of preference in the EC market for imports from developing countries associated with the EC (Harris, Swinbank and Wilkinson, 1983). This justification is not thought to be an adequate reason for the maintenance of preference by the food industry. In effect, EC consumers are being penalised in order to provide trade preferences for Third Country producers.

Whether or not the Uruguay Round will bring an improvement in this situation cannot be judged, however, until the outcome of the detail country-by-country negotiations on tariff offers is known.

9.7 AVOIDANCE OF MARKET SHARING ARRANGEMENTS

The British food industry (FDF, 1988) was prescient when it wrote in its principal submission on the Uruguay Round:

> The FDF does not find acceptable and warns against any solution to the problems of agricultural trade which avoids taking hard decisions over levels of agricultural support by 'fudging' the issue, i.e. through some combination of cartelisation of international trade (market sharing/market management) and the imposition of quotas for domestic production as a long term solution.

One part of the 'Final Act' appears, however, to result in international market sharing. The imposition of volume limits (and, indeed, cuts) in subsidised exports is a strange concept of market liberalisation. As the Financial Times (1992) argued in a leader, 'it would be better to focus on reductions of assistance, letting quantities go where they will'.

The pressure for such volume limits on exports came from the USA who were (and are) particularly concerned to regain market share in the world wheat market. The US loss of market share was held to be due to an expansion of EC exports. As the Uruguay Round price cuts were judged unlikely to rein back EC exports sufficiently to allow the USA to regain the market share it believed it was entitled to, the concept of volume limits on subsidised exports emerged.

Two comments are in order. First, the application of export volume limits is tantamount to international market sharing. If this is what the USA had wanted, then it could have been achieved more quickly and more efficiently through a bi-lateral deal with the EC, so saving both sides large amounts of taxpayers' funds in export subsidies (including the US EEP payments, as well as the EC's export refunds) in the six years of negotiations for the Uruguay Round.

Second, the meeting at which volume limits on exports were agreed was held at the Hague in November 1990. The understanding of the Dutch Prime Minister who attended the meeting was that the deal only concerned wheat. It is extremely unfortunate, therefore, that the Director General of GATT decided to extend the proposal for volume limits to all subsidised agricultural exports.

This limitation has been one of the sticking points for the EC, not only in terms of a straightforward argument as to how many million tonnes of wheat it should be allowed to export, but also in terms of the limitation being applied to other exports. Thus, while the argument over wheat was principally a French affair, the extension of volume limits to all agricultural commodities affected other important EC agricultural exporters – such as Denmark (pigmeat), the Netherlands (dairy products) and Ireland (beef).

Such volume limits on exports and the connotation of international market sharing that go with it are concepts the food industry can only deplore.

9.8 CAP REFORM

In this regard, the EC's CAP Reform measures agreed in May 1992 have confirmed the EC's gradual move towards support measures used in the USA. Thus, the principal CAP Reform mechanisms for cereals are a lowering in market support prices for cereals combined with the introduction of compensatory payments to make up farm incomes and the introduction of land set-aside requirements to control production levels (Council of the European Communities, 1992). From the point of view of EC agricultural policy-makers the move is sensible, as the more closely EC agricultural policy mimics that of the USA the less subject to challenge will it be, either bi-laterally in any discussions with the USA or multilaterally in the GATT.

For the food industry, the CAP Reform package is two-edged. On the one hand, the reform for cereals will deliver lower domestic market prices. This can only be to the benefit of food manufacturers using cereals either directly, or indirectly through the livestock products (pigs and poultry) heavily dependant on cereals. On the other hand, however, as the FDF feared in 1988, the reforms do appear to extend quota type approaches to a larger sector of agriculture: not only cereals through the set-aside arrangements, but also for beef and sheep through the premium arrangements, while the already-existing dairy quotas were tightened.

The attraction of supply control management through physical measures affecting the level of production is that it allows the maintenance of higher support prices than would otherwise be possible while keeping levels of surplus production (and, maybe, budget costs) under control. But it was just this outcome that food manufacturers wished to avoid as being unlikely to control surpluses properly and not encouraging efficient production in the areas best suited.

This ambivalence about CAP Reform reflects the confusion in its origins. When originally proposed, CAP Reform was to be the means for implementing the Uruguay Round outcome; so it would have been, had the original timetable been adhered to and the Uruguay Round completed in December 1990. Over the next year and a half as the Uruguay Round dragged on, however, CAP Reform became the pre-condition for a successful Uruguay Round, with the EC insisting that CAP Reform was being undertaken for internal reasons. Other GATT Contracting Parties had to wait until they saw the outcome of the reform to decide whether the Community was serious about negotiating an agricultural deal and whether what the Community could offer as a result of the reform would be sufficient to make the Uruguay Round interesting for them.

In the event the EC claims that the restrictions in its production which will flow from the CAP Reform measures will enable it to fit within the GATT outcome without further measures. This may, or may not, prove to be the case, but it is clear that the food industry will face increasing restrictions on supply as a result of CAP Reform, even though market prices may be lower than they would have been without the deal.

9.9   IMPROVED ACCESS TO THIRD COUNTRY MARKETS

Obviously the food industry would see improved access to Third Country markets as being an important outcome of the Uruguay Round. Priority areas for improved market access identified by the food industry included the newly industrialised countries of S E Asia (the NICs) as well as Brazil, Turkey, the USA, the EFTA countries and Japan.

It is notable that many of the countries in question do not carry their protestations as to their belief in trade liberalization so far as to encompass imports of manufactured foodstuffs. The food industry finds its ability to gain access to these markets restricted by significant barriers – whether through tariffs or, often just as important, through non-tariff barriers (in particular, health requirements).

How successful the Uruguay Round has been in improving market access will not become clear for some time to come. (The negotiations on tariff rates imposed on imports of specific products by individual countries have yet to be completed, while the success of the agreement on sanitary and phytosanitary measures embodied in the 'Final Act' will only be assessable after some years of operation.) It should not be surprising, however, that the EC's food industry believed that improved access to its domestic market for manufactured food stuffs should bring with it improved access to Third Country markets.

9.10   THE TREATMENT OF DEVELOPING COUNTRIES

The food industry had several concerns about the treatment of developing countries. These essentially related to:

1. the ability to distort the relationship between raw material and processed product prices;
2. the ability to delay access to their markets for manufactured foodstuff exports, as a result of the longer timescale (up to ten years) proposed for the adoption of GATT disciplines and the lower levels of reductions required (two thirds of the full levels);
3. the self-selecting nature of the process as to which countries fall in the category of developing countries for GATT purposes.

On the problem of the distortion of the relationship between raw material and processed product prices, the British food industry (FDF,

1988) stated that 'Improved access to the EC for manufactured products should not be granted when the finished product is being exported by countries which distort the price relationship between raw materials and finished product exports in favour of the latter. Solutions to the problem of distortion which extend to products in addition to tropical products should be sought'.

The issues are very clear. Many developing countries see the creation of domestic food processing industries as an important step in the development process. This has meant a willingness in some cases to restrict exports of raw materials to ensure they are exported in value added form. The USDA has pointed-out, as an example, that 'in both Brazil and Argentina, soybean meal exports have been encouraged by policies that create incentives for the export of soybeans in meal rather than bean form' (Burfisher and Missiaen, 1990). As the FDF put it, 'Any agreement allowing freer access to the EC of processed or semi-processed tropical products must allow an equivalent improvement in access to raw materials for manufacturers in the EC'.

The issue of access to developing-country markets for EC exports has been touched upon above. The point here is that there should be some differentiation between developing countries. The European food industry (CIAA, 1988) expressed this thought when it stated that for 'the newly industrialised countries ... any concessions should be linked to the abandonment of unfair trade practices in importing and exporting'. Whereas GATT policy should be 'selective and benefit, in particular, the least advanced countries'. The food industry's urgings do not seem to have had any marked degree of success, despite paralleling the proposals of the USA that there should be 'full compliance with commitments and implementation by advanced developing countries' (GATT, 1990).

While it is a fundamental criticism of the GATT structure that there are no criteria laid down for defining which countries should be treated as developing countries with access to 'special and differential' treatment, this problem has not been addressed. Although the commitment to help the development of poorer countries is accepted, it is not clear that countries should be able to continue to benefit from such special treatment when they have progressed very substantially and, in many aspects, increasingly share the characteristics of the developed, industrialised nations. In this regard, it should also be recognised that the GATT does not provide any 'effective limits on what a developing country can do' (Finger, 1991). This is a further serious criticism of the GATT's ability to control developing country policies.

9.11 THE TREATMENT OF EXPORT REFUNDS FOR PROCESSED PRODUCTS

It may appear inconsistent that despite the food industry's broad support for the objectives of the Uruguay Round in terms of agricultural disarmament and market liberalisation, it has had to defend the EC's use of export refunds for the raw material content of manufactured foodstuff exports. The position the EC's food industry finds itself in, however, has to be recognised. The export refunds granted on manufactured foodstuff exports are not granted on the products as such. They are granted on the raw material content of manufactured foodstuffs, and represent compensation to food manufacturers for the EC's continued use of a two price system of agricultural support. The refunds are calculated to put EC food manufacturers on an equal competitive footing with Third Country manufacturers, by giving the EC's food industry exporters their raw materials at close to world prices.

It was disingenuous of US negotiators to claim that such export refunds were GATT illegal (especially when the US itself employs GATT illegal measures, such as its Article 301 provisions). The claim ignores completely the fact that US food manufacturers already have access to world price raw materials because of the different system of US agricultural support. Thus, for those agricultural commodities where deficiency payments are made available to farmers, US domestic market prices for these commodities are at, or very close to, world levels. Even for commodities such as sugar and peanuts, where deficiency payments are not used, refund arrangements exist for manufactured foodstuffs exports containing these products, so giving a net result equivalent to that in the EC.

Table 9.2. illustrates the operation of the EC export refunds mechanism for a biscuit product containing 16 per cent sugar, 18 per cent butter, 61 per cent wheat flour and 5 per cent other ingredients. It is perfectly clear that without the payment of compensation for the raw material cost disadvantage suffered by EC food manufacturers (that is, the export refunds) they would be unable to compete on world markets. The importance of the refunds can be easily demonstrated: in 1989, for example, the export refunds were equivalent to between 42 per cent and 63 per cent of the invoice price for lower value added milk products, while even for highly processed products such as confectionary the refunds were worth some 10 per cent to 11 per cent of the invoice price.

Table 9.2   Operation of EC export refund mechanism

Basic CAP Product	Export refund for basic CAP product (£/100kg)	Proportion of CAP product in biscuit by weight	Export refund for the biscuit (£/100kg)
Butter	110	18%	19.8
White sugar	13	16%	1.9
Wheat flour	4	61%	2.4
Other ingredients	nil	5%	nil
Total		100%	24.10

The issue revolving around the use of export subsidies for the raw material content of processed products arises because of the GATT ban on export subsidies for 'products other than certain primary products' (Article 9 of the GATT Subsidies Code). Primary products are defined as 'any product of farm, forest or fishery, in its natural form which has undergone such processing as is customarily required to prepare it for marketing in substantial volume in international trade' (Ad Article XVI of the General Agreement, Section B, paragraph 2).

The question as to how tightly the definition of primary products should be drawn and whether processed foodstuffs were, or were not, covered, was addressed in the GATT Panel findings on the EC's use of export subsidies for pasta (GATT, 1983). The Panel held that 'durum wheat incorporated in pasta products could not be considered as a separate "primary product" and that the export refunds paid to exporters of pasta products could not be considered to be paid on the export of durum wheat'. The Panel's findings were not implemented, however, as not all the GATT Contracting Parties were prepared to accept them.

The resulting curious limbo over the use of export subsidies for the raw material content of processed products is settled in the Uruguay Round draft 'Final Act'. Specific provision is made for cutting by 36 per cent 'aggregate budgetary outlays in respect of subsidies on agricultural primary products incorporated in exported products'. By imposing a discipline on such spending the 'Final Act' effectively concedes the legitimacy of the use of such export subsidies. This must be viewed as a definite gain for the food industry as legal uncertainty is removed, especially so, as the 'Final Act' goes further in stipulating that domestic support and export subsidies subject to reduction commitments are 'presumed' not to cause 'serious prejudice' in terms of the GATT. This protects the exporting country against any countermeasures in the GATT. In principle the exporting country is protected against any countermeasures in the GATT, so long as its agricultural support measures fall within the Uruguay Round commitments.

9.12   THE ELIMINATION OF NON-TARIFF BARRIERS TO TRADE

The EC food industry was particularly concerned to control the use of sanitary and phytosanitary measures as barriers to food imports. It suggested (CIAA, 1988) that the existing GATT rules in this area should be strengthened and that a country 'wishing to introduce new rules in this field should be required to provide scientific proof concerning their necessity, otherwise adequate compensation should be provided'.

Article XX of the GATT states that Contracting Parties may introduce trade restrictions only where 'necessary to protect human, animal or plant life or health' as long as these do not 'constitute a means of arbitrary or unjustifiable discrimination between countries where the same conditions prevail or [constitute] a disguised restriction on international trade'. But, in practice, animal and plant health and food safety measures have increasingly become a source of barriers to trade, as other more traditional agricultural support measures have come under pressure.

The Standards Code introduced as part of the outcome of the Tokyo Round of the GATT negotiations was designed principally to prevent technical product standards, specifications and certification systems being used as barriers to trade, broadly by requiring signatory countries to base such measures on relevant international standards, where they existed. While the Standards Code has been effective in controlling the use of standards in industrial trade it has been less successful in the area of sanitary and phytosanitary restrictions.

The 'Final Act' of the Uruguay Round includes a specific 'Decision on Sanitary and Phytosanitary Measurers'. This section introduces the key measure demanded by the food industry that 'sanitary and phytosanitary measures are applied only to the extent necessary to protect human, animal or plant life or health, are based on scientific principles and are not maintained against available scientific evidence'. To this end, the Decision requires that sanitary and phytosanitary measures shall be based on 'international standards, guidelines and recommendations, where they exist'. The Decision specifies that international bodies setting such standards include the Codex Alimentarius Commission, the International Office of Epizootics and organisations operating within the framework of the International Plant Protection Convention.

The decision is a significant step forward. Its application should, in particular, make more difficult the adoption of sanitary and phytosanitary measures for political rather than scientific reasons. Examples of such measures include the EC's ban on all meat to which hormones have been added, and its refusal to grant permission for the use of BST.

A major failing of the Decision is, however, that it does not address 'green protectionism' arising from environmental concerns. Issues such as animal welfare codes and consumer health concerns are not covered. A recent example of such actions is the US ban on imports of tuna from countries which cannot certify that the tuna was not caught by nets which also catch sea mammals, such as dolphins. It is clear for the future that differing environmental legislation, imposing varying levels of compliance and production costs, will potentially be the trigger for protectionist demands (Sorsa, 1992).

9.13 THE PREVENTION OF TRADE DISPUTES

The food industry has had one very particular reason for wishing for a successful conclusion to the Uruguay Round. This is that the agricultural agreements in the 'Final Act' should help to prevent the eruption of future trade disputes. In the 1970s and 1980s, many (if not most) international trade disputes arose from agricultural problems.

The food industry's concern arises as, when agricultural disputes degenerate into warfare, it is normally food industry products which are targeted for 'retaliation' with existing trade concessions being withdrawn and/or penal duty rates being applied to the import of specific items. Manufactured foodstuff and drink items feature largely on such retaliation lists as, because of the multiplicity of products, it is much easier to get a group of products together which meet the required value of the trade total specified for retaliation and because it is much easier to target exports from specific countries.

It is not surprising that, for example, the exporters of French cognac should strongly object when they are targeted for retaliation by the

USA in agricultural trade disputes related to completely unrelated products.

As the Director General of GATT (Dunkel, 1992) told a meeting of the International Wheat Council, 'a major objective of the approach to commitments in the three main areas [domestic support, import access, export competition] is to establish a system which is less dispute prone. The commitments that would result from the negotiations would be incorporated in the legal schedules of individual participants. They would thus enjoy the same degree of permanence and security as other GATT concessions. This would include the protection of the improved consultation and dispute settlement procedures that would be part of the overall Uruguay Round package that is on the table'.

For the food industry any agreement that would prevent agricultural trade disputes erupting into open warfare, with retaliation and counter-retaliation, must be warmly welcomed. As the Director General of GATT (Dunkel, 1992a) pointed out, 'A number of potentially explosive agricultural trade disputes have been held more or less in suspense as long as the negotiations offered the hope of comprehensive solution. If this hope remains unfulfilled, there is reason to fear a return to a cycle of subsidy wars, escalating trade barriers and retaliation, more savage than we have seen since the 1930s. The consequences would not be confined to agriculture'.

It is notable that the US/EC bilateral deal on agriculture of November 1992 provided for a strengthend 'Peace Clause' to be included in the agricultural settlement in the Uruguay Round. This should help prevent disputes such as the five year US/EC dispute over oilseeds from erupting in the future.

9.14 CONCLUSION

Given the wide scope of the agricultural negotiations, an overall assessment is difficult to draw `(particularly so as the final details have not yet been established). Some tentative conclusions are below:

1. The Uruguay Round has brought agriculture within the normal GATT disciplines for the first time ever. This is a major development.
2. Nevertheless the Uruguay Round itself will not have delivered a major reduction in agricultural support. This should follow in succeeding rounds of GATT negotiations: the next set of negotia-

tions is already provided for at the end of the Uruguay Round implementation period.

3. That major reductions in agricultural support did not result from the Uruguay Round is a function of two factors. First, the levels of reduction specified in the Uruguay Round were all that countries would accept: in the case of the USA and the EC, the reductions are claimed to be no more than their domestic policy actions would deliver in any case. Thus, the EC argues its 1992 CAP Reform programme would produce the support cuts required by the Uruguay Round, while the USA says the support cuts already made since 1986 mean further cuts in internal support are not necessary to fulfil the Uruguay Round targets (USDA, 1992). Second, it is clear a considerable degree of ingenuity will be applied to interpreting the flexibility built into the Uruguay Round texts, so that 'sensitive sectors' (such as the sugar and dairy product industries) will continue to be significantly shielded.

4. It is unfortunate that the deal has involved the fixing of quantitative limits on export volumes. This not only made the conclusion of the deal unnecessarily difficult, it is also a step away from freeing international trade. This outcome, in particular, can only be deplored.

5. Again, the EC's domestic CAP Reform measures also appear to lean toward supply control by physical means, with the introduction of set-aside for cereals and increasing levels of control for livestock. Although the food industry will gain from the lower domestic market prices which should result from CAP Reform, it will remain wary of the supply control measures, fearing any fixing of patterns of production and the pressure to reduce the intensity of production even if this reduces competitivity.

6. The treatment of developing countries seem unnecessarily broadbrush in that all developing countries are treated alike. While there is a strong case for recognising the least developed countries and providing differentiated treatment for them, the same cannot be said of the more advanced developing countries which increasingly share characteristics with the developed nations. The case for providing special treatment for them is not self-evident. Rather there is a strong case for providing the same GATT disciplines for them as for developed countries, at least for those food commodities where they are major exporters.

7. Although the Uruguay Round agreement tightens-up on the treatment of sanitary and phyto-sanitary measures, the issue of

'green protectionism' has not been dealt with. It is already clear that this will be a major issue for the next round of GATT negotiations, where the apparent conflict between the trade rules of GATT and environmental concerns will have to be addressed.

The overall conclusion must be that while agriculture has, indeed, been brought within the GATT disciplines for the first time, there will still be a lot to do for future rounds of GATT negotiations on agriculture. For the food industry, the outcome is helpful in that trade disputes should be avoided and some progress will be made in improving conditions for international trade for food and agricultural products and in delivering somewhat lower agricultural raw material prices.

10 Perspectives on EC Agricultural Policy Reform

Secondo Tarditi[1]

10.1 INTRODUCTION

The EC position on the agricultural policy issues raised by the Uruguay Round of the GATT negotiations has been closely linked to the long-standing but still unresolved problem of the reform of the Common Agricultural Policy (CAP). In order to simplify the issues at stake, two principal points of view on the CAP reform problem will be discussed and analysed in this chapter, namely the 'social' and the 'sectoral' perspective. These two perspectives are not openly and distinctly spelled out by the Eurocrats working in the Commission or by the Council of Ministers; nevertheless they are implicit in official EC documents.

The CAP has always been, and still is, the result of a continuous compromise between people looking at agricultural problems from the point of view of the whole society or from a more narrow, private standpoint, no wonder then that implemented policy measures may be contradictory. For example, actual policies promote a better allocation of resources by subsidizing structural adjustment and, at the same time, misallocate resources by distorting market prices or setting-aside a large share of fertile land in order to protect farm incomes; promote research and widespread application of new technologies to increase productivity, while subsidizing farmers to reduce their average yields in order to control domestic supply and maintain a high level of domestic prices.

The Uruguay Round negotiations have exerted strong external pressure for the reform of the CAP, and a compromise between these two contrasting perspectives acceptable by world trade partners. In the author's opinion, adopting this analytical approach facilitates the understanding and appraisal of the short and long run effects of the present reform of the CAP derived from the MacSharry proposal, as well as the EC strategy in the GATT agricultural negotiations.

After illustrating these two perspectives on the solution of different problems concerning agriculture in Northern and Southern Europe, the crucial problem of compensating farmers for the income loss generated by drastic reductions in price support will be addressed by analysing the likely effects of the policy measures decided by the Council of Ministers of Agriculture, predominantly conceived in a 'sectoral' perspective, as compared to the effects of an alternative approach to compensation proposed by the Land Use and Food Policy InterGroup (LUFPIG) of the European Parliament, which is more coherent with the 'social' point of view.

10.2   THE 'SOCIAL' PERSPECTIVE

Agricultural problems are often looked at from the point of view of the whole of society. Farmers are considered as a praiseworthy group of citizens, and policy makers should take account of their personal and group interests in the same way as those of any other class of citizen. From this point of view the problems facing agriculture should be tackled in such a way as to solve them gradually by reaching a stable network of sound intersectoral economic relations in the long run. Such an objective can be reached by adjusting the structure of all economic sectors according to the evolution of consumers' demand, technological progress, and general economic development.

This perspective has been repeatedly referred to in numerous documents produced by policy makers and academics, and is the most common point of view in official documents where declarations of principles are stated. In essence it supports the idea that governments should not hinder the dynamic intersectoral reallocation of resources, labour in particular, requested by economic development. Rather, the role of government should be that of promoting economic development by reducing the adjustment costs which inevitably afflict the labour force when looking for another job.

According to this point of view present agricultural price support should be reduced in such a way as to maintain a reasonable stability on the domestic market, without generating costly surpluses, while the CAP should contribute to economic development by favouring intersectoral labour mobility and encouraging the creation of economically viable farms in order to reduce production costs and increase the competitiveness of European agriculture.

Farmers should be remunerated on a permanent basis for the positive externalities they produce especially in economically disadvantaged regions. Such environmental concerns have become more important in the Eighties and are perfectly consistent with the objective of maximizing the overall social welfare in the short as well as in the long run.

To quote only a few major EC documents, these social perspective principles were spelled out at the Stresa Conference in 1958, by the Mansholt Plan in 1968 (CEC, 1968) and by the Green Book in 1985 (CEC, 1985). Consumer associations and a large number of scholars share this point of view which has often been emphasized by individuals as well as by groups (Wageningen, 1973; Siena, 1984; NCFAP, 1991; various authors, 1988).

Northern and southern standpoints

Agriculture in the EC member states is characterized by very different geographical and climatic conditions, historical backgrounds, and ethnic and institutional features. From an economic and agricultural point of view, a remarkable difference exists between the northern and southern countries of the Community.

Figure 10.1 shows the existing correlation between GDP per capita, measured in terms of purchasing power standards (PPS), and agriculture's share of total civilian employment in EC member countries. Together with Ireland, southern states of the EC have a lower level of per capita income and a markedly higher agricultural employment share than remaining northern states (Marsh et al., 1991).

The north–south split in agricultural structure among EC member states is even more apparent in Figure 10.2, where the net value added per agricultural working unit (AWU = equivalent full-time workers) is plotted against total assets per AWU. Compared with the northern countries, Mediterranean countries are all characterized by lower average asset endowments per unit of labour leading to lower average productivity of people employed in agriculture.

These fundamental differences in the economic structure of EC agriculture are likely to be one major explanation of the different weight given to particular policy objectives by policy makers representing different member countries. This, in turn, is often a major reason for diverging opinions about the best policy measures to implement. The reduction of surplus agricultural labour is a particularly important objective in less developed member countries and regions, where the

Figure 10.1   Economic development and agricultural employment share in the EC

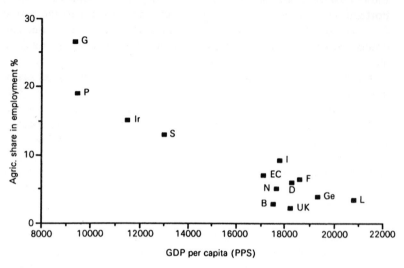

Source: EC Commission, 1991c

Figure 10.2   Farm assets and incomes per agricultural working unit in the EC

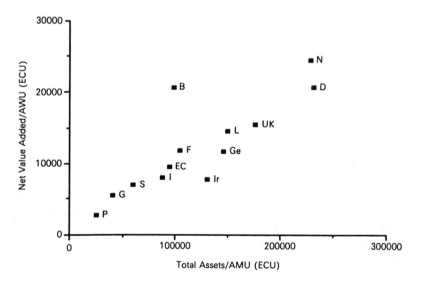

Source: EC Commission, 1990.

share of agriculture in total employment is still very high. Figure 10.3 shows how different the distribution of family farm incomes is between Portugal and the Netherlands, respectively the poorest and the richest EC member states in terms of per capita farm income. From this observation it may be inferred how much the distribution of farm incomes could improve in less developed regions if agricultural structural adjustment and rural diversification were pursued as major policy objectives.

Value added per working unit in agriculture is often less than 50 per cent of non agricultural value added. Considering that farm prices in the EC are supported at 50 per cent above the free market level, the average social productivity of one working unit in agriculture should be estimated at less than one third of a working unit in the rest of the economy. Easing and providing incentives for the intersectoral mobility of labour would therefore substantially increase the average social productivity of working units leaving agriculture.[2]

On the other hand, a reduced labour/land ratio would directly favour increased farm sizes, leading to higher labour productivity in agriculture as well and to higher per capita agricultural incomes. Figure 10.4 shows how in the EC average farm incomes of 'equivalent full-time workers' change in relation to farm size expressed in terms of European size units (ESU). The scope for improving intersectoral and intrasectoral resource allocation is therefore still very wide, especially in less developed regions mostly concentrated in southern European countries.

While in southern regions the long term solution of CAP problems is more related to structural adjustment, implying a reduction in agricultural employment, the perspective of northern policy makers is oriented more towards environmental problems. The outstanding issue is more frequently the danger that, in disadvantaged agricultural areas, the reduction in agricultural price support will result in excessive depopulation.

Notwithstanding these different standpoints between the northern and southern regions of the EC, the long-term perspective is wholly consistent with advocating both the improvement of incentives to encourage a greater intersectoral labour mobility leading to a substantial reduction in numbers of farmers in less developed regions, and the permanent subsidization of farmers in those disadvantaged areas where depopulation and environmental damage may occur as a consequence of lower support of agricultural prices. The central issue is to avoid indiscriminate policy instruments such as

Figure 10.3   The distribution of farms by family farm income per person in The Netherlands and Portugal

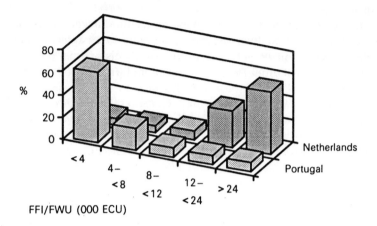

Source: EC Commission (1990).

Figure 10.4   Relation between labour income and farm size

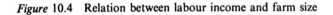
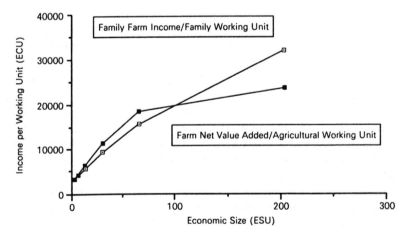

Source: EC Commission, 1990.

product price support or uniform unearned permanent subsidies to farmers which would generate contrasting effects on different European regions.

With reference to the Uruguay Round agricultural negotiations, the dominance of the 'social' perspective would point to an agreement on the phased reduction of policy measures which distort markets and trade (amber box) in order to concentrate aid to farmers in the form of 'production neutral' policy measures designed to achieve social and environmental objectives (green box). Consistent with this line of thinking, the tariffication of border measures could prove a useful device for use in implementing a gradual long term programme of agricultural reform fundamentally to restructure the EC economy.

10.3 THE 'SECTORAL' PERSPECTIVE

On the other hand, numerous policy decisions are taken by looking at present CAP problems from the private point of view of many farmers whose interests, however, are not homogeneous. Nevertheless, different pressure groups usually find a common political ground for defending existing privileges and income transfers to the agricultural sector.

Efficient farmers are frequently endowed with larger farms allowing reduced average costs. Although such farmers could withstand a reduction in prices, as landowners they benefit greatly from the economic rent derived from price support. In contrast, inefficient farmers, frequently running small farms at high average costs, earn low incomes and would be better off in alternative employment elsewhere in the economy. Nevertheless, the uncertainty and the adjustment costs of finding and adapting to another job makes most of them prefer present policies and the existing agricultural structure to a probably better but uncertain future in a restructured economic system. In this respect the 'sectoral' perspective is very much a 'short run' perspective.

It is understandable that most farmers' organizations regard present agricultural problems from this second point of view, and also look for possible opportunities to keep a large number of people in farming by promoting the fundamentalist opinion that farmers deserve income support, preferably via higher market prices. After all, farmers' organizations are groups of private citizens, and it is quite consistent with the traditional principles of a market economy if they try to increase their electoral power and income by means which are (for them) the most convenient, without being too much concerned with the costs of policies borne by society as a whole.

In principle it is less understandable that the farmers' sectoral perspective could be shared by policy makers who are ultimately responsible for policy decisions, and who have often declared, or even officially sworn, to pursue in their public duty only the interests of society as a whole.[3] In practice, the personal interests of policy makers are often strictly related to private interest groups, who support them in election campaigns or control the keys of their promotion in bureaucratic or political careers.

Even if wisely programmed by the government, structural adjustment is however costly and unpalatable for many farmers compelled to seek a non-agricultural job, sometimes outside their home area. Ever since the foundation of the EC, price support has been the dominant policy instrument and farmers have become accustomed to it. Lip service has been paid to the need for structural reform, but never seriously implemented in practice by the EC, notwithstanding the major efforts of the first Commissioner for Agriculture, Sicco Mansholt.

From a sectoral point of view, if the social costs generated by the distortions in resource allocation caused by agricultural policies are not taken into account, the easiest way to reach an agreement in the GATT negotiations and reduce the budgetary cost of the CAP could well be to offset the distorting effects of price support only in relation to its impact on foreign trade, without changing the domestic intersectoral and intrasectoral systems of domestic prices, rents and employment.

This goal may be reached by means of the quantitative control of supply, so limiting surplus production either directly, by administrative means, or by controlling the cultivated area. By limiting supply through administrative devices, the exportable surpluses may be directly reduced to the desired size, together with the reduction of budget outlays on export subsidies which pose the problems most easily perceived by EC policy makers.

But this sectoral perspective is essentially short-sighted, as it does not solve the basic structural problems troubling Community agriculture. These problems must inevitably be tackled in the long run and postponing the solution will only increase the cost of adjustment.

If compared with reduction in price support, supply control as a rule increases the overall misallocation of resources, by reducing their yield or their intersectoral as well as intrasectoral and territorial mobility. This is obvious for land set-aside, directly sterilizing a basic factor of production such as land, and for extensification, subsidizing a reduction of at least 20 per cent of the output for five years or more. In practice also production quotas worsen resource allocation, reducing overall welfare, especially if they are not traded and where the production structure is very inefficient due to a large number of small not economically viable, farms. (See Appendix for further details on this subject.)

Moreover a substantial amount of administrative work, usually performed by public agencies, is needed. However, the taxpayer's cost of this extra administrative cost is often overlooked by EC policy makers as it is often born mainly by national budgets. The budgetary cost of administrative measures is much higher in regions where farms are small and numerous and their book-keeping is very poor, than in regions where farmers are well acquainted with accountancy, which becomes increasingly useful when farms get larger.

Increased opportunities for fraud and lack of faith in free entrepreneurship and markets may be seen as negative externalities generated by a larger diffusion of administrative practices, especially in regions where the public administration has often been inefficient and corrupt.[4] These intangible negative effects both in the short and long run could be even more detrimental to social welfare than the proliferation of public servants in rural areas and their administrative cost.

10.4 EC COMMITMENTS IN GATT AND CAP REFORM

Although the EC negotiators in the GATT have maintained that the Uruguay Round negotiations and the CAP reform were two separate issues, the Commission's most recent reform proposals – eponymously dubbed the 'MacSharry' Plan – approved to a large extent by the Council of Ministers on 21 May 1992 can only be regarded as a major effort to enable the EC to escape from the impasse reached in the GATT negotiations on agriculture (EC Commission 1991 a, b) . The Community's GATT offer in December 1990 was a 30 per cent cut in domestic agricultural support expressed in terms of an Aggregate Measure of Support (AMS) over the period 1986–95. The Community estimated that, in order to honour this commitment, the current 1991–2 support level would need to be lowered by 23 per cent on average by 1996.

According to some estimates (*Agra Europe*, 4 October 1991), the impact of the Commission's latest CAP reform proposals upon levels of support would, by 1996, meet the commitment offered to the GATT by the EC fairly well. But this conclusion hinges upon the assumption that the compensatory payments which the EC farmers would get for the lowering of price support under the MacSharry Plan are classed as being 'production neutral', and therefore qualify for 'green box' treatment under the GATT rules.

But if, contrary to this assumption, MacSharry compensatory payments failed to qualify for exemption from the AMS cuts to which the EC was committed, the implementation of the MacSharry plan would fall short of matching the EC 's 1996 GATT offer by 5 per cent. However, the effects of the compensatory payments upon resource allocation, income distribution and other intangibles affecting welfare, could vary considerably depending upon precisely how they are defined and implemented.

The 'Sectoral' perspective

The decisions taken by the Council of Ministers of Agriculture on 21 May 1992 for reforming the CAP (Regulations [EEC] N. 1765/92, 1766/92, 2078/92, 2079/92, 2080/92 , 30 June 1992), although essential in order to reform the CAP by substantially reducing price support and transforming invisible income transfers into visible subsidies, still present a number of features more akin to the sectoral rather than to the social perspective.

The main aim of the Commission's proposed compensatory payments is to offset year by year the reduction in price support upon farmers' incomes, in order to keep a large[5] number of farmers on the land. As it is generally understood that price support policy mostly benefits the better off farmers, the tapering off of compensation in relation to increasing farm size was foreseen by the former Commission's proposal on the grounds of achieving greater equity in the distribution of farm income, but was rejected by the Council of Ministers for its adverse impact on resource allocation. The granted compensation is not modulated according to the size of farm. Small farms producing less than 92 tons of cereals are however exempted from setting aside 15 per cent of the cultivated area.

One drawback of annually defined direct payments to farmers is the administrative costs of their implementation. The well known textbook argument – that because production subsidies (for example, deficiency payments) do not distort consumption they are preferable to equivalent import tariffs – may be very misleading for practical policy making.

Although the gain in social welfare on the consumption side is undeniable, it could be quite modest due to the low price elasticity of demand for most agricultural products, and could be easily offset by a larger welfare loss due to added public and private deadweight costs of implementing the policy. These implementation costs could be substantial, especially in less developed regions where administration tends to be less efficient. Moreover, these social costs may be further increased by the extension of fraud often associated with the expansion of administration.

The more complicated and difficult to control direct payments are, the larger will be the social costs which are ignored by conventional models of policy analysis. If compensatory payments are confined only to selected agricultural products and are permanent, but must be re-calculated every year due to changes at the farm level in land use or crop rotation, the difficulty of maintaining effective cost controls, as well as achieving effective policing to prevent fraud, are likely to be huge.

A second drawback of annually computed compensation is the unavoidable trade-off between efficiency and equity that policy makers have to face. If compensations are not modulated, a more efficient structural adjustment in the longer run is not hindered, but income transfers to agriculture will continue to be inequitable as they will continue to flow mainly towards large farms and better-off farmers.

The early Commission proposals favoured a substantial degree of modulation, but ultimately the choice of the Council of Ministers was to accept largely the point of view of Northern member states that there should be no discrimination against large farmers in granting compensation for set aside. Existing privileges benefiting better-off farmers have not been substantially reduced and compensation has not been fully decoupled from production as requested by counterparts in the GATT negotiations.

On the other side, if an equitable and fine modulation in compensation is implemented, it will necessarily have a negative impact on the process of structural adjustment due to smaller farms being privileged when compared to larger and more economically viable farms. This will slow down the attainment of economies from larger scale production, the reduction of average costs and, eventually, the 'policy objective which guarantees the competitiveness and efficiency of Community agriculture' (COM[91]100, p. 11).

Inefficient allocation of resources in the short and longer run would be particularly dangerous in various Mediterranean regions where the crop mix is very diverse, adding to the difficulties of accounting and administrative controls, and the average farm size is still very small and inefficient (less than 5 ha or 4 European size units).

The 'social' perspective

The compensatory payments for the reduction of price support could be differently conceived in a long term perspective, with the aim being to enhance their positive effects on income distribution, to reduce their administrative costs and to transmute their negative consequences on agricultural adjustment into positive effects.

According to the decisions of the Council of Ministers of Agriculture, the substitution of compensatory payments for price support would apply only to the principal commodity sectors, accounting for three quarters of the total value of agricultural production subject to market organization, such as cereals, oilseed and beef. The reduction in marginal revenue in these sectors will most probably generate a shift of resources, labour and capital in particular, towards the remaining 25 per cent of agricultural production such as fruit and vegetables, where support will not be reduced. Such a shift will disrupt the existing equilibria on those markets, leading to higher budget expenditures and/ or to lower prices and farm revenues. Moreover, in the qualifying sectors, the annual administration and control of crop areas and livestock units eligible for compensation will be very costly and allow numerous opportunities for fraud, the negative effects of which are accountable in terms not only of additionally budgetary costs but also a reduced quality of life in regions where corruption and fraud will be more diffused.

These drawbacks could be substantially reduced if reductions in price support and compensatory payments were (Marsh *et al.*, 1991)[6]:

1. Granted on all farm land and livestock, since the whole agricultural sector will be affected, directly or indirectly, by the planned substantial reductions in agricultural price support.
2. Calculated only once on the basis of the crop areas and livestock recorded when the CAP reform is implemented; guaranteed to farmers for a pre-defined period (e.g.10 or 20 years).
3. Administered through bonds issued to the farmers concerned, on the basis of which the Commission would make annual payments over the relevant period, in the same way as it proposed to manage the compensation for milk quota reduction (COM[91]258, p. 21).

The bondholding farmers should be permitted, if they wish, to sell their bonds on financial markets in order to capitalize their future income flow entitlement.

This approach to compensatory payments offers several advantages compared to the present Commission proposal, for the following reasons:

1. Compensatory payments would be planned and computed as a lump sum, without lingering effects upon the productive decisions taken by farmers after the CAP reform has started and levels of compensations have been determined. This would qualify the payments for being classed as fully decoupled from future decisions on the amount of agricultural production and therefore eligible for 'green box' treatment in the GATT negotiations.

2. The financial burden of CAP reform on the EC budget would be spread over decades, while individual farmers could realize the benefit to themselves at any time, allowing substantial liquidity for enlarging farm size, where this is a viable option, or, if the existing farm size is too small, for selling the farm and investing the proceeds of the sale either in some non-farm business activity, or in the purchase of a life annuity to be added to early-retirement or other pension benefits. This increased mobility of financial resources is likely to stimulate the intersectoral and intrasectoral mobility of labour and land, so improving productivity both in agriculture itself and in the non-agricultural sector, especially in rural areas of backward regions where present farm structures are less efficient and under-employed resources could be activated by external investments in non-agricultural activities.

3. Administrative costs would be lower since the enumeration of crop areas, livestock numbers and average yields needed to determine the compensatory payment entitlements of individual farmers would need to be carried out only once, instead of every year. The probability of fraud would be reduced for the same reason, due to the elimination of annual re-assessments of payment entitlements.

4. Compensatory payments could be limited to a time period long enough to allow the majority of older farmers to retire and younger farmers either to restructure their farm or leave farming altogether in order to take up another more rewarding occupation. Some with jobs outside agriculture might wish to continue with farming as a part-time occupation, but it is difficult to justify permanent state

support of part-time farmers except, possibly, in particular areas where the social objectives like protection of the rural environment, including the prevention of rural depopulation, are paramount. The compensation would be guaranteed by the EC and would not depend on future market or policy developments, consequently the uncertainty for farmers about the amount of future compensatory payments would be eliminated. This approach would actually pursue the 'policy objective which guarantees the competitiveness and efficiency of Community agriculture' as indicated by the Commission.

5. A rapid restructuring of agricultural production will lower average costs and allow a quicker reduction of surpluses. The need for land set-aside to reduce export surpluses would therefore be much less and it could be used as a temporary policy measure for a few years.

6. Movements to larger and consequently 'economically viable' farms does not necessarily mean more agricultural pollution. Anti-pollution measures and a better financed agri-environmental action programme would enable socially desirable targets on environmental preservation and improvement to be attained at the minimum social cost, without unduly hindering agricultural and economic development in rural areas.

Moreover, as the administrative work needed to assess payment entitlements would be done only once, a more finely graduated modulation of compensations would be feasible. By fully compensating smaller farms and reducing the unit amounts of compensatory payments with increasing farm size, the cost of reform could be better controlled and reduced, whilst the target of a more equitable distribution of farm income could be attained without unduly hindering the agricultural adjustment process towards a more viable farm structure in the longer term.

However, in view of the significant differences in farm structure which exist amongst member states of the EC, a mutually acceptable balance between 'equity' and 'efficiency' considerations, in deciding about the modulation of compensation, is likely to be hard to find.

Summarizing, with reference to Figure 10.5, while the sectoral approach tends to shift the agricultural supply to the left, from S_0S_0 to S_1S_1, the social approach operates in the opposite direction, especially in the longer run, shifting the supply curve to S_2S_2. Even if the total compensation to farmers for the price reduction (areas $a+b+c+d$) were the same in both options, the economic effects

Figure 10.5 Structural impact of alternative prices

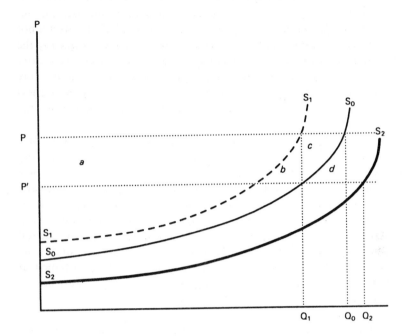

on production structure would be very different. Thanks to improved resource allocation in the economic system, the social approach would allow a net increase in welfare indicated by the area between $S_0 S_0$ and $S_2 S_2$ below the price level P'.

This improvement would benefit the whole society allowing reduction in price support, remunerative and better distributed per capita farm incomes and, altogether, lower budget (Community + national + regional) expenditure if compared with the result of the sectoral approach.

10.5 PROSPECTS AND CONCLUSIONS

If the sectoral perspective were to prevail amongst EC policy makers in the Uruguay Round negotiations, the future of European agriculture would not be greatly different from the past. Major investment distortions would prevail in the domestic market, together with the survival in agriculture of substantial economic inefficiency in the short term, and with a reduced rate of structural adjustment both in agriculture itself and in the overall economy. A relatively large number of farmers would remain in rural areas, but their per capita income, although heavily subsidized, would continue to be inadequate, giving rise to continuous problems and further pressures for reform of the CAP.

It is likely that jobs in public administration would proliferate at all levels: Community, national, regional, local. But the extra jobs in agriculture so preserved, and the consequent additional numbers of bureaucrats working in both the public and private sector, would add little to the amount of goods and services enjoyed by consumers. It is unlikely that overall social welfare would be significantly increased as a result of these activities. On the contrary, the social costs of production constraints upon the activities of farmers, the social costs of bureaucratic practices and of frauds, would probably be increasing.

Furthermore, if the 'sectoral' perspective prevails, special interest privileges and income disparities in agriculture will persist which are not beneficial to the majority of farmers in the long run as well as being very costly for taxpayers and other sectors which could employ redundant agricultural resources more productively.

On the other side, if the social, long term, perspective would prevail both in the Uruguay Round negotiations and in settling the details of CAP reform, the chronic problems afflicting European agriculture could be gradually solved. The reduction in price support would allow a more balanced system of relative market prices, and the amounts of agricultural surpluses would gradually be reduced through a sound process of structural adjustment in agriculture. Land set-aside could be limited to only a very short term policy measure.

Appropriate programmes of environmental improvement could provide farmers with extra income and incentives to continue with suitable forms of agriculture in all areas where environmental problems already exist, or could arise as a consequence of lower agricultural market prices. Lower consumer food prices and, in the long term, reduced budget expenditure on agriculture are likely to have a beneficial effect on the EC cost of living, on real wages and international competitiveness of EC exports with positive effects on total employment.

The bureaucratic and structural difficulties encountered in implementing milk quotas, especially in Mediterranean countries, are likely to prevent the implementation of a part of the policy measures taken on 21 May by the Council of Agricultural Ministers. Hopefully these

failures will convince Agricultural Ministers to redefine these measures, looking at them from a more socially oriented perspective.

APPENDIX: WELFARE EFFECTS OF SUPPLY MANAGEMENT

Limiting the quantity supplied in order to generate higher market prices is the most typical feature of monopolistic behaviour, the negative effects of which on social welfare are spelled out by microeconomics textbooks. It is therefore surprising to encounter the argument that, in terms of social welfare, the imposition of a production quota can be more efficient, and therefore preferable, to a reduction in market prices. This argument is sometimes advanced by supporters of the 'sectoral' perspective, but its truth needs to be proven to alter the orthodox view that supply control is systematically inimical to social welfare.

Due to the economic and political importance of this issue, some recent studies of the impact of agricultural production quotas on social welfare deserve careful attention and discussion (for example, De Gorter and Meilke, 1989; De Filippis, 1990)

In Figure 10.6, using the letters occupying various spaces in the figure to follow the conventions of partial equilibrium welfare analysis, D is aggregate domestic demand for an agricultural commodity, S is the aggregate supply curve without supply control, and P_w is the world demand facing a 'small' exporter. The farming industry is assumed to

Figure 10.6   Welfare effects of alternative policy measures

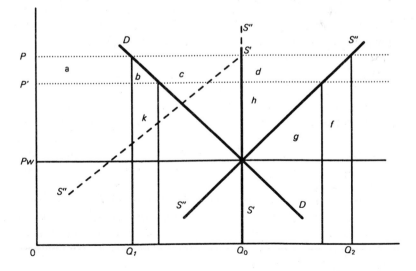

consist of identical farms. At a support price of P, aggregate production is OQ_2, of which OQ_1 goes to domestic consumption and Q_1Q_2 is exported with the aid of a unit export subsidy of $P-P_w$.

The problem is to compare the social welfare effects of two policy options: (1) partial price liberalization from P to a lower support price of P', and (2) the imposition of an aggregate production quota Q_0, limiting domestic production to the quantity which would be produced under free market conditions at world price, P_w.

In order to have a simpler diagram let us also assume self sufficiency at P_w and in order to focus on social costs and benefits let us assume that the producer surplus is the same in both policy options ($a+b+c = h$).

The net welfare effects of the policy alternatives of partial price support equilibrium and a production quota are as shown in Table 10.1. With the net welfare gain of $e+f$ common to both policy options, the choice between the options depends upon the relative magnitudes of the social welfare gain on the consumption side due to the reduction of price support ($b+k$) and the social cost of resource misallocation (g), i.e., if ($b+k$) > g then partial price liberalization is preferable; if on the contrary ($b+k$) < g then the production quota is preferable in terms of generating a higher level of social welfare.

The basic model presented by Figure 10.6 arbitrarily assumes efficient identical firms with minimum average total costs at or below P_w. The aggregate supply curve SS is the horizontal summation of the marginal cost curves of a population of homogeneous identical farms. However, since the quota has an implicit market value of $P-P_w$ per unit of production to the original owners, a shadow supply curve, reflecting the supply price to new entrants, can be visualized lying at a constant gap of $P-Pw$ price units above the original owners' supply curve SS, but only up to the aggregate output level Q_0. In Figure 10.6 the shadow supply curve is shown by $S''S''$.

Table 10.1   Welfare effects of policy alternatives

Partial Price Liberalisation							
Producer surplus	$-a$	$-b$	$-c$	$-d$			
Consumer surplus	$+a$	$+b$					
Taxpayer income	$+b$	$+c$		$+d$	$+e$	$+f$	$+k$
Net social welfare	$+b$				$+e$	$+f$	$+k$
Production Quota							
Producer surplus				$-d$		$-h$	
Consumer surplus	no change						
Taxpayer income				$+d$	$+e$	$+f$ $+g$	$+h$
Net social welfare					$+e$	$+f$ $+g$	

Although quota restrictions raise the private cost of new entrants (who have to buy quota), this is a transfer payment within the agricultural sector and not a social cost attributable to the quota scheme. Nevertheless it will reduce the intersectoral mobility of resources and hinder structural adjustment.

If the efficient identical farm assumption is dropped, inefficient farms, with minimum average total cost corresponding with a price level anywhere in the range between P and P_w, may coexist with efficient farms provided, of course, that the quota premium, $P - P_w$, and the right to produce, i.e. the quota, both remain intact. In Figure 10.7a, where the world price is 2 price units, Farm 1, an inefficient farm with minimum average total costs (ATC) of 2.5 price units, coexists with Farm 2, an efficient farm with minimum ATCs of one unit. Whereas Farm 2 enters production with 3 units at an incentive price of 1, Farm 1 does not enter below a price of 2.5, with the production of 1 unit. Given a support price (P) of 3 without quota restriction, Farm 1 is in production equilibrium at 1.5 units and Farm 2 at 4.5 units. The horizontal summation of marginal cost curves gives the aggregate supply curve of the 2-farm industry. Thus in Figure 10.7b, given $P = 3$, and the absence of quotas, the aggregate supply curve is $abcS$, and aggregate production equilibrium occurs at a total of 6 units.

Now assume that an equiproportional quota scheme is introduced to reduce production by one third. The individual quotas allocated to Farm 1 and 2 are 1 and 3 units respectively, giving an aggregate quota of 4 units. Assuming that the quotas are non-tradable, Farm 1 will remain in

Figure 10.7 Impact of non-tradable quotas at firm and industry levels

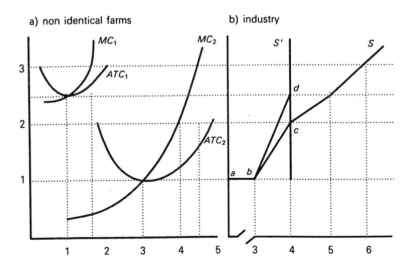

production with a marginal cost (MC) of 2.5 price units. This is reflected in Figure 10.7b by point *d* on the aggregate supply curve *abdS'*.

The actual aggregate supply function in Figure 10.7 will therefore be located to the left of *abdS'* according to the distribution of farms by size and consequently of their efficiency level. Therefore when analysing the welfare effects of quotas, the social costs due to resource misallocation must be taken into consideration, especially when the high-cost share of total production is large as compared to the low-cost share. In the dairy sector, for example, the share of holders with a presumably inefficient size of their herd, lower than 10 head of dairy cows, is slightly over 50 per cent in the EC as a whole, but is much higher in southern countries: over two thirds in Italy, over three fourths in Spain and over 90 per cent in Greece and Portugal. Consequently the efficiency costs of maintaining price support by limiting production are likely to be remarkable.

However, if the quotas are tradable, and producers are rational, it will pay Farm 1 (Figure 10.7) to cease production by selling its quota of 1 unit to Farm 2. This will enable Farm 2 to increase quota-constrained production from 3 to 4 units . The trading price will be the difference between P_s and P_w, i.e., 1 price unit per quota unit. For farm 2, buying quota to expand production from 3 to 4 units is not only privately profitable, but also socially efficient, as marginal costs equate with P_w after trading. The quota trading transaction shifts the aggregate supply curve from its pre-trading position at *abdS'*, *to a post-trading position at . abcS'*. Thus transferring quotas from inefficient Farm 1 to efficient Farm 2 eliminates the dead-weight supply side cost of price support represented by triangle *bcd*. Burrell (1989) gives a clear account of the theory of transferable quotas.

To summarize the argument, where quotas are transferable, the welfare conclusions of the efficient identical farm model can effectively be applied also to the non-identical farm model. That is, if trade in quota rights is allowed and is fully exploited by high-cost producers selling or leasing out quota to low-cost producers, the deadweight supply side cost of price support (the area *bcd* in Figure 10.7b) may be eliminated.

However in practice quota transferability is hampered by political, administrative and institutional barriers, particularly at frontiers between EC member states. Moreover high-cost producers may not sell their quota or even buy quota as a speculative asset if they have non-agricultural sources of income or easier access to capital, or due to the growth dynamics of the family business (Burrell, 1989, p. 103). Consequently in the real world the actual quota supply function is unlikely to be vertical but positively sloped, entailing a loss in social welfare more or less important according to the existing structure, institutions, information and transparency on local markets. Even without taking into consideration the administrative costs necessary to implement the quota regime, the constraints on the allocation of resources imposed on producers and the opportunities for fraud, the probability that a quota regime could be preferable to an equivalent (in terms of producer surplus) reduction of price support is likely to be practically irrelevant in the real world.

11 Agricultural Policy Reform after the Uruguay Round

D. R. Harvey

11.1 INTRODUCTION

Whatever the outcome of the Uruguay Round, the future of agricultural policy reform after 1993 will continue to reflect a mixture of internal or domestic and external, trade-related pressures, and will continue to be driven by politics rather than economics. Although the Uruguay Round is not yet concluded, or pronounced dead, the scope of the agreement (or agreement to differ) is now reasonably clear. In either case, there will remain considerable trading pressure for the continued reform of domestic policies on both sides of the Atlantic (not to mention the Pacific). Arguably, the pressure will be the more intense in the event of collapse of the Uruguay Round, though with the possibility that responses will be more insular and protective, and thus destructive of the world market, at least in the short run. But, as far as the EC is concerned, other pressures, especially those from the enlargement of the Community to include elements of the CIS and other Eastern and mid-European States, could potentially press for reform along more libertarian lines.

On the basis of previous experience, the driving pressures for reform will continue to be domestic budgetary costs and farm income preservation, increasingly tinged with environmental considerations and with trade consequences of domestic policy. On both sides of the Atlantic, it is arguable that these pressures have simply been expressed in the Uruguay Round, rather than the design and existence of the Round having had a substantive effect on domestic policy. Under this argument, the EC, for instance, would be hypothesised to have undertaken the MacSharry reforms in any event, regardless of the existence of the GATT negotiations, as has been argued in the past by the Commission. In fact, at the beginning of the negotiations over the MacSharry proposals, the Council and the Commission strongly denied any direct link with the GATT round, and maintained that internal reforms needed to precede any GATT agreement. Indeed, the Commission (1991) based its reform proposals on the following conclusions:[1]

- existing price guarantees, through their direct link to production, lead to growing output;
- this extra output could be accommodated only by adding to intervention stocks, already at excessive levels, or by exports to already oversupplied world markets;
- the in-built incentive to greater intensity and further production, provided by present mechanisms, puts the environment at increasing risk;
- rapidly rising budgetary expenditure, devoted in large part to a small minority of farms, provides no solution to the problems of farm incomes generally.

Later, however, the Ministers were reported as arguing that completion of the agreements on CAP reforms would have to await a GATT agreement, suggesting the reverse connection between the two negotiations.[2] It is difficult, and not of much more than intellectual interest, to distinguish between genuine linkages and connections and bargaining tactics in these reports.

A more fruitful approach is to the political economy of the agricultural reform process (as developed, for instance, by Rausser and Irwin, 1989). According to this argument, the principal advantage of multilateral agreement on agricultural policies is to resolve the prisoners' dilemma associated with the net benefits of unilateral liberalisation compared with those of either multilateral liberalisation or continued isolated protection in the face of other states' liberalised policies. A binding external agreement on the scope and level of policies is one (perhaps the only) way of resolving this dilemma, and forms a strong reason for countries to commit themselves to such negotiations. This will remain a strong reason for continued multilateral negotiations over agriculture whatever the outcome of the present round. However, as Rausser and Irwin point out, such external pressure, even if ultimately producing binding constraints on domestic policy behaviour, is not sufficient to produce liberalising reforms in the absence of domestic policy and policy process changes. The key internal changes identified by Rausser and Irwin are: (i) transparency and greater information on the costs of policies; (ii) at least partial compensation for the losers from policy change; and (iii) restructuring of institutions to ensure maintenance of reforms once in place.

Furthermore, it is inconsistent with both the logic of political economy and with past experience to expect the overall framework for agricultural policy reform to be set in the multilateral negotiation arena. Rather, the direction and strategy of reform will be set through the domestic internal policy process, which can be seen as responding to international or external pressures among a variety of others. Although the existence of the GATT Round could have been used by domestic politicians as a device to 'shift the blame' for unpopular domestic policy change, there is little evidence that this has occurred to any marked extent among the developed countries participating in the present round. Such an argument merely allows desirable domestic policy reform to be undertaken at lower cost, rather than providing the external pressures with increased valency. Similarly, the depressive effects of strongly supportive policies on world prices eventually return external effects of such policies to the internal (domestic) agenda, via the budgetary implications.

Thus, it is argued that policy reform after the Uruguay Round will continue to be driven, as it has been in the past, by internal or domestic pressures, and that the continuation of multilateral negotiations on agricultural trade reform will have to take appropriate account of these internal pressures and the policies which they produce. According to this argument, the incorporation (not to say leading role) of agriculture in the Uruguay Round was due to the realisation by two principal trading partners (the US and EC) that their own domestic agricultural policies were politically unsustainable at home, and that reform could be potentially cheaper or easier through the assistance of multilateral negotiations than without. In that sense, multilateral considerations must always take second place to internal pressures, though they may either constrain or assist the domestic policy reform process. This chapter will therefore consider the internal policy process and then return to the implications for the future of the GATT (or other) multilateral negotiations within the context of these internal pressures. Particular attention will be paid to the MacSharry reforms of the CAP, which seem on the surface to be more radical than any of the more evolutionary reforms in the US, and more directly associated with the GATT talks. The Rausser/Irwin framework is adopted for this analysis, since it provides a recent and concise (though not rigorous) outline of the political economy considerations relevant to the present discussion.

11.2 INTERNAL POLICY PROCESSES

11.2.1 Transparency and information

It seems obvious that clarification of the winners and losers from policy can be expected to assist in policy reform, while transparency of transfers (of either PERT or PEST nature)[3] is also expected to make political debate and judgements about them more socially rational. Hence, transfers which are made solely at the expense of the exchequer, rather than at the (partial) expense of the consumer, and those which occur as identifiable transfers rather than concealed within distorted market prices, are held to be more socially controllable. The major reasons for these assertions are that information and transactions costs are reduced and that free-rider problems associated with group (political) action are minimised. The latter are more easily overcome if the transfer is identified with the specific line-item in a government's budget, and is hence overseen by both the exchequer and competing spending departments' interests. Hence deficiency payments, commonly regarded as more efficient than the equivalent market price distortion through, for example, import levies (Josling, 1969; Gardner, 1983), are also more likely to be effectively policed through the political system.

This argument, however, ignores the importance in practice of political constituencies' understanding and valuation of information. For instance, economic cost calculations of farm policies have been prolific in the European Community for some time, but have not been noticeably important in triggering policy change. This fact would be expected from political economy analysis, since this information does little to resolve the disparity between the per head/household consumer gains and producer losses and hence the political power and resources devoted to change versus maintenance of the status quo by these opposed interest groups. More plausibly, the change in the characteristics of the supported industry and the changing social importance attached to non-productive elements of it by society at large appear to have been major forces in promoting reform of the CAP. Persistent surpluses in a 'world' of plenty and environmental damage attributed to modern intensive systems have become more important through the 1980s, while, at least for some, the maldistribution of benefits among the farming population has also grown in importance as a cause for concern and reason for change. These pressures are explicitly recognised in the European Commission document on reform of the CAP, quoted above (European Commission, 1991).

11.2.2 Compensation

To the extent that policy change involves significant redistribution of income and wealth, some form of compensation of the losers by the gainers is required. There are two major reasons for this compensation. First, the traditional welfare theory, based on the Pareto Criterion, can only be employed to demonstrate a *theoretical* improvement in welfare if there is net welfare gain. Without specifying the form and mechanisms for compensation, the policy change can only be recommended as providing the *potential* for welfare improvement. Actual welfare improvement, according to the Pareto Criterion, requires compensation to be carried out. Otherwise the policy change will involve losers and a value judgement is required in order to pronounce the change beneficial. Once a mechanism for the provision of compensation is suggested, this mechanism becomes a new policy, and the welfare implications of the policy change should now involve a comparison of the existing policy and the new (compensation) policy. The second reason is the political imperative. Political acceptance of possible policy alternatives requires that the losses resulting from the policy change be minimised, which implies some form of compensation. As Rausser and Irwin argue 'reform proposals need to facilitate adjustment and to consider compensating those disadvantaged by the removal of domestic programmes in order to neutralise their resistance to change' (1989, p. 360).

The first of these reasons argues for full compensation. However, there are a number of arguments for no compensation at all, including an apparently powerful one that it is not necessary to single out policy changes from the numerous other socio-economic changes for compensation. The second, political, reason for compensation treats it as a necessary cost of change, and as such, to be minimised to that level just sufficient to allow the change to be made. Thus change becomes likely as and when the necessary costs of compensation fall below the potential benefits of the change. Once agreed, however, compensation packages carry their own dangers, especially of moral hazard – that the likelihood of compensation encourages both opposition to change and disproportionate claims for damage resulting from the proposed change – and compensation seeking, by farmers anticipating compensation associated with existing resource allocation and seeking to increase this allocation (and thus associated compensation) prior to the policy change. It is not difficult, therefore, for compensation packages originally designed as PERTs to become PESTs through the operation of political–economic markets. Compensation for policy change has certainly been a feature of the present CAP reforms, with considerable attention being paid both to the levels and the consequences, as will be discussed below.

11.2.3 Institutional change

Typically, institutional changes or requirements have been ignored in conventional economic welfare analysis, but they are of potentially critical importance. Rausser and Irwin argue that some institutional change is a pre-requisite for policy reform, in the sense that it is through such change that previously ineffective opposition to current policies becomes articulate and effective, while institutional defence of present policies also needs undermining. While this is a plausible argument, it is difficult to identify critical institutional changes which have led to the present CAP reforms. However, four potential candidates can be suggested. First, in contrast to the arguments at the beginning of this chapter, the existence of the Uruguay Round of negotiations as an institution obliged the Council of Ministers to respond to offers and proposals for support reduction and policy reform, and hence to consider alternative systems of support (or compensation). Second, the emergence of the Single European Act and, more recently, the moves towards economic and political union (the Maastricht Treaty), have obliged the Community to review existing policies. Third, the incorporation of Finance Ministers into the ratification of annual farm price-setting agreements in 1988 should have led to increased pressure on limiting budget spending under the policy, though the direction of the present reforms is in direct opposition to this pressure. Fourth, the unification of Germany, and associated incorporation of a large scale and potentially productive agriculture sector, and the potential entry of a number of other Eastern (Central) European countries to the Community, forced reconsideration of the political–economic sustainability of a protectionist agricultural policy.

With the exception of the GATT negotiations, none of these changes have been explicitly recognised in the official reports from the Commssion. However, it seems likely that all have played some part in the reform process, with the last (eastern European expansion) being particularly important. Such an expansion presents a greater potential difficulty for the CAP system than either the domestic or international pressures. The inclusion of one actual major exporter (Hungary, which exports one third of its agricultural production) and several potential agricultural exporters cannot be contemplated within the old structure of the CAP. To deny Eastern Europeans the chance to exploit their potential comparative advantages in food production would be to deny them the chance to benefit from letting the market system work. Yet inclusion of these countries within the old CAP system would have done just that, since the cost of disposing of the consequent greatly enlarged surpluses would have been out of the question. The design and implementation of a different system of support for a wider European agriculture thus becomes an increasingly pressing imperative, yet one which has received very little overt attention from Europe's policy makers.

11.2.4 MacSharry reforms

In the light of the above, what can be said about the MacSharry reforms? The progress of the reform package is outlined for the major commodities in Table 11.1, which shows the principal changes in prices, compensation and supply control measures between the first (leaked) draft proposal in January 1991 through the formal proposals of July 1991, to the eventual agreement in May 1992. The draft proposal contained substantial price reductions, especially in cereals, with the intervention price set to reflect a Commission view of an expected free trade world price (European Commission, 1991, p. 9). Coupled with these price reductions were proposals for compensation which were heavily 'modulated' in favour of smaller and also more extensive producers. The supply control measures for milk were retained (and tightened) and also introduced for cereals. Given that the cereals' intervention price had been reduced to the expected free-trade world price level, it is difficult to follow the logic of adding a set-aside component. Presumably the supply control element represented some uncertainty about the power of market prices to resolve structural market imbalances and also provided a potential bargaining counter in the 'stabilisation' of world markets (to use the Commission's term). However, neither of these possible justifications are mentioned in official reports from the Commission, although the 'Reflections' paper (European Commission, 1991a, p. 7) does express serious concern about the Community's cereal imbalance.

The leaked proposals of the Commission raised a storm of protest, and the subsequent release of the official 'Reflections' document omitted mention of specific levels of support or details of compensa-

Table 11.1 Progress of MacSharry reform proposals, EC

Commodity	Measure	Draft Proposal, January 1991	Final Proposal, July 1991	Agreement, May, 1992
Cereals	Target Price	100ecu/t	100ecu/t	110ecu/t
	Intervention Price	90ecut/t (from 155 ecu/t)	90ecu/t	100ecu/t
	Threshold Price	ns	110ecu/t	155ecu/t
	Co-responsibility	abolished	abolished	abolished
	Set-aside	≤30ha: 0; 31–80ha: 25% > 80ha: 35% (rotational)	≤20ha: 0; > 20ha: 15% (rotational)	≤20ha: 0; > 20ha: 15% (non-rotational allowed at higher rate; + regional base)
	Compensation Payments			
	Price	≤30ha: full; 31–80ha: −25% > 80ha: −35%	full	full
	Set aside	none	≤50ha: full; > 50ha: none	full
Oilseeds & Protein Crops	as for cereals	as for cereals	as for cereals	
Milk	Quota	cut by 4.5 to 5% (with 'extensive' modulation)	cut by 5% (inc 91/2 price agreement cut of 2%)	cuts to be determined later
	Prices: Target	reduced by 10%	reduced by 10%	none
	Butter	reduced by 15%	reduced by 15%	reduced by 5%
	SMP	reduced by 5%	reduced by 5%	none

	Compensation Payments	≤15 cows (≤1LU/ha) 45 ecu/cow	Quota: 100ecu/kg over 10 years as a bond price: 75ecu/cow, ≤40 cows s.t. stocking rates	none
	Co-responsibility	abolished	abolished	retained
Beef	Intervention Price	reduced by 15% with safety net	reduced by 15%	reduced by 15% with safety net
	Compensation male beef premium	raised by 80ecu/h. limited to 1LU/ha, ≤90LUs	raised by 140 ecu/hd limited to 1LU/ha, 90 LUs	raied by 140 ecu/hd ≤2LUs/ha; ≤90LUs
	suckler cow premium:	no change in rate; limited by 1LU/ha, ≤90LUs	raised by 35 ecu/hd limited by 1LU/ha, ≤90LUs	raised by 0ecu/hd ≤2LUs/ha; no headage limit
	special premia:	none	none	i) early season slaughter ii) Extensive (≤1.4LU/ha) 60 ecu, 30ecu/hd respectively
Sheep	Ewe premium:	≤350hd(750 in LFAs)	≤350hd. (750 in LFAs)	≤500hd. (1000hd in LFAs) 50 % premia payable over these limits.

Notes: The Draft proposal, January 1991, was not officially released but was reported, inter alia, in *Agra Europe*, January 18th, 1991. The Final Proposal: European Commission: Development & Future of the CAP COM (91) 258 Final, 22.7.91, a follow up to the Reflections Paper (COM(91) 100, 1.2.91), which contained no specific proposals for levels of support, rather concentrated on the framework for reform.

The Agreement was reported in *Agra Europe*, 22.5.92, followed by various regulations in the EC Official Journal (eg. cereals – OJ No. L 181/p12 – 39, 1.7.92). Only full post-transitional changes are recorded here.

231

tion, although the principles of substantial support price reductions coupled with heavily modulated compensation were stoutly defended. In the event, however, the power of the commercial sector of the industry (strongly supported by the UK) succeeded in reducing the extent of modulation substantially in the final proposal of July 1991, with some increase in the proposed levels of compensation, especially in beef, at a potentially substantial increase in exchequer cost of the reform. Throughout the negotiations over this proposal, the commercial sectors of the industry, representing mainly larger scale producers, continued to object to the remaining and substantial elements of modulation, particularly with respect to the combinable crops set-aside provision, and beef and sheep premia, while the traditional agricultural lobbies, representing mainly smaller-scale farmers, protested the depth of the price cuts and quota reductions for milk.

The final outcome reflects these pressures on the Commission. The milk regime has been left largely untouched, while the cereals price reductions have been reduced and compensation increased, with set-aside compensation stripped of its major modulation provisions. Similarly, the upper limits on premia entitlement for beef and sheep producers have been relaxed markedly from the original proposal (especially pleasing to the UK) and the special interests of Ireland have been catered for in the special premia for beef. The addition of a ewe premium at half the full rate for flocks greater than the (increased) upper limits makes the very existence of these limits somewhat suspect. The general principles of the Commission's reform package have been retained. It remains a radical reform, but only just. The exchequer cost of the package has been increased substantially from the original proposal, both through the increased levels of, and broader entitlements to, compensation and through less substantial cuts in support prices. It is this fact which promises most pressure for continued reform of the policy in the future, at least from an internal perspective.

For some time the reform of the CAP has been poised between a direction of increased supply control and isolation from world markets, and the alternative of world prices and de-coupled support. The introduction of milk quotas in 1984 was a clear step in the former direction, reflecting the power of the vested producer interests against those more dispersed interests of the consumers. The 1988 'stabiliser' package signalled an attempt, albeit modest, to introduce more explicit price pressure, related to over-production though not explicitly to world prices. The MacSharry reforms can still be interpreted, in spite of the substantial weakening since the original proposals, as a significant move towards world prices and de-coupled support. However, as the budgetary pressure entailed in the present reform package begins to bite, it remains an open question as to whether this rather radical policy direction can be sustained.

There is substantial scope within the present reformed system for the PERTs of the compensation package to become PESTs. Elements of moral hazard are already evident in the progress of the reform negotiations, with compensation amounts and eligibilities consistently increased from the original proposals. The current package seems prone to compensation-seeking. The major questions are: (i) the extent to which paper re-definitions of farms, flocks and herds can be tailored to allow a greater proportion of the industry to qualify for compensation payments; and (ii) the extent to which current (and future) production decisions can influence the compensation payments per farm.

Since the full legal texts for the regulations are not presently available, it is difficult to make a judgement on these issues. However, some comment is possible on the combinable arable crops legislation.[4] Since this legislation incorporates a simplified scheme for 'small' producers (those with an average of less than 20 hectares of combinable crops), which excludes them from the set-aside provisions, it is to be expected that there will be some producers able to convince the authorities that their farms were really two or more separate units (under control of wives or other relations and partners) during the base period, thus converting existing holdings to the 'small' category and avoiding the set-aside restrictions – an example of compensation seeking under the first count above. Similar arguments are also possible with respect to the headage limits for beef and sheep producers. However, this is a once-and-for-all slippage in the compensation arrangements. More important is the extent to which the compensation payments depend on current production decisions, and thus encourage further production.

The regulations are such that producer compensation for both the price reductions and for the set-aside is clearly to be based on historical areas of crops (between 1989 and 1991) and historical yields (between 1986/7 and 1990/91, excluding the highest and lowest). The compensation is then to be set as the fixed compensation per tonne (45ECU from 1995/96 onwards) times the average yield figure for the region times the eligible historic area, *providing that the producer sows the area*. Thus, while eligibility for, and computation of, compensation payments per hectare appear to be divorced from current production decisions, entitlement to payment requires current sowings. Article 15 of the regulation makes further provision for altering payments and set-aside areas 'in the light of developments in production, productivity and the markets', which opens the door for future changes which may well depend on current production levels, albeit in an uncertain and, for the individual producer, an indirect fashion.

So long as the Community remains a net exporter, so that the floor in the domestic price is determined by the intervention price (100ECU/ tonne less any buying-in discount), there is every incentive for producers to participate in the voluntary scheme, setting aside 15 per cent of their arable area in order to receive compensation payments on all of this set-aside area, plus the compensation payments on their current sown area. Only if production falls sufficiently to place the Community on a net-import basis (with a domestic market floor price then rising to the threshold level of 155ECU/tonne) does this logic collapse. Since entitlement to compensation depends on the current sown area, it is to be expected that this decision, at least, will depend on the market price plus the compensation payment, and thus will not be decoupled from production (area planted) decisions. However, the historic areas define the eligible areas for both compensation and set-aside, so planted areas should be subject to this upper limit. The sowing condition thus ensures that the historic area will continue to be used for arable purposes, while the dependence of the compensation system on historic arable areas encourages maximum allocation of historic areas to the arable classification.

Variable inputs applied at and after sowing should be applied in response solely to market prices (the intervention price), since compensation is based on historic rather than current yields. However, there is a possibility that eligibility conditions will be changed (updated) in the future Thus current areas and yields may influence entitlements in the future. This re-enforces the incentive to plant the full entitlement area (or risk allocation of a smaller area in the future). But the logic argues against individual farmers maximising yield on their 'permitted' area, since the present yield (and thus likely future) calculations for compensation are based upon average yields, both over time and across farms (regions). Thus, economic logic points to the reduction of variable inputs on the sown area to the point were marginal benefit of inputs is just greater than the market price.

Since producers are obliged to sow their permitted crop area (historic area minus set-aside) in order to qualify for full compensation payments, the compensation payments are clearly *not* fully 'decoupled'. However, the compensation for cereals, protein crops and oilseeds combined is clearly limited in total to historic production levels (base period areas times average yields) and is fixed in total amount (according to the pre-set compensation figures per tonne). In that sense the compensation is limited and independent of current production decisions, though with no incentive to reduce planted areas. Similarly, it seems that there is no incentive for most producers to reduce their herds and flocks of beef and sheep, since compensation depends on the existence of these animals up to the herd and flock size limits and stocking rate densities. However, the reform package does remove the incentives to expand herds and flocks *above* these limits unless warranted by market prices, which remain supported though at reduced levels. As reported in *Agra Europe*, the Commission is committed to obtaining 'green box' status for these reformed subsidies. The new compensatory payments are seen as an 'integral part of the CAP', compensatory aids 'cannot fulfil that essential role unless they are free from any disciplines associated with the reduction of internal support agreed as part of multilateral trade negotiations' – hence the EC will 'continue to press in the course of negotiations on the Uruguay Round for their inclusion in a special category of the green box, i.e. aids not subject to reduction'.[5]

Pressure in the future for modification of these measures seems likely to come from three major sources: (i) budgetary limits on agricultural spending; (ii) potential expansion of the present European Community to include mid and eastern European states with major (actual or potential) agricultural industries; and (iii) the GATT or successor multilateral negotiations. One projection of the budgetary cost of the reform agreement[6] is that the present ceiling on agricultural spending (set in the 1988 round of price-fixing) will be breached within four years. However, this projected overshoot of the present guideline is relatively modest and limited. History suggests that a mild overshoot will lead to changes in the budgetary guideline rather than the policy. However, there is an unanswered question about the extent to which the taxpayers of Europe, and their representatives in the national exchequers, are willing to continue paying farmers to do nothing, as is implied in the compensation payments for the set-aside part of the present package. Aside from this point, current budgetary projections suggest that future budgetary pressure will be modest, so long as remaining export refunds can be contained, and consequently that further reform from this quarter will be limited. The reform package does contain substantial elements which should limit budgetary spending in the future, through more-or-less fixed compensation payments to farmers for cereals, oilseeds, protein crops, beef and sheep (even if still rather high by some standards), while the milk regime remains 'capped' with quotas, although again left at a level which will continue to produce structural surpluses. Budget exposure is now limited, both through the prospect of a substantially lower export refunds on cereals and through limited surplus disposal costs for milk, though costs of support for Mediterranean crops remain relatively open-ended.

Expansion of the CAP to include mid eastern European states, either on a full membership basis or, more likely in the medium term, a free-trading basis, is likely to put the remaining export refund and surplus disposal elements of the budget under further pressure. Extension of the compensation/support measures to these states would clearly give rise to substantial additional budgetary costs, with little political logic or constituency support. As far as common trading prices are concerned, there is little doubt in logic that the only sustainable set of prices for such trade are those determined in a free interplay of supply and demand conditions on a genuinely world-wide market. Much has been written about the agricultural potential of these newly liberalising states, with the prospect that the bloc could become a major exporter (at least for cereals) in the medium term.[7] An obvious market for at least some of this potential export surplus would be in Western Europe, traditionally the destination of important European grain exports prior to the 'great socialist experiment'. It seems politically inconceivable that the West European market could remain protected against the agricultural production potential of Eastern Europe, regardless of the formal economic and political links between the present European Community and the liberalising states. The conclusion is that this Eastern European pressure will ensure that EC markets become progressively more liberalised, at least within an enlarged European bloc, whatever the outcome of the present GATT round and any of its successors. It is to this final pressure on policy reform, and to the obverse – the implications for future multilateral negotiations – that the next section turns.

11.3 IMPLICATIONS FOR MULTILATERAL NEGOTIATIONS

11.3.1 Identification and measurement problems

Multilateral agricultural policy 'disarmament' under the GATT potentially allows countries to achieve domestic policy goals more effectively by offering the prospect of improving world market prices. Because the GATT is the legal code governing international trade relationships, it does not have authority over domestic policies other than through their trade distorting effects. The achievable objective of multilateral negotiations is, therefore, to minimize trade distortions, not necessarily to eliminate protection or domestic income support. Indeed, this objective has been central to the repeated declarations of intent from the GATT participants, that *trade distorting* agricultural support be substantially reduced, if not eliminated. It is now recognised that domestic support of agriculture must be allowed to continue within this constraint, given national desires so to do.

This objective, however, raises a serious issue for agricultural policy and trade analysts. Conventional analysis provides measures of protection, either nominal or effective, and of agricultural support, traditionally through measures of producers' surplus gain and more recently, and arguably, through the Producers' Subsidy Equivalent (PSE). But the literature does not identify trade distortion specifically. There is a question of whether the concepts of agricultural protection and agricultural support are interchangeable and of the relationships between them. The question is clearly important. Much of the debate within the GATT negotiations has been concerned with the appropriate definition and possible use of an Aggregate Measure of Support (AMS).

Josling (1973, 1975) refined and extended the nominal rate of protection (NRP) concept in developing PSEs for the FAO. The OECD have applied and modified the concept further under the Trade Mandate Study, and this has now become popular as a potential aggregate measure for negotiation under GATT. However, inasmuch as PSEs and NRPs are similar, neither are unambiguous measures of protection or distortion.[8] In part, this fact has promoted the search for aggregate measures of protection other than the PSE. In addition, the need to separate protection from trade distortion has also implicitly encouraged the development of alternative aggregate measures for the GATT purposes. These include the Effective Rate of Assistance (ERA) and Price Adjustment Gap (PAG) by Australia, the Trade Distortion Equivalent (TDE) by Canada, and the Support Measurement Unit (SMU) by the European Community.

As a result, there is an ongoing debate about whether an aggregate measure is useful for the negotiating process, and if so, what an appropriate aggregate measure might be and what role it should play.[9] This debate cannot ignore the differences between support, protection and distortion. If an aggregate measure has any role in the negotiations, it would seem necessary that it focus on trade distortion. Traditional conceptual analyses fail to recognise that equivalent levels of protection involving different policy instruments, economic supply/demand characteristics and world market conditions might generate different levels of support and still different levels of trade distortion. The argument here is that policy intervention is carried out for a variety of domestic reasons, with economic efficiency of secondary importance. Such intervention will not be negotiated away, certainly not in a multilateral forum. In this event, the analytic objective is to seek those forms of intervention which generate minimal international externalities; that is, minimize trade distortion. A prior task is to develop the analytical framework for the explicit measurement of distortion as opposed to protection and support. Such a framework can be used to condition the choice of aggregate measure of protection commitments, and help keep expectations about the results of their reduction more realistic. It also sheds more light on the distribution of gains and losses from the multilateral reduction of trade-distorting protection in the absence of the introduction of non-distorting compensatory programmes.

11.3.2   Measuring distortion, protection and support[10]

Protection, support and trade distortion are not necessarily the same things. Protection is defined on the basis of a difference between domestic and border prices. So long as protection changes incentive prices facing producers and consumers from their free trade levels, resulting trade volumes will be distorted from free trade levels. Thus protection implies distortion. But, different policy instruments yielding the same levels of protection can lead to different levels of distortion. Similarly, protection implies support to the domestic production sector, at the expense of the consumer, taxpayer and trading partner. Again, different methods of protection for the same level can afford different levels of support. Concepts of protection and support involve considerations of price and cost differences from free trade conditions, where different definitions of the scope of free trade lead to different measures of protection and support. But market distortion arises from differences in trade volumes compared to free trade, albeit related to price and cost differences. Thus it should be possible to measure distortion directly through comparisons of trade volumes under different market and policy conditions.

Consider Figure 11.1, which represents a stylised representation of the EC cereals market. The present support price is shown as $190/tonne, equivalent to the new (MacSharry) threshold price of 155ECU/tonne. Five different policies are identified which could implement this level of price support:

1. an export subsidy (of $90/tonne against a current world price of $100/tonne);
2. a production quota of 130m. tonnes plus a prohibitive import tariff of at least $78/tonne imposed above a world price of about $112/tonne and with both producer and consumer prices at $190/tonne, giving a quasi-supply curve as S_q: this is illustrative of applying the milk quota approach to the cereals regime, with the difference that the quota is set equal to domestic EC consumption in this case, as opposed to some higher level, as with milk;
3. a deficiency payment or production subsidy of around $82/tonne with consumer price set by a world market price of $108/tonne;
4. a set-aside programme linked to price reductions and compensation, as an approximation to the reform agreement, where set-aside is assumed to reduce production by 8 per cent, support prices are

Figure 11.1 Stylized representation of different support instruments (EC, cereals)

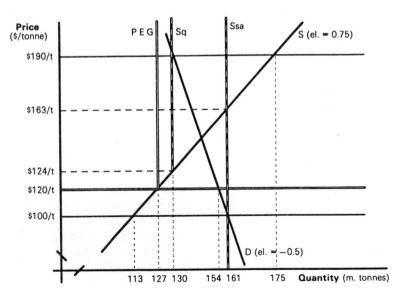

reduced to $120/tonne (100 ECU/tonne, the European Commission's expected free trade price) and compensation is paid to farmers to cover 100 per cent of both price reduction and the set-aside requirement. The 'old' import levy/export refund system continues to apply between the world price of around $110/tonne and the new floor price of $120/tonne. Notice that it is assumed here that the total cereals area is constrained by the compensation/set-aside provisions, giving a quasi-supply curve as Ss_a;

5. a 'producers' entitlement guarantee' scheme (PEG),[11] under which support is fixed and limited to no more than that quantity which would be produced under free trade (that is, at a price of $120/tonne), and paid direct to farmers from the exchequer, with all other market interventions removed.

Tables 11.2 and 11.3 illustrate some key measures associated with these policy options, calculated on the basis of a supply elasticity of 0.75 and a demand elasticity of -0.5 at current quantities/prices, using linear approximations. Table 11.2 shows the assumed data values associated with each policy option as already discussed, as well as the effects of each policy option on world prices which are treated here as endogenous. The actual world price ($100/t) and the free trade world price of $120/t are taken as given. For the other policy options the world price lies between these two figures, being lower the higher is the volume of EC exports. For each of the policy options involving less than full liberalisation (production quota; production subsidy; set-aside/compensation), the change in the world price from current policy is derived from the slope of the implicit excess demand curve.

Table 11.2   Base data and primary illustrative calculations

	1 PW ($/t)	2 Pp ($/t)	3 Pc ($/t)	4 S (mt)	5 D (mt)	6 X (mt)	7 PSE (%)	8 NRP (%)	9 TD (mt)
Ex. sub.	100.00	190.0	190.0	175.0	130.0	45.0	47	90	72
Prod. Q	112.4	190.0	190.0	130.0	130.0	0.0	41	69	27
Prod. sub	107.8	190.0	107.8	175.0	158.1	16.9	43	76	44
Comp/SA	110.5	190.0	120.0	161.0	153.9	7.1	42	72	34
PEG @ FT	120.0	190/120	12.0	126.6	153.9	−27.3	37	58	0
Free Trade	120.0	120.0	120.0	126.6	153.9	−27.3	0	0	0

Table 11.3   Illustrative policy measures

	1 Total PSE *($m)*	2 PSG *($m)*	3 Tax cost *($m)*	4 Cons. cost *($m)*	5 Net soc. cost *($m)*	6 Trans. eff. TE *(norm=1)*	7 Trans. cost TC *(norm=0)*
Ex. sub.	15750	10558	4050	9938	3431	0.67	0.32
Prod. Q	10082	9093	0	9938	845	0.90	0.09
Prod. sub.	14388	10558	14388	−1958	1873	0.73	0.18
Comp/SA	12800	11396	12317	0	921	0.89	0.08
PEG @ FT	8865	8865	8865	0	0	1	0
Free Trade	0	0	0	0	0	0	0

On this basis, the percentage PSEs and NRPs differ somewhat among the policy options considered (Table 11.2, columns 7 and 8). However, the usual method of estimating PSEs and NRPs treats world prices as exogenous. Had this methodology been used here, with the fixed and given world price at $100/tonne, all five policy options would be characterised as having identical PSE and NRP values, of 47 per cent and 90 per cent respectively.

Much of the technical debate within the GATT has been concerned with an appropriate measure of trade distortion. It is clear from this simple example that traditional measures do not discriminate between policies with different effects on trade volumes, and hence with different effects on world markets. That is, they do not discriminate between policies with different trade distorting effects. This point has not been lost on negotiators, who have been keen to adjust measures such as the PSE to account for trade distorting differences (for example, adjustments for supply control measures). It seems more sensible, and more direct, to try and measure trade distortion directly, as the difference between current (policy distorted) trade volumes and those which would occur under free trade.

Such a measure of trade distortion (TD) is shown in the ninth column of Table 11.2, following the above discussion.[12] TD is here defined as the difference between policy generated trade volumes and those which would occur under free-trade with no policy intervention (that is, an import quantity of 27m. tonnes in Figure 11.1), expressed in million tonnes. Thus, the export subsidy option results in the EC exporting 45m. tonnes compared with the import of 27m. tonnes under free trade. Thus the total effect of the export subsidy is to deny the EC's trade competitors exports of 72m. tonnes, which is a measure of the trade distortion caused by the export subsidy option. Notice that this measure includes the distorting effects of the policy on both consumption *and* production (termed CDE and PDE respectively by de Gorter and McClatchy), and also includes directly the consequences of any supply control policies (as shown by the TD value for production quotas). In contrast, by concentrating on differences between producers prices and world prices, most other measures purporting to measure distortion actually only measure the potential distortion arising from intervention on the supply side of the market (assuming that there are no production controls in the case of the NRP).

When the TD measure is used as a basis for comparison, all the remaining policy options are less distorting than the export subsidy option (that is, the pre-MacSharry CAP). The PEG option is (quasi) non-distorting *ex hypothesi*. The compensation/set-aside option would also be non-distorting under this measure if production were limited to 125m. tonnes, though here remains substantially distorting, given the assumption for these calculations that the set-aside only reduces production by 8 per cent. The treatment of the compensation/set-aside option here assumes that the compensation payments are seen by producers as deficiency payments, and thus determine their domestic production levels according to the floor price plus the compensation payments. In the event that these payments are perceived as fixed and independent of current production (as is arguably the intent of the reforms and certainly the implication of their acceptance as 'green box' measures), then production levels would be determined by the new floor price ($120/tonne). In this case, the level of trade distortion (and subsequent calculations of costs and benefits) are more closely approximated by the PEG option, rather than those shown here for the compensation/set-aside option, with the exception of the tax cost (see below) which is a reasonable reflection of the tax cost of the MacSharry reforms. The reality, perhaps, will lie somewhere between these two extremes, depending on the extent to which the compensation payments are treated as fixed and invariant with production levels.

However, all policy options look alike against a fixed world price, under both the NRP (the simplest measure of protection) and the PSE (frequently suggested as a base Aggregate Measure of Support, or AMS, for GATT negotiations). The point of these illustrative estimates is that, once the terms of trade effects of large country policy choices are allowed for, the policies are rather different both in terms of the support offered to the agriculture sector (measured by Producers Surplus Gain, PSG, Table 11.3) and also in terms of their trade-distorting effects, with which the GATT is primarily concerned.

No doubt there are difficulties with the precise measurement of trade distortion, not least because any trade volume measure requires knowledge of supply and demand responses to price and other policy changes, and (as measured here) knowledge of the free trade world price, in contrast to both the NRP and PSE measures, which only require information about current prices and quantitites. However, recognition of these difficulties does not justify the dismissal of attempts to measure trade distortion altogether, since the very concept of trade distortion must carry with it some notion of what an undistorted market would look like. It is surely not beyond the wit of man to agree to estimates of the required parameters for negotiation purposes, even if it is necessary to recognise that these estimates cannot be accurate reflections of reality.

Table 3 shows some indicators of policy effectiveness and efficiency for the policy options. The total PSE figures (in $ million) do differ between policies, since the total production levels differ. The quota, compensation/set-aside and PEG options result in lower levels of the production than the other three policies. It is of passing interest to note that the EC's offer to the GATT of reducing its PSE by 30 per cent (basis 1986) is comparable with these illustrative figures which involve a reduction in total PSE of 25.7 per cent for the quota option and 27.6 per cent for the PEG option.

The common measure of support is the producers's surplus gain (PSG), here measured in $ million relative to the free-trade price of $120/tonne. Under this measure, both the quota and PEG option score lower than the other policies (Table 11.3, column 2). In both cases, however, the PSGs for these policies could be adjusted upwards through an increase in the support price to offset the loss in PSG resulting from the quantity reductions. Notice, too, that the PSG for the PEG option is only 16 per cent lower than that for the export subsidy, and 13.9 per cent lower for the quota option, in contrast to the total PSE measure for these policies (Table 11.3, column 1), as a result of the cost savings in production. The PSG for the compensation/set-aside option is higher than the other options because of the assumption that the set-aside area is fully compensated (by the difference between the support price of $190 and the free trade world price of $120 applied to the foregone production of 175m.–161m. tonnes) while producers do not incur any measurable costs due to set-aside.

The tax cost of each policy option (Table 11.3, column 3) is here measured against the corresponding world price (Table 11.2, column 1). The tax cost is highest for the producer subsidy option as would be expected, and nearly as high for the compensation/set-aside option (which ghosts the MacSharry reforms), while the export subsidy option (reflecting the pre-MacSharry CAP) is relatively tax-effective, though not compared with the quota option as specified here, where the production quota is restricted to domestic requirements, so avoiding the need for export subsidies (in contrast to the present dairy situation in the EC).

The consumer cost (Table 3, column 4) is measured as the consumer surplus loss in the accepted fashion measured with respect to a free-trade world price of £120/tonne. As such, it applies only to the first three options analysed here (the traditional CAP instrument of export subsidies and import taxes, the production quota and the producer subsidy options). While the last option is usually considered not to affect consumers, under the methodology used here there is a consumer effect which results from the consequences of the subsidy on export volumes, and thus on world prices and domestic consumer prices. Measured against free trade world prices, and recognising that consumption is higher under this option than under free-trade conditions (because market and world prices are lower), this results in a consumer surplus gain (negative loss) under this option.

The net social cost of the policy options is identified in Table 11.3, column 5 in $million. This cost, as conventionally defined, is the sum of PSG, tax cost and consumer cost. Under this measure, the old CAP option appears the most inefficient. It should be noted that the compensation/set-aside tax cost includes an export refund (of around $10/tonne) paid on the export surplus under this option of 7.1m tonnes (columns 1 and 6 of Table 11.2). If production does not respond to the compensation payments (that is, the payments are truly de-coupled) then this export surplus will not materialise, and world prices will be higher (according to the assumptions used here), so the present figure may over-estimate the tax costs of this policy option. Nevertheless, the MacSharry ghost option (as represented by compensation/set-aside) shows a net social cost only marginally higher than the quota option in this analysis.

Clearly, if a policy base other than free-trade were to be used against which to measure producer gains and consumer losses, then the resulting measures would be different from those illustrated here. The problem of choice of the appropriate base is slightly more subtle than the familiar issue of the choice of first or second-best as the policy norm. Given an objective of the Uruguay Round to eliminate (eventually) all trade-distorting support, the choice of free-trade is at least defensible as a potentially acceptable policy norm, even though such an objective seems impossible to achieve quickly or easily. While a more immediately relevant policy base might be a predicted outcome of the present Round, it is beyond the bounds of this chapter to predict the outcome and assess the consquences for world prices. Nevertheless, it is accepted that the choice of policy base will influence the measures of support, protection and distortion, a fact which has not escaped negotiators.

The final two columns of Table 11.3 illustrate the efficiency and cost of making the transfers to producers under these policy options. Transfer efficiency relates PSG to total PSE, which is otherwise interpretable as the sum of the consumer and taxpayer costs of the policy, where the former is measured as total Consumer Subsidy Equivalent (CSE) rather than consumers' surplus. The PEG option has TE of 1, *ex hypothesi*. Of the remaining options, the most efficient by this criterion are the production quota (perhaps explaining its attraction in previous reforms of the CAP, notably the dairy reform of 1984), closely followed by the compensation/set-aside option. The 'old' CAP is least efficient under this measure.

Transfer cost (TC) relates the total PSG to the net social cost of the policy (defined as the net sum of PSG, consumers' surplus loss – CSL – and taxpayer cost of the policy) and hence measures the social cost per dollar transferred to producers. Apart from the PEG option, for which TC = 0 *ex hypothesi*, the compensation/set-aside and quota options are the most efficient.

While the analysis presented here is merely illustrative and partial, the general implications seem likely to be robust. Two points are worthy of emphasis. First, as Tables 11.2 and 11.3 demonstrate, many of the internal pressures on the CAP could be resolved with an insular policy development of production quotas limiting production to domestic consumption levels. Apart from the (probably severe) policing and implementation problems of such a policy, as evidenced already in the EC's dairy policy, the major force operating against such a policy direction is the international pressure for more liberal markets, including market access and expansion of market *demand*. Second, the present compensation/set-aside policy appears in this analysis to be a step in an acceptable direction. Although its domestic acceptability within Europe was in doubt and many of the original proposals have been dropped or weakened, the new policy should lead to some reduction in trade distortion and some improvement in transfer cost. Does it go far enough? The illustrative calculations here suggest not from the international point of view. But hinderances to pushing it further depend only partly on the compensation payments being declared non-distorting. Of equal if not more importance are the problems of finding acceptable compensation packages (especially in terms of budgetary costs) for greater reductions in prices or production levels and thus of substantially reducing the trade distortions of the present policy. In simple terms, either the price reductions and/or the set-aside provisions are presently insufficient to eliminate trade distortion. But there are likely to be considerable difficulties in extending the present policy to achieve non-distortion. However, the PEG option does provide a possible direction in which the policy could be developed.

As a concluding comment on this section, it should be emphasised that these illustrative calculations are partial and comparative-static. They ignore the potentially substantial effect that the history of protection and support has had on the structure and economic performance of the EC agricultural sector, and also the potential long-run and dynamic effects alternative policies would have on the sector. It seems intuitively plausible that the history of support has resulted in a shift of EC supply curves to the right of where they otherwise would have been, through the encouragement and enabling of technical and structural change. Thus the free-trade scenario depicted here continues to incorporate distortions built into the EC supply sector through the history of support. While this might be defensible on the grounds that it is unrealistic to expect multilateral negotiations to incorporate recompense for such historical 'embodied' distortions, present reports of the final negotiating meetings between the US and the EC on oilseeds seem to be dealing with just such issues, albeit on a commodity restricted basis.

Of potentially more importance are the possible future dynamic effects of the policy options. In particular, the PEG option has been labelled here as 'quasi' non-distorting. So long as the PEG payments are treated as independent of production decisions, then current production levels will be determined by current world prices. Hence it can be argued that the payments are non-distorting. Nevertheless, to the extent that they enable resources to remain in agriculture rather than be encouraged to leave, as they would be under genuine and uncompensated free trade, then the agricultural sector will be larger than without the compensation payments and hence remain distorted compared with free trade. It is difficult to be sure that such a large sector would not also exhibit more 'competitive' supply conditions than would exist without the payments, thus distorting product markets as well as resource allocation. The same arguments apply to the production quotas and compensation/set-aside policy options. However, so long as de-coupled compensation payments (whatever the method of delivery) do not increase the level of support (measured through PSG) compared with the present situation, then it can be argued: (i) that distortion is clearly substantially reduced under these options than the border protection systems characterising the 'old' CAP; and (ii) that the compensation payments 'merely' preserve historic embodied distortion. Furthermore, once de-coupled support payments become accepted, there are good reasons to argue that: (i) these payment entitlements should be tradeable; and (ii) that they should be capitalised to lump sum entitlements. Both of these extensions would allow the release of 'protected' resources from the industry (while providing for the appropriate compensation), thus disembodying historic distortions.

11.4 IMPLICATIONS FOR POLICY REFORM

11.4.1 Information

Returning to the political–economy framework outlined at the beginning of this chapter, the prominence of agriculture in the Uruguay Round has clearly resulted in a massive volume of technical and general information on agricultural protection, support and distortion and its consequences. This increase in information has done much to make even opaque policy instruments more transparent, an advance which cannot easily be undone even by the stoutest opponents of reform. However, it also contains dangers. First, the opposition can use (or perhaps misuse) selected parts of this information for its own ends (as referred to in Chapter 3 on the US), which is arguably the price that has to be paid for more and better information. Second, and more subtly, the existence and promulgation of the information does not guarantee that people will believe it. There are still major groups and important individuals in the agricultural policy process around the world who choose to ignore or disbelieve the information. Information is necessary but a long way from being sufficient for policy reform.

Over and above these considerations are the specific requirements for key information for future policy reform. The Uruguay Round clearly demonstrates the need for such measures: the AMS, the 'green, red, amber and blue boxes', and tariffication, are all ways of classifying and/or measuring policy intervention as a prelude to doing something about it. Underlying this debate is another one concerning the fundamental objectives of multilateral negotiations: to eliminate (trade distorting) support or reduce it. Whatever other lessons can be learnt from the Round, it should be clear that elimination is not something which is going to be easily agreed to. For those who would pursue it, stealth and flexibility would seem to be more appropriate than head-on attack. One outcome of the Round is that states will continue to seek ways of supporting their domestic agricultures, and will do so to the point of compromising the international trading system if necessary. Therefore, a definition and measure of acceptable and unacceptable policies is required – hence the boxes. Some will continue to try and use multilateral negotiations to achieve what they see as desirable domestic policy reform (especially substantial reduction, if not elimination, of support), as arguably did the US in the present Round. But the course of the Uruguay Round should convince them that multilateral negotiations can only play a supporting role in domestic policy reform. They cannot be used as the prime lever, since they require too much agreement from too many different interests, most of which are unconnected with the domestic problems, issues and constituencies.

However, multilateral negotiations can provide important and politically objective information necessary for domestic reform. There is little doubt that the world is better informed about the effects and effectiveness of domestic agricultural policies as a result of the Uruguay Round, and that domestic policy reform is thus both more possible and more likely to take socially desirable directions than before. But information requirements are not static. It seems possible that the ubiquitous PSE has now served its useful purpose and that other measures are now required, both to further the realistic objectives of multilateral negotiations (reduction/elimination of trade-distorting support) and to improve domestic reform. The PSE has been useful in pointing up the extent of agricultural support around the world, at least in terms of the costs of this support borne by consumers and taxpayers, if not the relative amounts actually received by the agricultural sectors. However, it is not a useful measure of the extent of trade distortions, as has been pointed out above; neither is the standard if imperfect measure of protection (the nominal rate of protection). While both these measures have the considerable advantage of being measurable in terms only of directly observable support and current world prices, and in the case of the PSE, observable quantities produced and consumed, they cannot distinguish between the different effects of agricultural policies either in terms of their trade distortion (the objective of multilateral negotiations) or in terms of their effectiveness for support of the industry (the primary concern of domestic policy makers).

A different measure is now required to highlight the trade-distorting effects of policy, and hence to place various policy instruments in particular categories for action in multilateral negotiations. In addition, more robust measures of policy costs and effectiveness are also required for domestic policy purposes. The elements of a trade-distortion measure have been outlined above and are further explored in a growing literature. The framework for measuring policy effectiveness and cost are already well established in the literature and need little further comment here. Unfortunately, these measures rely on more questionable bases, especially supply and demand responses and price linkages, and are therefore subject to more debate as to their accuracy than is the case for the PSE and NRP. Nevertheless, the argument here is that the uncontroversial nature of the latter measures is superficial. Once they are used for negotiating or policy reform purposes, their simplicity and generality proves to be their downfall.

11.4.2 Instrumentation and compensation

The critical link between domestic policy reform and trade distortion is the nature and extent of compensation. Compensation is a necessary part of domestic reform (*pace* the recent New Zealand experience, where compensation was expected to be delivered through the growth of the domestic economy and the liberalisation of trade). But the form and extent of the compensation is critical for the extent to which the new policy remains trade-distorting. Dunkel's provisions for green box treatment (that is those instruments to be regarded as non-distorting) require that support be based only on fixed base-period values, and that eligibility for continued support should not be conditional on continuation of production. Reference to Figure 11.1 above, and the associated concept of trade-distortion as depending on the difference between trade flows under the policy and those which would exist in the absence of policy, indicate that these provisions are at least necessary. It is possible, however, even within these conditions, to design a fixed-base and production-unconditional support system which might appear to support an excess supply above free-trade flows. Although traditional economic theory suggests that the enforcement of Dunkel-type conditions would guarantee that current production will be independent of the level of support, whatever this might be, there is little evidence that policy makers and negotiators are sufficiently convinced of this theory to base their decisions on it. Evidence for this assertion comes from the inclusion in the MacSharry reforms of the set-aside provision, even though the market intervention price is to be reduced to the Commission's expected free-trade world price.

The PEG option is an attempt to design a policy instrument which allows states to continue support with minimal trade distortions, in the light of political concerns about the level of production eligible for support in other countries. The key feature of the PEG proposal from this point of view is that the level of production eligible for support should be no greater than that which would occur under free trade, in addition to fixing the basis of support to some (non-distorting) fraction of historic production levels. There are two major problems with this proposal. First, the history of support in many countries has probably resulted in some rightward shifts of supply curves compared with the no-support alternative. Restricting production eligible for support to amounts based on existing levels of production will enshrine this historical distortion within the future levels of support. In that sense, the PEG can only be described as a 'quasi non-distorting' instrument. However, it is unrealistic to expect states to be willing to reduce distortion on a retrospective basis, even if the extent of this could be agreed. Rather than let the best be the enemy of the good, the PEG proposal admits of this imperfection and seeks to place a rigid limit on its exploitation in the future.

There is a stronger version of this argument (for example, Weiss, 1992) which holds that 'direct income de-coupled support' must result in more people (at least, if not also capital and land) remaining in the industry than without such support, and therefore the payment of support, even if de-coupled, must result in greater output than would be the case without the compensation. In other words, the supply curve in Figure 11.1 is shifted to the right as a result of direct income (or in this case, PEG) payments. Weiss presents an econometric model and simulation results for Austrian agriculture which demonstrates this argument. The Weiss results occur largely through the estimated influence of net farm income and profits on capital investment, labour use (especially retention of self-employed labour within the sector) and land use. Given that direct payments increase farm incomes, then the result that compensated price reductions lead to much less substantial reductions in output than uncompensated price reductions follow automatically.

However, such results contradict the conventional neoclassical response, namely that productive factors will only be employed to the point where marginal revenue is exceeded by marginal cost. If product prices are reduced and compensatory de-coupled support is independent of current and future production levels, then marginal revenues must fall, and levels of economically justifiable resource use must also fall. Market forces are expected to enforce this conclusion over time, in that those who do not behave in this fashion will find profits reduced and wealth declining compared with alternatives. In other words, a genuinely de-coupled support system may well result in more people continuing to live in the countryside than would otherwise be the case (which is, after all, often a major objective), but should not result in greater allocation of resources to farm production than would otherwise be the case. If these conclusions are wrong, then the implication is that the whole edifice of theoretical support for free trade itself is also wrong.

The second major problem with the PEG proposal is the determination and subsequent agreement on the PEG levels for each state. Clearly, whatever precise definition of distortion is chosen leaves considerable room for argument and disagreement. Nevertheless, it does seem reasonable to suppose that countries could: (i) agree in principle that long term support of agriculture will only be regarded as non-distorting (and thus acceptable within GATT rules) if PEGed; and (ii) negotiate a schedule of non-distorting production levels (country PEGs) with reference to evidence/argument about the effects of support on trade levels. Once negotiated, such PEG levels could be bound within modified GATT rules (which would perforce apply specifically to agriculture).

A related problem concerns the international policing of PEGs (or any alternative negotiated measure of support/distortion). So long as the individual farm PEG licences to receive support are freely tradable, then the rental price one would expect to observe for these licences would be the difference between the PEG support payment and the internal market price for the commodity in question.[13] The logic of the industry supply curve suggests that if this rental value turns out to be less than the government PEG payment, then the PEG limit is set 'too high', that is, to the right of the PEG constraint identified in Figure 11.1 above. Even in the absence of a formal market in PEG licences, the market system is likely to result in informal trades for which rental prices would be obtainable. Thus, rental values of PEG licences could form a valuable vehicle for the policing of the system, and the importance of this could even be recognised in negotiating PEG levels, through bargaining for lower PEG limits if PEG licenses are not allowed to be tradeable.[14]

As an illustration of possible levels of PEGs in relation to historic production levels, Figure 11.2 shows the estimated adjustment of current world prices towards free trade levels for selected commodities, with PEGs established at either 100 per cent of 1986 production (PEG100) or at 80 per cent (PEG80) of production. In both cases, the actual level of producer support per unit is kept at that actually estimated for 1986 through the Producer Surplus Equivalent (PSE),[15] with all other market intervention eliminated so that consumers pay market prices.

The results show that all sectors would experience at least 80 per cent of the free-trade change in world prices under PEG100. On average,

Figure 11.2   Percentage adjustment of world commodity prices towards free trade levels under PEGs at 100% and 80% of 1986 quantities

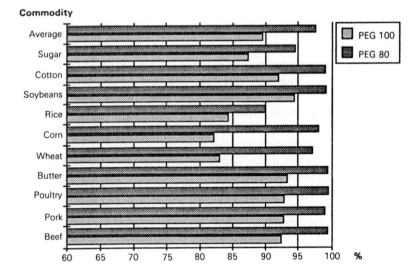

almost 90 per cent of the free-trade world price change would have occurred (top line in Figure 11.2). In the case of a PEG80 scheme, over 90 per cent of the full free-trade world price adjustment would have taken place in all cases, and over 95 per cent of the full adjustment would occur for all but two commodities (rice and sugar) with an overall average of 98 per cent. Hence, a PEG of 80 per cent of 1986 production levels provides a rough indication of the appropriate goal for a negotiated PEG quantity if historical levels of support are maintained, while still achieving the vast majority of the benefits of full liberalisation of world trade.[16] The results suggest that the PEG limit on support needs to be lower than 80 per cent of 1986 production levels for sugar and rice, and more detailed analysis would reveal the different levels required in different countries for the PEG supports to be minimally trade-distorting.

Current elements of the GATT negotiations have close links with the PEG proposal, especially tariffication and the identification of 'green box' instruments. Tariffication is an obvious approach to liberalisation with a long and mostly honourable tradition within the GATT negotiations. The IATRC (undated) concludes that

> tariffication . . . is a change in trade policy beneficial to the GATT but requiring domestic policy modifications. . . . Tariffs would be transparent, bound and easily negotiable, [tariffication] would have considerable advantage to the exporting countries [but] is unlikely to be welcomed by the importing countries [since] non-tariff barriers are usually there for a purpose, to stabilise the domestic economy or to support a particular system of domestic marketing.

The idea, closely connected with the AMS, is to identify a single measure around which GATT rules, bindings and negotiations can focus and constrain domestic action within these clearly defined rules. This is precisely what the PEG proposal offers. However, the proposal offers some advantages over the tariffication option, especially provision for the continued support or compensation of the agricultural sector. In this sense, the PEG option explicitly recognises that elimination of support is an unattainable objective for the GATT, while the logic of the tariffication option implies eventual elimination, whatever the rhetoric.

The 'green box' classification requires the identification of policies which are non-distorting, especially instruments which provide for the compensation or continued support of the industry. The PEG option not only provides such an instrument, it also provides a mechanism, through the limitation of support payments to a fixed quantity of production bound under GATT rules, by which existing support instruments can be brought under the GATT umbrella.

The above arguments have side-stepped the issue of whether future GATT-consistent policies are to be regarded as compensation or continued support. It is argued here that this is largely a domestic rather than international decision. From a domestic perspective the question is clearly important. However, so long as the support is strictly limited, the question is not relevant to the GATT negotiations, *pace* those who argue that the primary purpose of the GATT should be to remove domestic support for agriculture.

Under compensation, the losses from price reductions, however large they may be, are not infinite, so compensation implies a finite payment system rather than an indefinite stream of payments. In addition, a key element of compensation payments should be that such payments are totally independent of current production decisions – that is, they should be fully 'de-coupled'. Given these pre-conditions, there would be considerable administrative and economic advantage in converting the finite annual stream of compensation payments to a capital sum, issuing farmers with a 'government bond' and allowing farmers to either keep their bonds and clip the coupons to receive the annual payment, or sell the bonds, realising their capital value of the compensation and re-organising their business and personal affairs as they see fit. This method of payment would also allow the authorities to redeem the compensation bill through purchase of the outstanding bonds as and when required. This is the proposal made by Professor Tangermann (1990a) to the European Parliament's working group on CAP reform, and included in the final Commission proposals for milk, though excluded from the CAP reform agreement. The objection that such a scheme would be too expensive seems to miss the point entirely, since by definition it can be no more expensive than a commitment to compensate through annual payments (unless the intention is to reduce annual payments from their announced levels).

It seems clear, however, that the domestic reform process has not yet proceeded far enough in most countries for remaining support to be considered purely as compensation for price cuts. The EC, for instance, while mentioning compensation as the reason for continued support, makes no concessions to making such support finite, and indeed prefaces reform papers with arguments in favour of continued support for rural areas and (particularly) smaller and disadvantaged farms.

Thus, 'modulation' of support plays a large part in the principles of the reform package (though not so much in the final agreement). Modulation in this context means explicit re-distribution and, by implication, limitation of support to smaller or otherwise 'deserving' farms and farmers, and is a natural consequence of limiting compensation to something less than 100 per cent of the losses associated with support price reductions. However, there continue to be substantial problems on the domestic front for general agreement to these principles, as witnessed by the difficulties and progress of the EC reform process. There is little reason to suppose that the EC is atypical of developed countries (especially importers) in this regard. Nevertheless, state discretion about targeting payments towards specific farmers or regions on the basis of historic production patterns and levels is maintained through the PEG option, in a way which is not possible through tariffs.

Rausser and Irwin (1989) also raise the question of multi-country or international transfers, on the grounds that countries which expect to gain from trade liberalisation (mostly exporters) might be expected to contribute towards compensating those that lose (mostly importers). These authors comment that 'international tax arrangements appear difficult to arrange for various reasons' (p. 362), and suggest that concessions on service or non-agricultural trade might take the place of straight compensation. However, the PEG option provides a mechanism through which international compensation could occur. As pointed out above, it is to be expected that a formal or informal rental market (or associated asset market) would appear for PEG licences. If an exporting country (or group of countries) regards the negotiated PEG level as insufficiently low, it would be technically possible for it to buy licences in the importing country, thereby appropriately compensating those farmers who sell their licence to receive support and simultaneously reducing the overall quantity supported in the importing country. No doubt such international transfers of PEGs would be regarded with suspicion (to say the least) by politicians, but may provide a useful bargaining counter in the negotiations over the PEG limits.

11.4.3 Institutions

Although Rausser and Irwin stress the need for institutional reform as part of the conditions necessary for effective and sustainable policy reform, they are less clear about the processes through which institutional reform might be expected to occur. Here and elsewhere (Rausser and Zusman, 1992), Rausser appears to argue that constitutional or institutional reform needs to precede policy reform. In an ideal world this might be true. However, a casual reading of the history of agricultural reform might indicate that policy reform breeds institutional change rather than *vice versa*. Mention has already been made of the potential institutional reforms which might be expected to trigger farm policy change in the EC, with special emphasis on Eastern European expansion of the Community. At the international level, however, it is difficult to foresee imminent institutional changes of similar magnitude, unless spawned by international agreement on both the need for, and the form of, policy change. A GATT agreement which contained substantial changes in rules and procedures as far as agriculture is concerned, which presently seems unlikely during the Uruguay Round, would be expected to trigger a change in the status and role of the GATT (or its monitoring/policing agency) in domestic policy formation. Is it reasonable to expect contracting countries to agree to such a change in status and role without agreement on rules and procedures? It seems very doubtful.

At a less dramatic level, however, the prominence of the OECD in measuring and popularising measures of domestic support through its calculations of PSEs and associated material may well have played an important part in maintaining the pressure for some form of the GATT agreement, while the Uruguay Round itself can be regarded as a modest change in status of GATT as far as agricultural policy is concerned. Both are clearly candidates for recognition as real agitators for domestic policy reform. An increasing prominence to international agreements and associated institutions could further domestic pressures for more liberal reform. In this sense, failure of the Uruguay Round could prove a major disaster, leading not only to the commonly predicted increased pressures for protectionism and thoroughly destructive trade wars (the worst outcome of the prisoners' dilemma), but also to an undermining of international authority and removal of pressure for (beneficial) institutional change, which might prove even more destructive in the longer run. It is plausible to argue that collective common sense might limit the damage on the first count, but the destruction of an apparently emerging trust in international agencies and agreements would, if history is any guide, require substantially more effort and time to repair.

Assuming for the purposes of constructive argument, if nothing else, a more or less positive outcome to the Uruguay Round, progress towards liberalisation of world agricultural trade and re-coupling domestic to international prices will raise two key issues to the top of the multilateral agenda: international market stability and food security. The former must become more important as the devices employed by countries to stabilise internal markets are progressively reformed and domestic markets become increasingly and more directly tied to world markets – the object of liberalisation. Food security will also emerge as an increasingly important issue if markets are to be charged with the task of holding emergency stocks. It is far from clear that the market place will be reliable in the face of historically high real interest rates around the world and the apparent divergence of interests in holding stocks between those for whom it is cheapest and easiest (the major exporters) and those for whom the existence of stocks is most critical (the developing country importers, for whom storage is expensive and resources limited). The World Food Organisation represents a possible embryonic international institution which could become increasingly important in taking responsibility for securing and holding international food security stocks (or equivalently, contracts for the delivery of supplies conditional on particular circumstances). As such, it might become an important agency for the stabilisation of international markets, and hence in shaping future domestic policies.

A further potential for international institutional change arises from concerns over the global environment. International agreements on environmental protection which directly affect agriculture could be expected to generate considerable opposition from established farm lobbies. Nevertheless, pressure for environmental controls are growing, at least in the developed and richer parts of the world which have traditionally (and understandably according to political–economic arithmetic) governed the shape of international agreements. Typically, these seem to consist of concerns over short-term commercial exploitation of natural resources (especially rainforests) and over-intensive use of common lands and of marginal land in over-populated regions characterised by small-scale peasant agricultures. It is interesting to note that thoroughgoing liberalisation of world markets and establishment of more direct market mechanisms for the less developed countries, encouraging them to make the most of market opportunities, might under some circumstances lead to more rather than less environmental damage in the absence of appropriate definition and distribution of property rights. However, it is beyond the scope of this chapter to consider possible directions which such international reform (or associated institutions) might take.[17]

11.5 CONCLUSIONS

It seems, to the outside observer, that the course of the present negotiations has run and that they are approaching a dead end. Certainly the negotiating teams must be approaching terminal fatigue. Re-assessment and regrouping cannot now happen within the present negotiations. It requires a new start. Such a new start requires a 'success' to build on, not a failure to overcome. The outlines of a possible new start have been presented in this chapter, namely:

1. a more direct focus on trade distortion, accompanied by the development of, and agreement to, a new (quantity-based) measure, capable of being bound within GATT rules, if necessary made specific to agriculture, where the basis for such a measure has been referred to above;
2. recognition that continued support of at least parts of farming systems is a matter for domestic policy decision and not a matter to be resolved in the GATT or other multilateral fora;
3. development of explicit policy instruments to satisfy the twin requirements of minimal trade distortion and continued, if selective, agricultural support, with the means of translating existing instruments to these new ones, where the PEG is offered as an example.

Domestic pressures for reform will continue regardless of the outcome of the Uruguay Round. Furthermore, whatever the outcome of the Round it is apparent that it will not solve all the problems of present domestic (and thus international) market distortion. It follows that future policy reform will continue to depend, as it has in the past, on domestic pressures, but that these and the reforms they generate will continue to interact on the world market, thus recycling domestic issues around the world. These interactions, especially the world price depressing effects of domestic protective market intervention policies, which lead to the inclusion of agriculture as a major part of the Uruguay Round, have not diminished during the course of the Round and will continue to play a major part in successive initiatives.

Returning to the conditions for policy reform outlined at the beginning of the chapter, it seems that information-needs for policy reform are now largely met with further developments in the OECD and elsewhere promising to expand and develop the major database which already exists. Informal contact with staff in the OECD suggests that this organisation, at least, is taking the problem of measuring trade distortion (as opposed to either protection or support) seriously, and is also interested in developing character profiles of non- or minimally distorting policies. Compensation issues are now at the forefront of the agenda, through the appropriate classification of 'green box' measures to include subsidy payments which replace open-ended price support. The direction of the negotiations towards the creation of a 'blue box' is, perhaps, a recognition that these issues will not be fully resolved during the present Round, and will therefore remain important issues in the future. As yet, and perhaps to be expected, no real progress towards institutional change is apparent. For policy change to be sustained, however, it is clear that authoritative countervailing bodies have to be established against the powerful hegemonies which have historically controlled agricultural policy both within and between states. Here lies the crucial importance of the Uruguay Round. It is vital that the outcome does not undermine the nascent authority of the GATT process as far as agriculture is concerned. This requires an agreement, though the precise details are of much less importance. Failure of the Uruguay Round will not halt farm policy reform, but may well propel it in directions which are against both national and world interests, and substantially delay beneficial reform. It is to be hoped that the major protagonists are aware of these dangers and react accordingly.

12 Agriculture in the Uruguay Round: an Assessment

K. A. Ingersent, A. J. Rayner and
R. C. Hine

In this final chapter of the book, the editors draw upon the views and conclusions of the invited contributors in order to present a summary view of the Uruguay Round agricultural negotiations. This emphasises the reasons for slow progress with the negotiations and why the final outcome fell short of what the most ambitious and optimistic advocates of agricultural policy and trade reform had initially hoped for. After a brief introduction, the chapter opens with a section in which the initial positions of the major Uruguay Round participants on the question of agricultural policy and trade reform are compared and contrasted. The next section details the partial convergence of initial positions achieved by the negotiations. A fourth section deals with the conjunction of the GATT negotiations, in their later stages, with growing domestic pressures for agricultural policy reform in a number of developed countries. A fifth section summarises the GATT Secretary-General Dunkel's draft agreement on agriculture and assesses its impact upon the Uruguay Round negotiations. A sixth section summarises the 'final sticking points' which, in mid-1992, appeared to stand in the way of a final UR agreement on agriculture. The chapter closes with an assessment of the UR agricultural negotiations which seeks to identify what was achieved and the lessons learned for the future. A postscript outlines the provisions of the Washington Accord under which, on 20 November 1992, the EC and the US resolved their outstanding UR disagreements on agriculture bi-laterally.

12.1 INTRODUCTION

As emphasised by Greenaway in Chapter 2, the Uruguay Round was very ambitious in its aims. It embraced a total of fifteen areas of contention, including three completely new ones not covered in previous rounds. It is tempting to argue that the very complexity of this, the eighth round of MTNs under the GATT, reduced the chances of its success.

Though hardly a 'new issue', agriculture had remained largely unaffected by previous GATT rounds. But it was now 'centre stage', at the insistence of the US and other smaller agricultural exporting countries with less market power. These countries ostensibly wanted major reductions in agricultural protection and to see trade in agricultural products brought fully under the GATT rules and disciplines comparable with those applying to trade in manufactured products, as agreed in earlier rounds of MTNs.

The Punta del Este Declaration, which officially marked the inauguration of the Uruguay Round in July 1986, proclaimed that reforming the conduct of agricultural trade was a central objective of the negotiations. Furthermore, this was to be achieved by 'bringing *all* [our emphasis] measures affecting import access and export competition under strengthened and more operationally effective GATT rules and disciplines'. This form of words clearly committed all parties to the negotiations to placing their *domestic* agricultural policies on the international negotiating table, as well as policy measures specifically concerned with limiting imports and assisting exports. Yet it may be questioned whether any of the countries with highly protected domestic agricultures, such as the EC, Japan, Canada, or even the US, were really prepared for such a drastic step. Certainly, little had been done to prepare domestic agricultural producers, and others with a vested interest in maintaining the *status quo*, for the consequences of the withdrawal of protection. It was fairly apparent that when the major parties to the negotiations tabled their initial positions on agriculture, they would prove to be far apart on fundamental issues. Yet little or no preparatory work had been done upon how the yawning gaps amongst national positions could conceivably be bridged.

12.2 CONTRASTING INITIAL POSITIONS

Although more than 100 contracting parties to the GATT took part in the Uruguay Round, we attempt to simplify analysis of the course of the agricultural negotiations by confining attention to the positions of five major contestants: these are the United States (US), the European Community (EC), the Cairns Group (CG), Canada and Japan. Canada is, of course, a member of the CG. But due to a major divergence between the Canadian position on agriculture and that of the remaining CG countries, particularly during the later stages of the negotiations, at some points it is necessary to deal with Canada separately.

Hillman (Chapter 3) emphasises that despite an ambivalent attitude towards the removal of domestic agricultural protection and the liberalisation of farm imports dating back to the 1930s, the US entered the Uruguay Round with an apparent willingness to sweep away all forms of trade distorting protection, provided its trading competitors were prepared to follow suit. However, the 'zero option' does not appear to have been actuated by purely ideological motives, that is, trade liberalisation is 'good' and protection is 'bad'. Rather, the advance of self-interest played a major role, with the US entering the agricultural negotiations in 1986 determined to reverse the declining share of global agricultural trade it had suffered during the previous decade. The occurrence of this decline was beyond dispute, but the reasons for it were contentious. The US government blamed the predatory policies of competing exporters, particularly export subsidies paid by the EC. But critics attributed the decline of US agricultural market share mostly to excessively high interest rates and an over-valued US exchange rate, particularly during the early 1980s, as well as the loss of confidence in the US as a 'reliable' source of agricultural imports, following the temporary embargo on US exports of soybeans when supplies were exceptionally short and prices high in the early 1970s. As remarked by Hemmi (Chapter 7), this loss of confidence was particularly marked in Japan. Whether the US government ever really believed that it could succeed in persuading the EC and Japan to accept the *elimination* of agricultural protection, including trade distorting domestic support, is an interesting question. Hillman (Chapter 3) inclines to the view that the zero option was no more than 'an ideological trial balloon'. But if this is accurate, why, despite the implacable opposition of the EC and Japan in particular, and the failed attempt at mediation by the Cairns Group, did the US refuse to compromise on this issue for more than three years, and only did so after a change of President? With the benefit of hindsight, the zero option appears to have been no more than a futile and time-wasting tactic lacking in political credibility. Moreover, as also noted by Hillman, Paarlberg's argument that opponents of agricultural liberalisation within the US encouraged the Administration to persist with the zero option, secure in the belief that it would never go through, and might even succeed in protecting their interests by completely derailing the negotiations, carries considerable conviction. Opponents of agricultural policy reform could perceive the unreality of the US position even though those responsible for maintaining it apparently could not.

The EC's initial position on agriculture in the Uruguay Round was essentially defensive in reaction to the extreme reforming posture adopted by the US. Thus, although the Community was aware of the need for further modifications of the CAP, mainly for budgetary reasons, it was determined to protect it from *external* reform pressures. The essence of the EC's position was that although it was prepared to contemplate some reduction of domestic support and external protection affecting 'the most problematic commodities' (like cereals, oilseeds, sugar, dairy products and beef) in the *longer* term, it considered that a more urgent *short-term* priority was to improve international market stability by entering into market management agreements. By this means, the Community apparently hoped, at this stage, to maintain high domestic price supports, protect its domestic market and safeguard its agricultural export market share, possibly at the cost of tightening some domestic production constraints. The Community's preference for constraining production over reducing farm product prices was also revealed by one of two provisos it laid down for considering, for the longer-term, the possibility of reduced levels of protection being *bound* in the GATT. This was that the aggregate measure of support (AMS) employed to measure protection must give explicit credit for domestic supply constraints imposed by the government, as well as allowing for the effects of world price and exchange rate fluctuations. The second proviso, to which the Community probably attached even more importance, concerned the 're-balancing' of external protection. As a *quid pro quo* for agreeing to lower border protection of most commodities, the EC insisted on being permitted to *raise* tariffs on oilseeds and cereal substitutes which, since the Dillon Round, had entered the Community virtually duty-free. Above all it was clear that, despite having signed the Punta del Este Declaration, the Community was not prepared, at the initial stage of the agricultural negotiations, to yield on the fundamental principles of the CAP. Specifically, it was resolved to continue using the instruments of the variable import levy and the variable export subsidy to maintain high domestic price support and Community Preference to exclude imports from third countries. However, the Community's initial position also contained a hint that in the longer-term it might be prepared to substitute direct income payments for price support.

Tyers (Chapter 5) emphasises that despite major differences in size, economic structure and levels of development, the Cairns Group of 14 agricultural exporting countries had a common interest in ensuring that agriculture received unprecedented attention during the Uruguay Round with the object of arresting the declining trend of agricultural export earnings. As joint architect of the Tyers–Anderson model, Tyers quotes model results indicating that, in 1990, the net value of CG food export earnings were depressed by more than 50 per cent due to trade distortions resulting from agricultural protection in industrial countries. The CG identified the 'disputation between the EC, and the US' and the consequent agricultural trade war, as the principal cause of its agricultural trade problem. Tyers is also bold enough to argue that, due to the strength of its trading links with the 'big three' (the US, the EC and Japan), the CG could block any Uruguay Round 'deal' between the major players which neglected its vital interest in the liberalisation of agricultural trade. Initially, the CG sought to play a mediating role between the US and the EC. Thus, in its initial proposal for agriculture, the CG followed the US in asking for the eventual elimination of trade-distorting support and protection, but was prepared to settle for a longer phase-out period. The CG was also less dogmatic than the US about the outlawing of particular policy instruments as well as about the precise role of AMSs in domestic agricultural policy and trade reform.

Tyers highlights the fact that in Canada the role of agriculture in the total economy, in terms of both the sector's share of GDP and its share of total exports, is smallest amongst all the CG countries. Warley (Chapter 6) explains that with no less than 70 per cent of its exports going to its next door neighbour, it is essential for Canada to marry a satisfactory bi-lateral trading relationship with the US to its multilateral commitments to the rest of the world through the GATT. Even more crucially, attempts at agricultural policy reform in Canada have recently been dominated by an extremely delicate constitutional crisis in which the province of Quebec has threatened to withdraw from the federation. It so happens that Canada's least-competitive and most highly protected agricultural sectors of dairy and poultry production are dominant in Quebec, where political pressure for the retention of import quota protection of these sectors is consequently very intense. Thus, as Warley so aptly puts it, Canada's position both in the Uruguay Round and the Cairns Group has been shaped by 'the dichotomy between the attempt to foster the interests of export sectors – grains, oilseeds and red meats – while preserving protection for less competitive sectors – dairy and poultry'. Despite this divergence of view on the retention of import quotas to limit market access, in the initial stage of the agricultural negotiations Canada succeeded in preventing the CG position paper from asking for the abolition of Article XI:2(c)(i) and the QRs it permits. Rather, to quote Warley, the CG position 'used language which called only for the elimination or reduction in market access barriers 'not explicitly provided for in the GATT'.

According to Hemmi (Chapter 7), Japan's main motivation for supporting the launch of the Uruguay Round was to back continued expansion of its exports of manufactured goods. On agriculture, Japan's strategy was essentially defensive, like the EC's. Although Japan's food imports are the largest in the world, some sectors of Japanese agriculture, particularly rice, are very highly protected. In these sectors very high domestic price support is bolstered by rigid border protection in the form of import quotas. Hemmi also argues that Japan saw the Uruguay Round of multilateral trade negotiations as a means of escape from a long-standing bi-lateral pressure from the United States to liberalise its imports of rice and other highly protected farm products. Japan calculated that multilateral negotiations were preferable because of the support it expected to receive for its position on agriculture from other large food importers such as th EC. The core of Japan's strategy on agriculture was to make the minimum of concessions necessary to ensure the success of the Round as a whole. As well as continuing to expand its exports of manufactures, Japan was also very keen to see trade in services brought under the GATT rules and disciplines. Hemmi explains that Japan's attitude to national self-sufficiency in basic foodstuffs is still influenced by recollection of the food shortages experienced in the aftermath of the Second World War, as well as the temporary embargo imposed upon US exports of soybeans in the early 1970s. Thus Japan's initial position on agriculture in the Uruguay Round put much stress on the necessity of maintaining national food security. To this end, Japan was keen to see that agricultural import quotas were *not* outlawed by GATT rules and disciplines, by the retention of a clause in the spirit of Article XI:2(c)(i). A further reason advanced by Hemmi to explain Japan's low profile on agriculture in the Uruguay Round is government scepticism as to whether the negotiations would in fact succeed in yielding significant world-wide reductions in agricultural protection. Why offer to make 'unnecessary' concessions?

In summary, the contrasting initial positions on agriculture at the outset of the Uruguay Round were such that the highly idealistic and uncompromising position taken up by the US and the very defensive position of the EC were at opposite poles. Although the position of the CG bloc of agricultural exporting countries was really closer to the US than to the EC, their idealism was better tempered by pragmatism. Hence, at this stage, the CG attempted to play a mediating role between the two giants. However, the CG's attitude to import quotas was made ambiguous by the aberrant stance of Canada. Japan chose to maintain as low a profile on agriculture as possible, being much more interested in other areas of the negotiations. However, it would appear that Japan covertly hoped to bolster its very conservative position on admitting imports of rice and other basic foodstuffs by forming an alliance with the EC, or even Canada.

12.3   CONVERGENCE OF INITIAL POSITIONS

Very little movement in the initial positions on agriculture of the major Uruguay Round contenders occurred until after the stalled Montreal Mid-term Review in December 1988 and the Geneva Accord (GA) of April 1989, which at least succeeded in unblocking the logjam to restart active negotiations. The text of the GA contained no reference to the *elimination* of trade distorting support and protection, but only to its progressive reduction, with credit being allowed for measures already taken since 1986. These features of the GA represented concessions by two of its principal signatories, the US and the EC. The US implicitly gave up the zero option and the EC surrendered its claim for credit to be given for measures already taken since the earlier year of 1984. But a revised US position paper, tabled in October 1989, did not reflect abandonment of the zero option. The only concession made at that stage was the proposal that, unlike so-called 'red' agricultural support policies which the US still wanted to eliminate over 10 years, and non-trade-distorting 'green' policies which could be permitted to continue without discipline, less trade-distorting 'amber' policies should be subject only to monitored reduction and GATT discipline. A second major feature of the revised US position was the proposed 'tariffica-tion' of all agricultural import barriers not explicitly permitted by the GATT. The use of instruments like VILs, VERs and MIPs would be prohibited, to be replaced only by simple tariffs. 'Permitted' NTBs (that is, import quotas authorised by Article XI:2(c)(i) of the General

Agreement) would have to be converted to expanding tariff quotas in the short run and simple tariffs in the longer term. After ten years the US wanted a bound tariff, at a relatively low rate to be the only form of protection.

A little unexpectedly perhaps, the EC's post-GA position paper, tabled at the end of 1989, responded to the US tariffication proposal with a partial tariffication proposal of its own, subject to a number of provisos. The essence of the EC proposal was that border protection should consist of two elements. First, there would be a fixed tariff calculated relative to an external reference price – effectively the world price expressed in domestic currency at a fixed exchange rate. Second, there would be a 'corrective factor' to offset world price and exchange rate fluctuations beyond certain limits. When it was first unveiled, this second element of the EC's tariffication proposal was derided by other parties to the negotiations, particularly by spokesmen for the US. But later, in agreeing upon the form of the AMS to be used in monitoring the reduction of domestic support, the critics implicitly agreed that it is not inappropriate to insulate border protection from the effects of exchange rate movements, at least in the short run. See O'Connor et al.(1991) for a fuller discussion of this point. The two main provisos attached to the partial tariffication offer concerned the rebalancing of protection, which the EC continued to insist upon, and the retention of a reformulated Article XI in the General Agreement to permit the use of import quotas in exceptional circumstances. Critics of the offer also suspected that, regardless of tariff cuts, the EC intended to continue protecting its own farmers by applying a Community Preference margin to keep the price of imports above the domestic price level. Illustrative price data in documents subsequently issued by the Commission, showing reductions in support and protection the EC was prepared to make, lend some support to this suspicion. But despite these reservations, it is quite clear in retrospect that the EC's partial tariffication proposal of December 1989 was a substantial concession to the US position on this aspect of the negotiations.

The US delayed complete abandonment of the zero option until the autumn of 1990 when it presented its 'final' position paper on agriculture in response to the draft Framework Agreement on Agriculture tabled by the chairman of NG5 earlier in the year. Under the reduction of internal support, the US was now ready to accept cutting 'red' support measures, such as deficiency payments and production-linked input subsidies, by only 75 per cent over 10 years. In parallel with this offer under the reduction of border protection, the

US was prepared to settle for all bound tariffs and TEs being similarly reduced by 75 per cent over 10 years with the added proviso that no tariff should then exceed 50 per cent *ad valorem*. The relaxation of the US position was least marked with respect to the reduction of export subsidies. As regards subsidised exports of primary agricultural products, a 90 per cent reduction over 10 years was now demanded, in terms of both budgetary expenditure on export assistance and the aggregate quantity of exports subsidised (compared with the previous US demand for subsidy *elimination* over 5 years).

The CG position on the issue of tariffication was similar to that of the US until the 'final' phase of the negotiations when Canada broke away from the rest of the group by tabling a separate proposal calling for a smaller tariff reduction of only 50 per cent over 10 years and, even more significantly, for the retention of Article XI:2(c)(i) to permit the continuation of import quotas. Thus on issue of import quotas, Canada lined up with the EC and Japan, rather than with the remainder of the CG and the US, its natural allies in the battle for export market liberalisation. At the final stage, Japan offered to continue reducing tariffs on most agricultural products at the same average rate as agreed in the Tokyo Round. But an exception was made of rice. Here Japan rejected, on food security grounds, the very notion of converting internal support and border protection to tariff equivalent form, as a preliminary to progressive tariff reduction.

The CG had never fully endorsed the US zero option. Thus it had little difficulty in accommodating to its eventual abandonment. Japan continued to keep a low profile or, as Hemmi (Chapter 7) puts it, 'to shelter behind the EC in the agricultural negotiations'. But, broadly speaking, Japan appeared prepared to make concessions equivalent to those conceded by the EC, whilst attempting to maintain import restrictions as near as possible to their existing level.

With the positions of the other major participants staked out as the planned conclusion of the Uruguay Round in December 1990 approached, pressure mounted on the EC to clarify its final position on agriculture. In particular, the US and the CG had been pressing the EC for firm, quantitative and separate commitments with respect to the reduction of internal support, the lowering of border protection, and the curtailment of export subsidies. In the event, the EC was last in tabling its 'final' position paper on agriculture, shortly before the final Ministerial meeting of the Uruguay Round, scheduled to be held in Brussels in December 1990. The EC paper was very disappointing to the US and the CG in that it failed to respond to the pressure for separate quantitative commitments in all three of the most sensitive areas. The only firm undertaking the EC was prepared to make was a 30 per cent reduction in internal support for main agricultural products over 10 years, expressed in terms of an AMS (presumably the EC's own SMU). Moreover, the EC proposed backdating this offer to 1986, with credit being claimed for support reductions already implemented between 1986 and 1990. Thus only residual reductions would remain to be honoured between 1991 and 1995. In explanation of its failure to offer firm commitments to lower border protection and curtail export subsidies, the EC continued to argue that, having regard to how the CAP operates, the benefits its adversaries desired in these areas would flow naturally from the firm commitment to reduce internal support. Almost inevitably, the US and the CG were unwilling to accept this argument and continued to press for firm commitments in all three areas.

12.4 DOMESTIC PRESSURES FOR AGRICULTURAL POLICY REFORM

The 'final' Ministerial meeting of the Uruguay Round, duly held in Brussels in December 1990, ended in disarray. The entire round of negotiations collapsed as a direct result of the failure to reach any agreement on agriculture. The crux of the agricultural problem was that the US and the CG were unable to accept the EC's continued refusal to offer firm quantitative commitments to the lowering of border protection and the reduction of export subsidies. The specific issue upon which the meeting foundered was the EC's refusal to accept a compromise solution on agriculture tabled unofficially by Mats Hellstrom, chairman of the agricultural negotiating group and minister of agriculture in Sweden. Hellstrom proposed an agreement based upon a commitment to make uniform support reductions of 30 per cent over 5 years in all three of the critical areas of internal support, border protection and export assistance. But the EC refused to accept Hellstrom's 30:30:30 compromise. Acceptance would have involved reducing the implementation of its existing offer to cut internal support by 30 per cent from 10 to 5 years, as well as making a matching commitment in the remaining two areas. The Community was not prepared to take this step and its refusal to do so precipitated the end of the meeting. Led by Argentina and other CG members, other participants simply walked out from all areas of the negotiations.

Despite the collapse of the Uruguay Round at the end of 1990, domestic pressures for fundamental agricultural policy reform were increasing in several parts of the world, including the EC, the US, Canada and Japan. The main reason for the pressure was budgetary. Thus, for example, in the US the final form of the 1990 Farm Bill was determined by the size of the federal government's budget deficit which, for reasons of macroeconomic policy, the President was determined to reduce. In effect, the Omnibus Budget Reconciliation Act of 1990 amended the Farm Bill even before it became law. Whereas the budget cost of the Farm Bill originally agreed by the Congress was estimated at around $54 billion over five years from 1991 to 1996, the overriding budget reduction legislation cut this amount by more than $13 billion to around $41 billion. For this reason, the 1990 Food, Agriculture, Conservation and Trade Act appeared to offer a substantial federal budget saving compared with the cost of the previous bill, the 1985 Food Security Act. This implied reduced expenditure on farm income support and, possibly, an actual reduction in farm income.

Warley (Chapter 6) explains the background to a number of recent agricultural policy reviews in Canada culminating with a national conference in December 1989 signalling that 'the government required the agrifood sector to become more market-oriented and self-reliant'. This resulted in a number of new policy initiatives to prepare Canadian agriculture 'to compete successfully in an environment of reduced support and protection' even though, for overtly political motives, the federal government made a fresh commitment to the retention of special protection for the dairy and poultry industries involving import quotas and supply management. Similarly, Hemmi (Chapter 7) argues that, with the notable exception of rice, Japanese agricultural imports have been substantially liberalised in recent years. Moreover, due to rising living standards and changing tastes, the structure of Japanese agriculture has been gradually shifting away from traditional staples, which have attracted high support, towards higher production of newer food crops and decoratives, which are unsupported, but for which demand is growing rapidly. Hemmi believes that the current of opinion in Japan against the unquestioned support of agriculture is growing and that even the rice sector possesses the ability to survive without price support in the long-term, as larger and more efficient rice farms absorb land abandoned by large numbers of very small and inefficient producers.

Lastly, we come to internal pressures from within the EC for the reform of the CAP. The perceived necessity of controlling the size of agricultural budget had been a major issue in the Community from long before the inauguration of the Uruguay Round. But little effective action had been taken until the introduction of milk quotas in 1984. This was followed, early in 1988, by the introduction of 'stabilisers', intended to limit support expenditure on practically all agricultural commodities subject to CAP regulation. But these efforts to control the agricultural budget were of limited effectiveness – so much so that shortly before the Uruguay Round negotiations collapsed in Brussels, in December 1990, the EC Agricultural Commissioner, Ray MacSharry, unveiled a further green paper on CAP reform. This document, entitled 'Development and the Future of the CAP: Reflections Paper of the Commision', reiterated the fundamental imbalance inherent in the CAP system of income support, as well as its inequity. These flaws were attributed to guaranteeing product prices far above market clearing levels, rather than supporting farm incomes *per se*. With production consequently far in excess of the domestic market's absorption capacity, the growing costs of holding rising stocks and subsidising a growing volume of exports had both borne heavily on the budget. The green paper argued that the only way to remove the incentive to ever higher production inherent in the present system of support was to lower market prices. But direct income aids, to compensate producers for reduced prices, would be needed to give *political* viability to this scheme of reform. The green paper also argued that, in order to safeguard the basic CAP principle of 'real financial solidarity', the distribution of direct income aids should be biased or 'modulated' according to the needs of different classes of farmer, judged according to farm size, income, regional situation or other relevant factors. Thus, a further critical element of the MacSharry Plan was that, in order to qualify for direct income support, larger scale producers of cereals, oilseeds and protein crops would be required to *set aside* a designated proportion of their arable land. Moreover, compensation for set-aside (distinct from compensation for reduced market prices) would be limited to a relatively low acreage ceiling. Large producers, required to set aside more than the ceiling area to qualify for direct income support on their remaining crop area, would have to bear the full marginal costs of set-aside above the ceiling.

Publication of the MacSharry Plan was delayed for some time by controversy within the Commission. According to reports leaked to the press, some commissioners took the view that the suggested reductions in support prices were too drastic and others that the proposed bias in the distribution of compensation towards small producers was 'unfair' to larger producers, as well as penalising efficiency. The first version, released for publication and communicated to the Council in February 1991, confined itself to stating the case for CAP reform and the adoption of different policy instruments, without actually quantifying either support reductions or proposed levels of compensation. After several months in which member state governments and other interested organisations communicated their views to the Commission, a revised version was published in July 1991 with specific proposals for reform affecting most commodities covered by the CAP. Central to the reform package was a proposal to lower the administered price of cereals by 35 per cent, phased over the 3-year period, 1994–6. Producers would be eligible to receive full or partial compensation for this price cut, depending upon their scale of production, in the form of direct income payments based on the product of the difference between the 'old' and 'new' prices times the amount of production. However, with the exception of 'small producers', eligibility to receive compensation would be limited to those volunteering to participate in set aside, to be set initially at 15 per cent of the farm's 'base area' of cereals, oilseeds and protein crops.'Small producers' were defined as those with an annual production of not more than 92 tonnes of cereals (approximately 20 ha at the Community average cereal yield). Compensation for set aside participation was proposed, at the same rate per unit of land area as the compensation for price reduction, but only up to a maximum of 7.5 ha. of set aside land per farm. Thus, compared with small producers to be exempted from set aside participation, the largest producers were to be doubly penalised by (i) being obliged to participate in set aside in order to qualify for price reduction compensation; and (ii) being eligible to receive no more than partial set aside compensation.

As well as advancing plans for reforming the major CAP crop regimes (except sugar), the revised MacSharry Plan also made proposals for dealing with milk, beef and sheepmeat which, on the whole, were less 'revolutionary' than the arable crop proposals. Rather than proposing any major support price reduction, the milk proposal emphasised the tightening of production quotas. The beef and sheepmeat proposals emphasised switching away from price support to limited headage payments based upon herd or flock size and its location (upland or lowland). The plan's budgetary implications were also discussed. The Commission estimated that, despite the high budget costs of compensating farmers for the reduction of consumer-financed price support in the short term, there would be a budget saving when the new arrangements came fully into force after 1996.

The ultimate fate of MacSharry's Plan was to remain uncertain until May 1992, when the Council finally accepted a CAP reform package 'in the spirit of MacSharry', but with certain major revisions which we refer to later in the chapter. But, in the middle of 1991, the outcome of the Uruguay Round agricultural negotiations appeared to be intimately tied up with the fate of MacSharry's proposals at the hands of the EC Council, notwithstanding the fact that any connection between these two issues was being vigorously denied by official Community spokesmen who insisted that the sole purpose of on going CAP reform discussions was the achievement of budget savings and other purely domestic policy objectives.

12.5 DUNKEL'S DRAFT AGREEMENT ON AGRICULTURE

During February 1991, GATT Secretary-General Dunkel succeeded in re-activating the Uruguay Round by persuading all the contracting parties to agree to the resumption of agricultural negotiations on the basis of reaching 'specific binding commitments to reduce farm supports in each of the three areas: internal assistance, border protection and export assistance'. But, despite this initiative, the agricultural negotiations made little further progress in 1991. Then, in a further attempt to break the stalemate and force the Uruguay Round to a successful conclusion, the GATT Secretary-General re-intervened by tabling a draft 'Final Act' covering all areas of the negotiations, including agriculture. However, Dunkel's draft Agreement on Agriculture differed from the remainder of the Final Act because, in contrast to the position in other areas, where provisional agreements had already been reached in most negotiating groups, in agriculture no consensus view had emerged on the critical issue of the amounts and time-scale of cuts in government support and protection. The Secretary-General consequently took it upon himself to devise his own draft agreement on agriculture, including the relevant 'numbers', for consideration by the negotiators.

The main body of the Dunkel text on agriculture specifically dealt with improving market access, reducing domestic support and improving export competition. It was suggested that a common *implementation* period of 1993–9 be applied to all the proposed cuts in support and protection. But two different base periods of 1986–8 and 1986–90 were proposed, respectively applying to (i) domestic support reduction and improved market access; and (ii) export subsidy reduction. The key provisions were:

1. Improved market access: an average reduction of 36 per cent in customs duties, including those resulting from the tariffication of NTBs, such as import quotas and variable levies, subject to minimum reduction of 15 per cent in every tariff line. Customs duty reductions to be supplemented by *minimum access opportunities*, set at 3 per cent of the importer's base period consumption in the first year of implementation and rising to 5 per cent in the final year. *Special safeguard provisions* were also included to cushion the effects of unusually large import surges or reductions in import prices.

2. Domestic support reduction: a uniform cut of 20 per cent, expressed in terms of an AMS and applying individually to all supported commodities, with credit allowed for actions already taken since 1986. But Dunkel did *not* allow any credit for supply control as envisaged by the EC's SMU proposal. Exempt 'green box' policies were defined as those 'having no, or at most minimal, trade distortion effects', including publicly financed R & D, early retirement schemes for farmers and land retirement (subject to a minimum retirement period of three years). Dunkel also prescribed a set of criteria for use in determining whether particular schemes of direct payments to farmers qualified as *de-coupled payments* eligible for green box treatment.

3. Export competition improvement: twin requirements that *budgetary outlays* on export subsidies be cut by 36 per cent and the *volume* of subsidised exports by 24 per cent. The cuts were to be *commodity specific*.

The 'Final Act' also set 1 January, 1993 as the target date for the implementation of a Uruguay Round Agreement. To allow the minimum time needed for ratification and implementation by national governments, a deadline of 15 April 1992 was set for the conclusion of all negotiations. But the timetable for *agriculture* required all participants to submit, by 1 March 1992, product-specific lists of their base period positions and support reduction commitments drawn up as if in compliance with the parameters of Dunkel's draft agreement in each of the three critical areas of market access, domestic support and export competition. As well as being ready to accept Dunkel's draft agreement as a basis for a successful conclusion to the agricultural negotiations, the US and most of the CG countries (but not Canada) were prepared to adhere to this timetable. But the EC held back for a number of reasons. First, on improved import access, Dunkel made no concession towards either meeting the Community's demand for 're-balancing' or, in specifying the formula for converting NTBs into tariff equivalents, making provision for the retention of a Community Preference margin. Second, on domestic support reduction, the AMS definition recommended by Dunkel for use in gauging reduction commitments failed to reflect the EC's desire to have credit allowed for supply control. Third, because it is easier to control the CAP budget than the volume of agricultural production and, by implication, agricultural exports, the EC was unwilling to commit itself to any firm restriction on the *quantity* of its subsidised exports. In responding to Dunkel's 1 March deadline, the EC consequently confined itself to submitting commodity-specific lists showing its base period positions in each of the three critical areas, without making any new support reduction commitments. Due to the failure of the EC and a number of other countries, including Canada and Japan, to adhere fully to the conditions he had laid down for moving swiftly to an agreement on agriculture, Secretary-General Dunkel was obliged to abandon the timetable set by the Final Act for concluding all substantive Uruguay Round negotiations by 15 April 1992. Hemmi (Chapter 7) briefly discusses why the Japanese government rejected Dunkel, and Warley's analysis in Chapter 6 of the Canadian government's earlier position on agriculture readily explains (but does not excuse, from Warley's standpoint) the rejection from that quarter.

12.6 FINAL STICKING POINTS

A currently controversial issue in international trade discussions is the power conferred on the President by recent US legislation to impose trade sanctions *unilaterally* upon trading partners with whom the US is in dispute. It has been reported unofficially that the EC has been pressing for a 'peace clause' to be written into any Uruguay Agreement which may emerge, whereby the US would undertake to abandon the use of this power in favour of resolving all trade disputes through the GATT.

The EC has already made a number of concessions during the course of Uruguay Round agricultural negotiations (see Chapter 4). If the US and other contestants were to press for further concessions to the point where the EC risked losing face by surrendering *all* its residual claims, this might be decisive in causing a final and irrevocable collapse of the Round. For several years, attempting to control aggregate cereals output has been an intractable problem for the EC. Now, in the aftermath of the MacSharry reform of the cereals sector and intense external pressure to reduce subsidised exports, it may be politically unrealistic to expect the EC to permit increased imports of cereal substitute products, at least for a number of years. Thus it might be wise for the EC's adversaries in the agricultural negotiations to yield ground on this issue by assenting to what remains of the Community's bid for 'rebalanced' support, that is, the restriction by quota of cereal substitute imports to their current level.

In addition to being unwilling to give way on rebalancing, the retention of Community preference and limiting the volume of subsidised exports, as discussed in the previous section, there were two further obstacles to EC acceptance of Dunkel's proposed agreement on agriculture. First, an ambiguity appeared to exist concerning how MacSharry's proposed 'compensatory payments', to offset producer losses due to both the reduction of the cereals-support price and participation in arable set aside, would be treated in measuring internal support. Would they be classed as 'amber', that is, production-linked and therefore subject to AMS reduction? Or could they escape AMS measurement by being classed as production neutral and therefore 'green'? It was important for the EC to have this ambiguity resolved in its favour since 'green box' treatment of the compensatory payments would make it much easier to accept Dunkel's proposed 20 per cent reduction of internal support. The US had a similar problem with its existing deficiency payment scheme for cereals and certain other crops, which the government claimed bore many of the hallmarks of 'decoupled payments', judged by the criteria laid down by Dunkel. Thus there appeared to be the possibility of the EC and US reaching some mutually acceptable bi-lateral agreement on this issue. The EC had been claiming that, despite being linked to set aside, US deficiency payments were an implicit export subsidy. For its part, the US appeared likely to oppose according 'green box' treatment to MacSharry-style compensatory payments *unless* some mutually acceptable understanding could be reached with the EC. Thus, rumours appeared in the press of a 'blue box' compromise permitting the EC and the US both to obtain AMS exemption for non-decoupled deficiency payments at their base period level for a limited period, after which they would 'count' and be subject to reduction But, of course, such a mutually convenient arrangement between the two largest players might well be objected to by other participants, such as the CG, on the grounds of perceived damage to their interests.

The second further obstacle to EC acceptance of Dunkel's proposals for agriculture was that the MacSharry Plan itself remained only tentative. Domestic opposition to the MacSharry proposals was still very active, particularly on the part of farm organisations throughout the Community which continued to campaign for tighter supply control as their preferred alternative to lower market prices combined with direct income support. A further obstacle to Council acceptance of the MacSharry Plan was that some member states, particularly those with relatively large farms, like the UK and the Netherlands, opposed the modulation of compensation in favour of small producers, on the ground that this discriminated against 'efficiency' and international competitiveness.

There was one further major obstacle to the acceptance of Dunkel's draft agreement as the basis for reaching an accord on agriculture which could not be attributed to the EC. This was the disarray in the CG resulting from the maverick position of Canada concerning the retention of agricultural import quotas within the GATT as a 'special case'. Tyers (Chapter 5) and Warley (Chapter 6) both explain why Canada got into an anomalous position on this issue within the CG. Warley's analysis suggests that, for domestic political reasons, finding a solution to the anomaly is likely to be an intractable problem, particularly in the short term. Thus, if this were to be the only remaining obstacle to an agricultural agreement, this might be circumvented by some kind of special GATT provision allowing Canada to continue imposing quota restrictions on imports of dairy and poultry products for a limited period. A similar arrangement might be sought by Japan to stave off the liberalisation of rice imports there. Thus Canada and Japan might be expected to form an alliance on the issue of defending their 'right' to restrict imports of especially 'sensitive' agricultural products, at least for the time being.

Uncertainty about the precise nature of CAP reform was finally overcome in May 1992 when, after a marathon session of four days' duration, the Council agreed upon a somewhat modified version of the MacSharry Plan. There were two main changes from the draft plan. First, the reduction in the cereals support price, spread over three years, was reduced from 35 per cent to only about 29 per cent. Thus the projected amount of compensatory payments per unit area of cereals, for set aside participants, was also somewhat reduced. Second, it was decided that compensatory payments on arable land set aside would *not* be 'modulated' by scale of production. All set aside participants, regardless of size, would be fully compensated. Whereas the first change might be expected marginally to reduce the budget costs of reform, the second one appeared likely to increase it substantially, at least in the short term. Moreover, taken together the changes appeared likely to weaken any constraining influence the reform might have upon the Community's aggregate production of cereals. By the same token it appeared likely that the changes would exacerbate the difficulty of reducing the size of the export surplus in order to meet Dunkel's proposed 24 per cent reduction in the volume of subsidised exports over six years. It is also worthy of note that compared with proposals made in the the revised draft of the MacSharry Plan, reform of the milk sector was watered down (no pun intended!) in the final version. The cuts in dairy product support prices and global production quotas were both smaller than proposed by the Commission. Moreover, the cow headage payment, originally intended to partially to compensate producers for the price cut subject to a stocking rate ceiling, was suppressed. Thus, unlike the EC beef and sheepmeat regimes under which producers of these products now have to rely mainly upon direct income support, in the form of headage payments, the milk support regime continues to rely exclusively upon price support, subject only to supply control by production quota.

By tending to add to the budgetary costs of compensating producers for the reduction of price support, the final version of MacSharry appeared likely to strengthen the Community's resolve, in the GATT negotiations, to get all compensatory payments excluded from the 'amber' box, that is, exempt from AMS reduction. Also, because the final revisions appeared to weaken any constraining effect the reform might have on aggregate cereals production, it seemed probable that the Community would stand its ground on the linked issues of: (i) rebalancing imports of cereal substitutes, possibly with a tariff quota; (ii) giving domestic agricultural production some competitive advantage over imports by maintaining an element of Community Preference, for example, by omitting CP from any tariff reductions to which it subscribes; and (iii) holding out on the issue of not being committed to any reduction in the *volume* of subsidised cereal exports, or at least not the 24 per cent reduction proposed by Dunkel and endorsed by the US and the CG.

Thus, at the time of writing (autumn 1992), obtaining even a limited Uruguay Agreement on agriculture appeared to depend upon five major sticking points, as follows:

1. The EC, US and CG agreeing upon the AMS classification of direct income payments to farmers, as currently made in the US and due to be adopted shortly in the EC under the MacSharry reform.
2. Resolution of the import quota problem which has caused Canada to dissent from the position of the rest of the CG and in which Japan also claims to be vitally interested.
3. EC insisistence on rebalancing (now reduced to restricting imports of cereals substitutes).
4. EC insistence on continuing to levy a Community Preference Margin on imports of competing agricultural products. The final version of the MacSharry Plan defines CP as the difference between the threshold price and the target price.For cereals this is set at ECU 45 per tonne, or 35 per cent above the target price set for 1993/4 of ECU 130 per tonne. N.B. Prior to the MacSharry reform the target price was set *above* the threshold price. But now this relationship is reversed with the target price *lower* than the threshold price. The target price is still the notional price producers may expect to receive from the market but, for set aside participants, it is supplemented by a *deficiency payment* which restores the total return per unit of production close to the 'old' level.
5. EC refusal to be committed to commodity specific 24 per cent reductions in agricultural export volumes.

It would appear that, in principle, any or even all of these sticking points could be surmounted by some kind of interim ageement postponing a final solution until a later date. So, for example, direct income support as currently practised by the US, and now adopted by the EC, could be exempted from AMS reduction for a period of, say, five or six years, after which it would be classed as 'amber' unless modified to comply with *all* Dunkel's de-coupled payment criteria. Similarly, the import quota problem could be resolved by granting Canada and Japan a temporary and commodity-specific derogation from the provisions of a revised GATT, withdrawing the privileged status of agricultural import quotas under Article XI:2(c)(i). The EC could be permitted to apply quota restrictions to cereal-substitute imports, again for a limited period beyond which imports would cease to be regulated. The EC could similarly be permitted to continue, for an interim period, with some element of Community preference in its border pricing policy. Lastly, in order to realise the goal of an overall agreement on agriculture, the US and the CG might agree to some temporary modification of Dunkel's proposed commodity-specific 24 per cent reduction in agricultural export volumes which was also agreeable to the EC. So, for example, the implementation period for achieving the 24 per cent reduction could be extended from the 6 years proposed by Dunkel to a longer period. Alternatively, more space for negotiating an agreement on this issue might be achieved by not insisting that the 24 per cent export subsidy reduction must be commodity specific. So, for example, it has been suggested that the EC might be prepared to agree to a 24 per cent volume reduction in subsidised exports of *all cereals*, provided averaging was permitted between wheat and coarse grains. Another option might be to permit averaging amongst dissimilar products like dairy, beef and sugar.

From the point of view of capturing the benefits of global trade liberalisation, the difficulty with these and many other compromises which might be struck is that they reduce the short-term gains from reduced support and protection, whilst garnering the full benefits of policy and trade liberalisation remains uncertain, even in the long term. The 'most difficult' problems remain to be resolved in the future. The trade-off between a certain short-term gain and an uncertain long term one is always difficult to evaluate.

A further asymmetry between the EC and US positions on agricultural trade liberalisation is that, regardless of its form, EC *producers* are bound to lose whereas US producers might actually gain from a multilateral liberalisation agreement. This conclusion is backed by the results of a recent global agricultural trade simulation model (Anderson and Tyers, 1991) which indicates that if the US was to liberalise its agriculture *unilaterally*, US farmers as a whole would lose welfare. But, if the US succeeded in negotiating a *multilateral* agricultural policy and trade liberalisation agreement, it is likely that US farmers would actually gain welfare, due to a combination of higher world prices and increased export volumes. But, in contrast to the US position, farmers in the EC would lose out from both unilateral and multilateral liberalisation. Thus, in terms of the political costs of buying off farmer hostility to agricultural policy and trade reform, the work of Anderson and Tyers explains very clearly why the US has been so keen to realise the multilateral liberalisation of agricultural trade, as well as why the EC has remained hostile. Whilst it is true that EC consumers stand to gain handsomely from any form of farm liberalisation, their political influence remains comparatively weak for reasons well explained by public choice theory. Thus, despite the *net* welfare gains from agricultural policy and trade reform shown by the results of both Anderson and Tyers and other modellers, realistic assessment of the EC's overall position in the Uruguay Round points to the conclusion that it is unlikely to yield significant ground on agriculture except, possibly, in exchange for major gains in one or more other areas of the negotiations. Greenaway (Chapter 2, Table 5) indicates the nature of trade-offs between agriculture and other areas in which the EC might be interested.

The Anderson and Tyers model results pre-date the recent MacSharry reform of the CAP. What difference does this make? Although this reform provides direct income support to compensate EC farmers for the reduction of price support, it remains to be seen what effect it has on aggregate EC production and exports. Although, in principle, the set aside provision is intended to reduce or even eliminate excess supply, the experience of the US with set aside as a policy instrument suggests that, due to various 'leakages', this goal may not be realised in practice. The aggregate output of cereals is also affected by other factors, such as possible changes in opportunity costs (especially the relative profitability of oilseeds), the trend in yields due to technological progress and, not least, the substitution of direct income support for a proportion of former price support. The claim of some commentators that, in the aftermath of the price cuts proposed by Dunkel and now imposed by MacSharry, the EC can 'easily' meet Dunkel's 24 per cent cut in the volume of subsidised exports appears to rest upon questionable assumptions concerning the values of critical parameters such as the efficiency of set aside and the trend in agricultural productivity (see, for example, the European Commission's GATT compatibility paper, as reported by Agra Europe, 27 November 1992; Josling and Tangermann, 1992). With the latest CAP reform confronting European farmers with several new policy instruments as well as a sizable price cut, the behavioural assumptions underlying any attempt to estimate future production can only be heroic. But, without a marked reduction of EC production/exports, the US and other competing exporters will gain little if anything from the CAP reform.

Although, at the time of writing, there still appears to be a reasonable chance that the Uruguay Round will eventually be brought to a successful conclusion (though falling short of the most optimistic goals), it is prudent to consider the most likely consequences of failure. Any view of this eventuality must, of necessity, be largely speculative. However, it is at least plausible to argue that, as far as agriculture is concerned, failure could well result in increased protectionism and the escalation of trade wars, with possible very adverse consequences for national exchequers. Any expansion of trade would most likely be within regional trading blocs rather than upon a multilateral basis. On a more optimistic note, it may be argued that the untoward consequences of failure in the latest round of MTNs might be expected to increase pressure for the early initiation of the new round, directed towards achieving the same objective of achieving major reductions in agricultural protection.

12.7   THE URUGUAY ROUND AGRICULTURAL NEGOTIATIONS: AN ASSESSMENT

What, if anything, has been achieved by the Uruguay Round of agricultural policy and trade negotiations? What lessons have been learned for the future? We attempt to give brief answers to these questions in this the final section of the chapter.

In making our assessment, we stress that ours is essentially an outsiders' view of achievements without much regard for the effort expended in their realisation. As outsiders we are not in a position to evaluate or even describe in detail the process of negotiations leading up to the Uruguay Round's limited achievements in the sphere of agriculture. Such an evaluation must be left to 'insiders', such as those personally involved in the negotiations or with access to unpublished information. However, we take this opportunity of acknowledging the very large expenditure of time and effort made by many people in attempting to bring the agricultural negotiations to a successful conclusion. Key players, to whom the international community is much indebted, obviously include GATT Secretary-General Dunkel and NG5 Chairman Aart de Zeeuw, architect of the 1990 Framework Agreement on Agriculture. But, in addition to these named individuals, due acknowledgment is also owed to many anonymous public officials, and their academic advisers, who were involved in both intra- and inter-governmental consultations at many levels, and who worked with considerable zeal to prepare blueprints of possible alternative solutions to problems arising from the negotiations for consideration by those ultimately responsible for decisions, that is, politicians. Thus, to the extent that we are critical of the organisation and conduct of the negotiations, that criticism is aimed not at public servants but at their political masters.

12.7.1 Achievements

First, the Uruguay Round succeeded in obtaining an implicit agreement that domestic agricultural policy cannot reasonably be withheld from international negotiations. The EC had been particularly unwilling to concede this point in earlier GATT rounds, but effectively did so by subscribing to the 1986 Punta del Este Declaration, which committed its signatories to bringing *all* measures affecting import access and export competition under strengthened and more operationally effective GATT rules and disciplines. This commitment was reinforced in 1989 when, in concert with all other parties to the agricultural negotiations, the EC signed the Geneva Accord which declared that, henceforth, *all* internal support measures which affect trade would be subject to GATT disciplines. It carries conviction to argue that by subscribing to the GA the EC effectively surrendered its freedom to continue using, in the long run, major CAP support instruments like the VIL and the VES. It can similarly be argued that, merely by subscribing to instruments incidental to the the Uruguay Round negotiations and playing second fiddle to the EC during negotiations, Japan also effectively surrendered complete sovereignty over its domestic agricultural policy.

Second, although the OECD's pioneering work on PSEs, to standardise the aggregate measurement of all forms of agricultural support and protection, started some years before the inauguration of the Uruguay Round, the high profile given to this work by the agricultural negotiations has ensured that support measurement and monitoring will continue on a regular and permanent basis. That is, levels of support and protection accorded to agriculture by governments will, in future, be much more *transparent* than in the past. Other things being equal, greater transparency should be conducive to the reduction of support.

Third, it may be claimed that a near consensus has been achieved on the issue of 'tariffication'. With the possible exception of Canada and Japan, virtually all the GATT parties appear now to be prepared to abandon NTBs to agricultural commodity imports in favour of an equivalent tariff, though with 'safeguards' to counter the adverse effects on producers of extreme fluctuations in import prices or volumes (as under the EC's partial tariffication offer).

Fourth, even without a Uruguay Round agreement on agriculture, the Dunkel 'draft agreement', a very carefully crafted document, could be useful as a blueprint in forming the basis of a subsequent round of negotiations.

Fifth, the Round fostered the emergence of the Cairns Group to co-ordinate the views of the more efficient and lower-cost agricultural exporting countries and press their 'rightful' claims to a larger export market-share. Even if the attainment of this objective is frustrated by the blocking tactics of larger and more powerful parties to the negotiations this time round, the CG may live to fight another day.

Sixth, although the EC claims officially that the Uruguay Round did not accelerate the most recent CAP reform (MacSharry) or influence its nature, which they claim was actuated purely by domestic pressures (mainly budgetary), detached observers may find this denial unconvincing. By substituting direct income support for product price support, the reform will certainly benefit EC consumers and, regardless of the outcome of the Uruguay Round, makes it easier to liberalise trade – if not sooner, then later. However, despite MacSharry, some sectors of EC agriculture covered by the CAP, such as dairy and sugar, remain largely unreformed. Turning from the EC to the US, it is difficult to argue that the Uruguay Round has hastened the domestic reform of agricultural policy there. Despite the rhetoric of the US position on agriculture in the GATT negotiations, the support reductions embodied in the 1990 Farm Bill were driven by the macroeconomic policy objective of cutting the federal budget. Moreover, as in the EC, important sectors of US agriculture, which are supported by consumers rather than taxpayers, survived the 1990 farm legislation virtually unscathed.

Seventh, although the developing countries were not major players in the Uruguay Round agricultural negotiations, they were effectively drawn in partially due to the potential benefits of market liberalisation for net agricultural exporters. They also stood to gain from the potential advantages of trade-offs between concessions on agriculture and gains in other areas of the negotiations like textiles and non-agricultural tariff reductions. Before the Uruguay Round, the developing countries generally preferred to negotiate internationally on trade through the United Nations Conference on Trade and Development (UNCTAD), rather than through the GATT, which they tended to regard as a 'rich man's club'. However, the UNCTAD strategy of pressing the developed countries to grant them 'special trade preferences', on a strictly *non*-reciprocal basis with no trade concessions given in return, was not conspicuously successful, particularly in agriculture. Another UNCTAD strategy of negotiating international commodity agreements (ICAs) was even less successful. Thus, in recent years, developing countries have joined the GATT in increasing numbers, in order to be directly involved in negotiating 'special and differential treatment' of their interests in the Uruguay Round. The broad result has been not the *exemption* of developing countries from the trading rules accepted by others, but rather an extension of the transition period before the same rules and degrees of trade liberalisation must be accepted by them. In the case of agriculture, the Dunkel draft agreement not only granted developing countries an extended transition period (ten years instead of only six), but also 'easier' support reduction commitments in the three areas of market access, domestic support and export competition, of only two-thirds the rates required of developed countries. Only the *least developed* countries would be completely exempt from reduction commitments.

12.7.2 Lessons learned

With agriculture centre-stage, the Uruguay Round was intended to be different from previous GATT rounds. A principal reason why agriculture had previously escaped serious scrutiny and reform is that, due to the entrenchment of farm support, and the complexity of the divergent interests involved, agriculture is difficult enough to reform at the purely domestic level. Thus the temptation to shy away from attempting reform at the *international* level is not difficult to understand. However, by the early 1980s, much of the international community was no longer willing to tolerate the concessions previously made to agriculture. Nevertheless, at the beginning of the Uruguay Round, the EC's CAP remained as a serious obstacle to the reform of agriculture. Thus, the CAP reform which, after a quite prolonged internal battle, eventually received domestic assent in 1992, nearly six years after the start of the Uruguay Round, might be viewed as a precondition of success. This argument is not intended to imply that protection in the EC was the *sole* obstacle to serious reform, but only that the EC was a key player behind which others with similar protectionist agricultural policy stances tended to hide.

With the benefit of hindsight it is now possible to identify serious errors in negotiating tactics made by the major participants in the agricultural negotiations. For the US, the 'zero option' was hopelessly unrealistic from the beginning. For the EC, the MacSharry Plan came too late. The CG appeared mistakenly to believe that it held a casting vote and its position was weakened by divisions between Canada and the remaining members of the group. In some ways Japan was most 'successful', by keeping a low profile and sheltering behind the more exposed EC position. An interesting question to pose is whether these tactical errors could have been avoided by better advance planning.

It could be argued that, as far as agriculture is concerned, the Uruguay Round started 'too soon'. Too little work had been done on preparing the framework of the negotiations to pave the way to a successful outcome. After the main contestants had staked out their largely incompatible positions at an early stage, virtually no serious negotiations took place to find the compromises needed to break the stalemate, either in preparation for the Montreal Mid-Term Review in December 1988, or even during the run up to the Brussels Ministerial Meeting, which was supposed to bring the Round to a successful conclusion in December 1990.

It was only after the collapse of the Round at this meeting, as a direct consequence of the disarray on agriculture, that some semblance to proper negotiations on agriculture commenced. But, even then, in an attempt to force the pace of the negotiations, it was eventually necessary for GATT Secretary-General Dunkel to intervene by tabling a draft 'Final Act' covering all aspects of the Round, including a draft Agreement on Agriculture. Had the negotiators acted to have a document along these lines prepared and tabled three years earlier, at the Mid-Term Review, the chances of bringing the Round to a successful conclusion by the planned date of December 1990 would have been much improved. But, due to the entrenched positions of the main contestants and their unwillingness to compromise, this may not have been a feasible option at an earlier stage of the Round. Although preliminary discussion of Agricultural Commissioner MacSharry's plan for a fundamental reform of the CAP had already started, the intensity and complexity of intra-EC bargaining was virtually bound to prevent an early decision resulting in tangible policy adjustment.

International negotiations to lower agricultural protection and liberalise trade are inherently difficult due both to the many economic and political interests involved and to numerous technical complexities. In the Uruguay Round the necessity of tying in the results of the agricultural negotiations with those of parallel negotiations in fourteen other areas added greatly to the difficulty of achieving success. Thus a first lesson to be learned from the experience of the Uruguay Round is that a detailed negotiating framework needs to be in place before actual negotiations commence. Ideally, a draft agreement needs to be in place from the beginning so that the negotiators' main task is limited to finding agreement upon the 'numbers' to be entered within 'square brackets'.

A second lesson for the future is that better tactics need to be developed for overcoming political opposition to agricultural policy reform. Simulation models of the welfare implications of agricultural trade liberalisation, like Anderson and Tyers (1991), have been valuable in demonstrating that in virtually all countries where agriculture is protected liberalisation would result in a net welfare gain. However, even though *in principle* the gainers could compensate the losers and still be better off than under the status quo, the losers (that is, agricultural producers) tend to be unconvinced that they would be adequately compensated *in practice*. Thus the political credibility of producer compensation needs to be improved. This task is likely to fall primarily upon the national governments of countries where agriculture is most highly protected, such as the EC and Japan. But, due to the high budget cost of compensation, such governments could be encouraged to undertake this task if some means of sharing the costs of compensation *internationally* could be worked out and agreed upon. So, for example, it might be feasible for a proportion of producer compensation in the EC to be funded by means of some system of internationally approved tariff rebalancing within agriculture. Direct budgetary transfers would probably be inappropiate in this context It may be objected that any such scheme risks encouraging the use of protection as a weapon of international blackmail and that it is unreasonable for a country to expect external assistance with compensating its own producers for the reduction of agricultural protection, except indirectly from gains made in other areas of the negotiations as a consequence of the concessions given on agriculture. Moreover, it would clearly be inequitable for 'poor' countries,whose farmers benefit from agricultural liberalisation, to transfer income to 'rich' countries where farmers lose from liberalisation. Although we acknowledge the weight of these arguments against redistributing the costs of producer compensation internationally, we still believe that this proposal has merit as a possible inducement to more rapid liberalisation of agriculture world-wide, and that its feasibility merits careful examination, with appropriate safeguards to minimise the risk of blackmail or other abuses. A more practical difficulty with this proposal is that

agricultural exporting countries who stand to gain most from liberalisation, such as members of the CG, will doubtless argue that they have
'already paid' more than enough for the protectionist policies of the
EC, Japan and other countries where farmers stand to lose from trade
liberalisation.

Quite apart from the political problem of convincing farmers that
they will be compensated for the loss of protection, there is the related
one of persuading them that switching from market price support to
taxpayer support is compatible with maintaining their social standing
in the wider community. This will not be an easy task in countries
where, until now, farmers have taken it for granted that they are
entitled to earn an adequate livelihood 'in the market place', and that
low farm incomes signify that food is 'too cheap'. Nor can it necessarily
be taken for granted that farmers can be reconciled to accepting direct
income support in compensation for 'safeguarding the rural environment'. Although not averse to being seen by the general public as
'custodians of the countryside', larger scale farmers in particular tend
to regard themselves primarily as technologically advanced commercial
food producers. They have no wish to be 'national park keepers'. As
well as being unacceptable to farmers, the substitution of direct income
payments for product price support may also encounter the resistance
of *taxpayers* for two reasons. First, there is the general problem that
national exchequers are limited and increased budgetary expenditure
on agriculture is in competition with claims from many other areas.
Second, taxpayer voters might be especially reluctant to sanction direct
payments to farmers in their purest form, that of 'de-coupled
payments'. One of the criteria generally laid down for these (for
example, in the Dunkel draft agreement on agriculture) is that
eligibility to receive such payments must depend solely upon *past*
production. Present production, which could be zero, is quite
irrelevant. In other words, farmers of non-retiring age, with a base
period production record, qualify to receive a state pension 'for doing
nothing'. Why should farmers be singled out for such philanthropy at
the expense of taxpayers?

It is on the basis of these arguments that we suggest that a third
lesson to be drawn from the Uruguay Round agricultural negotiations
is that, before further cuts in trade distorting agricultural support and
protection are contemplated, possibly in a subsequent GATT round,
more research needs to be conducted on how to lower the political and
social barriers to extending further direct income support to compensate farmers for the loss of price support. An important component of

such research might be to explore the economic and political feasibility of de-coupled payments. A further need is to explore alternative methods of supporting agriculture to prevent undue depopulation of rural areas and even to discourage methods of farming considered to be socially harmful. As the budget costs of subsidising farmers to increase production above the competitive market level declines, it is more than likely that public expenditure on subsidies to encourage farmers to adopt more 'environmentally friendly' practices will increase. Moreover, environmental subsidies are likely to be regionally differentiated, rather than being granted to all farmers indiscriminately, to allow for differing degrees of environmental sensitivity between regions. To the extent that small-scale farmers in some environmentally sensitive areas may be unable to survive commercially without state assistance, subsidising farmers to remain on the land to benefit the environment, or maintain rural infrastructure, may also be linked with the relief of rural poverty for social reasons.

12.8   POSTSCRIPT

The bi-lateral agreement on agriculture, struck between the EC and the US in Washington DC on 20 November 1992, covered more than the Uruguay Round agricultural negotiations. It also resolved the long-standing dispute between the parties concerning EC protection of oilseeds. This postscript is confined to the five provisions of the Washington Accord specifically concerned with the Uruguay Round.

On *market access* the EC agreed to conform with the Dunkel draft agreement subject only to the inclusion of a 10 per cent Community Preference margin in the calculation of tariff equivalents, i.e. $TE_{EC} = 1.1P^I - P^W$, where P^I is the internal producer price and P^W is the world price. This implies that a 10 per cent CP would remain as barrier to exports seeking access to the EC market, even if P^I were eventually to achieve parity with P^W, i.e. given $P^I = P^W$, $TE_{EC} = 0.10$.

On *internal support*, the EC agreed to conform with Dunkel draft provisions, except that crop area and livestock headage payments under CAP reform will be excluded from AMS calculations, that is, these direct income payments will go into the 'green box', even though they do not conform with all the criteria laid down by Dunkel for classification as de-coupled payments. This aspect of the accord raises the question of the AMS treatment of direct income payments in the US. Presumably from now on these will also be excluded from AMS calculations (though they have not been so excluded in past OECD calculations of PSEs).

On *export assistance*, the EC again agreed to abide by Dunkel draft provisions, except that the quantitative export subsidy reduction commitment will be relaxed from 24 per cent of base period exports to only 21 per cent. Thus, on what is probably the most critical aspect of the Dunkel draft for the EC, it has gained a small but possibly quite significant concession.

On the issue of *rebalancing*, the Washington Accord provides that, should EC imports of non-grain feed ingredients rise to a level which undermines the implementation of CAP reform, there will be bi-lateral consultations. In other words, the rebalancing issue appears to have been shelved, at least for the time being.

Lastly, the Washington Accord includes a so-called '*peace clause*' which appears to commit the US to not initiating further proceedings against the EC under Article XVI of the GATT (concerning subsidy rules) so long as the provisions of the accord are 'respected'.

Taking an overall view of the Washington Accord, it would appear that with the US already committed to acceptance of the Dunkel draft agreement on agriculture, the EC is now equally committed to the same agreement, except where the bi-laterally agreed WA amends it.

The long-term significance of present disagreement amongst member states of the EC, regarding the 'acceptability' of the Washington Accord, is difficult to assess. However, it seems most likely that, one way or another, the dissident minority will eventually fall in with the majority by accepting a Uruguay Round agricultural settlement based on the Dunkel draft, as amended by the Washington Accord.

It goes without saying that the Washington Accord does *not* represent a Uruguay Round agreement on agriculture. To convert the accord to a multilateral agreement it would have to be endorsed by *all* the GATT's contracting parties including, for example, the Cairns Group and Japan. This cannot be taken for granted. Nevertheless, the accord does represent a major step towards the conclusion of a multilateral agreement.

Notes and References

1. Introduction

1. Article XVI of the GATT provided an escape clause for primary products as regards domestic and export subsidies, provided that a country did not obtain more than an 'equitable' share of world export trade. Article XI:2 of the GATT permitted quantitative restraint on imports of farm products without parallel action to restrict domestic production. Finally, primarily because the Western Powers wished to encourage European integration as a bulwark against the spread of Soviet communism, the introduction of the protectionist CAP (Common Agricultural Policy) of the EC was not effectively challenged in the GATT.
2. A group of 14 agricultural exporting nations who, in general, have a comparative advantage in agriculture, and hence an interest in agricultural trade liberalisation.

2. Agenda, Expectations and Outcomes

1. 'Liberalisation' refers to a cut in the mean tariff, for a given variance; whilst 'harmonisation' refers to a cut in the variance for a given mean. EC concern with the greater number of tariff peaks in the US tariff schedule was instrumental to the adoption of a harmonisation formula. For an analysis of the properties of alternative harmonisation formulae, see Ennew, Greenaway and Reed (1991).
2. The term 'structural adjustment' is generally associated with policy conditionality in developing countries, the conditionality applying to supply side adjustments. Insofar as supply side adjustments were prompted by the first oil shock and the consequences of shifting comparative advantage, the description is quite appropriate.
3. This is not to argue that they are necessarily straightforward at the bilateral level: witness the complexity and breadth of the recent 'Structural Impediments Initiative' negotiated between the US and Japan.
4. For an assessment of alternative means of tariffication, see Takacs (1991).
5. For an assessment of agriculture in the Uruguay Round, see Hine, Ingersent and Rayner (1989).
6. Deardorff (1990) provides an interesting review of the welfare issues raised by TRIPs.

3. The US Perspective

1. This chapter was written principally while I was Visiting Professor, Lincoln University, New Zealand. Special thanks are due to Jan Clark and Elnora Fairbank for their assistance with the manuscript. Since the end of the Tokyo Round I have observed an increasing volume of quantitative econometric analysis with respect to agricultural trade in

general and the Uruguay Round in particular. In the end, the assistance of such analyses in helping to resolve the fundamental issues dividing the United States, Europe, Japan and the Cairns Group on farm and trade issues has been unclear. Hence it was my decision to approach the US perspective of the Uruguay Round via a politico-economic statement.

2. For a detailed discussion and updating of Section 22 legislation and activities, see Hillman (1991) pp. 19, 66ff, 98–9, and Appendix C.

3. For example, see US Senate Committee on Finance, Subcommittee on International Trade (1989).

4. Section 301 of the 1974 Trade Act covers unfair trade practices by foreign governments affecting US products. These often are cases that cannot be covered by the escape clause, dumping duties, countervailing duties, or Section 337 of the same Act. The Section 301 cases are administered by the President's Special Representative for Trade Negotiations (STR), and many have involved complaints against the EC's Common Agricultural Policy (CAP).

5. Under Fast-track legislation Congress gives the President authority to negotiate with foreign governments without meddling in the process or second-guessing the deals being made. After the negotiation has been completed and in order that the 'package' or 'deal' become legally binding, the Congress must vote 'yes' or 'no' on the entire agreement and cannot vote on items selectively.

6. Two other very significant studies are: National Center for Food and Agricultural Policy (1991) and CARD (undated).

7. Anderson and Hayami (1986) show that as the relative importance of agriculture declines the cost of supporting it is spread over a growing non-agricultural population within which the costs of organized opposition to farm subsidies are such that most people choose to opt out (or free ride). Also, they present compelling evidence to back their hypothesis that the relationship between agricultural protection and comparative advantage (as reflected by agriculture's relative importance in the economy) is inverse. Tullock and Hillman (1991) have explained through public choice theory why a dwindling number of American farmers have maintained political power.

4. The EC Perspective

1. OECD agricultural trade statistics indicate that, during 1985–7, total EC-12 agricultural *imports* averaged $US13.75 billion per annum compared with imports of $US11.35 billion by Japan. Over the same period total EC-12 agricultural *exports* averaged $US13.49 billion per annum compared with exports of $US17.56 by the US (OECD, 1990, Annex Table III.5).

2. 1985–7 average import market shares (OECD, 1991, Annex Table VI.32).

3. 1985–7 average export market shares (OECD, 1991, Annex Table VI.31).

4. The montant de soutien was defined similarly to the Producer Subsidy Equivalent (PSE) developed in the early 1980s for use in the Uruguay Round.

5. For a fuller explanation of how the SMU allows credit for supply control, see Rayner et al. (1990).

6. As used here the term 'direct income support' merely signifies that producer prices are maintained with deficiency payments instead of

administered market prices. It does *not* signify that the total value of support is necessarily decoupled from current production.
7. Trade policy negotiators may find it expedient to ignore supply control measures, provided that they are not used to justify import restrictions. But such measures are 'illiberal' because they distort the allocation of resources. There is also the danger that as long as supply control remains 'respectable', governments will be tempted to use it as a prop to support producer prices as the preferred alternative, at an acceptable budget cost, to complete market liberalisation.

5. The Cairns Group Perspective

1. Thanks are due to Don Gunasekera, Richard Higgott and T.K. Warley for useful discussions on the subject of the paper, and to Prue Phillips for access to the resources of the ANU International Economic Databank. The introductory parts of the chapter draw on Tyers (1992b), though the analysis presented here is more extensive and the results differ as a consequence of the use of a recently up-dated and extended version of the Tyers–Anderson model, combined with more recent estimates of incentive distortions in agriculture. Constructive suggestions from the editors are appreciated.
2. See Tyers and Anderson (1992) Chapter 1.
3. For more complete accounts of the origins of the Cairns Group, see Oxley (1990, Chapter 9) and Higgott and Cooper (1990).
4. An alternative view is that both the EC and the United States are fundamentally protectionist of their agricultural sectors and that for each the aggression of the other is an excuse to maintain protection through export subsidisation. This view would suggest that punitive import restrictions warrant further consideration.
5. The performance of the model has been tested and found adequate in ex post simulations over the period 1983–9. See Tyers and Anderson (1992) Chapter 5 and appendices.
6. A key property of the simulation model is its incorporation of the market-insulating components of agricultural policy. It is these which cause the levels of protection to fluctuate from year to year as international prices rise and fall.
7. Indirect effects, due to exchange rate distortions and protection in other sectors, are approximated in the manner of Tyers and Anderson (1992, Chapter 6) and Anderson and Tyers (1993). Based on work summarised by Schiff and Valdes (1992), the equivalent nominal protection coefficients for food products are adjusted downward by 10 per cent for Thailand and 20 per cent for the other developing members of the Group.
8. See Cairns Group (1986).
9. This was the 'Geneva Accord', the events following which are clearly summarised by O'Connor et al. (1991).
10. Commodity prices had improved somewhat since 1986 and the level of assistance to EC farmers, measured relative to world markets, had fallen accordingly. The extent to which real reform was embodied in the proposal was modest indeed.

11. More background on this is offered by Warley in Chapter 6.
12. I have been aided in this characterisation of the EC unilateral reforms by reference to CARD (1991), Josling and Tangermann (1992) and Helmar et al. (1992), as well as by personal communications with staff at the Australian Bureau of Agricultural and Resource Economics, who have been conducting a more detailed analysis of the proposal than is reported here.
13. The representation of the reforms is at its most approximate in the livestock sector, where the coincidence of reduced beef and veal prices with herd reduction incentives makes the reform quite complex. In the simulation presented, these are represented by permanent supply curve shifts which are not accompanied by reductions in underlying productivity growth in the sector. To the extent that investments in cost-reducing technical change could abate following the reforms, the results presented understate the likely long term reductions in EC livestock production, and hence the beneficial effects on other countries exporting livestock products.
14. The pattern and modesty of the gains is consistent with results from analyses of negotiable approaches to the reduction of EC surpluses by Tyers (1990b) and subsequently Guyomard et al. (1992).
15. For the Cairns Group members which remain net exporters of foods as defined here (cereals, livestock products and sugar), particularly Argentina, Australia, Canada, New Zealand and Thailand, the increase in net earnings is a more modest 13 per cent and the corresponding increase in net cereal exports is just 6 per cent.
16. Outside the Cairns Group, higher food prices bring gains to the rural sector though these are most often outweighed by consumer losses. In the United States, most cereal farmers are paid at 'target' prices which are higher than border prices and set administratively. Higher cereal market prices therefore benefit taxpayers at the expense of consumers, while the net gains to farmers are small.

6. The Canadian Perspective

1. The treaty is called the United States–Canada Free Trade Agreement. A national perspective, recognition that the agreement does not create 'free' trade, and the desire for a pronounceable acronym leads to general use of the term 'CUSTA' in Canada.
2. At some $200 billion a year, Canada–US trade in goods and services is the world's largest bi-lateral trade flow. Ontario–US trade alone is larger than US–Japan trade.
3. Agriculture was a necessary but difficult component of the comprehensive bi-lateral trade agreement. Its provisions for liberalizing trade in agriculture are broad but not deep. It provides for: eliminating tariffs on farm and food products; the easing of some non-tariff measures (import quotas on poultry, beef and sugar products, grain import licensing and discriminatory pricing of wines); abjuring the use of export subsidies in bi-lateral trade; improved dispute settlement mechanisms; and the harmonization of technical standards. Neither country was required by the Agreement to make fundamental changes in its domestic agricultural support policies. In particular, Canada retained its Article XI rights under the GATT (though it soon became apparent that it was unclear

what these were) and the question of whether Canada's farm income stabilization programmes distort trade was left to be resolved in the multilateral trade negotiations.

4. The CUSTA replaces national judicial reviews of countervail and anti-dumping actions with binding appeals to bi-national panels. Eight technical groups are working towards the harmonization of technical standards, acceptance of the equivalence of results of different national systems, and appeal to scientific knowledge in resolving disputes.

5. The major national stabilization programmes are the Agricultural Stabilization Act, the Western Grains Stabilization Act, the National Tripartite Stabilization Program, crop insurance and the underwriting of the Canadian Wheat Board's initial prices. Most provinces also operate their own price stabilization schemes. Some of these programmes will eventually be superceded by the Gross Revenue Insurance Plan and the Net Income Stabilization Accounts introduced in 1991.

6. The freight subsidy provided under the Western Grains Transportation Act, and some related public expenditures on the western transportation system, are commonly known as 'the Crow Benefit' – a reference to the use of the Crow's Nest Pass as the basing point for regulated rail freight rates.

7. The proceedings of the Growing Together conference and the reports of the task forces are available from Communications Branch, Agriculture Canada, Ottawa, K1A 0C5.

8. The UPA is the sole authorized bargaining agency for Quebec agriculture. Its President is a declared separatist, and the organization has publicly endorsed 'sovereignty – association'.

9. The Cairns Group has been extensively studied by Canadian political scientists. The work of Cooper (with Higgott) and Findlayson and Weston is especially notable.

10. Canada's agrifood exports at C\$9–10 billion are only 3 per cent of the world total. Canada has a significant position in world trade in wheat, barley, canola, flaxseed and pork. However, in the larger markets for grains, oilseeds and meats Canada is a price-taking, small country supplier of these products.

11. At the time of this writing Canada's offer has been published only in synoptic form in a news release. The account that follows is based on this and various interpretive public statements made by Ministers and others.

12. No attention is paid here to the matter of agricultural sanitary and phytosanitary measures. Along with the US, Australia and New Zealand, Canada is a major architect of the widely-endorsed draft agreement.

13. Moreover, producers don't receive all the subsidy since a proportion of it is 'held back' as 'within quota' levies to finance the loss incurred by the Canadian Dairy Commission in dumping milk products abroad.

14. The effect of paying the subsidy to the railways is to raise the on-farm price of feed grains in the Prairie region. This discourages livestock production and value-added processing. The alternative of paying the transport subsidy directly to grain farmers has been successfully resisted by them, thus far.

15. The formula is said to be $R = \dfrac{32 + D}{5}$ where R is the reduction and D the base rate.

16. There is a federal ban on the importation of margarine. Additionally, some provinces forbid the sale of milk-like drinks or cheese analogues. They also require that margarine be coloured to look either like lard or a by-product of petroleum distillation! Butter–margarine blends are banned in some jurisdictions.

17. The perception is that the LDCs have enjoyed the benefits of the GATT system while assuming few of its obligations. For instance, the tariffs levied by most LDCs are generally high and unbound, and many of them have sought exemptions for their import controls on balance of payments grounds under Article XVIII:B. For an excellent treatment of this subject see Whalley (1989).

18. The devaluation of assets would affect land and quota values. How far land prices would fall has not been estimated. The aggregate values of milk and poultry marketing quotas are about C$5.0 billion and C$1.5 billion respectively.

19. The NISA programme enables farmers to contribute a proportion of their farm income to individual, interest-bearing, tax-sheltered, trust accounts. The farmer's contribution is matched by federal and provincial governments. Withdrawals from the accounts can be made when farm income is low or when the farmer quits farming.

20. The GRIP programme provides two types of income protection for farmers who enrol. Crop insurance kicks in if yields fall below a percentage of the farmer's long-term average, while revenue insurance payments are made if prices fall below a multi-year moving average. Thus a farmer can establish his/her minimum gross revenue for each crop covered by the programme in advance of planting. (The support level differs by crop and province.) Provincial Governments pay 67 per cent of the premiums.

21. Michael Hart, who is a senior trade official, reports the charge but does not say whether he thinks it is justified.

7. The Japanese Perspective

1. The author wishes to thank the editors of this volume for valuable suggestions and efforts to improve his English.

2. For the details, see Anderson and Hayami (1986). Egg imports were liberalised in 1962; bananas, sugar and 23 other commodities were liberalised in 1963; pork and pork products and a further 19 items were liberalised in 1971. No further major progress with liberalisation occurred between 1972 and 1987. Note that price support levels increased in response to an appreciating yen–dollar exchange rate, especially after 1985.

3. Japanese journalists specialising in agricultural policy have a much poorer command of English and other foreign languages than journalists working in other fields.

4. The price support formula was revised mainly by eliminating smaller-sized rice producers from the sample used in calculating the cost of production base of price support levels.

5. No official English translation of the Japanese offer has yet been published. Thus the author's own translation may differ from the official version when it appears.
6. A recent report of the Economic Deliberation Council shows that the annual rate of economic growth in Japan declined from 4.6 per cent in the latter half of the 1980s to between 3.75 per cent and 1.50 per cent in 1990, depending upon the attainment of various possible targets concerning CO_2 reduction in the air, the reduction of individual working hours and assumptions concerning the success of anti-pollution measures and other technological developments (Economic Deliberation Council, 1991, pp. 19–20).
7. The author has been misunderstood by Professor Egaitsu who counts him amongst those Japanese agricultural economists who are pessimistic about Japan's ability to reduce the costs of agricultural production (Egaitsu, 1989). The reason for the misunderstanding is that Professor Egaitsu overlooked the author's assumption that present government programmes to improve the efficiency of agricultural production would continue (see Hemmi, 1987, p. 38). The author is also of the opinion that, by modifying its current price/income support programmes, the Japanese government could substantially *accelerate* the cost reduction process. But, at the same time, it is probably beyond the bounds of political feasibilty to suppose that the producer price of rice could be reduced to the world market level within ten years.
8. In Japan those who cultivate 10 ares or more, or whose gross sales of agricultural products exceed Y 150 000, are defined as farmers. As a result of setting the minimum size of farm so low and rising standards of living throughout the economy, two-thirds of Japanese farm households are getting more than half their income from non-farm activities. These should really be classified as non-farm households. Table 7.2 shows that while the

Table 7.2   Percentage changes in numbers of farms by size, 1980–1990

Farm Size (hectares)	Distribution in 1990	1980–1985	1985–1990
Less than 1.0	69.6	−5.8	−9.7
1.0 to 2.0	20.9	−9.9	−11.4
2.0 to 3.0	5.9	−2.5	−5.1
3.0 to 5.0	2.7	13.4	7.5
More than 5	0.7	42.7	38.1
Total	100.0	−5.7	−6.1

Farms in Hokkaido are not included in the table because the average size of farms there (comprising 2.5% of all Japanese farms) is far in excess of the average for the remainder of Japan.

Source: MAFF Statistics and Information Service, 1991, p. 47.

total number of Japanese farms (excluding those in Hokkaido) declined by only around 6 per cent in the past 5 years, the number of those exceeding 3 hectares in size increased very rapidly (in Hokkaido the number of farms with less than 20 hectares has decreased). While the total number of rice farms declined by more than 10 per cent during 1985–90, the number of rice farms with more than 5 hectares increased by more than 14 per cent during the same period (MAFF, 1991, p. 75).

9. While indirectly controlled rice can be sold in the open market at market-determined prices, directly controlled rice has to be sold to the government at administered prices.

10. In April 1991 the rate of import duty on beef stands at 70 per cent. The rate will be reduced to 60 per cent in April 1992 and 50 per cent in April 1993. An obstacle to reducing the costs of beef production and dairying in Japan is that they are land-intensive enterprises. For this reason, with rice, these enterprises form the crux of the agricultural negotiations for Japan.

11. The core of the Staple Food Control System is to support the price of rice at a level which covers all costs, including payments for land use, capital and labour. Due to the surplus of rice above consumption requirements at the administered price level, a proportion of the rice area has been set aside, under a government scheme, since 1971. As consumption has declined, so the area set aside has increased. In 1988 about 27 per cent of the total rice area was set aside. Due to the adverse effect of set aside on their scale of operation, rice farmers are very reluctant to accept any further increase in the proportion of land required to be set aside.

12. The 'normal' trade pattern is a (hypothetical) grain export and import pattern at world market prices undistorted by government intervention, derived by simulation. In 1985, Japanese grain imports were 4.42 tonnes per capita , compared with an average of 1.92 tonnes in 20 developed countries and an average of 4.53 tonnes across a total of 41 countries both developed and developing. The rather large deviation of Japanese imports above the average of developed countries may be explained by the large size of Japan's protected livestock sector.

13. This note updates section 7.4.3 by discussing the impact of the Dunkel Text on Agriculture on the Japanese position.

14. The author considers that a 15 per cent reduction of the tariff on rice would necessitate the abolition of the present rice production control programme.

15. This figure derives from a publication by the United States International Trade Commission (United States International Trade Commission, April 1990).

8. The LDC Perspective

1. Editors note: the author of this chapter would like readers to know that it is based on information available at the time of the April 1990 conference (see Preface).

2. While I refer to objectives some commentators prefer to think of these factors as constraints. So long as the constraints bind but are not absolutely rigid, the distinction hardly matters for the rest of this paper.
3. See Winters (1987b, 1990) for some answers.
4. That the burden has not been fully passed on previously reflects the fact that until it becomes a choice between taxes rather than whether to tax or not, politicians pay regard to the political and economic costs of imposing taxes, even implicit ones. That is, 'burden shifting' of this kind is more likely as a means to avoiding expenditure cuts than as a means of directly financing expenditure increases.
5. It must be admitted that it is even more difficult to predict trade reversals than the other effects of liberalisation. Not only does reversal depend on the developing countries' own policies, but also on the wedges between import and export prices, which, in turn, depend on trading costs, the discounts necessary to break into new markets, etc. Overall, however, at least some trade reversal looks likely.
6. This mercantilist, or quantity-based, conception of trade problems besets the whole of the EC's agricultural policy and has coloured the Round significantly to date.
7. The positions, but not their attribution, is based on de Zeeuw (1989).
8. Effective EC wheat prices were the same in 1988 as in 1980 in terms of ECU but rose by 25 per cent in terms of local currencies. This arises from a complex interaction between MCAs and green exchange rates (Field, Hearn and Kirby, 1989).
9. The only serious exceptions to this arise from countries' concerns for guaranteed supplies of 'essentials' such as food and fuel, in which case export prohibitions suddenly become acceptable and trading partners are held to have a duty to maintain unrestricted supplies.
10. Trade reversal is possible with tariffs as the only policy instruments if trade in intermediate goods is heavily distorted, but it does not seem particularly likely.
11. This point is relevant given the likely bureaucratic resistance to tariffication.
12. Of the 787 non-tariff barriers on imports for which one of the US, Japan, or the EC was the principal supplier, 166 referred to agriculture/food. The barriers were defined at four-digit SITC level and the importers covered were Argentina, Brazil, Chile, Hong Kong, Korea, Pakistan, Philippines and Singapore.
13. A proper interpretation of Schuh is probably that for any individual country macro economic stabilisation should come prior to agricultural liberalisation, although even this view poses some dangers of the sort alluded to in the text.
14. Incremental earnings might be defined relative to, say, 1990 exports.
15. For practical purposes the tax could be defined by the nominal protection co-efficients of certain products multiplied by consumption.

9. The Food Industry Perspective

1. The author is Director for Corporate Affairs, British Sugar, plc. He is Chairman of the International Trade Policy Working Party of the Food

and Drink Federation (of the UK) and a member of the External Trade Committee of the CIAA (of the EC).

10. Perspectives on EC Agricultural Policy Reform

1. Research supported by National Research Council of Italy, Special Project RAISA, Sub-project N. 1., Paper N. 438. The final version has been substantially improved by the co-editor Ken Ingersent in the whole text and especially in the appendix.
2. Lower food prices would increase real wages and improve domestic demand and international competitiveness of non-agricultural sectors. According to the results of numerous general equilibrium models, total employment is likely to increase.
3. This is the case of Italian Ministers when they take office.
4. In some rural areas of Southern Italy, for example, public administration is still unfamiliar, considered as a consequence of the Piedmontese occupation of the territory more than a century ago, and is not fully trusted.
5. In the early, unofficial, leaked version of the MacSharry Plan, the first objective mentioned started with the assertion: 'It is necessary to keep a large number of farmers on the land'. In the later official version (COM[91]100) the adjective 'large' became 'sufficient'.
6. A proposal characterized by these features was presented in 1990 by the Land Use and Food Policy InterGroup (LUFPIG) of the European Parliament.

11. Policy Reform after the Uruguay Round

1. European Commission, 1991, p3.
2. Agra Europe, 22.11.91.
3. Rausser, 1982, first suggested these terms to distinguish between policy transfers or interventions legitimately and logically designed to correct for market failure (so called Political Economic Resource Transactions – PERTs) and those which, whatever their original intention, result in identifiable economic losses but are subject to rent-seeking, thus resulting in a form of political failure (in that originally intended benefits become outweighed by economic costs and captured by unintended beneficiaries – hence termed Political Economic-Seeking Transfers – PESTs).
4. Official Journal of the European Communities, No. L 181/12–20, 1.7.92.
5. Agra Europe report on EC statement on legal texts of CAP reform agreement and 1992/93 price package, 1.7.92. Later press reports have indicated that the US is willing to accept 'green box' status for these compensation payments.
6. Agra Europe, 26.6.92, P/1–P/2, not noted for pro-European Commission comment.
7. See, as a recent example, Kirschke (1991) and references therein; also Tangermann (1990b).
8. A study by Peters (1990) provides a densely argued analysis of the differences between rates of protection and PSEs. An earlier study by de

Gorter and McClatchy (1984) included a review of the relationship between the PSE and a rate of protection.

9. GATT Mid Term Review, Tangermann et al. (1987).

10. An early version of these arguments is provided by de Gorter and Harvey (1990). A more recent exposition and extension of the arguments is in de Gorter (1991).

11. This proposal is further discussed by Blandford, deGorter and Harvey (1989).

12. Several authors have addressed the problem of defining a trade distortion index, including de Gorter and McClatchy (1984), de Gorter, McClatchy and Lahoar (1987), de Gorter and Harvey (1990), Roningen and Dixit (1991) and de Gorter (1991).

13. The PEG is here discussed as if introduced on a commodity-by-commodity basis. However, implementation might eventually be on a farm-by-farm basis if this turns out to be more politically acceptable.

14. In fact, theory suggests that non-tradable farm PEG licences may result in supported production exceeding the national PEG limit, unless PEG payments are completely decoupled, that is, they do not require some current production as a condition for payment. In this case there is additional reason for negotiating lower national PEG limits. Conversely, those PEG programmes which are freely tradable and which are also independent of current production levels may deserve higher PEG levels.

15. As defined and calculated in OECD (1987). These estimates are based on the Roningen et. al. (1989) analysis.

16. These results come from empirical analysis by the International Agricultural Trade Research Consortium (IATRC) 1988. This suggests that soybeans and soybean meal are the only exceptions to the general prediction that world prices would rise following trade liberalization by industrial countries (see IATRC, Assessing the Benefits of Trade Liberalization, August 1988). Trade liberalization would lead to an increase in world prices above current support prices for several commodities in several countries.

17. A recent issue of World Economy (15, 1, January 1992, pp. 101–171) contains four articles relating the GATT and agricultural trade to environmental issues, which explore most of the general issues, particularly the issue of appropriate pricing of environmental goods and the prerequisite of establishing property rights over these goods.

Bibliography

AGRICULTURE CANADA (1989) *Growing Together: A Vision for Canada's Agrifood Industry*, Ottawa, Supply and Services Canada, Agriculture Canada Publication 5269/E, November.

ANDERSON, K. and YUJIRO HAYAMI (1986) *The Political Economy of Agricultural Protection*, Sydney and London.

ANDERSON, K. and R. TYERS (1991) *Global Effects of Liberalising Trade in Farm Products*, Harvester Wheatsheaf, Brighton.

ANDERSON, K. and R. TYERS (1993) 'How developing countries could gain from food trade liberalisation in the Uruguay Round', *Journal of Agricultural Economics*, forthcoming.

Asahi Shimbun, 11 and 21 January 1992.

ASIAN DEVELOPMENT BANK (1991) *Asian Development Outlook* 1991, Manila, April.

BALASUBRAMANYAM, V. N. (1991) 'Trade in Service: The Real Issues', in D. Greenaway *et al.* (eds) *Global Protectionism*, London, Macmillan.

BHAGWATI, J. (1990) 'Multilateralism at Risk: The GATT is Dead; Long Live the GATT', *The World Economy*, 13, pp. 149–169.

BLACKHURST, R., et al. (1977) *Trade Liberalisation, Protectionism and Interdependence*, Studies in International Trade No. 5, GATT, Geneva.

BLANDFORD, D. (1990) 'The Costs of Agricultural Protection and the Difference Free Trade Would Make', in F. Sanderson (ed.), *Agricultural Protectionism in the Industrialized World*, Washington DC, Resources for the Future.

BLANDFORD, D., H. DE GORTER and D. R. HARVEY (1989) 'Farm Income Support with Minimal Trade Distortions', *Food Policy*, 14 August, pp. 268–273.

BURFISHER, M. and M. MISSIAEN (1990) 'Developing countries' high-value agricultural trade: implications for US exports', Economic Research Service Agriculture Information Bulletin, No. 615, USDA, Washington DC.

BURRELL, A. (1989) 'The microeconomics of quota transfer', in A. Burrel (ed.), *Milk quotas in the European Community*, CAB International, Wallingford.

CAHILL, S. A. (1991) 'Implications for Canada of One Possible Outcome: Results from a Multicommodity Analysis with the Trade Simulation Analysis System (TASS)', Working Paper 10/91, Ottawa, Agriculture Canada, August.

CAIRNS GROUP (1986) *Declaration of the Ministerial Meeting of Fair Traders in Agriculture*, Cairns, August.

CAIRNS GROUP (1988) *A Time for Action, A Proposal for a Framework Approach for Agriculture*, made available in Canada as News Release No. 148, Ottawa, Department of External Affairs, 13 July.

CAIRNS GROUP (1989) *Comprehensive Proposal for the Long-term Reform of Agricultural Trade*, made available in Canada as News Release No. 292, Ottawa, Minister for International Trade, 23 November.

CAIRNS GROUP (1990) *Proposal for a Multilateral Reform Program for Agriculture*, Geneva, 15 October.

CARD (1991) 'An analysis of the EC Commission plan for CAP reform', GATT Research Paper 92-GATT-4, Center for Agricultural and Rural Development, Ames, Iowa State University, November.

CARD (1991), 'Determining winners and losers from a GATT agreement: the importance of base periods and rules', GATT-Research Paper 91-GATT 2, Iowa State University, May.

CARD (1991) 'Implications of a GATT Agreement for World Commodity Markets 1991–2000', GATT Research Paper 91-GATT-1, Ames, Iowa State University.

CEPR (1992) 'Monitoring European Integration 3: Is Bigger Better? The Economics of EC Enlargement', Annual Report, Centre for Economic Policy Research, London, September.

CHINO, JUNZABURO, 1991, 'Costs of Production of Rice in 2000 and 2010' ('Inasaku Kosuto Teigen no Kanosei'), in Ken Morishima (ed.), *Possible Impacts of Import Liberalization of Rice on Japanese Agriculture* (Kome Yunyujiyuka no Eikyo Yosoku), Tokyo.

CIAA (1988) 'CIAA Position Paper on the GATT Multilateral Negotiations', page 2, REX-35/88 final, 5 July, Brussels.

COOPER, A. F. (1990) 'The Cairns Group, Agricultural Trade and the Uruguay Round: A 'Mixed' Coalition in Action', Ottawa, Occasional Paper in International Trade Law and Policy, Centre for Trade Policy and Law, Carleton University, November.

COUNCIL OF THE EUROPEAN COMMUNITIES (1992) 'Press Release following the 1579th meeting of the Agricultural Council', 6539/92 (Presse 85), 18 to 21 May, Brussels.

DAIRY FARMERS OF CANADA (1989) 'Necessary GATT Principles for Supply Management', Ottawa, 19 October.

DEARDORFF, A. (1990) 'Should Patent Protection be Extended to All Developing Countries', *The World Economy*, Vol. 13, pp. 492–503.

DE FILIPPIS, F. (1990) 'La revisione della PAC tra controllo della produzione e riorientamento al mercato', in M. GORGONI and A. ZEZZA, *Scarsita e sovraproduzione nell'economia Agroalimentare*, INEA, Il Mulino, Bologna.

DE GORTER, H. (1991) 'Agricultural Policies and the GATT: Towards a Theory of Trade Distortion', paper to International Conference on Mechanisms to Improve Agricultural Trade Performance under the GATT, Kiel, October 28–29, Cornell University.

DE GORTER, H. and K. D. MEILKE (1989) 'Efficiency of Alternative Policies for the EC's Common Agricultural Policy', *American Journal of Agricultural Economics*, August.

DE GORTER, H. and D. R. HARVEY (1990) 'Agricultural Policies and the GATT: Reconciling Protection, Support and Distortion', International Agricultural Trade Research Consortium Working Paper, 90-6, Department of Agricultural Economics, Cornell University.

DE GORTER, H. and D. McCLATCHY (1984) 'Rates of Distortion as an Alternative to Rates of Protection for Analysing Trade Effects of Agricultural Support Policies', Appendix 1 to paper presented to International Agricultural Trade Research Consortium, Wye Woods, Maryland, August.

DE GORTER, H., D. McCLATCHY, and J. LAHOAR (1987) 'Analysis of International Trade Distortions Arising from Agricultural Policies', *Agriculture and Economic Instability*, M. BELLAMY and B. GREENSHIELDS (eds), Gower, Brookfield, VT.

DE ZEEUW, A. (1989) 'GATT and agriculture', *European Affairs*, 1:13–17.

DEATON, LARRY, BOB RIEMENSCHNEIDER, SHANE MATT and LEE ANN STACKHOUSE (1990) 'GATT trade liberalization: the US proposal', USDA, ERS, Agricultural Information Bulletin No. 596.

DRABENSTOTT, MARK, ALAN BARKEMA and DAVID HENNEBERRY (1989) 'Agriculture and the GATT: the link to US farm policy', *Economic Review*, Federal Reserve Bank of Kansas City, Vol. 74, No. 5, Table 2, p. 17.

DUNKEL, A. (1991) Address to the 1991 annual meeting of the World Economic Forum, Davos, Switzerland, 4 February. Excerpts reprinted in GATT Newsletter, No. 78, January–February, Geneva.

DUNKEL, A. (1991a) Speech to the European Atlantic Group, London, 15 May.

DUNKEL, A. (1992) Address to the International Wheat Council Seminar on the Future of World Grain Trade, 24 June, London.

DUNKEL, A., (1992a) Address to the World Farmers Congress, 3 June, Quebec.

EAST WEST CENTER (1986) 'Asia-Pacific Report: Trends, Issues, Challenges', Honolulu, Hawaii: East West Center.

EC COMMISSION (1968) 'Memorandum on the reform of agriculture in the EEC,' COM(68)1000, Bruxelles.

EC COMMISSION (1985) 'Perspectives for the Common Agricultural Policy', COM(85)333, Bruxelles.

EC COMMISSION (1988) 'Agricultural negotiations. Short-term measures (other than immediate measures) in the framework of the measures proposed by the European Communities', MTN/GNG/NG5/W/62, Geneva.

EC COMMISSION (1990) 'Economic results of agricultural holdings', N. 5, 1986–7, Bruxelles.

EC COMMISSION (1991) 'The development and future of the Common Agricultural Policy', Communication of the Commission to the Council and to the European Parliament, July.

EC COMMISSION (1991a) 'The Development and Future of the CAP: Reflections Paper of the Commission', COM(91)100 final, Bruxelles.

EC COMMISSION (1991b) 'The Development and Future of the Common Agricultural Policy: Follow-up to the Reflections Paper', COM(91)285 final, Brussels.

EC COMMISSION (1991c) 'The Agricultural Situation in the Community' 1990 Report, Bruxelles.

ECONOMIC DELIBERATION COUNCIL (1991) 'Option Toward Year 2010 – A Message for the Earth and Human Beings' Report of the 2010 Sub-Committtee *(2010 Nen eno Sentaku – Messeiji)*, Tokyo.

EGAITSU, FUMIO (1989) Book Review in *American Journal of Agricultural Economics*, 71 (1).

ENNEW, C., GREENAWAY, D. and REED, G. V. (1991) *Tariff Liberalisation and Harmonisation: Do the Negotiators Get What They Want?*, CREDIT Research Paper, 91/9, Department of Economics, University of Nottingham.

EUROSTAT (1992) *Europe in Figures*, p. 179, Office for Official Publications of the European Communities, Luxembourg.

FDF (1988) 'The Uruguay Round of GATT Multilateral Negotiations', 2 January, London.

FIELD, H., S. HEARN and M. G. KIRBY (1989) 'The 1988 EC Budget and Production Stabilisers', Discussion Paper 89.3, Australian Bureau of Agricultural and Resource Economics, Canberra.

FINGER, J. and MURRAY, T. (1990) 'Policing Unfair Imports: The US Example', *World Bank Working Paper*, WPS 401.

Financial Times (1992) leader on 'Bridging the final GATT gap', issue for 14 April, London.

FINGER, J. M. (1979) 'Trade Liberalisation: a public choice perspective', in R. C. AMACHER, G. HABERLER and T. C. WILLETT, (eds), *Challenges to a Liberal International Economic Order*, American Enterprise Institute, Washington D.C.

FINGER, J. (1991) 'The old GATT magic no more casts its spell', in *Journal of World Trade Law*, p. 20, Vol. 25, No. 2, Geneva.

FINLAYSON, J. A. and A. WESTON (1990) *The GATT, Middle Powers and the Uruguay Round*, No. 5 in the series 'Middle Powers in the International System', Ottawa, North–South Institute, June.

FUJITA, NATSUKI (1991) 'Resource Endowments and Grain Imports: An International Comparison' (*'Kokumotsu Yunyu no Tekisei Suijun ni Tsuite: Yosofuson Karamita Nogyohogo no Kokusai Hikaku'*), in KEN MORISHIMA (ed.) (1991) *Possible Impacts of Import Liberalization of Rice on Japanese Agriculture*, Tokyo.

GARDNER, B. (1983) 'Efficient Redistribution through Commodity Markets', *American Journal of Agricultural Economics*, 65, pp. 225–34.

GATT (1983) *European Economic Community – Subsidies on export of pasta products: Report of the Panel*, SCM/43, Geneva.

GATT (1987) *Report of the Panel on Japanese Restrictions in Imports of Certain Agricultural Products*, L/6253, 18 November.

GATT (1989) *Canada – Import Restrictions on Ice Cream and Yoghurt*, Report of the Panel, L/6568, 27 September.

GATT (1989) *Submission of the United States on comprehensive long-term agricultural reform*, MTN.GNG/NG5/W/118, Geneva.

GATT (1990) *Synoptic Table of Negotiating Proposals Submitted Pursuant to Paragraph 11 of the Mid-term Review Agreement in Agriculture*, GATT Secretariat, MTN.GNG/NG5/W/ 150/Rev 1, 2 April.

GATT (1991) *'Final Act' of the Uruguay Round Trade Talks. L. Text on Agriculture*, MTN.TNC/W/FA, Geneva.

GATT (1990) *International Trade 1989–90*, Geneva, GATT.

GIFFORD M. J. (1989) Statement, *Minutes of Proceedings and Evidence of the Standing Committee on Agriculture*, House of Commons, Second Session of the Thirty-fourth Parliament, Issue No. 21, 13 December, p. 21:7.

GOVERNMENT OF CANADA (1990a) 'Canada tables proposals for strengthening and clarifying GATT Article XI in support of supply management programs' Press Release, Ottawa, 14 March.

GOVERNMENT OF CANADA (1990b) 'Canada tables offer for agricultural trade reform in multilateral trade negotiations', News Release, Ottawa, 15 October.

GRAHAM J.D., B. STENNES, R.J. MACGREGOR, K.D. MEILKE and G. MOSCHINI (1990) *The Effects of Trade Liberalization on the Canadian Dairy and Poultry Sectors*, Working Paper 3/90, Ottawa, Agriculture Canada, June.

GREENAWAY, D. (1983) *International Trade Policy*, London, Macmillan.

GREENAWAY, D. (1986) 'Estimating the Welfare Effects of Voluntary Export Restraints and Tariffs: An Application to Non Leather Footwear in the UK', *Applied Economics*, 18, pp. 1065–1084.

GREENAWAY, D. (1990) 'TRIMs: Political Economy Aspects and Consequences for GATT', *The World Economy*, Vol. 13, pp. 363–82.

Green Europe (1991) February, Agra Europe, Tunbridge Wells, Kent.

GROUP W/74 (1989) 'Ways to take account of the negative effects of the agriculture reform process on net food importing developing countries', unnumbered paper, 25 October 1989, Geneva.

GUYOMARD, H., L.P. MAHE and T. ROE (1992), 'The EC and the US agricultural trade conflict and the GATT Round: petty multilateralism?', presented at the 31st European Seminar of the European Association of Agricultural Economists, Frankfurt, Germany, December 7–9.

HAMILTON, C. and WHALLEY, J. (1991) *The World Trading System after the Uruguay Round*, Washington, Institute of International Economics.

HARRIS, S. (1989), 'Agricultural policy and its implications for food marketing functions', pp. 289–93 in C. SPEDDING, *The Human Food Chain*, Elsevier Applied Science, London and New York.

HARRIS, S. and A. SWINBANK, (1991) 'Dried grapes: a case study in EC market disruption', pp. 10–16, in *British Food Journal*, Vol. 93, No. 9, Bradford.

HARRIS, SIMON, ALAN SWINBANK and GUY WILKINSON (1983) *The Food and Farm Policies of the European Community*, John Wiley & Sons.

HART, M.M. (1989) 'The Future on the Table: The Continuing Negotiating Agenda under the Canada – United States Free Trade Agreement' in R.G. DEARDEN, M.M. HART and D.P. STEGER, *Living with Free Trade: Canada, the Free Trade Agreement and the GATT*, Ottawa and Halifax, Centre for Trade Policy and Law and the Institute for Research on Public Policy.

HART, M.M. (1990) 'Mercantilist Bargaining and the Crisis in the Multilateral Trade System', Occasional Papers in International Trade Law and Policy, Ottawa, Centre for Trade Policy and Law, Carleton University.

HATHAWAY, D.E. (1987) *Agriculture and the GATT: Rewriting the Rules*, Washington DC, Institute for International Economics.

HELLSTROM, MATS (1990) 'GATT Non-paper on Agriculture', Brussels, 6 December.

HELMAR, M.D., D.L. STEPHENS, K. ESWARAMOORTHY, D.J. HAYES and W.H. MEYERS (1992) 'An analysis of reform of the CAP', presented at the 31st European Seminar of the European Association of Agricultural Economists, Frankfurt, Germany, December 7–9.

HEMMI, KENZO (1987) 'Agricultural Reform Efforts in Japan', in D. GALE JOHNSON (ed.), *Agricultural Reform Efforts in the United States and Japan*, New York and London.

HEMMI, KENZO (1990) 'Future of Japanese Agriculture', in FOOD AND AGRICULTURE POLICY RESEARCH CENTRE (ed.), *Agricultural Policies of Japan*, Tokyo.

HERTEL, T. W. (1989) 'PSEs and the mix of measures to support farm incomes', *The World Economy*, 12(1):17–28.

HIGGOTT, R. A. and A. F. COOPER (1990) 'Middle Power Leadership and Coalition Building: Australia, the Cairns Group and the Uruguay Round of Trade Negotiations', International Organization, 44, 4, Autumn, pp. 589–632.

HILLMAN, JIMMYE S. (1991) *Technical Barriers to Agricultural Trade*, Westview Press.

HINDLEY, B. (1988) 'Dumping and the Far East Trade of the European Community', *The World Economy*, Vol. 11, pp. 445–64.

HINE, R. C., INGERSENT, K. A. and RAYNER, A. J. (1989) 'Agriculture in the Uruguay Round', *Journal of Agricultural Economics*, Vol. 50, pp. 385–96.

INTERNATIONAL AGRICULTURAL TRADE RESEARCH CONSORTIUM (1988) 'Designing Acceptable Agricultural Policies', Summary Report for Symposium on Bringing Agriculture into the GATT, Annapolis, Maryland.

INTERNATIONAL AGRICULTURAL TRADE RESEARCH CONSORTIUM (undated) 'Tariffication and Rebalancing', Commissioned Paper 4, 'Bringing Agriculture into the GATT', Dept. Ag.& Applied Econ. University of Minnesota.

JACKSON, J. (1990) *Restructuring the GATT System*, London, RIIA.

JOSLING, T. E (1969) 'A Formal Approach to Agricultural Policy', *Journal of Agricultural Economics*, 20 (2), pp. 175–96.

JOSLING, T. E. (1973) 'Agricultural Production: Domestic Policy and International Trade', Supporting Study No. 9, FAO, Rome.

JOSLING, T. E. (1975) 'Agricultural Protection and Stabilisation Policies: a Framework for Measurement in the Context of Agricultural Adjustment', FAO Mimeograph, October.

JOSLING, T. and S. TANGERMANN (1992) 'MacSharry or Dunkel: Which Plan Reforms the CAP?' International Agricultural Trade Research Consortium, Working Paper No. 92-10.

KANO, YOSHIKAZU (1987) 'Toward an Independent and Healthy Agricultural Industry', *Journal of Japanese Trade and Industry*, (2).

KIRSCHKE, D. (1991) 'Perspectives for the grain economy in Eastern Europe and implications for the world market', paper to International Conference on Mechanisms to Improve Agricultural Trade Performance under the GATT, Kiel, October 28–9, Technical University of Berlin.

KNIGHT, STEPHEN and A. P. DOW-JONES (1990) 'US threatens trade war over subsidies', as reported in *National Business Review*, Vol. 21, No. 197, October 26, p. 3, Auckland, New Zealand.

KRUEGER, A. O., M. SCHIFF and A. VALDES (1983) 'Agricultural incentives in developing countries: measuring the effect of sectoral and economy-wide policies', *World Bank Economic Review*, 2:255-271.

LAIRD, S. and YEATS, A. (1990) *Quantitative Methods for Trade Barrier Analysis in Developing Countries*, London, Macmillan.

LANGHAMMER, R. J. and A. SAPIR (1987) *Economic Impact of Generalised Tariff Preferences*, Thames Essay No. 49, Gower Press for Trade Policy Research Centre, London.

LOO, T. and E. TOWER (1988) 'Agricultural protectionism and the less developed countries: the relationship between agricultural prices, debt servicing capacities and the need for development aid', Working Paper No. 36, Duke University Programme in International Political Economy.

MADDALA, G. S. (1990) 'Estimation of dynamic disequilibrium models with rational expectations: the case of commodity markets', chapter 2 in WINTERS, L.A. and D. SAPSFORD (eds), Primary Commodity Prices: Economic Models and Policy, Cambridge University Press, pp. 21-37.

MADIGAN, EDWARD (1991) 'US Dairy Policy: Pointing it in the Right Direction', *Choices*, Third Quarter.

MAFF (1990) *Our Views on GATT Agricultural Negotiations and the Rice Issue (GATT Nogyo Kosho to Komemondai o Kangaeru)*, Tokyo.

MAFF Statistics and Information Service (1991) *Summary of 1990 Agricultural Census, Vol. 1 (1990 Nen Sekai Noringyo Sensus Kekkagaiyo [1])*, Tokyo.

MARSH J., B. GREEN, B. KEARNEY, L. MAHÉ, S. TANGERMANN and S. TARDITI (1991) *The Changing Role of Common Agricultural Policy*, Belhaven Press, London.

MATTHEWS, A. (1985) *The Common Agricultural Policy and the Less Developed Countries*, Gill and Macmillan, Dublin.

McCLATCHY D. (1988) 'The Trade Distortion Equivalent (TDE): An Aggregate Indicator of Adverse Trade Effects of Measures of Support and Protection for Agriculture', Technical Discussion Paper, Ottawa, Agriculture Canada, 11 February.

MEILKE, K. D. and B. LARUE (1989) 'A Quantitative Assessment of the Impacts of Trade Liberalization on Canadian Agriculture', in *Agriculture in the Uruguay Round of GATT Negotiations: Implications for Canada's and Ontario's Agrifood Systems*, Department of Agricultural Economics and Business, University of Guelph, July.

MEILKE K. D. and E. VAN DUREN (1990) 'Economic Issues in the US Countervail Cases Against Canadian Hogs and Pork', in G. Lermer and K. K. Klein (eds), *Canadian Agricultural Trade: Disputes, Actions and Prospects*, University of Calgary Press.

MESSERLIN, P. (1989) 'The EC Anti Dumping Regulations: A First Economic Appraisal', *Weltwirtschaftliches Archiv*, Vol. 125, pp. 563–87.

MESSERLIN, P. (1990) 'Anti Dumping Regulations or Pro Cartel Law?', *The World Economy*, Vol. 13, pp. 463–91.

MINISTER OF INTERNATIONAL TRADE (1989) 'Canada tables first comprehensive proposal for new GATT subsidy – countervail rules', News Release No. 158, Minister of International Trade, Ottawa, 28 June.

MINISTERIAL TASK FORCE ON PROGRAM REVIEW (1985) *Agriculture: A Study Team Report*, Ottawa, February.

NABBS-ZENO, CARL and NINA M. SWANN (1991) *Bibliography of Research on Agricultural Trade Policy Reform*, ERS-USDA, Washington DC, September.

NARAYANAN S., A. ANDISON, D. PERVIS and M. RODIER (1989) 'Evaluating the Potential Farm Level Implications of Multilateral Agricultural Free Trade on Selected Farm Sectors in Canada', *Canadian Journal of Agricultural Economics*, 37, 4 (Part II), December, pp. 975–91.

NATIONAL CENTER FOR FOOD AND AGRICULTURAL POLICY (1991) *Should Agriculture go with the GATT?* Resources for the Future, Washington DC.

Nihon Keizai Shimbun (1992) 15 April.

NOGUES, J., OLECHOWSKI, A. and WINTERS, L. A. (1987) 'The Extent of Non-Tariff Barriers to Industrial Countries' Imports', *The World Economy*, 13, pp. 463–491.

NGUYEN, T., PERRONI, C. and WIGLE, R. (1991) 'The Value of a Uruguay Round Success', *The World Economy*, Vol. 14, pp. 359–74.

O'CONNOR, H., A. J. RAYNER, K. A. INGERSENT and R. C. HINE (1991) 'The Agricultural Negotiations in the Uruguay Round: Developments Since the Geneva Accord', University of Nottingam, CREDIT Research Paper, No. 91/8.

OECD (1987) *National Policies and Agricultural Trade*, Paris.

OECD (1989) 'Economy-Wide effects of Agricultural Policies in OECD Countries: Final Results', WP1 of Economic Policy Committee, March, (Restricted).

OECD (1990) *Agricultural Policies, Markets and Trade*, Paris.

OECD (1991) *Agricultural Policies, Markets and Trade: Monitoring and Outlook*, Paris.

OECD (1992) *Agricultural Policies, Markets and Trade: Monitoring and Outlook*, Paris.

OXLEY, A. (1990) *The Challenge of Free Trade* Hemel Hempstead: Harvester Wheatsheaf.

PAARLBERG, ROBERT (1991) *Why Agriculture Blocked the Uruguay Round: Evolving Strategies of a Two Level Game*, Harvard Center for International Affairs, April 1.

PARIKH, K. S. *et al.* (1987) *Towards Free Trade in Agriculture*, Nijhoff, Amsterdam.

PEARSON, C. (1983) *Emergency Protection in the Footwear Industry*, Thames Essay 36 London, Trade Policy Research Centre.

PETERS, G. (1989) 'The Interpretation and Use of Producer Subsidy Equivalents', *Oxford Agrarian Studies*, XVII.

POLICY REFORM FORUM (Seisaku Koso Forum) (1992) *On Possible Impacts of Rice Trade Barriers Tariffication: For Understanding Dunkel Proposal*, March.

POLICY REFORM FORUM (Seisaku Koso Forum), *Towards Success of GATT Uruguay Round*, January 1992.

PORTER, JANE M. and DOUGLAS E. BOWERS (1989) *A Short History of Agricultural Trade Negotiations*, Agriculture and Rural Economy Division, ERS, USDA Staff Report AGES 89-23, August.

PUBLIC RELATIONS OFFICER, Ministry of Foreign Affairs (1988) *Uruguay Round and Japan – Constructing a New World Trading System toward the 21st Century, (Uruguay Round to Nihon – Nijuisseiki ni Muketeno Aratana Sekaiboekitaisei no Kochiku)*, Tokyo.

RAUSSER, G. C. (1982) 'Political economic markets: PERTs and PESTs in food and agriculture', *American Journal of Agricultural Economics*, 64 (5), pp. 821–33.

RAUSSER, G. C. and D. A. IRWIN (1989) 'The political economy of agricultural policy reform', *European Review of Agricultural Economics*, 15, pp. 349–66.

RAUSSER, G. C. and P. ZUSMAN (1992) 'Policy Explanation and Prescription', *American Journal of Agricultural Economics*, 74 (2), May, pp. 247–57.

RAYNER, A. J., K. A. INGERSENT and R. C. HINE (1990) 'Agriculture in the Uruguay Round: Prospects for Long-term Trade Reform', *Oxford Agrarian Studies*, 18 (1).

REINSEL, ROBERT D. (1989) 'Decoupling: Not a New Issue', *Choices*, Vol. 4, No. 3.

RICE POLICY STUDY GROUP (1992) *Effects of Rice Tariffication*, February.

ROBERTS, I., G. LOVE, H. FIELD and N. KLIJN (1989) 'US Grain Policies and the World Market', Policy Monograph No.4, Australian Bureau of Agricultural and Resource Economics, Canberra, July.

RONINGEN, V. and P. DIXIT (1989) 'Economic Implications of Agricultural Policy Reforms in Industrialised Market Economies', Staff Report No. AGES 89-363, Washington DC, Economic Research Service, US Department of Agriculture.

RONINGEN V. O. and P. M. DIXIT (1989) 'How Level is the Playing Field? An Economic Analysis of Agricultural Policy Reforms in Industrial Market Economies', Foreign Agricultural Economics Report Number 239, Washington DC, US Department of Agriculture, December.

RONINGEN, V. and P. M. DIXIT (1991) 'A Simple Measure of Trade Distortion', *IATRC Working Paper*, No. 91-10, ERS, USDA, Washington.

RUNGE, C. F. and STANTON, G. H. (1988) 'The Political Economy of the Uruguay Round Negotiations, a view from Geneva', *American Journal of Agricultural Economics*, 70:1146–52.

SCHIFF, M. and A. VALDES (1992) *Synthesis: The Economics of Agricultural Price Interventions in Developing Countries*, Volume 4 in the series on Political Economy of Agricultural Pricing Policy, Baltimore: Johns Hopkins University Press.

SCHLUTER, G., and W. EDMONDSON (1989) *Exporting Processed instead of Raw Agricultural Products*, USDA, Washington DC.

SCHUH, G. E. (1988) 'Some neglected agricultural policy issues in the Uruguay Round of Multilateral Trade Negotiation', mimeo, presented at Eighth Agricultural Sector Symposium, The World Bank, January.

SIENA MEMORANDUM (1984) 'The Reform of the Common Agricultural Policy', *European Review of Agricultural Economics*, 11(2).

SKOGSTAD G (1990) 'The Political Economy of Agriculture in Canada', in H. J. MICHELMANN, J. C. STABLER and G. G. STOREY (eds), *The Political Economy of Agricultural Trade and Policy: Towards a New Order for Europe and North America*, Boulder, Westview Press, pp. 57–91.

SLATER, J. (1988) 'The food sector in the United Kingdom', in J. BURNS and A. SWINBANK (eds), *Competition Policy in the Food Industry*, Food Economics Study No.4, University of Reading.

SORSA, P. (1992) 'Gatt and Environment: Basic Issues and some Developing Country Concerns', in P. LOWE (ed.), *International Trade and the Environment*, World Bank Discusson Papers 159, The World Bank, Washington DC.

STUDY GROUP ON JAPANESE AGRICULTURE IN THE 21ST CENTURY (*Nijuisseiki Tenbo Iinkai*) (1990) *Agriculture in the Year 2000 (Zusetsu Nisennen no Nogyo)*, Tokyo.

TAKACS, W. (1991) 'Export Restraints: Proliferation and Options for Retariffication', in D. GREENAWAY, R. C. HINE, A. P. O'BRIEN and R. THORNTON (eds) *Global Protectionism*, London, Macmillan.

TANGERMANN, S. (1990) 'Options and prospects: a feasible package', presented at a conference on 'Agriculture in the Uruguay Round of the GATT Negotiations: The Final Stages', University of Guelph, February.

TANGERMANN, S. (1990a) LUFPIG Working Paper on 'A Bond Scheme for Supporting Farm Incomes'; background paper for *A Future for Europe's Farmers and the Countryside* (by Marsh, Green, Kearney, Mahé, Tangermann, and Tarditi), commissioned by the Land Use and Food Policy Inter-Group, European Parliament, November and published as *The Changing Role of the CAP: The Future of Farming in Europe*, Belhaven, London, 1991.

TANGERMANN, S. (1990b) LUFPIG Working Paper on 'Implications for the CAP of Developments in Eastern Europe'; background paper for *A Future for Europe's Farmers and the Countryside* (by Marsh, Green, Kearney, Mahé, Tangermann, and Tarditi), commissioned by the Land Use and Food Policy Inter-Group, European Parliament, November and published as *The Changing Role of the CAP: The Future of Farming in Europe*, Belhaven, London, 1991.

TANGERMANN, S., T. JOSLING and S. PEARSON (1987) 'International Negotiations on Farm Support Levels: the Role of PSEs', *IATRC Working Paper*, No. 87-3, June.

TANGERMANN, S., T. JOSLING and S. PEARSON (1987) 'Multilateral negotiations on farm support levels', *The World Economy*, 10:265–82.

TARDITI, S. (1985) 'The "Green Paper" in a long-term perspective', *European Review of Agricultural Economics*, 14(1).

TRACY, MICHAEL (1982) *Agriculture in Western Europe: Challenge and Response*, 1880–1980, Granada, London.

TRELA, I. and WHALLEY, J. (1990) 'Global Effects of Developed Country Trade Restrictions on Textiles and Apparel, *Economic Journal*, Vol. 100, pp. 1190–205.

TULLOCK, G. and JIMMYE S. HILLMAN (1991) 'Public Choice and Agriculture: An American Example', in P. DASGUPTA (ed.) *Issues in Contemporary Economics, Volume 3: Policy and Development*, Macmillan, London.

TYERS, R. (1990a) 'Implicit policy preferences and the assessment of negotiable trade policy reforms', *European Economic Review*, 34 (7): 1399–426.

TYERS, R. (1990b) 'Trade reform and price risk in domestic and international food markets', *The World Economy*, 13(2): 212–29.

TYERS, R. (1992a) 'Economic reform in Greater Europe and the former USSR: implications for international food markets', report to the International Food Policy Research Institute, Washington D.C., November.

TYERS, R. (1992b) 'The Cairns Group and the Uruguay Round of international trade negotiations', *Australian Economic Review*, forthcoming.

TYERS, R. and K. ANDERSON (1988) 'Liberalising OECD agricultural policies in the Uruguay Round: effects on trade and welfare', *Journal of Agricultural Economics*, 39:197–216.

TYERS, R. and K. ANDERSON (1992) *Disarray in World Food Markets: A Quantitative Assessment*, Cambridge University Press, July.

TYERS, R. and R. FALVEY (1989) 'Border price changes and domestic welfare in the presence of subsidised exports', *Oxford Economic Papers* 41:434–51.

USDA, OFFICE OF ECONOMICS (1991) *Economic Implications of the Uruguay Round for US Agriculture*, Washington DC.

USDA (1992) 'Outline of US–EC Agreement on oilseeds, Uruguay Round', fact sheet dated 20 November 1992, Washington DC.

US GATT DELEGATION (1989) 'Submission of the United States on Comprehensive Long-Term Agricultural Reform', a proposal tabled in Geneva, October 25.

US HOUSE OF REPRESENTATIVES COMMITTEE ON AGRICULTURE (1991) Hearing: 102nd Congress, First Session, March 13, Serial No. 102–17, p. 17.

US INTERNATIONAL TRADE COMMISSION (1990), *Estimated Tariff Equivalents of Nontariff Barriers on Certain Imports in the European Community, Japan and Canada*, April 1990.

US SENATE COMMITTEE ON FINANCE, SUBCOMMITTEE ON INTERNATIONAL TRADE (1989) 'Extending International Trading Rules of Agriculture', Hearing, Washington DC, November 3.

VALDES, A. (1992) 'Gaining momentum: economywide and agricultural reform in Latin America', Agricultural Division, Technical Department, Latin America and the Caribbean Regional Office, World Bank, Washington DC, June.

VALDES, A. and ZIETZ, J. (1980) *Agricultural Protection in OECD Countries: It's Cost to Less Developed Countries*, Research Report, No. 21, International Food Policy Research Institute, Washington DC.

VARIOUS AUTHORS (1988) 'Mutual disarmament in world agriculture – A Declaration on Agricultural Trade',. National Center for Food and Agricultural Policy and Resources for the Future, Washington DC.

VITALIANO, PETER (1988) Remarks of, quoted in *The Food and Fibre Letter*, Vol. 8, No. 43, November 7, p. 3.

VITALIANO, PETER (1991) Testimony before the Committee on Agriculture, US House of Representatives, May 13.

VOUSDEN, N. (1990) *The Theory of Trade Protection*, New York: Cambridge University Press.

WAGENINGEN MEMORANDUM (1973) 'Reform of the EC's Common Agricultural Policy', *European Review of Agricultural Economics*, 1(2).

WARLEY, T. K. (1976) 'Western Trade in Agricultural Products', in A. Schonfield (ed.) *International Relations in the Western World, 1959–1971*, Vol. 1, Oxford University Press, London.

WARLEY, T. K. (1988) *Agriculture in the GATT: Past and Future*, invited paper, XXth Conference of the International Association of Agricultural Economists, Buenos Aires, Argentina.

WEBB, A. J., M. LOPEZ and R. PENN (1990) 'Estimates of producer and consumer subsidy equivalents: government intervention in agriculture, 1982–87', Statistical Bulletin No.803, Economic Research Service, USDA, Washington DC, April.

WEISS, CHR. R. (1992) 'The Effect of Price Reduction and Direct Income Support Policies on Agricultural Input Markets in Austria', *Journal of Agricultural Economics*, 43 (1).

WHALLEY, J. (1989) *The Uruguay Round and Beyond*, London: Macmillan.

WHALLEY, J. (1990) 'Non Discriminatory Discrimination: Special and Differential Treatment under GATT for Developing Countries', *Economic Journal*, Vol. 100, pp. 1318–28.

WINTERS, L. A. (1987) 'The Road to Uruguay', *Economic Journal*, Vol. 100, pp. 1288–303.

WINTERS, L. A. (1987a) 'Negotiating abolition of non-tariff barriers', *Oxford Economic Papers*, 39:469–80.

WINTERS, L. A. (1987b) 'The economic consequences of agricultural support: a survey', *OECD Economic Studies*, No. 9, Autumn pp. 7–54.

WINTERS, L. A. (1990a) 'The so-called "Non-economic" Objectives of Agricultural Policy', *OECD Economic Studies*, 13:237–66.

WINTERS, L. A. (1990b) 'The Road to Uruguay', *Economic Journal*, Vol. 100, pp. 1288–303.

WORLD BANK (1990) *World Development Report 1990*, New York: Oxford University Press.

YEUTTER, AMBASSADOR CLAYTON (1986) Testimony on the Results of the GATT Ministerial Meeting before the Sub-committee on Trade, Committee on Ways and Means, US House of Representatives, Washington DC.

YEUTTER, CLAYTON (1989) Statement made on October 24, USDA, Washington DC.

ZIETZ, J. and A. VALDEZ (1988) 'Agriculture in the GATT: An Analysis of Alternative Approaches to Reform', Research Report No. 70, International Food Policy Research Institute, Washington DC.

Author Index

Agra Europe   169, 211, 231, 235, 281, 300
Agriculture Canada   122
Anderson, K.   88, 94, 98, 102, 106, 133, 159, 178, 280, 287, 292, 293, 296
Asahi Shimbun   156

Balasubramanyam, V. N.   20
Barkema, A.   41
Bhagwati, J.   13, 15, 23
Blackhurst, R.   186
Blandford, D.   133, 301
Bowers, D. E.   3
Burfisher, M.   195
Burrell, A.   41

Cahill, S. A.   134
Cairns Group   125, 126, 293
Center for Agricultural and Rural Development (CARD)   133, 292, 294
Centre for Economic Policy Research (CEPR)   102
Chino, J.   152
Confederation des Industries Agro-Alimentaires de la CEE (CIAA)   183, 184, 195, 198
Cooper, A. F.   90, 94, 293

Dairy Farmers of Canada   130
Deardorff, A.   291
Deaton, L.   40
De Filippis, F.   219
de Gorter, H.   219, 301
de Zeeuw, A.   299
Dixit, P.   3, 41, 133, 301
Dow-Jones, A. P.   46
Drabenstott, M.   41
Dunkel, A.   49, 200

East West Centre   91
Economic Deliberation Council (Japan)   297
Edmonson, W.   184
Egaitsu, F.   297
Ennew, C.   291
Eswaramoothy, K.   101, 106, 294
European Communities Commission   49, 63, 76, 101, 205, 206, 208, 211, 224, 226, 229, 300
Eurostat   183

Falvey, R.   97
Field, H.   102, 299
Financial Times   191
Finger, J. M.   14, 174, 178, 195
Finlayson, J. A.   305
Food and Drinks Federation of the UK (FDF)   184, 187, 191, 194
Fujita, N.   154

Gardner, B.   226
General Agreement on Tariffs and Trade (GATT)   14, 78, 126, 130, 182, 185, 195, 197
Gifford, M. J.   120
Government of Canada   126, 127
Graham, J. D.   134
Green, B.   205, 214
Greenaway, D.   12, 14, 20, 291
Green Europe   76
Group W/74   186
Guyomard, H.   101, 102, 294

Hamilton, C.   306
Harris, S.   57, 183, 191
Hart, M. M.   138
Harvey, D. E.   301
Hathaway, D. E.   3, 34
Hayami, Y.   88, 292, 296
Hayes, D. J.   101, 106, 294

Hearing: US House of
Representatives Committee on
Agriculture 34
Hearn, S. 299
Hellstrom, M. 47, 190
Helmar, M.D. 101, 106, 294
Hemmi, K. 146, 153, 297
Henneberry, D. 41
Hertel, T.W. 99
Higgott, R.A. 90, 94, 293
Hillman, J.S. 292
Hindley, B. 14
Hine, R.C. 291, 292, 293

Ingersent, K.A. 291, 292, 293
International Agricultural Trade
Research Consortium
(IATRC) 253, 301
Irwin, D.A. 224, 227, 255

Jackson, J. 10
Josling, T.E. 101, 102, 106, 164,
226, 237, 281, 294, 301

Kano, Y. 151
Kearney, B. 205, 214
Kirby, M.G. 299
Kirsche, D. 300
Klijn, N. 102
Knight, S. 46
Kreuger, A.O. 160, 162

Lahoar, J. 301
Laird, S. 13, 16
Langhammer, R.J. 177
Larue, B. 133
Loo, T. 159, 178
Lopez, M. 313
Love, G. 102

MacGregor, R.J. 134
Maddala, G.S. 160
Madigan, E. 50
Mahé, L.P. 101, 102, 205, 214, 294
Marsh, J. 183, 205, 214
Matt, S. 40
Matthews, A. 159
McClatchy, D. 125, 301

Meïlke, K.D. 129, 133, 134, 219
Messerlin, P. 14
Meyers, W.H. 101, 106, 294
Miner, W.M. 45
Minister of International Trade
(Canada) 127
Ministerial Task Force
(Canada) 122
Ministry of Agriculture, Forestry and
Fisheries (MAFF) (Japan) 150,
297, 298
Ministry of Foreign Affairs
(Japan) 141
Missiaen, M. 195
Murray, T. 14

Nabbs-Zeno, C. 41
Narayanan, S. 134
National Center for Food and
Agricultural Policy
(NCFAP) 205, 292
Nihon Keizai Shimbun 309
Nguyen, T. 24
Nogues, J. 14, 17

O'Connor, H. 293
Olechowski, A. 14
Organization for Economic
Cooperation and Development
(OECD) 1, 2, 30, 63, 116, 133,
164, 178, 187, 188, 292, 301
Oxley, A. 293

Paarlberg, R. 32, 34, 35, 51
Parikh, K.S. 159
Pearson, C. 14
Pearson, S. 164, 301
Penn, R. 313
Perroni, C. 24
Pervis, D. 134
Peters, G.H. 300
Policy Reform Forum (Japan) 156
Porter, J.M. 31

Rausser, G.C. 224, 227, 255, 256,
300
Rayner, A.J. 291, 292, 293
Reed, G.V. 291
Reinsel, R.D. 37, 44

Rice Policy Study Group
(Japan) 156
Riemenschneider, B. 40
Roberts, I. 102
Rodier, M. 134
Roe, T. 101, 102, 294
Roningen, V.O. 3, 41, 133, 301
Runge, C.F. 173

Sapir, A. 177
Schiff, M. 160, 162, 293
Schluter, G. 184
Schuh, G.E. 310
Siena Memorandum 205
Skogstad, G. 121
Slater, J. 182, 183
Sorsa, P. 199
Stackhouse, L.A. 40
Stanton, G.H. 173
Stennes, B. 134
Stephens, D.L. 101,106, 294
Study Group on Japanese
Agriculture in the 21st
Century 153, 155
Swann, N.M. 41
Swinbank, A. 57, 191

Takacs, W. 291
Tangermann, S. 101, 102, 106, 164,
168, 169, 172, 205, 214, 254, 281,
294, 300, 301
Tarditi, S. 205, 214
Tower, E. 159, 178
Tracy, M. 48, 57
Trela, J. 17
Tullock, G. 292

Tyers, R. 94, 95, 97, 98, 102, 106,
107, 133, 159, 178, 280, 287, 293,
294

United States Department of
Agriculture (USDA) 51, 52,
54, 201
United States International Trade
Commission 298
US GATT Delegation 41
US Senate Committee on Finance,
Subcommittee on International
Trade 292

Valdes, A. 107, 160, 162, 169, 170,
189, 293
Van Duren, E. 129
Vitaliano, P. 39, 50
Vousden, N. 88

Wageningen Memorandum 205
Warley, T.K. 57, 58
Webb, A.J. 313
Weiss, Chr. R. 250
Weston, A. 305
Whalley, J. 17, 22, 296
Wigle, R. 24
Wilkinson, G. 57, 191
Winters, L.A. 11, 14, 18, 157, 174,
178, 299
World Bank 313

Yeats, A. 13, 16
Yeutter, Clayton 35, 36, 40

Zietz, J. 160, 169, 170
Zusman, P. 256

Subject Index

aggregate measure of support
(AMS) 62, 69, 237, 263, 276
agricultural policy
objectives of industrial
countries 157
pressure for reform of 158, 270
price insulating effects of, in
industrial countries 161, 293
agricultural subsidies
'traffic light' categorisation
of 43–4, 65, 235, 248, 266
agricultural support and protection
costs of, in the US 28, 30 (Table
3.1)
'rebalancing' of 62, 66, 68, 80, 83,
263, 267, 275–6, 278, 290
agricultural trade distortion
measurement of 238 *et seq.*
agricultural trade reform
and domestic policy 225, 248

Cairns Group of agricultural
exporting countries 37, 63–4,
89 *et seq.*, 163–4, 264, 284, 293n,
294, 295
Canada
Canada–US Trade Agreement
(CUSTA) 110, 112 *et seq.*,
294, 295
domestic reform of agricultural
policy in 121 *et seq.*, 270
effect of agricultural trade
liberalisation on 133
effect of trade liberalisation on
agriculture 97–8
position of, within Cairns
Group 123 *et seq.*, 264–5,
277
position on agricultural trade
reform 90, 98, 100
compensation
as component of policy
reform 249 *et seq.*

feasibility of sharing costs of,
internationally 287–8
principle of, applied to analysis of
agricultural policy and trade
reform 227

decoupled payments 37, 43, 61, 79,
81–2, 215, 232–3, 244, 247,
250–1, 254, 274, 288–9
direct income support
administative costs of 211–13,
215
as a component of CAP
reform 75, 264
definition of 292–3
farmers' distrust of 81, 288
modulation of 213, 277–8
redeemable bonds, as instrument
of 214–15, 254
transparency of 283

environmental problems of
agriculture
environmental subsidies 289
implications for agricultural
policy 207, 218, 301
European Community (EC)
Common Agricultural Policy
(CAP): budgetary costs
of 62, 232, 235, 271, 278;
Commission proposals for
reform of 58–9, 74;
Community Preference 62,
72, 80, 267, 275, 278, 289;
decoupled payments
and 234; MacSharry
Plan 5, 49, 74 *et seq.*, 203,
211 *et seq.*, 223 *et seq.*, 271–3,
276–8, 281, 284, 286, 300;
oilseeds support 62, 289;
political economy of 224,
271; pressure for reform
of 56;

European Community (EC) CAP
(*cont.*)
variable import levies/export
subsidies 56–8, 62, 65, 83,
263
Community budget 56
Community enlargement,
implications for agricultural
policy 223, 228–9, 236
Dunkel draft agreement on
agriculture, Community
reaction to 80
world market shares of agricultural
trade 55–6
export subsidies/assistance
Canada's proposals on 127–8
EC proposals on 72–3
terms of Washington Accord
regarding 290
US proposals on 66, 70–1

farm structural adjustment and
reform 210, 218
food industry
implications of export subsidies on
agricultural raw materials
for 196–7
implications of Uruguay Round
draft text on agriculture
for 189–90
interest of in the prevention of
trade disputes 199–200
opposition of to market
sharing 191–2
view of on CAP reform 193–4
view of on special and differential
treatment of developing
countries 194–5
food security
EC attitude to 186
emphasis on in developing
countries 186
Japan's attitude to 140–1, 147,
154, 265
and stockholding costs 257

G7 Economic Summit
1990 communiqué regarding
agricultural trade reform 68

General Agreement on Tariffs and
Trade (GATT)
Article XI: Canada's attitude
to 125–6, 265
EC proposal for revision of 66
Japan's attitude to 265
provisions of 29, 31, 65, 291
Section 22 waiver of, granted to
US 31, 89, 292
Dillon Round 56
export subsidy rules (Article
XVI) 58, 66, 290, 291
Kennedy Round 11, 56–7
neglect of agriculture in 1
origins of 9
'Rounds' system of 10
Tokyo Round 11, 57–8
'green box' policies
definition of 79, 274, 276, 289,
300
green protectionism 198–9

information needs for policy
reform 247 *et seq.*
institutional change/reform
and policy reform 228–9, 255 *et
seq.*
internal/domestic support
Canada's proposals on 128–9
Dunkel draft agreement proposals
on 79
EC proposals on 71–2
terms of Washington Accord
regarding 289
US proposals on 65, 68–70
international markets
instability of 257
management of, as policy
strategy 61, 263

Japan
Basic Agricultural Law of 1961,
provisions of 142–3
changing structure of agriculture
in 152–3, 270
domestic farm support, recent
reductions of 143–4
effect of GATT agreement on
agriculture 151 *et seq.*

liberalisation of agricultural
    imports in 141, 270, 296, 298
opposition to liberalisation of rice
    imports 148–9, 265, 268, 277
tariffication of rice import barriers,
    attitude towards 149

market access/border protection
    Canada's proposals on 129–32
    Dunkel draft agreement proposals
      on 79
    EC proposals on 72, 84
    terms of Washington Accord
      on 289
    US proposals on 65–6, 70
minimum access opportunities 79,
    274

oilseeds, trade in
    dispute between US and EC
      regarding 5–6, 289

partial tariffication, EC proposal
    on 66
PERTs and PESTs 226–7, 233, 300
policy offsets
    definition 2
    wastefulness of 2–3
preferential trading
    arrangements 176–8
producer subsidy equivalent (PSE)
    definition 1, 164
    limitations of as policy reform
      instrument 164, 237 *et seq.*,
      248–9, 300–1
producers' entitlement guarantee
    (PEG) 240 *et seq.*, 301
producers' surplus gain (PSG) 243

Reciprocal Trade Agreements Act
    (1934)
    provisions of 26
rural depopulation
    implications for agricultural
      policy 207, 289

safeguards
    proposed special provisions
      for 79, 274, 283

sanitary and phytosanitary barriers
    to food imports 198–9, 295
set aside, as agricultural policy
    instrument
    as adopted by the EC 76, 229,
      271–2
    as adopted by Japan 298
    as adopted by the US 276, 281
Staple Food Control System 154,
    156
supply control
    and CAP reform 232
    and resource
      misallocation 210–11, 293
    EC claim for 'credit'
      regarding 63, 68, 79–80, 263,
      274–5
support measurement unit
    (SMU) 63, 79, 164, 172–3, 237,
    269, 274, 292

tariff snap-back mechanism 70
tariffication of NTBs 38,40, 70,
    168–71, 209, 248, 253, 266, 283
trade distortion equivalent
    (TDE) 241–2
transfer cost (TC) 245
transfer efficiency (TE) 245
Tyers–Anderson food trade
    model 94 *et seq.*, 159–60, 264,
    280, 287, 293

United States
    Export Enhancement Program
      (EEP) 89, 100, 102, 118
    Farm Bill (1990) 42, 50, 100, 270,
      284
    share of global agricultural
      trade 262
Uruguay Round
    achievements 283–5
    agenda of 15 *et seq.*
    aims of 8, 248, 261
    Cairns Group position on
      agriculture 99 *et seq.*, 268
    Canadian position on
      agriculture 126 *et seq.*, 262,
      268

chronology of 4 (Table 1.2)
collapse of agricultural
 negotiations in Brussels,
 December 1990 101, 269
consequences of failure 24–5,
 256, 282
developing country interests
 in 159 *et seq.*, 284–5
de Zeeuw framework agreement on
 agriculture 67, 267
Dunkel draft text on
 agriculture 5, 78 *et seq.*,
 155–6, 189, 273 *et seq.*, 281,
 286, 298
EC concessions on
 agriculture 86–7
EC position on agriculture 61 *et
 seq.*, 263, 267–9
food industry's aims in 184–5

Geneva Accord 4, 40, 64–5, 163
 et seq., 266, 283, 293
Japan's position on
 agriculture 63, 147 *et seq.*,
 265, 268
lessons learned from 285 *et seq.*
mid-term review of 4, 20, 38, 64,
 266, 286, 301
Punte del Este Declaration 1, 60,
 164, 261
reasons for placing agriculture at
 centre of 3
US position on agriculture in 4,
 33, 35–6, 40 *et seq.*, 51, 59,
 65–6, 69–71, 262, 266–8

Washington Accord/Blair House
 Agreement 101, 260, 289–90